The Princeton Review®

PSAT™ 8/9

PREP

with 2 Practice Tests

Second Edition

The Staff of The Princeton Review

PrincetonReview.com

Penguin Random House

The Princeton Review
110 East 42nd Street, 7th Floor
New York, NY 10017

Published in the United States by Penguin Random House LLC, New York.

Terms of Service: The Princeton Review Online Companion Tools ("Student Tools") for retail books are available for only the two most recent editions of that book. Student Tools may be activated only once per eligible book purchased for a total of 24 months of access. Activation of Student Tools more than once per book is in direct violation of these Terms of Service and may result in discontinuation of access to Student Tools Services.

ISBN: 978-0-593-51745-1
ISSN: 2693-0722

PSAT™ is a trademark of the College Board, which is not affiliated with, and does not endorse, this product.

The Princeton Review is not affiliated with Princeton University.

The material in this book is up-to-date at the time of publication. However, changes may have been instituted by the testing body in the test after this book was published. If there are any important late-breaking developments, changes, or corrections to the materials in this book, we will post that information online in the Student Tools. Register your book and check your Student Tools to see if there are any updates posted there.

Editor: Chris Chimera
Production Editors: Sarah Litt and Liz Dacey
Production Artist: Deborah Weber

Printed in the United States of America.

10 9 8 7 6 5 4 3 2 1

Second Edition

The Princeton Review Publishing Team
Rob Franek, Editor-in-Chief
David Soto, Senior Director, Data Operations
Stephen Koch, Senior Manager, Data Operations
Deborah Weber, Director of Production
Jason Ullmeyer, Production Design Manager
Jennifer Chapman, Senior Production Artist
Selena Coppock, Director of Editorial
Orion McBean, Senior Editor
Aaron Riccio, Senior Editor
Meave Shelton, Senior Editor
Chris Chimera, Editor
Patricia Murphy, Editor
Laura Rose, Editor
Isabelle Appleton, Editorial Assistant

Penguin Random House Publishing Team
Tom Russell, VP, Publisher
Alison Stoltzfus, Senior Director, Publishing
Emily Hoffman, Associate Managing Editor
Patty Collins, Executive Director of Production
Mary Ellen Owens, Assistant Director of Production
Alice Rahaeuser, Associate Production Manager
Maggie Gibson, Associate Production Manager
Suzanne Lee, Senior Designer
Eugenia Lo, Publishing Assistant

For customer service, please contact **editorialsupport@review.com**, and be sure to include:

- full title of the book
- ISBN
- page number

Acknowledgments

Special thanks to Kenneth Brenner, Sara Kuperstein, Amy Minster, and Scott O'Neal for their contributions to this edition.

Thanks also to Aleksei Alferiev, Tania Capone, Paul Christiansen, Remy Cosse, Stacey Cowap, Harrison Foster, Beth Hollingsworth, Adam Keller, Kevin Keogh, Ali Landreau, Christine Lindwall, Jomil London, Sweena Mangal, Sionainn Marcoux, Valerie Meyers, Jason Morgan, Acacia Nawrocik-Madrid, Robert Otey, Gabby Peterson, Kathy Ruppert, Jess Thomas, and Suzanne Wint.

The Princeton Review would also like to thank Deborah Weber, Sarah Litt, and Liz Dacey for their time and attention to each page.

Special thanks to Adam Robinson, who conceived of and perfected the Joe Bloggs approach to standardized tests, and many other techniques in this book.

Contents

Get More (Free) Content
at **PrincetonReview.com/prep**

As easy as *1•2•3*

1 Go to PrincetonReview.com/prep or scan the **QR code** and enter the following ISBN for your book: **9780593517451**

2 Answer a few simple questions to set up an exclusive Princeton Review account. *(If you already have one, you can just log in.)*

3 Enjoy access to your **FREE** content!

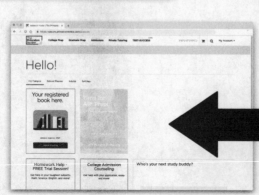

Once you've registered, you can...

- Access and print out one more full-length practice test as well as the corresponding answers and explanations

- Use our online tools to take your practice tests digitally or use our online proctor to time you while you take the test in the book, then enter your answers online

- Enter your answers in our online bubble sheet to get an approximate scaled score with explanations

- Get valuable advice about the college application process

- If you're still choosing between colleges, use our searchable rankings of *The Best 390 Colleges* to find out more information about your dream school

- Access printable resources, including a study guide, a score conversion table, and more

- Check to see if there have been any corrections or updates to this edition

Need to report a potential **content** issue?

Contact **EditorialSupport@review.com** and include:

- full title of the book
- ISBN
- page number

Need to report a **technical** issue?

Contact **TPRStudentTech@review.com** and provide:

- your full name
- email address used to register the book
- full book title and ISBN
- Operating system (Mac/PC) and browser (Chrome, Firefox, Safari, etc.)

Look For These Icons Throughout The Book

 ONLINE PRACTICE TESTS

 ONLINE ARTICLES

 PROVEN TECHNIQUES

 APPLIED STRATEGIES

 STUDY BREAK

 MORE GREAT BOOKS

Part I
Orientation

Chapter 1
What Is the Digital PSAT 8/9?

The Digital PSAT 8/9 is a standardized test given to eighth and ninth graders to give them a "preliminary" idea of how well they could do on SAT question types. This chapter will give you a general overview of the test and how it is used, along with the basics to start your preparation. We'll also give you a glimpse at the other tests in College Board's Suite of Assessments: the PSAT 10, PSAT/NMSQT, and the SAT.

THE DIGITAL PSAT 8/9

College Board's "Suite of Assessments" ranges from the PSAT 8/9 to the SAT. If you are reading this book, you are likely most interested in the PSAT 8/9 at this time, so we'll start there. Just like the other tests in the Suite, the PSAT 8/9 contains a Reading and Writing section and a Math section, each divided into two modules. The content of all the tests in the Suite is similar, and the number of questions and time per module are identical.

This is what College Board says about the Reading and Writing section:

"The section focuses on key elements of comprehension, rhetoric, and language use that the best available evidence identifies as necessary for college readiness and success. In this section, students answer multiple-choice questions requiring them to read, comprehend, and use information and ideas in texts; analyze the craft and structure of texts; revise texts to improve the rhetorical expression of ideas; and edit texts to conform to core conventions of Standard English."

Here is the Princeton Review's take: Be prepared to justify your selected answer with evidence from the passage and/or graph provided. This test is not about making up anything; it's about finding the correct answer based on the passage.

College Board has this to say about the Math section:

"The digital SAT Suite Math section focuses on key elements of algebra, advanced math, problem solving and data analysis, and geometry and trigonometry (except for the PSAT 8/9 which does not test trigonometry) that evidence identifies as necessary for college and career readiness and success. Over the course of the Math section, students answer multiple choice and student-produced response (SPR) questions that measure their fluency with, understanding of, and ability to apply the math concepts, skills, and practices that are most essential for readiness for entry-level postsecondary work."

Here is the Princeton Review's take: Expect to see Algebra I and II, some Geometry, and questions that have charts, graphs, data tables, scatterplots, or other forms of data.

The Digital Suite of Assessments has a built-in Desmos calculator that can be used on all Math questions. In addition, students may bring their own approved calculators if they prefer. Even though this tool is always at hand, it is up to the test-taker to determine whether the calculator will help solve a question. According to College Board, "students who make use of structure or their ability to reason will probably finish before students who use a calculator."

The bottom line: Write down your work and use the calculator for tedious calculations, but a calculator most likely will not be necessary to solve most of the questions.

All questions in the Reading and Writing section are multiple-choice. Most of the Math questions are multiple-choice, but about 25% of the questions are "student-produced responses," for which students enter their own answers. Each correct answer earns points, and there is no penalty for an incorrect response or a question left blank.

The bottom line: Don't leave anything blank!

When Is the Digital PSAT 8/9 Given?

The PSAT 8/9 is offered by schools. Prior to the switch to Digital, schools could choose the date of the test during the school year. Now, the Digital PSAT will be administered in a testing window of several days. Your school will announce the exact dates at the beginning of the school year, and you can find out more about the testing windows at PrincetonReview.com or through College Board at CollegeBoard.org.

How Do I Sign Up for the PSAT 8/9?

You don't have to do anything to sign up for the PSAT 8/9; your school will do all the work for you. Test registration fees can vary from school to school, so be sure to check with your school counselor if you have questions about how much the PSAT 8/9 will cost you.

What About Students with Special Needs?

If you have a diagnosed physical or learning disability, you will probably qualify for accommodations on the PSAT 8/9. However, it's important that you get the process started early. The first step is to speak to your school counselor who handles learning disabilities. Only your counselor can file the appropriate paperwork. You'll also need to gather some information (documentation of your condition) from a licensed practitioner and some other information from your school. Then your school counselor will file the application for you. You will need to apply for accommodations only once; with that single application you'll also qualify for accommodations on the PSAT 8/9, PSAT, SAT, and AP Exams. The one exception to this rule is that if you change school districts, you'll need to have a counselor at the new school refile your paperwork.

Does the PSAT 8/9 Play a Role in College Admissions?

No! The PSAT 8/9 plays no role in college admissions. It's really just a practice test for the SAT.

What Happens to the Score Report from the PSAT 8/9?

Only you and your school will receive copies of your score report. It won't be sent to colleges.

Who Writes the PSAT 8/9?

The PSAT 8/9 is written and administered by College Board. You might think that the people at College Board are educators, professors of education, or teachers. They're not. They are people who just happen to make a living writing tests. In fact, they write hundreds of tests, for all kinds of organizations.

The folks at College Board aren't really paid to educate; they're paid to make and administer tests. And even though you may pay them to take the PSAT 8/9, you're not their customer. The actual customers College Board caters to are the colleges, which get the information they want at no cost, and the middle and high schools, which are often judged based on how well their students do on these tests. Because you, the student, are not College Board's customer, you should take everything that College Board says with a grain of salt and realize that its testing "advice" isn't always the best advice. (Getting testing advice from College Board is a bit like getting baseball advice from the opposing team.)

WHAT DOES THE PSAT 8/9 TEST?

As you begin your prep, it's useful to remember that the PSAT 8/9 is not a test of aptitude, how good of a person you are, or how successful you will be in life. The PSAT 8/9 simply tests how well you take the PSAT 8/9 (and, by extension, how well you would have performed on the PSAT 10, PSAT/NMSQT, or SAT, if you had taken one of those tests instead). And performing well on the PSAT 8/9 is a skill that can be learned like any other. The Princeton Review was founded over 40 years ago on this very simple idea, and—as our students' test scores show—our approach is the one that works. These tests can be extremely daunting. However, remember that any standardized test is a coachable test. A beatable test.

The PSAT 8/9 doesn't measure the stuff that matters. It measures neither intelligence nor the depth and breadth of what you're learning in school. The PSAT 8/9 is an opportunity to start preparing for the tests that do matter: the PSAT/NMSQT and the SAT.

HOW IS THE PSAT 8/9 STRUCTURED AND SCORED?

Category	PSAT 8/9
Time Overall	134 minutes plus break
Components	• Reading and Writing section • Math section
Number of Questions	• Reading and Writing: 54, including 4 experimental questions • Math: 44, including 4 experimental questions
Answer Choices	• Reading and Writing: all multiple-choice with 4 answers per question • Math: 75% multiple-choice with 4 answers per question, 25% student-produced responses
Time by Section	• Reading and Writing: 64 minutes in two 32-minute modules • Math: 70 minutes in two 35-minute modules
Relationship Between Modules	• Module 1 has a broad mix of levels of difficulty. • Performance on Module 1 determines the difficulty of Module 2. • Students who do well on Module 1 will get a Module 2 that is harder, on average. • Students who do less well on Module 1 will get a Module 2 that is easier, on average.
Scoring	• The score is based on the number of questions correct and the difficulty of the questions seen. • Students who do well on Module 1 are put into a higher bracket of possible scores. • Students who do less well on Module 1 are put into a lower bracket of possible scores. • Section scores range from 120 to 720. • Total score is the sum of the section scores and ranges from 240 to 1440.

With the move to a digital suite of assessments starting in fall of 2023, College Board took the opportunity to alter not just the delivery format but the content of the test from its previous version. All Reading and Writing questions are now attached to short passages, with one question per passage. There will be a wide range of text complexities presented, and the passages will cover a variety of topics from history, science, and literature (even some poetry).

The Math content is fairly similar to the form it took on paper tests in 2022 and earlier. There is a strong focus on algebra, problem-solving, and analytical topics, and it includes some high-level content such as trigonometry. Some questions require student-produced responses, and these will be scattered throughout the Math modules. As previously stated, calculator use will be allowed on all Math questions.

As you can see from the table on the previous page, both sections (Reading-Writing and Math) are divided into two modules. On the Digital PSAT 8/9, your performance on the first module in each section will determine the makeup of your second module. Do well on the first module, and you will see a harder (on average) mix of questions on the second module. Miss more questions in the first module, and you will get an easier (on average) level of difficulty for the second module. You always want to do as well as possible, of course, but it's worth keeping in mind that you will need to get the hard second module on each section in order to earn a top score.

To help you do your best, we recommend that you review the explanations for the questions in the drills and the practice tests, even if you answer a question correctly. You may discover techniques that help to shave seconds from your solutions. A large part of what's being tested is your ability to use the appropriate tools in a strategic fashion, and while there may be multiple ways to solve a given problem, you'll want to focus on the most efficient path to a solution.

Scoring on the PSAT 8/9

The PSAT 8/9 is scored on a scale of 240–1440, which is the sum of the two section scores that range from 120–720. The two sections are the Reading and Writing section and the Math section. Wrong answers are not penalized, so you're advised never to leave a question blank—even if that means randomly picking a letter and clicking it for any uncompleted questions before time runs out.

So, how do the two modules work together to determine your score in a section? Well, if your raw score is high enough on the first module, you will automatically be bumped into a possible score range that is overall higher than you would be in if you had a lower raw score on the first module, though the two ranges may overlap some. Some questions within a module are also weighted, so doing better on those will increase your score more than doing well on easier, non-weighted questions. As such, your score is determined not only by how many questions you got right but also by how hard the questions were that you did. Although the scoring curve on each Digital PSAT 8/9 may calculate your score slightly differently, you will always have two jobs: understanding which questions can maximize your score and building your stamina to stay sharp through both modules in each section. Throughout this book, we will show you how to do just that.

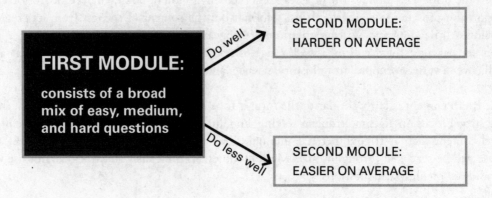

On the recent paper-and-pencil versions of the SAT Suite of Assessments, various subscores and cross-test scores were reported in addition to the section and overall scores. On the Digital Suite, only your section scores and total score will be reported.

What Does My PSAT 8/9 Score Mean for My PSAT and SAT Scores?

College Board has created what it calls a "Suite of Assessments" that starts with the PSAT 8/9. One of the ideas behind these tests is that each test prepares you for the next. To that end, the tests are more similar than different. All the tests in the Suite have the same structure, the same number of questions, and the same timing, so the main differences are the scale and level of difficulty. The PSAT 8/9 is scored on a 1440 scale, whereas the PSAT is scored on a 1520 scale and the SAT on a 1600 scale. However, because the PSAT 8/9, PSAT, and SAT are aligned by College Board to be scored on the same scale, your PSAT 8/9 score indicates the approximate PSAT or SAT score you would earn were you to have taken the PSAT or SAT on that same day. Since the difficulty of the PSAT 8/9 is lower than the other tests, you can't score quite as high on it as you can on the PSAT or SAT. Remember, though, no matter what score you get on your PSAT 8/9, you'll still have plenty of time to improve it before your PSAT or SAT!

HOW DOES THE PSAT 8/9 DIFFER FROM THE PSAT AND SAT?

So, if the PSAT 8/9, the PSAT 10, and the PSAT/NMSQT all have the same sections, number of modules, number of questions, and time to take them, what exactly ARE the differences between the tests? There are two main ones: the content covered on each test and the possible score ranges. See the chart below for a comparison of all the tests in the Digital SAT Suite of Assessments.

Test	PSAT 8/9	PSAT 10 and PSAT/NMSQT	SAT
Reading and Writing Content	Information and Ideas (≈26%) Craft and Structure (≈28%) Expression of Ideas (≈20%) Standard English Conventions (≈26%)	Information and Ideas (≈26%) Craft and Structure (≈28%) Expression of Ideas (≈20%) Standard English Conventions (≈26%)	Information and Ideas (≈26%) Craft and Structure (≈28%) Expression of Ideas (≈20%) Standard English Conventions (≈26%)
Text Complexity	Grades 6 through 11	Grades 6 through 14	Grades 6 through 14
Math Content	Algebra (≈42.5%) Advanced Math (≈20%) Problem-Solving and Data Analysis (≈25%) Geometry (≈12.5%)	Algebra (≈35%) Advanced Math (≈32.5%) Problem-Solving and Data Analysis (≈20%) Geometry and Trigonometry (≈12.5%)	Algebra (≈35%) Advanced Math (≈35%) Problem-Solving and Data Analysis (≈15%) Geometry and Trigonometry (≈15%)
Math Topics Excluded	Rational and Radical Equations, Trigonometry, Circles, Evaluating Statistical Claims and Making Inferences	Circles, Making Inferences from Statistical Samples	
Section Score Range	120 to 720	160 to 760	200 to 800
Total Score Range	240 to 1440	320 to 1520	400 to 1600

According to College Board, the SAT Suite of Assessments is designed to reflect how prepared you are for college and the working world. By creating a series of tests given over several years, College Board claims to measure a student's progress toward readiness for higher education and beyond.

College Board maintains that the best way to prepare for the test is to do the following:

- take challenging courses
- do your homework
- prepare for tests and quizzes
- ask and answer lots of questions

We at the Princeton Review are dubious about these claims, especially in regard to college and career readiness. Moreover, we think the best way to prepare for an exam is to know the content and structure of that exam. By reading this book, you are already on your way to improving your test scores.

HOW MUCH SHOULD I PREPARE FOR THE PSAT 8/9?

The PSAT 8/9 gives you insight into the PSAT and SAT. Your goal should be to prepare enough so that you feel more in control of the test and have a better testing experience. (Few things are as nerve-wracking as being dragged through a testing experience unsure of what you're being tested on or what to expect—except perhaps dental surgery.) The other reason to prepare for the PSAT 8/9 is that it will give you some testing skills that will help you begin to prepare for the test that actually counts, namely the SAT.

The bottom line is this: the best reason to prepare for the PSAT 8/9 is that it will help you get an early start on your preparation for the SAT.

WHAT IS THE PRINCETON REVIEW?

The Princeton Review is the nation's leading test-preparation company. In just a few years from our founding in 1981, we became the nation's leader in SAT preparation, primarily because our techniques work. We offer courses and private tutoring for all of the major standardized tests, and we publish a series of books to help in your search for the right school. If you'd like more information about our programs or books, give us a call at 800-2-REVIEW, or check out our website at PrincetonReview.com.

HOW TO USE THIS BOOK

This book is divided into five parts. The first three parts of the book contain Practice Test 1, general testing strategies, and question-specific problem-solving instruction. Use the first practice test as a diagnostic tool to see which sections of the test you need to work on when you read through the content chapters. The last part of the book contains drill answers and explanations. After working through the content chapters and checking your answers and the explanations to the chapter drills, take Practice Test 2 online and apply everything you've learned to improve your score. The "Session-by-Session Study Guide" starting on **page 12** will give you a plan to prepare for these tests and the rest of the book. There is no single plan that will fit everyone, so be prepared to adapt the plan and use it according to your own needs.

Practice Test 1 will give you an idea of your strengths and weaknesses, both of which can be sources of improvement. If you're already good at something, additional practice can make you great at it; if you're not so good at something, what you should do about it depends on how important it is. If the concept is one that frequently appears on the test, you should spend a lot of time on it; if it comes up only once in a while, you should spend very little time working on it and remember that it's something you should either put off until you've completed things you're better at or skip it entirely.

Study
If you were getting ready to take a biology test, you'd study biology. If you were preparing for a basketball game, you'd practice basketball. So, if you're preparing for the PSAT 8/9 (and eventually the PSAT and SAT), study the PSAT 8/9. The PSAT 8/9 can't test everything, so concentrate on learning what it does test.

Shortcuts
The Princeton Review's techniques are the closest thing there is to a shortcut to the PSAT 8/9. However, there is no shortcut to learning these techniques.

Use our online tools to take your practice tests digitally or use our online proctor to time you while you take the test in the book, then enter your answers online. Either way, you'll see your results and a breakdown of the question categories. See page 22 for more info.

How do you know what's important? We'll tell you throughout this book when we discuss techniques like Plugging In and so forth, but you can also get an idea of what to focus on simply by observing how this book is laid out. The Reading and Writing Introduction tells you how to jump to the questions you want to work on first. In the Math chapters, the most important concepts appear first. For example, if you're shaky on Reading, you know you'll need to devote some time to Reading questions because there is a total of 25–29 such questions on the test. And if you're not so confident when it comes to geometry, don't panic. Geometry questions appear only in the last math chapter, which tells you that this topic isn't as much of a priority as Plugging In or Math Basics.

One important note: In this book, the sample questions are in numerical order within a chapter. The question number does not indicate where you can expect to see a similar question on the test. As we'll show you later, what really matters is your *Personal* Order of Difficulty.

Time Management

To manage your PSAT 8/9 preparation, make use of the study guide on the following pages. This guide will break down the seemingly daunting task of PSAT 8/9 prep into bite-sized pieces we call "sessions." We have mapped out tasks for each session to be sure you get the most out of this book. The tests will be the first and last sessions, so you should be sure to plan to have about two-and-a-half hours for these sessions. Most other sessions will last between an hour and two hours, so plan to take a short break in the middle, and if it looks like the session is going to exceed two hours, feel free to stop and pick up where you left off on the next day.

When You Take a Practice Test

You'll see when to take practice tests in the session outlines. Here are some guidelines for taking these tests:

- If possible, take your practice tests online. Although one test is printed in this book, taking it online instead of on paper will allow you to become more comfortable with the online environment.
- When taking an online test, make sure to practice using the online tools. Use the annotation tool to mark important text in the passages and questions. Use the Answer Eliminator to get rid of the wrong answers. Mark questions you want to return to.
- Take a practice test in one sitting, under conditions similar to those of a proctored test. Sit in a quiet place and remove distractions like phones from the area. You need to build up your endurance for the real test, and you also need an accurate picture of how you will do. However, do take a 10-minute break between the Reading and Writing section and the Math section. On the real test you will have a break, so it's important not to skip it on the practice tests.
- If you take your tests online, you will be able to use the on-screen timer to keep track of the time remaining in each module. If you take the first test in the book instead of online, you will need to time yourself. Just make sure you do not allow yourself to go over time for any module.

For more information about how to take and score your practice tests, see page 22.

- Whether you take a test online or on paper, write down the things you need in order to answer the question. For the Digital PSAT 8/9, you will get three sheets of scratch paper. Make sure to write down calculations or make notes you need. Do not write on the questions or answers themselves on the paper test, as you will not be able to do so on the Digital PSAT 8/9.

Session-by-Session Study Guide

Session Zero You're involved in this session right now. Finish reading the first chapter so you'll know what the test is about, how it is used, and what to expect from the rest of the book. This step probably won't take you long, so if you have about two-and-a-half hours after you complete Chapter 1, you can go on to Session One and take the first practice test.

Session One Take Practice Test 1 and score it. You'll use this result to get an idea of your strengths and weaknesses and the parts of each section you should concentrate on. Note that our explanations refer to concepts discussed elsewhere in this book, so you may want to wait until after Session Four before reviewing this test.

Session Two Work through Chapter 2 of the Orientation and Chapter 5, Reading and Writing Introduction.

Session Three Read Chapter 6, Reading Comprehension, and Chapter 7, Rules Questions: Introduction.

Session Four Work through the Math Basics in Chapter 11 and the corresponding drills. Then do Chapter 8, Rules Questions: Punctuation.

Session Five Work through the Math Techniques section in Chapter 12 and associated drills. Take a look at Chapter 9, Rules Questions: Grammar.

Session Six Work through Advanced Math, Chapter 13. As you work through this chapter, be sure to apply techniques like Plugging In that you learned in Chapter 12. Since these techniques are central to doing well on the Math section, you can never practice them too much. If there's time, start Chapter 14.

Session Seven Work through Geometry in Chapter 14. When you finish, read through Chapter 10, Rhetoric Questions. This will complete your work in the content chapters.

Session Eight Take Practice Test 2, available online in your student portal. Use the techniques you've been practicing throughout the book. Score your test and go through the explanations, focusing on where you may have missed the opportunity to use a technique and your decisions about whether you should have attempted a question or not, given your pacing goals and Personal Order of Difficulty.

Some of the terminology in the study guide may be unfamiliar to you now, but don't worry, you'll get to know it soon. Also, you'll want to refer back to this study guide at each session to keep yourself on track.

So, what are you waiting for? Go ahead and dive into the Digital PSAT 8/9!

Chapter 2
General Strategies

The first step to cracking the PSAT 8/9 is to know how best to approach the test. The PSAT 8/9 is not like the tests you've taken in school, so you need to learn to look at it in a different way. This chapter will show test-taking strategies that immediately help to improve your score. Make sure you fully understand these concepts before moving on to the following chapters. Good luck!

BASIC PRINCIPLES OF CRACKING THE TEST

What College Board Is Good At

The folks at College Board have been writing standardized tests for nearly a century, and they write tests for all sorts of programs. They have administered the test so many times that they know exactly how you will approach it. They know how you'll approach certain questions, what sort of mistakes you'll probably make, and even what answer you'll be most likely to pick. Freaky, isn't it?

However, College Board's strength is also a weakness. Because the test is standardized, the PSAT 8/9 has to ask the same type of questions over and over again. Sure, the numbers or the words might change, but the basics don't. With enough practice, you can learn to think like the test-writers. But try to use your powers for good, okay?

The PSAT 8/9 Isn't School

Our job isn't to teach you math or English—leave that to your supersmart schoolteachers. Instead, we're going to teach you what the PSAT 8/9 is and how to crack the PSAT 8/9. You'll soon see that the PSAT 8/9 involves a very different skill set from the one you use in school.

> **No Penalty for Incorrect Answers!**
> You will NOT be penalized on the PSAT 8/9 for any wrong answers. This means you should always guess, even if this means choosing an answer at random.

Be warned that some of the approaches we're going to show you may seem counterintuitive or unnatural. Some of these strategies may be very different from the way you learned to approach similar questions in school but trust us! Try approaching the questions using our techniques and keep practicing until they become easier. You'll see a real improvement in your score.

Let's take a look at the questions.

Cracking Multiple-Choice Questions

What's the capital of Azerbaijan?

Give up?

Unless you spend your spare time studying an atlas or live in that part of the world, this may stump you. If this question came up on a test, you'd have to skip it, wouldn't you? Well, maybe not. Let's turn this question into a multiple-choice question—just like all the questions on the PSAT 8/9 Reading and Writing section and the majority of questions you'll find on the PSAT 8/9 Math section—and see if you can figure out the answer.

1 ☐ Mark for Review

What is the capital of Azerbaijan?

Ⓐ Washington, DC

Ⓑ Paris

Ⓒ London

Ⓓ Baku

The question doesn't seem that hard anymore, does it? Of course, we made our example extremely easy. (By the way, there won't actually be any questions about geography on the PSAT 8/9 that aren't answered by the accompanying passage.) But you'd be surprised by how many people give up on PSAT 8/9 questions that aren't much more difficult than this one just because they don't know the correct answer right off the top of their heads. "Capital of Azerbaijan? Oh, no! I've never heard of Azerbaijan!"

These students don't stop to think that they might be able to find the correct answer simply by eliminating all of the answer choices they know are wrong.

You Already Know Almost All of the Answers

Most of the questions on the PSAT 8/9 are multiple-choice questions, and every multiple-choice question has four answer choices. One of those choices, and only one, will be the correct answer to the question. You don't have to come up with the answer from scratch. You just have to identify it.

How will you do that?

It's Not About Finding the Right Answer

The Digital PSAT 8/9 tools will include an answer eliminator, so any wrong answers you find can be crossed off directly on the screen. If you need a more subtle system of rating the answers, write A, B, C, D on your scratch paper to mark them accordingly. Try using the following notations:

- ✔   Put a check mark next to an answer you like.
- ∼   Put a squiggle next to an answer you kind of like.
- ?   Put a question mark next to an answer you don't understand.
- A̶   Cross out the letter of any answer choice you KNOW is wrong.

You can always come up with your own system. Just make sure you are consistent.

Look for the Wrong Answers Instead of the Right Ones

Why? Because wrong answers are usually easier to find than the right ones. After all, there are more of them! Remember the question about Azerbaijan? Even though you didn't know the answer off the top of your head, you easily figured it out by eliminating the three obviously incorrect choices. You looked for wrong answers first.

In other words, you used the Process of Elimination, which we'll call POE for short. This is an extremely important concept, one we'll come back to again and again. It's one of the keys to improving your PSAT 8/9 score. When you finish reading this book, you will be able to use POE to answer many questions that you may not understand.

The great artist Michelangelo once said that when he looked at a block of marble, he could see a statue inside. All he had to do to make a sculpture was to chip away everything that wasn't part of it. You should approach difficult PSAT 8/9 multiple-choice questions in the same way, by chipping away everything that's not correct. By first eliminating the most obviously incorrect choices on difficult questions, you will be able to focus your attention on the few choices that remain.

PROCESS OF ELIMINATION (POE)

There won't be many questions on the PSAT 8/9 in which incorrect choices will be as easy to eliminate as they were on the Azerbaijan question. But if you read this book carefully, you'll learn how to eliminate at least one choice on almost any PSAT 8/9 multiple-choice question, if not two or even three choices.

What good is it to eliminate just one or two choices on a four-choice PSAT 8/9 question?

Plenty. In fact, for most students, it's an important key to earning higher scores. Here's another example:

---

2 🔖 Mark for Review

What is the capital of Qatar?

Ⓐ Paris

Ⓑ Dukhan

Ⓒ Tokyo

Ⓓ Doha

On this question, you'll almost certainly be able to eliminate two of the four choices by using POE. That means you're still not sure of the answer. You know that the capital of Qatar has to be either Doha or Dukhan, but you don't know which.

Should you skip the question and go on? Or should you guess?

Close Your Eyes and Point

There is no guessing penalty on the PSAT 8/9, so you should enter an answer for every question. If you get down to two answers, just pick one of them. There's no harm in doing so.

You're going to hear a lot of mixed opinions about whether you should guess at all. Let's clear up a few misconceptions about guessing.

FALSE: Don't answer a question unless you're absolutely sure of the answer.

> You will almost certainly have teachers and school counselors who tell you this. Don't listen to them! While the SAT used to penalize students for wrong answers prior to 2016, no tests in the current "Suite of Assessments" do this now. Put something down for every question: you might get a freebie.

FALSE: If you have to guess, guess (C).

> This is a weird misconception, and obviously it's not true. As a general rule, if someone says something really weird sounding about the PSAT 8/9, it's safest not to believe that person. (And we at the Princeton Review have gone through every PSAT 8/9, PSAT, and SAT and found that there isn't a "better" letter to guess, so just pick your favorite!)

FALSE: Always pick the [fill in the blank].

Be careful with directives that tell you that this or that answer or type of answer is always right. It's much safer to learn the rules and to have a solid guessing strategy in place.

As far as guessing is concerned, we do have a small piece of advice. First and foremost, make sure of one thing:

> Answer every question on the PSAT 8/9. There's no penalty.

GUESS AND GO

Sometimes you won't be able to eliminate any answers, and other times there will be questions that you won't have time to look at. For those, we have a simple solution. Guess and Go! Select an answer for all the questions for which you weren't able to eliminate any choices, then move on.

It's far more important and helpful to your score to eliminate answer choices if you can. But for those questions you don't know at all or get stuck on, Guess and Go is better than leaving the question blank.

Get Ready...
Check out *Digital SAT Prep* for everything you need to know about the SAT exam.

PACE YOURSELF

Guess and Go should remind us about something very important: there's a very good chance that you won't answer every question on the test. Instead, work at a pace that lets you avoid careless mistakes, and don't stress about the questions you don't get to.

Think about it this way. In each given module, there will be questions that you can tackle quickly and accurately and others that will take you more time and effort. Why should you spend 4 or 5 minutes on one question when you may get two or three questions that are easier for you in the same amount of time?

Another tool you can use on the Digital PSAT 8/9 to help pace yourself is the Mark for Review tool. If you see a question that looks like it might be time-consuming or that you aren't sure how to solve, but you still want to come back to it if there is time, mark it. You can see the marked questions at a glance both at the end of the section or by opening the section overview at any time. This will allow you to quickly find the ones you want to work after you've done all the questions you know you can do quickly and accurately.

Unless you're currently scoring in the 610+ range on the two sections, you shouldn't be working all the questions.

> Slow down, score more. You're not scored on *how many questions you do*. You're scored on *how many questions you answer correctly*. Doing fewer questions can mean more correct answers overall!

EMBRACE YOUR POOD

Embrace your *what* now? POOD! It stands for "Personal Order of Difficulty." The Digital PSAT 8/9 will put questions in a rough order of difficulty, by content domain on the Reading and Writing section and overall on the Math section. But this Order of Difficulty (OOD) is only what College Board thinks about the question levels, not how you will do on them. So, rather than doing the questions in order, you need to be particularly vigilant about applying your *Personal* Order of Difficulty (POOD).

Think about it this way. There's someone writing the words that you're reading right now. So, what happens if you are asked, *Who is the author of PSAT 8/9 Prep?* Do you know the answer to that question? Maybe not. Do we know the answer to that question? Absolutely.

So, you can't exactly say that that question is "difficult," but you can say that certain people would have an easier time answering it. Pace yourself. Work carefully on questions you know how to do to make sure you get them right. Mark questions you want to come back to later.

As we've begun to suggest with our Pacing, POE, and Letter of the Day strategies, the Princeton Review's strategies are all about making the test your own, to whatever extent that is possible. We call this idea POOD because we believe it is essential that you identify the questions that you find easy or hard and that you work the test in a way most suitable to your goals and strengths.

As you familiarize yourself with the rest of our strategies, keep all of this in mind. You may be surprised to find out how you perform on particular question types and sections. This test may be standardized, but the biggest improvements are usually reserved for those who can treat the test in a personalized, nonstandardized way.

Summary

o   When you don't know the right answer to a multiple-choice question, look for wrong answers instead. They're usually easier to find.

o   When you find a wrong answer choice, eliminate it. In other words, use Process of Elimination, or POE.

o   There's no penalty for wrong answers, so there's no reason NOT to guess.

o   There will likely be at least a few questions you simply don't get to or where you're finding it difficult to eliminate even one answer choice. When this happens, use the Guess and Go strategy.

o   Pace yourself. Work carefully on questions you know how to do to make sure you get them right.

o   Mark questions you want to come back to later. Guess and Go on any you know are not worth your time or effort or that you know you are unlikely to get right.

o   Make the test your own. When you can work the test to suit your strengths (and use our strategies to overcome any weaknesses), you'll be on your way to a higher score.

Part II
Practice Test 1

HOW TO TAKE THE DIGITAL PSAT 8/9 ON PAPER

The Digital PSAT 8/9 will be administered on a computer or tablet. Both tests associated with this book, the one that follows and a second one, can be found in your online portal. The best way to practice is to take your tests online in your student portal to mimic the real testing experience. However, should you decide to take Test 1 on paper either indicate your answers as described in the directions for print tests included with each module or by entering your answers as you go onto the answer sheet on pages 83–84.

On the Digital PSAT 8/9, you will only get two modules in each section, and the second module you get in each section will be determined by your performance on the first module in that section. Therefore, for both RW and Math, the following test contains a standard first module and two options for the second module, one easier and one harder. You should take the appropriate second module based on your performance in the first module, as detailed below, but you can feel free to use the other module for extra practice later.

In order to navigate the practice test in this book, take the following steps.

- ☐ Take Reading and Writing Module 1, allowing yourself 32 minutes to complete it.

- ☐ Go to the answer key on page 86 and determine the number of questions you got correct in RW Module 1.

- ☐ If you get fewer than 15 questions correct, take RW Module 2—Easier, which starts on page 36. If you get 15 or more questions correct, take RW Module 2—Harder, which starts on page 46.

- ☐ Whichever RW Module 2 you take, start it immediately and allow yourself 32 minutes to complete it.

- ☐ Take a 10-minute break between RW Module 2 and Math Module 1.

- ☐ Take Math Module 1, allowing yourself 35 minutes to complete it.

- ☐ Go to the answer key on page 86 and determine the number of questions you got correct in Math Module 1.

- ☐ If you get fewer than 14 questions correct, take Math Module 2—Easier, which starts on page 66. If you get 14 or more questions correct, take Math Module 2—Harder, which starts on page 74.

- ☐ Whichever Math Module you take, start it immediately and allow yourself 35 minutes to complete it.

- ☐ After you finish the test, check your answers to RW Module 2 and Math Module 2.

- ☐ Only after you complete the entire test should you read the explanations for the questions, which start on page 87 and are also available online.

- ☐ Go to your online student tools to see the latest information about scoring and to get your estimated score.

Chapter 3
Practice Test 1

PSAT 8/9 Test 1—Reading and Writing
Module 1

Turn to Section 1 of your answer sheet to answer the questions in this section.

1 ☐ Mark for Review

In 1913, approximately 91% of the roads in the United States were rural dirt roads. Experts recognized the need for improved surfaces and, as part of an ambitious _____, worked toward the completion of the Lincoln Highway in 1916: extending from New York City to San Francisco, the Lincoln Highway became the first coast-to-coast highway in the United States.

Which choice completes the text with the most logical and precise word or phrase?

Ⓐ treaty

Ⓑ undertaking

Ⓒ invention

Ⓓ failure

2 ☐ Mark for Review

Bill Morrison has dedicated his career to presenting archival film footage set to modern music. As part of his process, Morrison _____ several different composers, whom he asks to write a score that will allow him to present old, decaying footage as part of a new, integrated narrative. Among other accolades, his 2002 film *Decasia* was selected for preservation by United States National Film Registry.

Which choice completes the text with the most logical word or phrase?

Ⓐ works with

Ⓑ praises

Ⓒ argues with

Ⓓ cautions

CONTINUE

3 ☐ Mark for Review

Archaeologists have long believed that the first meaningful contact between East and West occurred with the opening of the Silk Road in the second century BCE, but new findings suggest otherwise. Archaeologists have recently excavated statues from China, and senior archaeologist Xiuzhen Li of the Emperor Qin Shi Huang's Mausoleum Site Museum believes the findings _____ previous conclusions: terracotta acrobats and bronze birds such as swans and cranes indicate a strong Greek influence and the involvement of Greek sculptors from as far back as the fifth century BCE.

Which choice completes the text with the most logical and precise word or phrase?

(A) contradict

(B) confirm

(C) investigate

(D) demonstrate

4 ☐ Mark for Review

The following text is adapted from Katherine Mansfield's 1922 short story "The Garden Party." The narrator is describing one part of a neighborhood that he has just arrived in.

That really was extravagant, for the little cottages were in a lane to themselves at the very bottom of a steep rise that led up to the house. A broad road ran between. True, they were far too near. They were the greatest possible eyesore, and they had no right to be in that neighbourhood at all. They were little <u>mean</u> dwellings painted a chocolate brown.

As used in the text, what does the word "mean" most nearly mean?

(A) Displeasing

(B) Welcoming

(C) Captivating

(D) Abusing

CONTINUE

5 ☐ Mark for Review

Missoula, Montana, is known for a children's theater that casts children in plays as the company travels from city to city. The Missoula Children's Theater (MCT) was founded in 1970 as a company of adults performing for children, but in 1972 the two founders realized there was a high demand for the kids themselves to perform the shows. Now touring nationally, the MCT goes to different cities and casts local children in each show, building a community experience in each location while keeping the spirit of the theater intact.

Which choice best states the main purpose of the text?

(A) To detail the surge in theater popularity in Missoula from 1970 onwards

(B) To contrast the Missoula Children's Theater with other theater companies in Missoula

(C) To describe the history and current contributions of the Missoula Children's Theater

(D) To advocate for people to raise funds for children's theater in Missoula

6 ☐ Mark for Review

The following text is from Jane Austen's 1814 novel *Mansfield Park*. Fanny, a 10-year-old girl, has recently moved in with her aunt and uncle.

From this day Fanny grew more comfortable. She felt that she had a friend, and the kindness of her cousin Edmund gave her better spirits with everybody else. The place became less strange, and the people less formidable; and if there were some amongst them whom she could not cease to fear, she began at least to know their ways, and to catch the best manner of conforming to them.

Which choice best states the main purpose of the text?

(A) To explain how Edmund and his family feel about Fanny

(B) To detail Fanny's adjustment to her situation

(C) To describe the fears that Fanny shares with Edmund

(D) To discuss how Fanny came to live at Mansfield Park

CONTINUE ➤

7 ▢ Mark for Review

Alloparental care occurs when an animal cares for offspring that are not its own. Most research on this behavior in other animals has focused on genetic relatedness of the adopted animal to its adoptive parent. However, biologist Marianne Riedman and Burney Le Boeuf showed that it can occur in unrelated pairs as well (i.e., not from the same family). In their study, which focused on a colony of northern elephant seals (*Mirounga angustirostris*) in California, the researchers further reported that some females adopted pups alongside their own or adopted multiple pups at the same time.

Which choice best describes the function of the first sentence in the text as a whole?

- Ⓐ It provides a theory that is confirmed by the text.

- Ⓑ It introduces an occurrence that is examined by the text.

- Ⓒ It states a challenge that is described by the text.

- Ⓓ It makes an argument that is contradicted by the text.

8 ▢ Mark for Review

The following text is from Sir Arthur Conan Doyle's 1892 novel *The Adventures of Sherlock Holmes*. Dr. John Watson has joined a disguised Holmes as they await a person of interest in an investigation.

It was already dusk, and the lamps were just being lighted as we paced up and down in front of Briony Lodge, waiting for the coming of its occupant. The house was just such as I had pictured it from Sherlock Holmes' succinct description, but the locality appeared to be less private than I expected. On the contrary, for a small street in a quiet neighbourhood, it was remarkably animated.

Which choice best states the main purpose of the text?

- Ⓐ It shows a character expressing a lack of surprise regarding a location.

- Ⓑ It demonstrates a character's response to a surprising situation.

- Ⓒ It details why a character has visited a certain neighborhood.

- Ⓓ It contrasts two different characters' assumptions about a location and its activity level.

CONTINUE ➡

9 ☐ Mark for Review

Between 1883 and 1914, architect Antoni Gaudí designed seven different residential properties inside and around Barcelona. <u>These buildings represent his personal style, which combined elements of Gothic and Baroque architecture with his own signature interest in flowing structures reminiscent of natural landscapes and features.</u> The buildings have the architectural hallmarks of the time but are also notable for pushing the boundaries of design into a new era, making Gaudí one of the first modernist architects.

Which choice best describes the function of the underlined sentence in the text as a whole?

(A) It explains how Gaudí's buildings were often featured in architectural magazines.

(B) It highlights Gaudí's desire to become one of the first modernist architects.

(C) It describes how Gaudí became involved in architecture.

(D) It details certain notable aspects of Gaudí's buildings.

10 ☐ Mark for Review

The discovery of human teeth and bones from a 700-year-old Pueblo in present-day Arizona has yielded new information about the people who once lived there. Using strontium isotope analysis, T. Douglas Price and his team were able to determine where the pueblo inhabitants originated. By comparing strontium in Pueblo rocks, human bones and teeth, and rock and bone samples from several different sites, Price and his team discovered that different groups of Native Americans from different parts of the Southwest all migrated to the Pueblo following a massive drought.

Which choice best states the main idea of the text?

(A) Prior to the development of strontium isotope analysis, scientists needed to dissect rock specimens in order to determine their origin.

(B) Due to an innovation, scientists can uncover and analyze more human bone and tooth remains than they could previously.

(C) Scientists have been successful in locating a Native American migration trail that was utilized 700 years ago.

(D) With the assistance of specialized technology, scientists have determined the origins of some members of the Pueblo tribe.

CONTINUE →

11 ☐ Mark for Review

The following text is adapted from E. M. Forster's 1908 novel *A Room with a View.* Lucy, a young British woman, is visiting the city of Florence, Italy.

Her first morning was ruined, and she might never be in Florence again. A few minutes ago she had been all high spirits, talking as a woman of culture, and half persuading herself that she was full of originality. Now she entered the church depressed and humiliated, not even able to remember whether it was built by the Franciscans or the Dominicans. Of course, it must be a wonderful building. But how like a barn! And how very cold!

Which choice best states the main idea of the text?

(A) Lucy is visiting a church in Florence because she has never been inside of a church before.

(B) Lucy is depressed until the warmth of the church raises her spirits.

(C) Lucy is upset and flustered by an experience she has had in Florence.

(D) Lucy is initially disappointed by the appearance of a church in Florence but is soon enamored with it.

12 ☐ Mark for Review

The American designer, screenwriter, and producer Polly Platt was a hugely influential force in film during the late twentieth century, but her contributions are often overlooked by those outside of the film industry. The lack of visible career opportunities for women in male-dominated Hollywood contributed to her being overshadowed by the men whose careers she supported. Notably, she launched the careers of famous directors such as Cameron Crowe, Wes Anderson, and her ex-husband Peter Bogdanovich through her creative roles behind the scenes that relegated her to the background despite her artistic genius.

Which choice best states the main idea of the text?

(A) Few of Platt's films are available for purchase today because she only worked on a small number of pictures.

(B) People may not be as aware of Platt's work as they should be because Crowe, Anderson, and Bogdanovich have received more attention.

(C) During Platt's career, her contributions to the film industry have been more frequently acknowledged than those of Crowe, Anderson, or Bogdanovich's.

(D) Platt worked on some of the same films as Crowe, Anderson, and Bogdanovich but used different filmmaking techniques than they did.

CONTINUE ➡

13 ☐ Mark for Review

Buddhists in Three Asian Countries
and North America

Country/Region	Approximate number of Buddhists (in millions)	Estimated % of world Buddhist population
India	9	2
China	244	50
Thailand	64	13
North America	4	1

Buddhism is a major world religion with an estimated 488 million adherents worldwide. It is a formally recognized religion in Thailand, India, China, and North America and is the primary religion of Thailand. This means that the majority of people in Thailand are Buddhist. Interestingly, even though Buddhism originated in India, there are other countries that contain a much larger number of Buddhists among their populations.

Which choice most effectively uses data from the table to support the underlined claim?

Ⓐ Approximately 50 percent of the world Buddhist population lives in China, while only about one percent of the world Buddhist population lives in North America.

Ⓑ Thailand has approximately 64 million practicing Buddhists, which is much more than the approximate number of Buddhists who live in India.

Ⓒ Thailand is estimated to have at most 16 million practicing Buddhists, while the country contains an estimated 13 percent of the world Buddhist population.

Ⓓ Buddhists make up 50 percent of the population of China, which has 244 million people.

14 ☐ Mark for Review

Octavia Butler's 1993 science fiction novel *The Parable of the Sower* has influenced literature in several different ways. Its Black female main character inspired other Black authors to write their own science fiction tales. Lauren Olamina, the main character, was also influential in starting a wider artistic movement. The depiction of a Black girl who eventually travels through space inspired other Black writers to explore the theme of future technology in their works, contributing to the development of Afrofuturism.

Which statement, if true, would most strongly support the claim in the underlined sentence?

Ⓐ Novels about Black characters by Black authors written since 1993 have often been compared to *The Parable of the Sower*.

Ⓑ In social media posts, a number of Black authors cite *The Parable of the Sower* as a primary influence in writing their own science fiction works.

Ⓒ In interview transcripts, several famous authors who are not Black claim that reading *The Parable of the Sower* helped them develop their approach to science fiction.

Ⓓ *The Parable of the Sower* won multiple awards upon publication and is considered by many readers to be the best science fiction book of the last 100 years.

CONTINUE →

15 ☐ Mark for Review

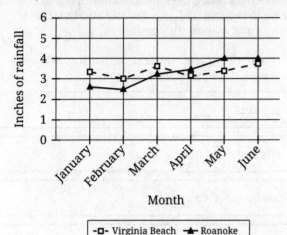

Monthly Inches of Rainfall from January to June in Roanoke and Virginia Beach, Virginia

-□- Virginia Beach ▲ Roanoke

A student is conducting research about inches of rainfall per month in cities across Virginia. While studying trends in Roanoke and Virginia Beach, the student concludes that rainfall in inches from the months of January to June in these cities follows a similar pattern.

Which choice best describes data from the graph that support the student's conclusion?

(A) Roanoke and Virginia Beach both have more than three monthly inches of rainfall from January to February but less than four monthly inches of rainfall from May to June.

(B) The monthly inches of rainfall in both Roanoke and Virginia Beach remain constant from March to April before beginning to increase in May.

(C) The monthly inches of rainfall in both Roanoke and Virginia Beach decrease from January to February and then increase from April to May.

(D) Roanoke and Virginia Beach both have less than three inches of rainfall from January to June.

16 ☐ Mark for Review

In writing her 2013 drama *The Flick*, playwright Annie Baker used a theater convention of inserting long, awkward silences into her plays. Baker takes this convention to an extreme; *The Flick* is three-and-a-half hours long with much of it taking place in silence. In the play, Baker pays homage to the "quiet" actors in Chekhov plays and silent film stars like Charlie Chaplin, who fill silence with emotion through body language and facial expressions. It might seem like including awkward silence would be too disquieting for the audience, and in fact, some people left *The Flick* in the middle. However, theater critics lauded *The Flick* for its acknowledgment of the history of theater and cinema and awarded Baker the Pulitzer Prize for the work. This reaction suggests that _____

Which choice most logically completes the text?

(A) Baker influenced many other playwrights to create works with long, awkward silences.

(B) many theater critics may have overlooked Baker's central message in *The Flick*.

(C) Baker's use of silence helped her complete a goal she had when making *The Flick*.

(D) silent film star Charlie Chaplin was one of Baker's favorite actors.

CONTINUE ➡

17 ⬚ Mark for Review

Created in 1978, the Cape Grim Air Archive is a collection of air samples obtained at the Cape Grim Baseline Air Pollution Station in Tasmania. The location was chosen because the air coming from the Southern Ocean is unaffected by local pollution from landmasses. Approximately every three months, researchers fill stainless steel flasks with air and _____ the samples to the archive.

Which choice completes the text so that it conforms to the conventions of Standard English?

(A) were adding

(B) added

(C) had added

(D) add

18 ⬚ Mark for Review

How do scientists classify fossils from millions of years ago as those of mammals or reptiles? Researchers _____ the teeth to help distinguish mammals from reptiles: mammals have only two sets of teeth, the baby set and the permanent set, while reptiles replace their teeth throughout their lives.

Which choice completes the text so that it conforms to the conventions of Standard English?

(A) to use

(B) using

(C) having used

(D) use

19 ⬚ Mark for Review

In the 2009 book *A Mighty Long Way*, Carlotta Walls LaNier describes how her attendance at Little Rock Central High School in Arkansas as one of the first to integrate the school _____ her life and the lives of her family and community members.

Which choice completes the text so that it conforms to the conventions of Standard English?

(A) to affect

(B) affected

(C) having affected

(D) affecting

20 ⬚ Mark for Review

Katherine Siva Saubel was a scholar, activist, and tribal leader dedicated to the preservation of Cahuilla language, history, and culture. She conducted research with linguists at UCLA as well as the University of Cologne in _____ with anthropologist Lowell John Bean, she wrote *Temalpakh (From the Earth): Cahuilla Indian Knowledge and Usage of Plants*.

Which choice completes the text so that it conforms to the conventions of Standard English?

(A) Germany, and

(B) Germany,

(C) Germany and

(D) Germany

CONTINUE ➡

21 ☐ Mark for Review

In 2011, British choreographer and dancer Sarah Michelson considered the space and context of the venue when designing the work she called _____in the performers' space, the audience is confronted with a new perspective and urged to identify with the dancers.

Which choice completes the text so that it conforms to the conventions of Standard English?

(A) _Devotion_. Sitting

(B) _Devotion_ sitting

(C) _Devotion_, sitting

(D) _Devotion_ sitting,

22 ☐ Mark for Review

While her husband worked as a mechanic with the Tuskegee Airmen, Azellia White learned to fly. She earned her pilot's license in 1946, making her one of the first African American women to earn a license in the United States. _____she and her husband, along with two other Tuskegee Airmen, founded the Sky Ranch Flying Service, a flight school and airport for African American aviators.

Which choice completes the text with the most logical transition?

(A) Moreover,

(B) In other words,

(C) Nevertheless,

(D) Still,

23 ☐ Mark for Review

Author Aleksis Kivi was one of the first prominent writers in the Finnish language. In 1864, he wrote the play _Heath Cobblers_. _____in 1870, he wrote the novel _Seitsemän veljestä_ (_Seven Brothers_), the first significant novel in Finnish. He is still regarded as the national writer of Finland.

Which choice completes the text with the most logical transition?

(A) However,

(B) On the other hand,

(C) For example,

(D) Later,

24 ☐ Mark for Review

American choreographer and conceptualist Ralph Lemon took ten years to create a trilogy of performances to present social issues. _____Lemon expressed himself through painting, but he found that movement through dance allowed him to communicate more thoroughly and accurately.

Which choice completes the text with the most logical transition?

(A) Initially,

(B) In effect,

(C) Hence,

(D) At any rate,

CONTINUE

25 ☐ Mark for Review

While researching a topic, a student has taken the following notes:

- Miguel Algarín was a Puerto Rican poet and writer.
- With other poets, he founded the Nuyorican Poets Café.
- The café was noteworthy for popularizing slam poetry, or spoken word poetry, by hosting poetry slams.
- Poetry slams are events at which poetry is performed and judged.

The student wants to describe what was noteworthy about Algarín's café. Which choice most effectively uses relevant information from the notes to accomplish this goal?

Ⓐ Algarín helped to found the Nuyorican Poets Café.

Ⓑ Slam poetry, or spoken word poetry, was popularized through events at which poetry is performed and judged.

Ⓒ Algarín's café popularized slam poetry by hosting poetry slams, events at which poetry is performed and judged.

Ⓓ A Puerto Rican poet and writer, Miguel Algarín helped found Nuyorican Poets Café.

26 ☐ Mark for Review

While researching a topic, a student has taken the following notes:

- Alodia was one of the three medieval Nubian kingdoms.
- It was located in what is now known as Sudan.
- Alodia was formed sometime after 350 CE when the Kingdom of Kush fell.
- In historical records, it was first mentioned in 569 CE.
- The capital of Alodia was Soba, which was a large trading hub.

The student wants to specify the year Alodia was first mentioned in the historical records. Which choice most effectively uses relevant information from the notes to accomplish this goal?

Ⓐ Alodia, a medieval Nubian kingdom, was first mentioned in historical records in 569 CE.

Ⓑ One of the three medieval Nubian kingdoms, Alodia formed after the Kingdom of Kush fell.

Ⓒ Soba, a large trading hub, was the capital of Alodia.

Ⓓ The Nubian kingdom Alodia formed sometime after 350 CE.

CONTINUE ➡

27   ◻ Mark for Review

While researching a topic, a student has taken the following notes:

- Conventionally, opera is a dramatic type of theater consisting of music and singers.

- The music is classical, and the singers learn the words from a *libretto*, or script.

- In the 1960s, the idea of a rock opera became appealing to various rock artists and groups.

- Rock operas use rock music and are typically released as concept albums.

- Rock operas do not have scripts, unless these operas are adapted for the stage.

The student wants to emphasize a difference between rock operas and conventional operas. Which choice most effectively uses relevant information from the notes to accomplish this goal?

(A) Operas have featured classical music but also rock music.

(B) Conventionally, an opera uses a *libretto* and consists of classical music, not rock music.

(C) Unlike conventional operas, rock operas use rock music and do not have scripts.

(D) Rock operas were developed in the 1960s and are generally released as concept albums.

YIELD

Once you've finished (or run out of time for) this section, use the answer key to determine how many questions you got right. If you got fewer than 15 questions right, move on to Module 2—Easier, otherwise move on to Module 2—Harder.

PSAT 8/9 Test 1—Reading and Writing
Module 2—Easier

Turn to Section 1 of your answer sheet to answer the questions in this section.

---

1 ☐ Mark for Review

Dame Zaha Hadid, an architect active during the second half of the twentieth century, was known for her organic and _____ building designs. Rather than adhering to the symmetry of traditional structural elements, she favored deconstructivism, which is defined by fragmented shapes and flowing movements.

Which choice completes the text with the most logical and precise word or phrase?

(A) logical

(B) unusual

(C) straightforward

(D) typical

---

2 ☐ Mark for Review

Each dolphin has its own whistle sequence, similar to a human name, that its mother teaches it when it is young. These individualized _____ help dolphins locate one another in murky water and other situations where visibility is poor.

Which choice completes the text with the most logical and precise word or phrase?

(A) contracts

(B) sizes

(C) ornaments

(D) arrangements

CONTINUE ➤

---

3 ☐ Mark for Review

Family Legacies: The Art of Betye, Lezley, and Alison Saar was an exhibit of mixed-media assemblages exploring the Saar family's history, traditions, and spirituality. The exhibit _____ two generations, tracing how daughters Alison and Lezley expanded their mother Betye's work.

Which choice completes the text with the most logical and precise word or phrase?

(A) disregarded

(B) adopted

(C) bridged

(D) criticized

4 ☐ Mark for Review

Alfred Hitchcock's successful movie career was aided by the _____ of accomplished composer Bernard Herrmann, whose musical works provided the perfect backdrop for Hitchcock's films such as the comedic *The Trouble With Harry* and the terrifying, award-winning film *Psycho*.

Which choice completes the text with the most logical and precise word or phrase?

(A) criticisms

(B) arguments

(C) talent

(D) retirement

5 ☐ Mark for Review

Canals, rivers, and storm drains carry garbage and debris out into the ocean. But the debris carried out by these waterways could not make it farther out to sea without the help of a strong ocean current. Researchers label these currents "gyres." These gyres carry debris along a consistent pathway, leading to significant accumulation of garbage at specific points in the ocean. Though oceanographers had long suspected the existence of one such garbage patch in the Pacific Ocean, it was Charles Moore, a racing boat captain, who discovered the Great Pacific Garbage Patch, which covers 1.6 million square kilometers.

Which choice best describes the function of the underlined portion in the text as a whole?

(A) It details the difference among three types of waterways.

(B) It highlights Charles Moore's opinion about the challenges he has overcome.

(C) It presents a scientific term that is relevant to the rest of the discussion.

(D) It highlights the intriguing nature of the discovery that is mentioned.

CONTINUE →

6 ☐ Mark for Review

Text 1

Joshua Plotnik and Frans B. M. de Waal observed 26 Asian elephants (*Elephas maximus*) to determine how they reacted to distressing stimuli. The researchers observed that when one animal was distressed, other elephants approached the distressed animal and touched it with their trunks. The researchers claimed that this behavior suggests that elephants can be altruistic, trying to console other elephants without any direct benefit to themselves.

Text 2

The idea of animals trying to console one another through touch in times of distress seems logical, particularly for a species such as elephants, which have been known to exhibit various forms of tactile behavior. However, it is quite likely that the animals are simply congregating following an event that distressed several individuals, with some perhaps showing a delayed reaction to the distressing stimuli and seeking social cohesion as a means of safety.

Based on the texts, how would the author of Text 2 most likely respond to the researcher's claim in Text 1 regarding the behavior of the Asian elephants?

(A) The behavior observed may be sufficiently explained without concluding that the elephants were exhibiting altruistic tendencies.

(B) The behavior observed may have been due to the confined nature of the elephant enclosure rather than to the distress of an individual.

(C) The behavior observed likely implies that the elephants were actively working to benefit themselves by seeking comfort in others.

(D) The behavior observed may not be evidence of altruistic behavior in *Elephas maximus* because only some of the elephants exhibited it.

7 ☐ Mark for Review

Los Angeles's Contra-Tiempo Activist Dance Theater, founded by Ana Maria Alvarez, creates dance works featuring multimedia in collaborations with artists such as choreographer Marjani Forté. For the company's *joyUS justUS* performance, Alvarez invites members of the audience to participate in dance and movement exercises and then create their own collaborative dance.

Which choice best states the main idea of the text?

(A) Alvarez invites members of the audience to create their own dance to illustrate the complexity of the task.

(B) The Contra-Tiempo Activist Dance Theater company performs dances from all over the United States but mostly performs dances choreographed by Los Angeles natives.

(C) Alvarez began the Contra-Tiempo Activist Dance Theater company to perform dances choreographed by Marjani Forté.

(D) The Contra-Tiempo Activist Dance company gives audience members the opportunity to both observe and participate in collaborative dance performances.

CONTINUE

8 ☐ Mark for Review

Species	Approximate molar diameter	Estimated average height
Homo sapien	10 mm	5′4″
Homo floresiensis	9.8 mm	3′6″
Homo luzonensis	8 mm	3′5″

The table shows data from anthropologist Florent Détroit's 2019 discovery of *Homo luzonensis* fossils, excavated from Callao Cave on the Island of Luzon, and those of two other hominin species: *Homo sapien* and *Homo floresiensis*. The fossils suggest that, compared to several other hominin species, *Homo luzonensis* had _____

Which choice most effectively uses data from the table to complete the claim?

- (A) a smaller molar diameter, and a taller average height.

- (B) a larger molar diameter, and a shorter average height.

- (C) a larger molar diameter, and a taller average height.

- (D) a smaller molar diameter, and a shorter average height.

9 ☐ Mark for Review

Celestial object	Primary atmospheric gas	Percentage of primary gas in atmosphere
Mercury	Oxygen	42%
Venus	Carbon dioxide	96%
Pluto	Nitrogen	90%
Earth's Moon	Argon	70%
Titan (Moon of Saturn)	Nitrogen	97%

Like Earth, some objects in the solar system have atmospheres composed of more than 80% nitrogen. Two examples of such objects are _____

Which choice most effectively uses data from the table to complete the statement?

- (A) Pluto and Earth's Moon.

- (B) Titan and Pluto.

- (C) Mercury and Titan.

- (D) Pluto and Mercury.

CONTINUE ➡

10 ☐ Mark for Review

Captain Dimitrios Kontos and his team of Greek sponge divers discovered the wreckage of a first-century cargo ship. One of the items recovered from the wreck was the Antikythera mechanism. This mechanism is a complex geared device from ancient times, and many scholars believe it is the world's first computer.

Which finding, if true, would most directly support the scholars' claim?

(A) Debris from other mechanisms has been found at the Greek site that were probably the work of inventors.

(B) Other versions of the same first-century mechanism have been found in the ruins of many residences in the area, including in one residence that may have belonged to an inventor.

(C) Similar mechanisms have been discovered at other sites dating to the same century whose people often shared ideas with those who lived near the Greek site.

(D) Descriptions of the mechanism from the same time period have been noted to claim that its primary purpose was to calculate complex mathematical approximations.

11 ☐ Mark for Review

Water without any dissolved particles appears blue because that is the color of light that is reflected from the water particles. Water containing sediment from broken-down rock looks brown or yellow because those are the hues most commonly reflected off of sediment. Water containing algae usually looks green because green is the primary color reflected off the algae. However, approximately one-third of rivers in the United States have changed color in the last 35 years, with normally algae-rich waters becoming more yellow. One team of researchers hypothesized that this phenomenon is the result of human activity, with dams and water runoff altering the composition of the dissolved particles in the water.

Which finding, if true, would most directly weaken the team's hypothesis?

(A) Algae-rich waterways can appear yellow if the algae are exposed to certain naturally occurring compounds.

(B) Yellow or brown water remains the same color when mixed with blue water due to existing sediment in the water.

(C) Dams and water runoff produce a deeper yellow water color in the United States than they do in other regions of the world.

(D) Yellow or brown water and green water are rarely mixed together in nature.

CONTINUE

12 ⬚ Mark for Review

Appalachian fiddle musicians, many of whom immigrated from Scotland and Ireland in the 1700s, gave rise to modern-day American bluegrass music. The genre is still popular today, with annual fiddle contests drawing up to 10,000 people at a time. However, historical recordings of the traditional fiddle music are few and far between, and those that do exist are largely stored on media that is susceptible to decay. This has led some historians to dedicate their time to implement safer storage practices for the recordings. By ensuring the security of these valuable sound and video records, they are also _____

Which choice most logically completes the text?

Ⓐ ensuring that listeners of fiddle music can attend concerts by their favorite performers.

Ⓑ protecting at least some of the history of Appalachian musical culture.

Ⓒ expanding awareness of Appalachian fiddle music beyond the lands of its origin.

Ⓓ assisting future Appalachian fiddle musicians who are interested in recording their own music.

13 ⬚ Mark for Review

Based on computer models of the collision that formed our moon, Keiichi Wada, Eiichiro Kokubo, and Junichiro Makino determined that the disk that eventually coalesced into the Moon must have been primarily solid or liquid particles. The team calculated that a disk made primarily of gas would have been vaporized in the collision and a satellite the size of our Moon would not have formed. In their models, the team set the impact velocity at approximately 15 km/s, leading to the development of a primarily gaseous disk and a very small satellite. Because collision velocity depends on the masses of the colliding bodies, the researchers concluded that _____

Which choice most logically completes the text?

Ⓐ the disk that eventually formed the Moon was of significant enough mass to also form the Earth.

Ⓑ the impact velocity at which the collision that formed the Moon occurred must be slower than the initial calculations suggested.

Ⓒ the mass of the bodies that collided to form the Moon must have been within a specific range.

Ⓓ if the impact velocity of the collision that formed the Moon had been faster, the moon would have been much larger than it is today.

CONTINUE ➡

14 ⬜ Mark for Review

Ramola Vaidya is a wastewater engineer. She studies ways to make treated wastewater flow into underground water sources called aquifers rather than into rivers. This allows aquifers that have run dry _____ and prevents local waterways from becoming polluted.

Which choice completes the text so that it conforms to the conventions of Standard English?

Ⓐ to refill

Ⓑ refilled

Ⓒ refills

Ⓓ have refilled

15 ⬜ Mark for Review

Critics of young adult literature have _____ *The Outsiders* by S. E. Hinton, a novel based on the author's own high school experiences in 1960s Tulsa, Oklahoma, as one of the pioneering works in the genre.

Which choice completes the text so that it conforms to the conventions of Standard English?

Ⓐ recognized.

Ⓑ recognized:

Ⓒ recognized

Ⓓ recognized,

16 ⬜ Mark for Review

Complete metamorphosis, or holometabolism, is a complex process used by some insects, such as butterflies and bees. You _____ the less complex partial metamorphosis, when insects change the shape of their bodies, in the previous chapter.

Which choice completes the text so that it conforms to the conventions of Standard English?

Ⓐ saw

Ⓑ will see

Ⓒ see

Ⓓ will be seeing

17 ⬜ Mark for Review

Foscadh, a movie in which the actors speak the Irish language, is based on Donal Ryan's novel *The Thing About December*. It was nominated for the 2022 Academy Awards in the category of Best International Foreign Film. In the movie, the character of John Cunliffe, played by Dónall Ó Héalai, suddenly _____ the responsibilities of adulthood after becoming an orphan and inheriting his parents' farm.

Which choice completes the text so that it conforms to the conventions of Standard English?

Ⓐ learns. About

Ⓑ learns about

Ⓒ learns, about

Ⓓ learns; about

CONTINUE ➡

18 🔖 Mark for Review

The marble lions on each side of the entrance to the Beaux-Arts Main Branch building of the New York Public Library are two of New York City's most famous and beloved works of public art. The library's website says that _____ named "Patience" and "Fortitude" by Mayor Fiorello LaGuardia in the 1930s after the virtues the city's residents would need during the ongoing Great Depression.

Which choice completes the text so that it conforms to the conventions of Standard English?

Ⓐ some were

Ⓑ it was

Ⓒ one was

Ⓓ they were

19 🔖 Mark for Review

GMO (Genetically Modified Organisms) foods can contain higher amounts of certain nutrients than non-GMO _____ critics of GMO foods claim that the long-term health risks are still unknown.

Which choice completes the text so that it conforms to the conventions of Standard English?

Ⓐ foods

Ⓑ foods, but

Ⓒ foods,

Ⓓ foods but

20 🔖 Mark for Review

When you first see the traditional Croatian pastry known as a licitar, you might not recognize it as something edible. It is often bright red and highly decorated, sometimes even used as a Christmas tree ornament. Licitars date back to the Middle Ages, and in the 18th and 19th centuries, _____ made by highly respected craftspeople.

Which choice completes the text so that it conforms to the conventions of Standard English?

Ⓐ these were

Ⓑ this was

Ⓒ they were

Ⓓ those were

21 🔖 Mark for Review

By utilizing single nuclei RNA-sequencing (sNuc-Seq), scientists can explore the previously unknown mechanism by which axolotl salamanders are able to regenerate brain matter. sNuc-Seq could be utilized as a method of single-cell sequencing that _____ the cells' nuclei instead of the entire cells.

Which choice completes the text so that it conforms to the conventions of Standard English?

Ⓐ has targeted

Ⓑ targets

Ⓒ targeted

Ⓓ is targeting

CONTINUE ➡

22 ☐ Mark for Review

Hippocamp, the smallest moon known to orbit the planet Neptune, _____ named after the same mythological sea-horse monster that inspired the name for the part of the human brain responsible for managing memory.

Which choice completes the text so that it conforms to the conventions of Standard English?

- (A) is
- (B) were
- (C) are
- (D) have been

23 ☐ Mark for Review

English materials scientist Nicola Spaldin studies multiferroics, materials that display multiple ferroic properties, such as ferromagnetism, ferroelasticity, and ferroelectricity. Spaldin was one of the first researchers to explain why there are so few multiferroics; _____ Spaldin was asked to join a team studying bismuth ferrite and its multiferroic characteristics.

Which choice completes the text with the most logical transition?

- (A) in other words,
- (B) in spite of this,
- (C) as a result,
- (D) likewise,

24 ☐ Mark for Review

Wildfires in the western United States affect the weather in the central United States. _____ wildfires produce increased levels of aerosol and heat, creating an environment more conducive to storms and causing heavy precipitation and large hail in the central United States.

Which choice completes the text with the most logical transition?

- (A) In addition,
- (B) Likewise,
- (C) Therefore,
- (D) Specifically,

25 ☐ Mark for Review

The Atlantic menhaden is an example of a keystone species, sometimes referred to as "the most important fish in the sea" despite its small size. Menhaden perform an important function within their environment by consuming large amounts of algae that can grow out of control and produce toxic "blooms" in the absence of menhaden. _____ they are a key food source for shorebirds and larger oceanic fish.

Which choice completes the text with the most logical transition?

- (A) Furthermore,
- (B) Indeed,
- (C) For instance,
- (D) Specifically,

CONTINUE ➤

26 ☐ Mark for Review

While researching a topic, a student has taken the following notes:

- Saturn's rings are about 45,000 miles wide and 1,000 yards thick.
- They are primarily composed of pure water ice.
- Multiple theories have been proposed to explain the origin of Saturn's rings.
- Some astronomers believe Saturn's rings were formed from the remnants of a moon.
- This moon may have drifted too close to Saturn and then been destroyed by tidal forces, resulting in the rings' formation.

The student wants to specify how Saturn's rings may have been formed. Which choice most effectively uses relevant information from the notes to accomplish this goal?

- (A) Saturn's rings were formed primarily out of pure water ice.

- (B) According to some astronomers, it's possible that when one of Saturn's moons got too close to the planet, tidal forces destroyed the moon, forming Saturn's rings.

- (C) Astronomers have proposed various theories to explain the formation of Saturn's rings.

- (D) Saturn's rings are 1,000 yards thick, 45,000 miles wide, and composed primarily of pure water ice.

27 ☐ Mark for Review

While researching a topic, a student has taken the following notes:

- The inland taipan (*Oxyuranus microlepidotus*) is a species of Australian snake that produces an extremely harmful venom.
- The inland taipan is a member of the Elapidae family of snakes, the majority of which are venomous.
- One bite from the inland taipan contains enough venom to kill more than 100 average-sized humans.
- It typically feeds on marsupials and rodents, as its venom is specifically adapted to kill mammals.
- After biting its prey, the inland taipan instantly releases its hold, unlike other snakes of the Elapidae family.

The student wants to emphasize how harmful the venom of the inland taipan can be. Which choice most effectively uses relevant information from the notes to accomplish this goal?

- (A) The inland taipan instantly releases its hold after biting its prey, unlike other members of the mostly venomous Elapidae family of snakes.

- (B) The inland taipan's venom is specifically harmful to mammals, such as marsupials and rodents.

- (C) The Elapidae family of snakes, the majority of which are venomous, includes Australia's inland taipan.

- (D) The venom from one bite of an inland taipan is extremely harmful, capable of killing more than 100 average-sized humans.

STOP

**If you finish before time is called, you may check your work on this module only.
Do not turn to any other module in the test.**

PSAT 8/9 Test 1—Reading and Writing
Module 2—Harder

Turn to Section 1 of your answer sheet to answer the questions in this section.

DIRECTIONS

The questions in this section address a number of important reading and writing skills. Each question includes one or more passages, which may include a table or graph. Read each passage and question carefully, and then choose the best answer to the question based on the passage(s).

All questions in the section are multiple-choice with four answer choices. Each question has a single best answer.

---

1 ☐ Mark for Review

A sculptor and designer, Isamu Noguchi was deeply affected by his international travels and _____ incorporating a range of cultural perspectives into his art pieces. He accomplished this by experimenting with different art mediums, studying traditional Japanese pottery and Chinese calligraphy, and utilizing a broad spectrum of materials such as bronze, aluminum, steel, and cast iron.

Which choice completes the text with the most logical word or phrase?

(A) skeptical about

(B) unfamiliar with

(C) focused on

(D) resistant to

---

2 ☐ Mark for Review

A single paragraph summary of Alan Paton's novel *Cry, the Beloved Country* can't possibly capture the _____ undertaken by James Jarvis, who goes from expressing ignorance towards the plight of those around him to providing aid and hope to those downtrodden by societal injustices.

Which choice completes the text with the most logical and precise word or phrase?

(A) burden

(B) precaution

(C) dormancy

(D) transformation

CONTINUE ▶

3 ▢ Mark for Review

The theremin, an unconventional and non-traditional instrument, is named for its inventor, Russian scientist Lev Theremin. This electronic instrument, a predecessor to the synthesizer, is made of a box that emits sound waves. The warbling musical tones produced are highly _____; the pitch and volume can be altered substantially by minute changes to the position of the musician's hands between two antennae on either end of the box.

Which choice completes the text with the most logical and precise word or phrase?

(A) neglected

(B) diverse

(C) commanding

(D) predictable

4 ▢ Mark for Review

In the 1990s, the rise in personal computers allowed artists greater access to MIDI devices that create electronic music, giving musicians such as Imogen Heap the ability to produce full albums on their own. Heap utilized this _____ access to creative technology to craft influential works that blend electronica and emotion, like her album *Speak for Yourself* (2005).

Which choice completes the text with the most logical word or phrase?

(A) routine

(B) expanded

(C) unstable

(D) expected

5 ▢ Mark for Review

Text 1

Over the past four decades, citizens of Saipan, one of the Northern Mariana Islands, have reported several sightings of invasive brown tree snakes (*Boiga irregularis*), although none have been confirmed. Amy Adams and colleagues conducted multiple active surveys for the snakes over a 19-year period. Surprisingly, they observed no brown tree snakes on the island. While this result does not prove that brown tree snakes do not occur on Saipan, it strongly suggests that there is not an established population of them.

Text 2

Not only have there been many reported sightings of brown tree snakes (*Boiga irregularis*) on Saipan since 1980, but multiple snakes also have been confirmed intercepted at ports of entry. The snakes are well camouflaged, and there were probably individuals hidden during the Adams team's surveys. Since it only takes a small number of this invasive species to devastate an ecosystem, the island of Saipan must continue to be surveyed so that appropriate countermeasures can be taken.

Based on the texts, Adams's team and the author of Text 2 would most likely agree with which statement about brown tree snakes?

(A) It may be difficult to locate brown tree snakes on the island of Saipan.

(B) Many brown tree snakes are better able to camouflage themselves on Saipan than they are on other islands.

(C) More brown tree snakes would probably be located on the island of Saipan if different types of surveys were conducted.

(D) Brown tree snakes are likely to be difficult to locate on Saipan because there is a much smaller population of them than of other snake species on the island.

CONTINUE ➤

6 ☐ Mark for Review

Los Angeles's Contra-Tiempo Activist Dance Theater, founded by Ana Maria Alvarez, creates dance works featuring multimedia in collaborations with artists such as choreographer Marjani Forté. For the company's *joyUS justUS* performance, Alvarez invites members of the audience to participate in dance and movement exercises and then create their own collaborative dance.

Which choice best states the main idea of the text?

Ⓐ Alvarez invites members of the audience to create their own dance to illustrate the complexity of the task.

Ⓑ The Contra-Tiempo Activist Dance Theater company performs dances from all over the United States but mostly performs dances choreographed by Los Angeles natives.

Ⓒ Alvarez began the Contra-Tiempo Activist Dance Theater company to perform dances choreographed by Marjani Forté.

Ⓓ The Contra-Tiempo Activist Dance company gives audience members to opportunity to both observe and participate in collaborative dance performances.

7 ☐ Mark for Review

Medical studies can be interventional, in which people are placed into treatment and control groups, or observational, in which people who may fall into such groups are observed without interference. Each type of study is valuable in different ways. Interventional studies allow researchers to directly investigate the efficacy of a new medicine, for example, with less potential for inaccurate data due to outside factors. Observation studies can help researchers determine the validity of diagnostic tests or the effects of an environmental change. However, if the results of an interventional and an observational study on patients who have undergone heart surgery are in opposition, there may have been bias in participant selection in one or both of the studies that affected the results produced.

Which choice best states the main idea of the text?

Ⓐ Conflicting results between interventional and observational studies of patients such as those who have undergone heart surgery are strong indicators of an error made by both studies that impacted the credibility of those studies.

Ⓑ When the results of an interventional study and those from an observational study of patients such as those who have undergone heart surgery conflict, the interventional study is more likely than the observational study to produce credible data.

Ⓒ Studying patients such as those who have undergone heart surgery in both interventional and observational modalities often leads to contradictory results that scientists struggle to reconcile.

Ⓓ Patients such as those who have undergone heart surgery can be studied in both interventional and observational modalities, but each has different advantages and must still account for the possibility of bias.

CONTINUE →

8 ☐ Mark for Review

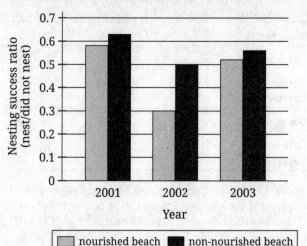

Nesting Success Rates of Loggerhead Sea Turtles Based on Presence of Nourishment

nourished beach ■ non-nourished beach

A section of beach in the Archie Carr National Wildlife Refuge in Florida was artificially nourished in 2002. Biologists Kelly A. Brock and colleagues investigated the nesting success of loggerhead sea turtles on the nourished beach and an adjacent non-nourished beach. They reasoned that the unfamiliarity of the loggerhead turtles to the artificial nourishment initially deterred them from nesting at the nourished beach, but that this effect was reduced as the turtles became more acclimated to the nourishment.

Which choice best describes data from the graph that support Brock and colleagues' reasoning?

Ⓐ The nesting success ratio at the nourished beach dropped from 2001 to 2002, but in 2003 it increased and became closer to the nesting success ratio at the non-nourished beach.

Ⓑ The lowest nesting success ratio at the nourished beach was approximately 0.3, and the highest nesting success ratio at the non-nourished beach was approximately 0.63.

Ⓒ The nourished beach had a greater nesting success ratio in 2001 than did the non-nourished beach, and this difference fluctuated significantly in 2002 and again in 2003.

Ⓓ The highest nesting success ratio for the non-nourished beach was in 2001, but the non-nourished beach achieved a nesting success ratio of 0.5 or higher for all three years studied.

9 ☐ Mark for Review

In 1965, Congress established the National Endowment for the Arts (NEA), which operates as an independent federal agency, to provide grant funds to schools, nonprofits, and individuals in an effort to democratize participation in the arts. A spokesperson for the NEA claims that its funds have resulted in a significant increase in the number of non-profit theater companies and symphony orchestras in the United States.

Which quotation from a work by an economist would be the most effective evidence for the spokesperson to include in support of this claim?

Ⓐ "The priority of the NEA was to promote the growth of the arts, and public records indicate that its funding has contributed to a six-fold increase in the number of non-profit theater companies over the last 50 years."

Ⓑ "Although the NEA started as a government initiative, activists successfully called for its establishment as an independent agency because they believed it could better accomplish its goal of promoting the arts that way."

Ⓒ "For decades, the subsidy of arts programs in foreign countries was supported by the citizens of those countries, but in the United States, the proposal to create the National Endowment for the Arts was initially met with skepticism by the general population."

Ⓓ "Congress's creation of an independent federal agency for the arts echoed a prevalent belief among US citizens that the role of a governing body is not only to legislate but also to enrich the lives of its populace."

CONTINUE →

10 ☐ Mark for Review

A primary pathway in the water cycle involves the evaporation of water from Earth's surface followed by its condensation in the atmosphere and return to the surface as precipitation. Hans Knoche and Harald Kunstmann used meteorological models with moisture-tagging capabilities to track the movement of moisture from a surface source to its eventual destination as precipitation. The researchers tagged the water in Lake Volta in Ghana, West Africa, and used the model to determine how much of the water evaporated from the lake returned locally (the regional recycling ratio). Average recycling ratios for other regions fall between 10 and 50%. They concluded that very little local precipitation comes from Lake Volta and most of the water that evaporates from the lake is transported elsewhere.

Which finding, if true, would most directly support the researchers' conclusion?

(A) Water evaporated from Lake Volta accounts for just 6% of the precipitation in the area surrounding the lake, and only 2% of the water evaporated from Lake Volta returns to the lake itself as precipitation.

(B) The water evaporated from Lake Volta contains higher quantities of saline, which causes water to evaporate more slowly, and has an average recycling ratio between 10% and 50%.

(C) In the valley surrounding Lake Volta, the average recycling ratio was above 10% near the lake's shoreline and below 10% farther from the lake.

(D) The majority of the area surrounding Lake Volta was found to have an average recycling ratio greater than 50%.

11 ☐ Mark for Review

Response	Initial percentage of respondents (%)	Final percentage of respondents (%)
Don't know	25	8
Approve	11	32
Strongly approve	2	6
Disapprove	24	16
Strongly disapprove	14	10

Researcher Simon Shackley and his team surveyed people in the UK to determine the public perception of offshore carbon dioxide capture and storage (CCS). The team asked respondents for their opinions on CCS at the beginning of the survey and then again at the end, after explaining the concept. They found that educating people about the process increased public approval. For example, 25% of respondents did not know what they thought about CCS at the start of the survey, while at the end, that number decreased to 8% and _____

Which choice most effectively uses data from the table to complete the text?

(A) 16% of respondents stated that they strongly approved of carbon dioxide capture and storage.

(B) 24% of respondents stated that they disapproved of carbon dioxide capture and storage.

(C) 32% of respondents stated that they approved of carbon dioxide capture and storage.

(D) 10% of respondents stated that they strongly disapproved of carbon dioxide capture and storage.

CONTINUE ➜

12 ☐ Mark for Review

The Rapa Nui people settled on the island of Rapa Nui, also known as Easter Island, sometime before 1200 CE and lived in isolation for hundreds of years. They are the only Polynesian civilization known to have developed writing, a pictorial script called Rongorongo, which researchers and linguists have been unable to decipher. Nevertheless, knowledge of the Rapa Nui people has been carried forward over time through archaeological artifacts, customs, and oral traditions. This suggests that _____

Which choice most logically completes the text?

Ⓐ investigating the culture's archaeological artifacts has enabled researchers to decode the culture's writing system.

Ⓑ researching a culture is more straightforward without an understanding of the culture's writing system.

Ⓒ deciphering a culture's writing system isn't a requirement in order to gain insight into that culture.

Ⓓ linguistics research should focus on uncovering archaeological artifacts rather than understanding pictorial scripts.

13 ☐ Mark for Review

In Brazil, capuchin monkeys have been found to use stones to open seeds and nuts. They choose stones based on their specific properties. For example, the stones the monkeys used as a hammer were four times heavier than average stones, while the stones used as anvils were over eight times heavier. When studying excavated stone tools that were used by monkeys about 600 to 700 years ago, archaeologist Michael Haslam found that the tools are similar to the ones used by monkeys today in terms of rock materials and weights, and both tool types had been arranged in small piles to be used again and again. This suggests to Haslam that _____

Which choice most logically completes the text?

Ⓐ monkeys have learned that both types of stone tools are more effective than their own teeth for opening seeds and nuts.

Ⓑ stone tools of both types are valuable enough for monkeys to keep and reuse as needed.

Ⓒ stones used as hammers are easier for the monkeys to use than stones used as anvils.

Ⓓ monkeys prefer to trade stones used as hammers but won't trade the stones they use as anvils.

CONTINUE

14 ☐ Mark for Review

Neil Gaiman's novel *Coraline* follows the adventures of a young girl who discovers a world that mirrors her own but holds a sinister secret. The book's depiction of children _____ the themes of developing courage and overcoming adversity even at a young age.

Which choice completes the text so that it conforms to the conventions of Standard English?

- (A) are exploring
- (B) explores
- (C) explore
- (D) have explored

15 ☐ Mark for Review

Wound care is a growing concern in the healthcare system due to costs and complications in the healing process. A team of scientists and engineers in the UK is working to create wound dressings that contain biosensors: these sensors monitor wound healing in real _____ prevent risk of infection, and save on healthcare costs.

Which choice completes the text so that it conforms to the conventions of Standard English?

- (A) time,
- (B) time;
- (C) time
- (D) time. And

16 ☐ Mark for Review

Gravity, an attraction that occurs between all objects that have _____ is significantly weaker than the other three fundamental forces but has the most obvious effect on humans' lives.

Which choice completes the text so that it conforms to the conventions of Standard English?

- (A) mass—
- (B) mass
- (C) mass and
- (D) mass,

17 ☐ Mark for Review

The technology of search engines has transformed the internet by allowing keywords or questions to be inputted and then generating a list of relevant sources within _____ the process of researching each source can be time-consuming in comparison to the more direct answers that an AI chatbot can provide.

Which choice completes the text so that it conforms to the conventions of Standard English?

- (A) seconds still,
- (B) seconds, still;
- (C) seconds, still,
- (D) seconds; still,

CONTINUE ➡

18 ☐ Mark for Review

A research initiative from Daniel Hermens and other Australian scientists, _____ can be predicted by analyzing young people's "brain fingerprints" over time.

Which choice completes the text so that it conforms to the conventions of Standard English?

- (A) the Longitudinal Adolescent Brain Study has used MRI scans to show that mental health outcomes

- (B) MRI scans—used by the Longitudinal Adolescent Brain Study—show that mental health outcomes

- (C) mental health outcomes, the Longitudinal Adolescent Brain Study has used MRI scans to show,

- (D) it was shown in the Longitudinal Adolescent Brain Study that mental health outcomes

19 ☐ Mark for Review

In the 1990s, Lebanese contemporary media artist Walid _____ instituted The Atlas Group, a fictional foundation that serves as an archive used to add context to pieces related to the Lebanese Civil Wars.

Which choice completes the text so that it conforms to the conventions of Standard English?

- (A) Raad,

- (B) Raad;

- (C) Raad:

- (D) Raad

20 ☐ Mark for Review

Ojibwe poet Heid Erdrich, _____ to illustrate themes related to modern Indigenous issues, has produced a number of award-winning video-poems with multi-disciplinary Ojibwe artist Jonathan Thunder.

Which choice completes the text so that it conforms to the conventions of Standard English?

- (A) hoping

- (B) hoped

- (C) hopes

- (D) is hoping

21 ☐ Mark for Review

Zoonotic diseases, including those caused by viruses and parasites, _____ infectious illnesses with a wide range of symptoms and effects and can be transferred between animals and humans.

Which choice completes the text so that it conforms to the conventions of Standard English?

- (A) is

- (B) has been

- (C) are

- (D) was

CONTINUE

---

22 ☐ Mark for Review

The Atlantic hurricane season officially runs from June 1 to November 30, and citizens living in affected areas know there is a higher risk of dangerous weather during this time. _____ a recent study found that hurricanes in the Atlantic basin have been trending about five days earlier per decade since 1979, suggesting the possibility of a need for a shift in what's considered the hurricane season.

Which choice completes the text with the most logical transition?

Ⓐ Therefore,

Ⓑ However,

Ⓒ Overall,

Ⓓ Otherwise,

23 ☐ Mark for Review

CAVES is a training course for astronauts that mimics some of the conditions of outer space. The goal of the course is to prepare astronauts for the challenging conditions that exist in long spaceflights. Jeanette Epps was the first African American woman to complete the CAVES course; _____ she became a role model for future female and African American candidates.

Which choice completes the text with the most logical transition?

Ⓐ specifically,

Ⓑ instead,

Ⓒ therefore,

Ⓓ rather,

24 ☐ Mark for Review

Bulgarian and Macedonian folkloric tradition includes Martenitsi, small adornments made of yarn in the shape of dolls, worn to celebrate the start of the spring season. An observer of the tradition puts on the Martenitsa on the springtime holiday Baba Mara Day and removes it after seeing a stork, a swallow, or a blossoming tree (symbols of the beginning of spring). After removing the Martenitsa, some tie it to a fruit tree's branch, a gesture meant to give the tree good fortune and health. _____ some place the Martenitsa on the ground under a rock, and the type of insect closest to the rock the following day is said to indicate what kind of fortune the wearer can expect for the rest of the year.

Which choice completes the text with the most logical transition?

Ⓐ Nevertheless,

Ⓑ For example,

Ⓒ Alternatively,

Ⓓ In fact,

CONTINUE ➡

25 ☐ Mark for Review

While researching a topic, a student has taken the following notes:

- Deciduous forests are found in two distinct biomes.
- Tropical deciduous forests experience seasonal rainfall variations.
- Temperate deciduous forests experience seasonal temperature variations.
- Temperate deciduous forests have been harvested for wood, timber, and charcoal.
- As a result of this harvesting, less than one-fourth of the original temperate deciduous forests remain today.

The student wants to emphasize a difference between tropical and temperate deciduous forests. Which choice most effectively uses relevant information from the notes to accomplish this goal?

Ⓐ Deciduous forests are found in two distinct biomes: tropical deciduous forests and temperate deciduous forests.

Ⓑ Tropical deciduous forests have variations in temperature, whereas temperate deciduous forests have variations in rainfall.

Ⓒ Although tropical and temperate deciduous forests are both deciduous forests, these forests do have some differences.

Ⓓ Less than one-fourth of the original temperate deciduous forests remain after being harvested for wood, timber, and charcoal.

26 ☐ Mark for Review

While researching a topic, a student has taken the following notes:

- The Eocene-Oligocene extinction event occurred a little over 33 million years ago.
- 63% of African mammals died out during this event.
- These extinct mammals included rodents and early primates.
- One possible cause for the event was a global cooling that decreased temperatures in a relatively short time frame.
- One reason for the declining temperatures was a decrease in carbon dioxide in the atmosphere.

The student wants to explain a possible cause of the Eocene-Oligocene extinction event. Which choice most effectively uses relevant information from the notes to accomplish this goal?

Ⓐ The Eocene-Oligocene extinction event occurred a little over 33 million years ago at a time of a global cooling.

Ⓑ 63% of African mammals, including rodents and early primates, died out during the Eocene-Oligocene extinction event.

Ⓒ The Eocene-Oligocene extinction event may have been the result of decreased levels of carbon dioxide in the atmosphere, which caused a global cooling.

Ⓓ An extinction event can occur when global temperatures decline.

CONTINUE ➡

27 ☐ Mark for Review

While researching a topic, a student has taken the following notes:

- Monoculture farming is the practice of growing one crop at a time.
- Polyculture farming grows a variety of crops.
- When a field has only one crop, the crop is at greater risk of damage by pests.
- When a variety of crops is grown, the threat of pests is lower.

The student wants to contrast monoculture farming with polyculture farming. Which choice most effectively uses relevant information from the notes to accomplish this goal?

(A) Polyculture faming—growing a variety of crops—yields a farm that is less susceptible to pests compared with monoculture farming—growing one crop at a time.

(B) Monoculture farming, which grows only one type of crop at a time, increases a crop's risk of damage by pests.

(C) Some styles of farming grow one kind of crop while others grow a variety.

(D) Monoculture farming and polyculture farming are two different practices that can be threatened by pests.

STOP
If you finish before time is called, you may check your work on this module only.
Do not turn to any other module in the test.

THIS PAGE LEFT INTENTIONALLY BLANK.

PSAT 8/9 Test 1—Math
Module 1

Turn to Section 2 of your answer sheet to answer the questions in this section.

DIRECTIONS

The questions in this section address a number of important math skills.
Use of a calculator is permitted for all questions.

NOTES

Unless otherwise indicated:

- All variables and expressions represent real numbers.
- Figures provided are drawn to scale.
- All figures lie in a plane.
- The domain of a given function f is the set of all real numbers x for which $f(x)$ is a real number.

REFERENCE

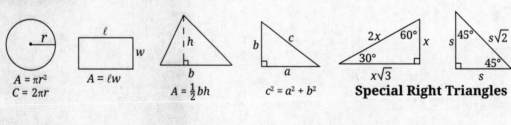

$A = \pi r^2$
$C = 2\pi r$

$A = \ell w$

$A = \frac{1}{2}bh$

$c^2 = a^2 + b^2$

Special Right Triangles

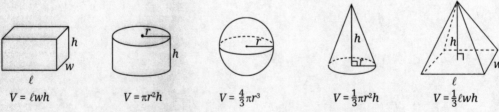

$V = \ell wh$

$V = \pi r^2 h$

$V = \frac{4}{3}\pi r^3$

$V = \frac{1}{3}\pi r^2 h$

$V = \frac{1}{3}\ell wh$

The number of degrees of arc in a circle is 360.
The number of radians of arc in a circle is 2π.
The sum of the measures in degrees of the angles of a triangle is 180.

CONTINUE

INSTRUCTIONS FOR PRINT TESTS

For multiple-choice questions, solve each problem, choose the correct answer from the choices provided, and then circle your answer in this book. Circle only one answer for each question. If you change your mind, completely erase the circle. You will not get credit for questions with more than one answer circled or for questions with no answers circled.

For student-produced response questions, solve each problem and write your answer next to or under the question in the test book as described below.

- Once you've written your answer, circle it clearly. You will not receive credit for anything written outside the circle or for any questions with more than one circled answer.

- If you find **more than one correct answer**, write and circle only one answer.

- Your answer can be up to 5 characters for a **positive** answer and up to 6 characters (including the negative sign) for a **negative** answer, but no more.

- If your answer is a **fraction** that is too long (over 5 characters for positive, 6 characters for negative), write the decimal equivalent.

- If your answer is a **decimal** that is too long (over 5 characters for positive, 6 characters for negative), truncate it or round at the fourth digit.

- If your answer is a **mixed number** (such as $3\frac{1}{2}$), write it as an improper fraction (7/2) or its decimal equivalent (3.5).

- Don't enter **symbols** such as a percent sign, comma, or dollar sign in your circled answer.

----

1 ⚑ Mark for Review

What is the value of $2a$ if $8a = 40$?

Ⓐ 5

Ⓑ 10

Ⓒ 44

Ⓓ 46

2 ⚑ Mark for Review

$$9 - x^3 - 4$$

Which of the following expressions is equivalent to the given expression?

Ⓐ $-x^3 - 36$

Ⓑ $-x^3 - 5$

Ⓒ $-x^3 + 5$

Ⓓ $-x^3 + 13$

3 ⚑ Mark for Review

The temperature, t, of a bowl of soup is 145 degrees Fahrenheit when the soup is first served. The soup cools at an average rate of 0.63 degrees Fahrenheit per minute for the first 10 minutes after it is served. If m is the number of minutes after the soup is served and t is the temperature of the soup, in degrees Fahrenheit, which equation best models this situation?

Ⓐ $t = -0.63m + 0.63$

Ⓑ $t = -0.63m + 145$

Ⓒ $t = 145m$

Ⓓ $t = 145m + 145$

4 ⚑ Mark for Review

The combined weight of Daniel and his father, Frank, is 240 pounds. Daniel weighs d pounds, Frank weighs f pounds, and Frank weighs three times as much as Daniel. Which system of equations represents this situation?

Ⓐ $d = 3f$
$d + f = 240$

Ⓑ $d = 240f$
$d + f = 3$

Ⓒ $f = 240d$
$d + f = 3$

Ⓓ $f = 3d$
$d + f = 240$

CONTINUE ➡

5 ☐ Mark for Review

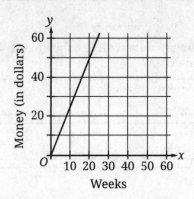

Weeks

The graph models the amount of money, in dollars, that a child adds to her piggy bank in x weeks, without removing any of the money. According to the graph, how much money on average, in dollars, does the child add to the piggy bank each week?

Ⓐ 2.50

Ⓑ 10

Ⓒ 25

Ⓓ 35

6 ☐ Mark for Review

A rectangle with a length of 6 centimeters has an area of 42 square centimeters. What is the width, in centimeters, of the rectangle?

Ⓐ 6

Ⓑ 7

Ⓒ 13

Ⓓ 36

7 ☐ Mark for Review

The relationship between the base and the height of a certain triangle can be expressed by the equation $\frac{1}{2}bh = 30$. If $b = 12$, what is the value of h?

8 ☐ Mark for Review

$$w = 72m$$

The given equation represents the number of words, w, typed by a court stenographer during a trial, where m represents the number of minutes spent typing. What is the best interpretation of the number 72 in this context?

Ⓐ The stenographer typed a total of 72 words.

Ⓑ The stenographer typed a total of $72m$ words.

Ⓒ The stenographer typed an average of $\frac{1}{72}$ words per minute.

Ⓓ The stenographer typed an average of 72 words per minute.

CONTINUE ➡

9 ⬚ Mark for Review

$$3x + y = 17$$
$$y = 5$$

Which ordered pair is the solution to the given system of equations when the system is graphed in the *xy*-plane?

Ⓐ (2, 3)

Ⓑ (3, 5)

Ⓒ (4, 5)

Ⓓ (5, 4)

10 ⬚ Mark for Review

$$144x^2 - 192x + 64$$

Which of the following expressions is equivalent to the given expression?

Ⓐ $(6x - 4)(6x - 4)$

Ⓑ $(6x + 4)(6x - 4)$

Ⓒ $(12x - 8)(12x - 8)$

Ⓓ $(12x + 8)(12x - 8)$

11 ⬚ Mark for Review

$$3, 12, 15, 21, 26, 37$$

All of the values in data set A are shown. What is the median of data set A?

Ⓐ 18

Ⓑ 19

Ⓒ 21

Ⓓ 34

12 ⬚ Mark for Review

$$g(x) = \sqrt{x} - 9$$

The function *g* is defined by the given equation. What is the value of $g(25)$?

⬚

CONTINUE

13 ☐ Mark for Review

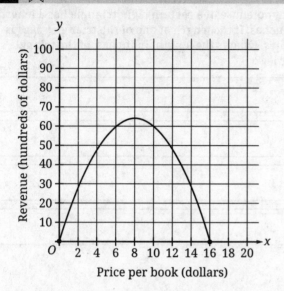

In an effort to maximize profits, an online used bookstore records revenue based on the price per book sold. The data is modeled in the graph shown. Based on the model, which table gives three values of x and their corresponding values of y?

Ⓐ

x	y
0	16
0	64
10	60

Ⓑ

x	y
0	0
6	60
8	−64

Ⓒ

x	y
0	16
6	60
64	8

Ⓓ

x	y
6	60
8	64
10	60

14 ☐ Mark for Review

The estimated value, in dollars, of a photocopier x years after the date of purchase is given by the function $p(x) = 7,466(0.80)^x$, where $0 < x \le 10$. In this context, what is the best interpretation of the statement "$p(2)$ is approximately equal to 4,778"?

Ⓐ When the estimated value of the photocopier is 4,778 dollars, it is $\frac{1}{2}$ of the estimated value of the photocopier in the previous year.

Ⓑ When the estimated value of the photocopier is 4,778 dollars, it is 2% greater than the estimated value of the photocopier in the previous year.

Ⓒ 2 years after the date of purchase, the value of the photocopier will be approximately 4,778 dollars.

Ⓓ 2 years after the date of purchase, the value of the photocopier will have decreased by a total of approximately 4,778 dollars.

CONTINUE ➡

15 ▢ Mark for Review

How many minutes are there in 4 days?
(1 day = 24 hours and 1 hour = 60 minutes)

16 ▢ Mark for Review

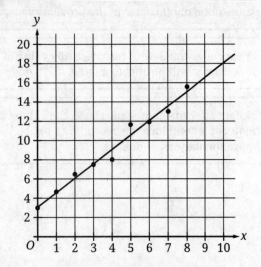

The scatterplot shows the relationship between two variables, x and y. A line of best fit is also shown. Which of the following is closest to the slope of the line of best fit?

Ⓐ −1.5

Ⓑ 1.5

Ⓒ −15

Ⓓ 15

17 ▢ Mark for Review

The hypotenuse of a certain right triangle has a length of 8 inches. If the length of one of the triangle's legs is 6 inches, what is the length, in inches, of the triangle's other leg?

Ⓐ $2\sqrt{7}$

Ⓑ 10

Ⓒ 14

Ⓓ 28

18 ▢ Mark for Review

$$37a + b = c$$

The given equation relates the positive numbers a, b, and c. Which equation correctly expresses b in terms of a and c?

Ⓐ $b = c - 37a$

Ⓑ $b = c + 37a$

Ⓒ $b = 37ac$

Ⓓ $b = \dfrac{c}{37a}$

CONTINUE ➡

19 ▢ Mark for Review

What is the product of the solutions to the equation $2x^2 + 30x - 12 = 0$?

(A) -15

(B) -6

(C) 6

(D) 15

20 ▢ Mark for Review

Linear function f is defined by the equation $f(x) = kx - 79$. If $f(7) = 40$ and k is a constant, what is the value of $f(11)$?

▢

21 ▢ Mark for Review

Enrollment in a certain park district program decreased by 70% from September 1997 to September 1998. Enrollment then increased by 110% from September 1998 to September 1999. What was the net percentage decrease in enrollment from September 1997 to September 1999?

(A) 33%

(B) 37%

(C) 40%

(D) 63%

22 ▢ Mark for Review

What is the value of $4x^2 + 8x$ if $x^2 + 2x - 20 = 0$?

▢

YIELD
Once you've finished (or run out of time for) this section, use the answer key to determine how many questions you got right. If you got fewer than 14 questions right, move on to Module 2—Easier, otherwise move on to Module 2—Harder.

PSAT 8/9 Test 1—Math
Module 2—Easier

Turn to Section 2 of your answer sheet to answer the questions in this section.

DIRECTIONS

The questions in this section address a number of important math skills.
Use of a calculator is permitted for all questions.

NOTES

Unless otherwise indicated:

- All variables and expressions represent real numbers.
- Figures provided are drawn to scale.
- All figures lie in a plane.
- The domain of a given function f is the set of all real numbers x for which $f(x)$ is a real number.

REFERENCE

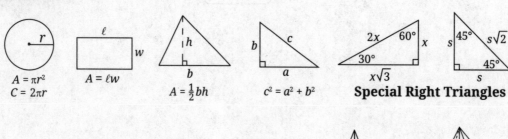

$A = \pi r^2$
$C = 2\pi r$

$A = \ell w$

$A = \frac{1}{2}bh$

$c^2 = a^2 + b^2$

Special Right Triangles

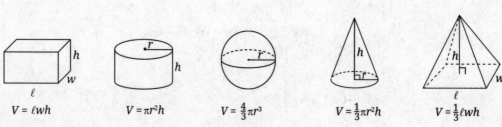

$V = \ell w h$

$V = \pi r^2 h$

$V = \frac{4}{3}\pi r^3$

$V = \frac{1}{3}\pi r^2 h$

$V = \frac{1}{3}\ell w h$

The number of degrees of arc in a circle is 360.
The number of radians of arc in a circle is 2π.
The sum of the measures in degrees of the angles of a triangle is 180.

CONTINUE

- -

INSTRUCTIONS FOR PRINT TESTS

For multiple-choice questions, solve each problem, choose the correct answer from the choices provided, and then circle your answer in this book. Circle only one answer for each question. If you change your mind, completely erase the circle. You will not get credit for questions with more than one answer circled or for questions with no answers circled.

For student-produced response questions, solve each problem and write your answer next to or under the question in the test book as described below.

- Once you've written your answer, circle it clearly. You will not receive credit for anything written outside the circle or for any questions with more than one circled answer.
- If you find **more than one correct answer**, write and circle only one answer.
- Your answer can be up to 5 characters for a **positive** answer and up to 6 characters (including the negative sign) for a **negative** answer, but no more.
- If your answer is a **fraction** that is too long (over 5 characters for positive, 6 characters for negative), write the decimal equivalent.
- If your answer is a **decimal** that is too long (over 5 characters for positive, 6 characters for negative), truncate it or round at the fourth digit.
- If your answer is a **mixed number** (such as $3\frac{1}{2}$), write it as an improper fraction (7/2) or its decimal equivalent (3.5).
- Don't enter **symbols** such as a percent sign, comma, or dollar sign in your circled answer.

CONTINUE ➤

1 ☐ Mark for Review

There are 45 gumballs of various flavors in a gumball machine: 12 grape, 14 strawberry, 10 lemon, and 9 watermelon. If one gumball is removed from the machine at random, what is the probability that it is a watermelon gumball?

(A) $\frac{9}{45}$

(B) $\frac{12}{45}$

(C) $\frac{14}{45}$

(D) $\frac{36}{45}$

2 ☐ Mark for Review

Most Recent Visit	Number of Patients
One week ago	3
One month ago	17
Three months ago	54
Six months ago	91
One year ago	135
Total	300

The table summarizes the approximate time of the most recent visit to the dentist's office by 300 patients of a certain dentist. According to the table, how many patients had their most recent visit to the dentist's office one month ago or three months ago?

(A) 17

(B) 37

(C) 54

(D) 71

3 ☐ Mark for Review

$$7a - 364 = 126$$

Which value of a satisfies the given equation?

(A) 34

(B) 70

(C) 364

(D) 483

4 ☐ Mark for Review

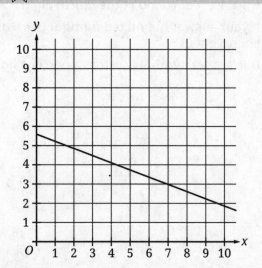

What is the y-intercept of the line graphed?

(A) $\left(0, -\frac{11}{2}\right)$

(B) $\left(0, -\frac{2}{11}\right)$

(C) $\left(0, \frac{11}{2}\right)$

(D) $\left(\frac{11}{2}, 0\right)$

CONTINUE ➡

5 ⬚ Mark for Review

The ratio of c to d is 35:22. To maintain this ratio, by what value must d be divided if c is divided by 5?

6 ⬚ Mark for Review

In a basket full of grapes, 50% of the grapes are black, and the rest are red. If there are 280 grapes in the basket, how many of them are black?

7 ⬚ Mark for Review

$$y = x - 5$$
$$y = 18$$

The given system of equations has one solution at (x, y). What is the value of x?

Ⓐ 13

Ⓑ 18

Ⓒ 23

Ⓓ 90

8 ⬚ Mark for Review

How many fathoms are equivalent to 132 feet? (1 fathom = 6 feet)

CONTINUE

9 ☐ Mark for Review

$$h(x) = 3x - 10$$

Function h is defined by the given equation. What is the value of $h(x)$ when $x = 50$?

- (A) 20
- (B) 43
- (C) 140
- (D) 150

10 ☐ Mark for Review

A robot at an automobile factory performs two tasks: welding seams and drilling holes. The robot takes 41.2 seconds to weld one seam and 15.5 seconds to drill one hole. If the robot spends 154.6 seconds welding s seams and drilling h holes, which equation represents this situation?

- (A) $s + h = 154.6$
- (B) $3.75s + 9.97h = 154.6$
- (C) $15.5s + 41.2h = 154.6$
- (D) $41.2s + 15.5h = 154.6$

11 ☐ Mark for Review

There are 2,750 trees in an apple orchard, and there are 110 trees planted per acre of land. How many acres does the apple orchard cover?

- (A) 25
- (B) 40
- (C) 250
- (D) 2,860

12 ☐ Mark for Review

The ratio of road bikes to mountain bikes at a bicycle shop is 7 to 3. If there are 24 mountain bikes at the shop, how many road bikes are there at the shop?

- (A) 8
- (B) 24
- (C) 56
- (D) 72

CONTINUE ➜

13 ☐ Mark for Review

A rectangle has a perimeter of 64 centimeters. What is the length, in centimeters, of one of the shorter sides of the rectangle if the length of each of the two longer sides of the rectangle is 22 centimeters?

14 ☐ Mark for Review

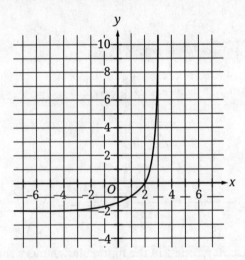

Which of the following is the x-intercept of the graph shown?

Ⓐ (0, 0)

Ⓑ (0, 2)

Ⓒ (2, 0)

Ⓓ (3, 3)

15 ☐ Mark for Review

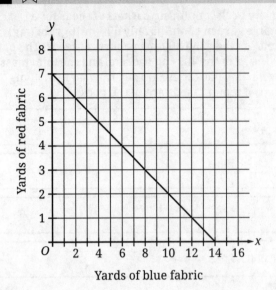

The possible combinations of the number of yards of blue fabric and number of yards of red fabric that can be purchased for $14 at a certain store are shown in the graph. How many yards of blue fabric did Jessica purchase if she purchased blue fabric and 6 yards of red fabric for a total of $14?

Ⓐ 2

Ⓑ 4

Ⓒ 8

Ⓓ 11

CONTINUE

16 ☐ Mark for Review

A variety pack containing packets of seeds for a vegetable garden contains only 600-milligram (mg) packets of seeds and 400-mg packets of seeds. The pack contains 20 of the 400-mg packets, and the total mass of the variety pack is 29,000 mg. How many 600-mg packets of tomato seeds are in the pack?

Ⓐ 20

Ⓑ 35

Ⓒ 400

Ⓓ 600

17 ☐ Mark for Review

A right triangle contains two acute angles. One of the acute angles measures 20°. What is the measure of the other acute angle, in degrees?

Ⓐ 20

Ⓑ 50

Ⓒ 60

Ⓓ 70

18 ☐ Mark for Review

Line a and line b are graphed in the xy-plane. Line a is defined by $2y = x - 24$, and line b is parallel to line a. What is the slope of line b?

Ⓐ −12

Ⓑ −2

Ⓒ $\frac{1}{12}$

Ⓓ $\frac{1}{2}$

19 ☐ Mark for Review

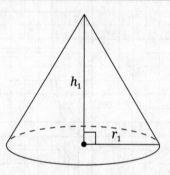

Right Circular Cone 1 in the figure shown has a radius of r_1 and a height of h_1. The volume of Right Circular Cone 2 (not shown) is 100 times the volume of Right Circular Cone 1. Right Circular Cone 2 has a radius of r_2 and a height of h_2. Which of the following could represent r_2 and h_2, in terms of r_1 and h_1, respectively?

Ⓐ $r_2 = 5r_1$ and $h_2 = 4h_1$

Ⓑ $r_2 = 25r_1$ and $h_2 = 4h_1$

Ⓒ $r_2 = 4r_1$ and $h_2 = 5h_1$

Ⓓ $r_2 = 4r_1$ and $h_2 = 25h_1$

CONTINUE

| 20 | ⚑ Mark for Review |

What is the area, in square centimeters, of an isosceles triangle with a height of 25 centimeters and a base length of 44 centimeters?

| 22 | ⚑ Mark for Review |

The number t is 30% less than the positive number u. The number v is 50% greater than t. How many times the value of u is the number v?

| 21 | ⚑ Mark for Review |

According to the triangle inequality theorem, the length of any side of a triangle must be greater than the difference between the lengths of the other two sides. Which inequality represents the possible lengths, p, of the third side of a triangle with side lengths of 9 and 11?

(A) $p < 2$

(B) $2 < p < 20$

(C) $p > 20$

(D) $p < 2$ or $p > 20$

STOP
**If you finish before time is called, you may check your work on this module only.
Do not turn to any other module in the test.**

PSAT 8/9 Test 1—Math
Module 2—Harder

Turn to Section 2 of your answer sheet to answer the questions in this section.

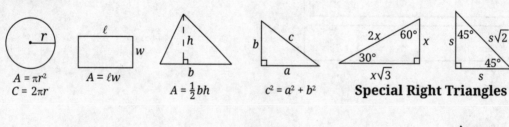
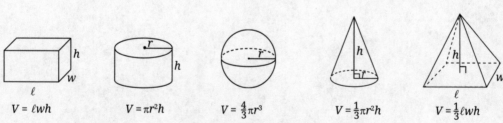
CONTINUE

INSTRUCTIONS FOR PRINT TESTS

For multiple-choice questions, solve each problem, choose the correct answer from the choices provided, and then circle your answer in this book. Circle only one answer for each question. If you change your mind, completely erase the circle. You will not get credit for questions with more than one answer circled or for questions with no answers circled.

For student-produced response questions, solve each problem and write your answer next to or under the question in the test book as described below.

- Once you've written your answer, circle it clearly. You will not receive credit for anything written outside the circle or for any questions with more than one circled answer.

- If you find **more than one correct answer**, write and circle only one answer.

- Your answer can be up to 5 characters for a **positive** answer and up to 6 characters (including the negative sign) for a **negative** answer, but no more.

- If your answer is a **fraction** that is too long (over 5 characters for positive, 6 characters for negative), write the decimal equivalent.

- If your answer is a **decimal** that is too long (over 5 characters for positive, 6 characters for negative), truncate it or round at the fourth digit.

- If your answer is a **mixed number** (such as $3\frac{1}{2}$), write it as an improper fraction (7/2) or its decimal equivalent (3.5).

- Don't enter **symbols** such as a percent sign, comma, or dollar sign in your circled answer.

CONTINUE ➤

---

1 🔖 Mark for Review

17 is what percent of 340?

[_____]

2 🔖 Mark for Review

At a local library, there is a fee of $1.85 for each overdue book. In addition, the library charges a fine of $0.21 for each day the book is overdue. A patron has only one overdue book and no other charges. If she is charged a total of $5 for the overdue book, how many days overdue is the book?

(A) 3

(B) 15

(C) 24

(D) 25

3 🔖 Mark for Review

Two teams of employees at a certain factory each produce the same specialized part. Team A produces the part at an average rate of 725 per day, team B produces the part at an average rate of 650 per day, and no other teams produce the part. The factory produces a minimum of 10,000 units of this part in one week. Which of the following inequalities represents this situation, where a and b are the numbers of days team A and team B produced this part, respectively?

(A) $650a + 725b \leq 10,000$

(B) $650a + 725b \geq 10,000$

(C) $725a + 650b \leq 10,000$

(D) $725a + 650b \geq 10,000$

4 🔖 Mark for Review

A long string of decorative lights has 10 clear lights, 45 solid color lights, 8 multi-color lights, and 45 blinking lights. If a single light is selected at random, what is the probability that the light selected is <u>neither</u> a clear light <u>nor</u> a multi-color light?

(A) $\frac{1}{6}$

(B) $\frac{2}{5}$

(C) $\frac{5}{6}$

(D) $\frac{25}{27}$

CONTINUE ➡

---

5 ⚑ Mark for Review

What is the side length, in inches, of a square that has an area of 5,184 square inches?

Ⓐ 18

Ⓑ 72

Ⓒ 1,296

Ⓓ 2,592

---

6 ⚑ Mark for Review

$$f(x) = x - 30$$

The function f is defined by the given equation. What is the value of $f(330)$?

Ⓐ 11

Ⓑ 30

Ⓒ 300

Ⓓ 360

---

7 ⚑ Mark for Review

Escape velocity is a measure that expresses the minimum speed an object needs to reach in order to escape the gravity of a planet. If the escape velocity at the surface of Mercury is 15,300 kilometers per hour, what is the speed that an object needs to reach in order to escape Mercury's gravity, in kilometers per second? (1 hour = 3,600 seconds)

---

8 ⚑ Mark for Review

The ratio of c to d is 35:22. To maintain this ratio, by what value must d be divided if c is divided by 5?

CONTINUE

---

9 ☐ Mark for Review

Line l passes through the points $(1, 15)$ and $(0, 17)$ in the xy-plane. Which of the following equations defines line l?

(A) $y = -2x + 17$

(B) $y = -\frac{1}{2}x + 17$

(C) $y = 15x - 2$

(D) $y = 15x - \frac{1}{2}$

10 ☐ Mark for Review

Two of the jets in a decorative water fountain shoot water at specific intervals. After the fountain is turned on, jet A shoots water every 405 seconds and jet B shoots water every 330 seconds. How much longer, in seconds, does it take for jet A to shoot water 64 times than it takes for jet B to shoot water 64 times after the fountain is turned on?

11 ☐ Mark for Review

If the value of k is 0.97 times 100, the value of k is what percent less than 100?

(A) 3

(B) 9.7

(C) 97

(D) 103

12 ☐ Mark for Review

What value of a is the solution to the equation $-\frac{7}{5}(a-2) + \frac{3}{2}(a-2) = 6$?

(A) -100

(B) -10

(C) 2

(D) 62

CONTINUE

---

13 ⚑ Mark for Review

Line *l* has an *x*-intercept of $\left(\frac{95}{2}, 0\right)$ and a *y*-intercept of $(0, -10)$ when graphed in the *xy*-plane. What is the slope of line *l*?

Ⓐ $\frac{2}{950}$

Ⓑ $\frac{4}{19}$

Ⓒ $\frac{19}{4}$

Ⓓ $\frac{950}{2}$

14 ⚑ Mark for Review

$$y = -\frac{1}{3}x$$
$$y = -5x$$

The given system of equations has one real solution at (x, y). What is the value of *y*?

Ⓐ −3

Ⓑ 0

Ⓒ 5

Ⓓ 15

15 ⚑ Mark for Review

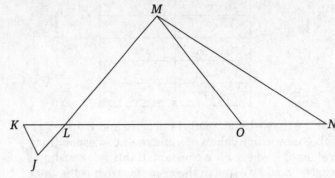

Note: Figure not drawn to scale.

In the figure, the measure of angle *JLK* is 27°, the measure of angle *MNO* is 17°, and $LM = MO$. What is the measure of angle *NMO*, in degrees?

‾‾‾‾‾‾

16 ⚑ Mark for Review

The amount of money in a bank account from the end of week 2 after the account was opened to the end of week 24 can be modeled by a linear equation. The model estimates that the amount of money in the account was \$2,278 at the end of week 5 and \$4,195 at the end of week 24. What is the amount of money, to the nearest dollar, that was in the account at the end of week 2?

‾‾‾‾‾‾

CONTINUE ➡

17 ☐ Mark for Review

x	y
c	0
$c - 25$	4
$c - 50$	8
$c - 75$	12

For the linear relationship between x and y, the table shows four values of x and their corresponding values of y, where c is a constant. If this relationship is represented by a line in the xy-plane, what is the slope of the line?

Ⓐ $-\dfrac{4}{2c + 25}$

Ⓑ $-\dfrac{25}{4}$

Ⓒ $-\dfrac{4}{25}$

Ⓓ $\dfrac{4}{c - 25}$

18 ☐ Mark for Review

Four data sets are represented by the following frequency tables. The mean is the least for which data set?

Ⓐ

Number	Frequency
5	3
10	3
15	3
20	3
25	3

Ⓑ

Number	Frequency
5	3
10	4
15	4
20	4
25	3

Ⓒ

Number	Frequency
5	6
10	2
15	2
20	2
25	6

Ⓓ

Number	Frequency
5	6
10	5
15	4
20	3
25	2

CONTINUE ➤

19 ☐ Mark for Review

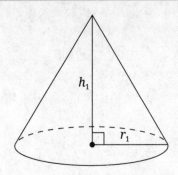

Right Circular Cone 1 in the figure shown has a radius of r_1 and a height of h_1. The volume of Right Circular Cone 2 (not shown) is 100 times the volume of Right Circular Cone 1. Right Circular Cone 2 has a radius of r_2 and a height of h_2. Which of the following could represent r_2 and h_2, in terms of r_1 and h_1, respectively?

Ⓐ $r_2 = 5r_1$ and $h_2 = 4h_1$

Ⓑ $r_2 = 25r_1$ and $h_2 = 4h_1$

Ⓒ $r_2 = 4r_1$ and $h_2 = 5h_1$

Ⓓ $r_2 = 4r_1$ and $h_2 = 25h_1$

20 ☐ Mark for Review

$$g(x) = 2c^x - k$$

The function g is defined by the given equation, where c and k are constants. If the graph of $y = g(x)$ in the xy-plane crosses the x-axis at $x = -56$ and crosses the y-axis at $y = 114$, what is the value of k?

☐

21 ☐ Mark for Review

Each student in a class with 25 students chose one of three sizes of slushy at the year-end party. There were 4 students who chose the 5-ounce slushy. The number of students that chose the 9-ounce slushy was 6 times the number of students t that chose the 12-ounce slushy. Which equation must be true for the value of t?

Ⓐ $5t + 9t + 12t = 25$

Ⓑ $6t + 4 = 25$

Ⓒ $7t + 4 = 25$

Ⓓ $9(6t) + 12t + 5(4) = 25$

22 ☐ Mark for Review

$$-10x + 6y = -22$$
$$-5x + 3y = -11$$

Each equation in the given system is graphed in the xy-plane. Which of the following represents a point that lies on each graph, for any real number n?

Ⓐ $\left(-\dfrac{3n}{5} - 22, \dfrac{3n}{5} - 11\right)$

Ⓑ $\left(\dfrac{n}{2} - 11, \dfrac{n}{2} - 22\right)$

Ⓒ $\left(n, \dfrac{3n}{5} + \dfrac{11}{5}\right)$

Ⓓ $\left(\dfrac{3n}{5} + \dfrac{11}{5}, n\right)$

STOP

If you finish before time is called, you may check your work on this module only.
Do not turn to any other module in the test.

PSAT 8/9, 2nd Edition
Practice Test

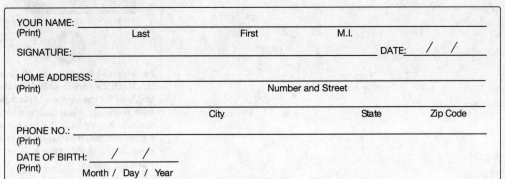

YOUR NAME: _____
(Print)   Last   First   M.I.

SIGNATURE: _____   DATE: ___/___/___

HOME ADDRESS: _____
(Print)   Number and Street

_____
                City   State   Zip Code

PHONE NO.: _____
(Print)

DATE OF BIRTH: ___/___/___
(Print)   Month / Day / Year

For both the Reading and Writing and the Math, be sure to only fill in the bubbles for the version of Module 2 that you took. If you took the Easier Module 2, only fill in the answer in the Easier column. If you took the Harder Module 2, only fill in the answers in the Harder column.

Section 1: Module 1
Reading and Writing

1. Ⓐ Ⓑ Ⓒ Ⓓ
2. Ⓐ Ⓑ Ⓒ Ⓓ
3. Ⓐ Ⓑ Ⓒ Ⓓ
4. Ⓐ Ⓑ Ⓒ Ⓓ
5. Ⓐ Ⓑ Ⓒ Ⓓ
6. Ⓐ Ⓑ Ⓒ Ⓓ
7. Ⓐ Ⓑ Ⓒ Ⓓ
8. Ⓐ Ⓑ Ⓒ Ⓓ
9. Ⓐ Ⓑ Ⓒ Ⓓ
10. Ⓐ Ⓑ Ⓒ Ⓓ
11. Ⓐ Ⓑ Ⓒ Ⓓ
12. Ⓐ Ⓑ Ⓒ Ⓓ
13. Ⓐ Ⓑ Ⓒ Ⓓ
14. Ⓐ Ⓑ Ⓒ Ⓓ
15. Ⓐ Ⓑ Ⓒ Ⓓ
16. Ⓐ Ⓑ Ⓒ Ⓓ
17. Ⓐ Ⓑ Ⓒ Ⓓ
18. Ⓐ Ⓑ Ⓒ Ⓓ
19. Ⓐ Ⓑ Ⓒ Ⓓ
20. Ⓐ Ⓑ Ⓒ Ⓓ
21. Ⓐ Ⓑ Ⓒ Ⓓ
22. Ⓐ Ⓑ Ⓒ Ⓓ
23. Ⓐ Ⓑ Ⓒ Ⓓ
24. Ⓐ Ⓑ Ⓒ Ⓓ
25. Ⓐ Ⓑ Ⓒ Ⓓ
26. Ⓐ Ⓑ Ⓒ Ⓓ
27. Ⓐ Ⓑ Ⓒ Ⓓ

Section 1: Module 2 (Easier)
Reading and Writing

1. Ⓐ Ⓑ Ⓒ Ⓓ
2. Ⓐ Ⓑ Ⓒ Ⓓ
3. Ⓐ Ⓑ Ⓒ Ⓓ
4. Ⓐ Ⓑ Ⓒ Ⓓ
5. Ⓐ Ⓑ Ⓒ Ⓓ
6. Ⓐ Ⓑ Ⓒ Ⓓ
7. Ⓐ Ⓑ Ⓒ Ⓓ
8. Ⓐ Ⓑ Ⓒ Ⓓ
9. Ⓐ Ⓑ Ⓒ Ⓓ
10. Ⓐ Ⓑ Ⓒ Ⓓ
11. Ⓐ Ⓑ Ⓒ Ⓓ
12. Ⓐ Ⓑ Ⓒ Ⓓ
13. Ⓐ Ⓑ Ⓒ Ⓓ
14. Ⓐ Ⓑ Ⓒ Ⓓ
15. Ⓐ Ⓑ Ⓒ Ⓓ
16. Ⓐ Ⓑ Ⓒ Ⓓ
17. Ⓐ Ⓑ Ⓒ Ⓓ
18. Ⓐ Ⓑ Ⓒ Ⓓ
19. Ⓐ Ⓑ Ⓒ Ⓓ
20. Ⓐ Ⓑ Ⓒ Ⓓ
21. Ⓐ Ⓑ Ⓒ Ⓓ
22. Ⓐ Ⓑ Ⓒ Ⓓ
23. Ⓐ Ⓑ Ⓒ Ⓓ
24. Ⓐ Ⓑ Ⓒ Ⓓ
25. Ⓐ Ⓑ Ⓒ Ⓓ
26. Ⓐ Ⓑ Ⓒ Ⓓ
27. Ⓐ Ⓑ Ⓒ Ⓓ

Section 1: Module 2 (Harder)
Reading and Writing

1. Ⓐ Ⓑ Ⓒ Ⓓ
2. Ⓐ Ⓑ Ⓒ Ⓓ
3. Ⓐ Ⓑ Ⓒ Ⓓ
4. Ⓐ Ⓑ Ⓒ Ⓓ
5. Ⓐ Ⓑ Ⓒ Ⓓ
6. Ⓐ Ⓑ Ⓒ Ⓓ
7. Ⓐ Ⓑ Ⓒ Ⓓ
8. Ⓐ Ⓑ Ⓒ Ⓓ
9. Ⓐ Ⓑ Ⓒ Ⓓ
10. Ⓐ Ⓑ Ⓒ Ⓓ
11. Ⓐ Ⓑ Ⓒ Ⓓ
12. Ⓐ Ⓑ Ⓒ Ⓓ
13. Ⓐ Ⓑ Ⓒ Ⓓ
14. Ⓐ Ⓑ Ⓒ Ⓓ
15. Ⓐ Ⓑ Ⓒ Ⓓ
16. Ⓐ Ⓑ Ⓒ Ⓓ
17. Ⓐ Ⓑ Ⓒ Ⓓ
18. Ⓐ Ⓑ Ⓒ Ⓓ
19. Ⓐ Ⓑ Ⓒ Ⓓ
20. Ⓐ Ⓑ Ⓒ Ⓓ
21. Ⓐ Ⓑ Ⓒ Ⓓ
22. Ⓐ Ⓑ Ⓒ Ⓓ
23. Ⓐ Ⓑ Ⓒ Ⓓ
24. Ⓐ Ⓑ Ⓒ Ⓓ
25. Ⓐ Ⓑ Ⓒ Ⓓ
26. Ⓐ Ⓑ Ⓒ Ⓓ
27. Ⓐ Ⓑ Ⓒ Ⓓ

PSAT 8/9, 2nd Edition
Practice Test

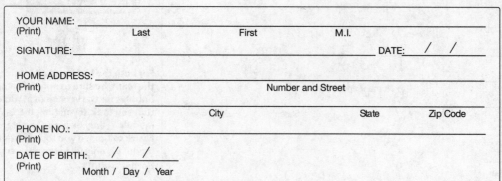

YOUR NAME: _____
(Print)   Last   First   M.I.

SIGNATURE: _____ DATE: __/__/__

HOME ADDRESS: _____
(Print)   Number and Street

_____
                City   State   Zip Code

PHONE NO.: _____
(Print)

DATE OF BIRTH: ____/____/_____
(Print)   Month / Day / Year

For both the Reading and Writing and the Math, be sure to only fill in the bubbles for the version of Module 2 that you took. If you took the Easier Module 2, only fill in the answer in the Easier column. If you took the Harder Module 2, only fill in the answers in the Harder column.

Section 2: Module 1
Math

1. Ⓐ Ⓑ Ⓒ Ⓓ
2. Ⓐ Ⓑ Ⓒ Ⓓ
3. Ⓐ Ⓑ Ⓒ Ⓓ
4. Ⓐ Ⓑ Ⓒ Ⓓ
5. Ⓐ Ⓑ Ⓒ Ⓓ
6. Ⓐ Ⓑ Ⓒ Ⓓ
7. _____
8. Ⓐ Ⓑ Ⓒ Ⓓ
9. Ⓐ Ⓑ Ⓒ Ⓓ
10. Ⓐ Ⓑ Ⓒ Ⓓ
11. Ⓐ Ⓑ Ⓒ Ⓓ
12. _____
13. Ⓐ Ⓑ Ⓒ Ⓓ
14. Ⓐ Ⓑ Ⓒ Ⓓ
15. _____
16. Ⓐ Ⓑ Ⓒ Ⓓ
17. Ⓐ Ⓑ Ⓒ Ⓓ
18. Ⓐ Ⓑ Ⓒ Ⓓ
19. Ⓐ Ⓑ Ⓒ Ⓓ
20. _____
21. Ⓐ Ⓑ Ⓒ Ⓓ
22. _____

Section 2: Module 2 (Easier)
Math

1. Ⓐ Ⓑ Ⓒ Ⓓ
2. Ⓐ Ⓑ Ⓒ Ⓓ
3. Ⓐ Ⓑ Ⓒ Ⓓ
4. Ⓐ Ⓑ Ⓒ Ⓓ
5. _____
6. _____
7. Ⓐ Ⓑ Ⓒ Ⓓ
8. _____
9. Ⓐ Ⓑ Ⓒ Ⓓ
10. Ⓐ Ⓑ Ⓒ Ⓓ
11. Ⓐ Ⓑ Ⓒ Ⓓ
12. Ⓐ Ⓑ Ⓒ Ⓓ
13. _____
14. Ⓐ Ⓑ Ⓒ Ⓓ
15. Ⓐ Ⓑ Ⓒ Ⓓ
16. Ⓐ Ⓑ Ⓒ Ⓓ
17. Ⓐ Ⓑ Ⓒ Ⓓ
18. Ⓐ Ⓑ Ⓒ Ⓓ
19. Ⓐ Ⓑ Ⓒ Ⓓ
20. _____
21. Ⓐ Ⓑ Ⓒ Ⓓ
22. _____

Section 2: Module 2 (Harder)
Math

1. _____
2. Ⓐ Ⓑ Ⓒ Ⓓ
3. Ⓐ Ⓑ Ⓒ Ⓓ
4. Ⓐ Ⓑ Ⓒ Ⓓ
5. Ⓐ Ⓑ Ⓒ Ⓓ
6. Ⓐ Ⓑ Ⓒ Ⓓ
7. _____
8. _____
9. Ⓐ Ⓑ Ⓒ Ⓓ
10. _____
11. Ⓐ Ⓑ Ⓒ Ⓓ
12. Ⓐ Ⓑ Ⓒ Ⓓ
13. Ⓐ Ⓑ Ⓒ Ⓓ
14. Ⓐ Ⓑ Ⓒ Ⓓ
15. _____
16. _____
17. Ⓐ Ⓑ Ⓒ Ⓓ
18. Ⓐ Ⓑ Ⓒ Ⓓ
19. Ⓐ Ⓑ Ⓒ Ⓓ
20. _____
21. Ⓐ Ⓑ Ⓒ Ⓓ
22. Ⓐ Ⓑ Ⓒ Ⓓ

Chapter 4
Practice Test 1:
Answers and
Explanations

PRACTICE TEST 1 ANSWER KEY

Reading and Writing			Math		
Module 1	**Module 2 (Easier)**	**Module 2 (Harder)**	**Module 1**	**Module 2 (Easier)**	**Module 2 (Harder)**
1. B	1. B	1. C	1. B	1. A	1. 5
2. A	2. D	2. D	2. C	2. D	2. B
3. A	3. C	3. B	3. B	3. B	3. D
4. A	4. C	4. B	4. D	4. C	4. C
5. C	5. C	5. A	5. A	5. 5	5. B
6. B	6. A	6. D	6. B	6. 140	6. C
7. B	7. D	7. D	7. 5	7. C	7. 4.25 or $\frac{17}{4}$
8. B	8. D	8. A	8. D	8. 22	8. 5
9. D	9. B	9. A	9. C	9. C	9. A
10. D	10. D	10. A	10. C	10. D	10. 4800
11. C	11. A	11. C	11. A	11. A	11. A
12. B	12. B	12. C	12. −4	12. C	12. D
13. B	13. C	13. B	13. D	13. 10	13. B
14. B	14. A	14. B	14. C	14. C	14. B
15. C	15. C	15. A	15. 5760	15. A	15. 10
16. C	16. A	16. D	16. B	16. B	16. 1975
17. D	17. B	17. D	17. A	17. D	17. C
18. D	18. D	18. A	18. A	18. D	18. D
19. B	19. B	19. D	19. B	19. A	19. A
20. A	20. C	20. A	20. 108	20. 550	20. −112
21. A	21. B	21. C	21. B	21. B	21. C
22. A	22. A	22. B	22. 80	22. 1.05	22. D
23. D	23. C	23. C			
24. A	24. D	24. C			
25. C	25. A	25. B			
26. A	26. B	26. C			
27. C	27. D	27. A			

PRACTICE TEST 1—READING AND WRITING EXPLANATIONS

Module 1

1. **B** This is a Vocabulary question, as it asks for a *logical and precise word or phrase* to fill in the blank. The blank should describe something that is ambitious, or grand, so look for and highlight clues in the passage about something that is large in scope. The passage states that *extending from New York City to San Francisco, the Lincoln Highway became the first coast-to-coast highway in the United States.* The "ambitious" thing in the passage is the Lincoln Highway project itself. Therefore, a good word to enter in the annotation box would be "project" or "development."

   - (A) and (D) are wrong because *treaty* and *failure* don't match "project."

   - (B) is correct because *undertaking*, or task, matches "project."

   - (C) is wrong because the passage doesn't describe the Lincoln Highway as an *invention*, or something newly created, but as a larger and more extensive road project.

2. **A** This is a Vocabulary question, as it asks for a *logical and precise word or phrase* to fill in the blank. The blank should describe Morrison's interaction with several different composers, so look for and highlight clues in the passage about this interaction. The passage states Morrison asks the composers *to write a score that will allow him to present old, decaying footage as part of a new, integrated narrative.* Therefore, a good phrase to enter in the annotation box would be "teams up with" or "gets together with."

   - (A) is correct because *works with* matches "teams up with."

   - (B) is wrong because *praised* goes beyond what the passage can support—it's not known from the passage that Morrison praises the composers who write for him or not.

   - (C) and (D) are wrong because *argues with* and *cautioned* are negative, which is the opposite tone of the positive phrase "teams up with."

3. **A** This is a Vocabulary question, as it asks for a *logical and precise word or phrase* to fill in the blank. The blank should describe the interaction between the findings and previous conclusions, so look for and highlight clues in the passage about this interaction. The passage states that the *new findings suggest otherwise*, meaning that they go against what was previously concluded. Therefore, a good word to enter in the annotation box would be "go against" or "disagree with."

   - (A) is correct because *contradict* matches "go against."

   - (B) and (D) are wrong because *confirm* and *demonstrate* are the opposite of what the findings do to the previous conclusions.

   - (C) is wrong because *investigate* doesn't match "go against."

4.   **A**   This is a Vocabulary question, as it asks what "mean" *most nearly means*. Treat "mean" as if it were a blank—the blank should describe the dwellings, or houses, so look for and highlight clues in the passage about the houses. The passage states that *They were the greatest possible eyesore, and they had no right to be in that neighbourhood at all.* Therefore, a good word to enter in the annotation box would be "unwelcome" or "unwanted."

   - (A) is correct because *Displeasing* matches "unwanted."

   - (B) and (C) are wrong because *Welcoming* and *Captivating* are the opposite tone of "unwelcome."

   - (D) is wrong because while *Abusing* something could be part of being *mean* to it, the houses are not described as actively abusing something.

5.   **C**   This is a Purpose question, as it asks for the *main purpose of the text*. Read the passage and highlight who or what the passage focuses on: the idea that *The Missoula Children's Theater was founded in 1970 as a company of adults performing for children.* The passage goes on to give more of the theater's history and what it does today. Therefore, a good main purpose of the passage to enter in the annotation box would be "gives the history of the theater company."

   - (A) and (B) are wrong because the passage only discusses the Missoula Children's Theater Company, not the *popularity* of theater or *other theater companies in Missoula.*

   - (C) is correct because it's consistent with the highlighting and annotation.

   - (D) is wrong because the passage does not encourage *people to raise funds* for children's theater.

6.   **B**   This is a Purpose question, as it asks for the *main purpose of the text*. Read the passage and highlight who or what the passage focuses on: the idea that *Fanny grew more comfortable.* The passage goes on to explain various ways that this growth took place. Therefore, a good main purpose of the passage to enter in the annotation box would be "describe how Fanny became more comfortable."

   - (A) is wrong because only *Edmund*, not the rest of *his family*, are mentioned in the passage, and Edmund's opinion of Fanny is not given.

   - (B) is correct because it's consistent with the highlighting and annotation.

   - (C) is wrong because only Fanny's fears are mentioned in the passage, not Edmund's.

   - (D) is wrong because the passage doesn't explain what brought Fanny to her current home.

7.   **B**   This is a Purpose question, as it asks for the *function of the first sentence in the text as a whole*. Read the passage and highlight clues that can explain the role of the underlined sentence. The second sentence expands on the first by mentioning that alloparental care research usually focuses on *genetic relatedness*, but the third sentence uses the word *However* to introduce that alloparental care *can occur in unrelated pairs as well.* Therefore, a good function of the underlined portion to enter in the annotation box would be "mention something people are debating about."

   - (A) and (C) are wrong because alloparental care is not described as a *theory* or a *challenge* in the first sentence, which only defines what alloparental care is.

- (B) is correct because it's consistent with the highlighting and annotation—discussing conflicting information on an occurrence such as alloparental care could mean that occurrence is being *examined*.

- (D) is wrong because this is the function of the second sentence, not the first.

8.   **B**   This is a Purpose question, as it asks for the *main purpose of the text*. Read the passage and highlight who or what the passage focuses on: the idea that the house Watson and Holmes are at *was remarkably animated*. The passage sets up this point by describing the setting of the house, called Briony Lodge. Therefore, a good main purpose of the passage to enter in the annotation box would be "explains house is more active than expected."

- (A) is wrong because a *lack of surprise* is the opposite of calling something "remarkable."

- (B) is correct because it's consistent with the highlighting and annotation.

- (C) is wrong because the reason for Watson and Holmes' visit is not given in the passage.

- (D) is wrong because only Watson's reaction to the situation is given, not that of *two different characters*.

9.   **D**   This is a Purpose question, as it asks for the *function of the underlined sentence in the text as a whole*. Read the passage and highlight clues that can explain the role of the underlined sentence. The sentence before states that *Gaudí designed seven different residential properties*. The underlined sentence goes on to describe the features of *These buildings*. Therefore, a good function of the underlined portion to enter in the annotation box would be "describe the buildings that Gaudí designed."

- (A) is wrong because there's no mention of *architectural magazines* in the passage.

- (B) is wrong because it goes beyond what the passage can support—while Gaudí did become *one of the first modernist architects*, it's not stated whether he had a *desire* to become one.

- (C) is wrong because the underlined sentence only describes the buildings that Gaudí designed, not how he *became involved in architecture*.

- (D) is correct because it's consistent with the highlighting and annotation.

10.   **D**   This is a Main Idea question, as it asks for the *main idea of the text*. Look for and highlight information that can help identify the main idea. The passage states that *Price and his team discovered that different groups of Native Americans from different parts of the Southwest all migrated to the Pueblo following a massive drought*. Since the other sentences set up the investigation of where the Pueblo may have come from, the last sentence serves as the main idea. The correct answer should be as consistent as possible with this portion of the passage.

- (A) and (B) are wrong because they go beyond what the passage can support—it's not known that it was necessary to *dissect rock specimens* before strontium isotope analysis or that this *innovation* allows scientists to study *more human bone and tooth remains* than before.

- (C) is wrong because it uses terms from the passage inaccurately—*migrated* describes the movements of the Native Americans, while *700-year-old* describes the bone and tooth remains.

- (D) is correct because it's consistent with the highlighted portion of the passage—the *specialized technology* could mean the *strontium isotope analysis*.

11.   **C**   This is a Main Idea question, as it asks for the *main idea of the text*. Look for and highlight information that can help identify the main idea. The passage states that *Her first morning was ruined, and she might never be in Florence again*. Since the other sentences mention that Lucy began the day with *high spirits* but is now *depressed and humiliated*, something has happened during the morning to change her mood and the first sentence serves as the main idea. The correct answer should be as consistent as possible with this portion of the passage.

- (A) is wrong because it makes too extreme of a statement—it's not known that Lucy has *never* been inside of a church before.

- (B) and (D) are wrong because they are the opposite of the passage, as Lucy is *depressed and humiliated* when entering the church and remarks upon it being *cold* and like a *barn*. Though she also says *it must be a wonderful building*, this is not strong enough given the other evidence to say that the church *raises her spirits* or that she has become *enamored*, or in love, with it.

- (C) is correct because it's consistent with the highlighted portion of the passage.

12.   **B**   This is a Main Idea question, as it asks for the *main idea of the text*. Look for and highlight information that can help identify the main idea. The passage states that *Polly Platt was a hugely influential force in film during the late twentieth century, but her contributions are often overlooked by those outside of the film industry*. Since the other sentences explain Platt's contribution but explain that she was overlooked because many roles for women in film at the time were behind the scenes, the first sentence serves as the main idea. The correct answer should be as consistent as possible with this portion of the passage.

- (A) and (D) are wrong because they each go beyond what the passage can support—it's not known what *number* of films Platt worked on or if she used *different filmmaking techniques* from other people.

- (B) is correct because it's consistent with the highlighted portion of the passage and the evidence in the last sentence regarding the fame achieved by Crowe, Anderson, and Bogdanovich.

- (C) is wrong because it's the opposite of the passage—Platt's work is *often overlooked*, not *more frequently acknowledged* than that of the others.

13.   **B**   This is a Charts question, as it asks for *data from the table* that will *support the underlined claim*. Read the title and variables from the table. Then, read the passage and highlight the underlined claim, which is that *even though Buddhism originated in India, there are other countries that contain a much*

larger number of Buddhists among their populations. The correct answer should offer accurate information from the table that offers evidence in support of this claim.

- (A) is wrong because it's consistent with the table but not relevant to the claim—the answer does not include *India*, which is one of the main focuses of the claim.

- (B) is correct because it's consistent with the table and the highlighted claim—Thailand is an example of a country that has a *much larger number of Buddhists* than India.

- (C) and (D) are wrong because they're not consistent with the table—Thailand has 64 million Buddhists, not *16 million.* Also, China does not have *244 million people* in its population, but rather, 244 million Buddhists. Additionally, for (D), the Buddhists are not 50% of China's population, but rather, China contains 50% of the world Buddhist population.

14. **B** This is a Claims question, as it asks which choice *would most strongly support the claim in the underlined sentence.* Look for and highlight the claim in the passage, which is that *The depiction of a Black girl who eventually travels through space inspired other Black writers to explore the theme of future technology in their works.* The correct answer should address and be consistent with each aspect of this claim.

- (A) is wrong because it's not relevant to the claim—other books being compared to *The Parable of the Sower* does not indicate that the novel *inspired* any of the authors of those books.

- (B) is correct because it's consistent with the highlighted claim—citing something as an *influence* could mean it *inspired* someone to write.

- (C) is wrong because it's also irrelevant to the claim—while it's possible that *The Parable of the Sower* may have inspired *authors who are not Black*, the correct answer must specifically mention *Black writers* as the claim does.

- (D) is wrong because it's also irrelevant to the claim—the awards and accolades achieved by *The Parable of the Sower* don't mean that it necessarily *inspired* any Black writers to write.

15. **C** This is a Charts question, as it asks for *data from the graph* that will *support the student's conclusion.* Read the title, key, and variables from the graph. Then, read the passage and highlight the conclusion containing the same information, which is that *rainfall in inches from the months of January to June in these cities follows a similar pattern.* The correct answer should offer accurate information from the graph that provides evidence in support of this conclusion.

- (A) is wrong because it's not consistent with the graph—Roanoke does not have *more than three monthly inches of rainfall* from *January to February* and it has exactly *four inches of rainfall* from *May to June*, not *less than* four inches.

- (B) is wrong because it's also inconsistent with the graph—both Roanoke and Virginia Beach do not have *constant* inches of rainfall from March to April. During that time, Roanoke's rainfall increases while Virginia Beach's decreases.

- (C) is correct because it's consistent with the graph and the highlighted conclusion.

- (D) is wrong because it's also inconsistent with the graph—both cities are above *three inches of rainfall* from March onwards.

16. **C** This is a Conclusions question, as it asks what *most logically completes the text.* Look for the main focus of the passage, which is the *theater convention of inserting long, awkward silences* into plays. Then, highlight the main points made regarding this focus: first, the passage states that Baker uses this convention to pay *homage to the "quiet" actors in Chekhov plays and silent film stars like Charlie Chaplin.* Then, the passage states that *theater critics lauded The Flick for its acknowledgment of the history of theater and cinema.* Therefore, critics appreciated how Baker used long, awkward silences to pay tribute to silent actors. The correct answer should be as consistent as possible with this conclusion.

- (A) is wrong because it goes beyond what the passage can support—it's not known from the passage that *Baker influenced many other playwrights.*

- (B) is wrong because it's the opposite of what's stated in the passage—critics *lauded*, or praised, Baker's message, so it was not *overlooked.*

- (C) is correct because it's consistent with what the highlighted sentences say about how Baker used the theater convention of long, awkward silences.

- (D) is wrong because it also goes beyond what the passage can support—it's not known if Charlie Chaplin *was one of Baker's favorite actors*, only that she chose to pay homage to him.

17. **D** In this Rules question, verbs are changing in the answer choices, so it's testing consistency with verbs. In this case, the verb is part of a list of two things that the researchers did, the first of which is *fill.* Highlight the word *fill*, which the verb in the answer should be consistent with. Eliminate any answer that isn't consistent with *fill.*

- (A), (B), and (C) are wrong because *were adding, added,* and *had added* aren't consistent with *fill.*

- (D) is correct because *add* is in the same tense and form as *fill.*

18. **D** In this Rules question, verb forms are changing in the answer choices, so it's testing sentence structure. The subject of the sentence is *Researchers*, and there is no main verb, so the answer must provide the main verb. Eliminate any answer that isn't in the correct form to be the main verb.

- (A) is wrong because a "to" verb can't be the main verb in a sentence.

- (B) and (C) are wrong because an *-ing* verb can't be the main verb in a sentence.

- (D) is correct because it's in the right form to be the main verb.

19. **B** In this Rules question, verb forms are changing in the answer choices, so it's testing sentence structure. In this case, the verb is part of a clause describing what *her attendance* did, so the answer must provide a main verb for the clause. Eliminate any answer that isn't in the correct form to be the main verb.

- (A) is wrong because a "to" verb can't be the main verb in a clause.

- (B) is correct because it's in the right form to be the main verb.

- (C) and (D) are wrong because an *-ing* verb can't be the main verb in a clause.

20. **A** In this Rules question, punctuation is changing in the answer choices. Look for independent clauses. The first part of the sentence says *She conducted research with linguists at UCLA as well as the University of Cologne in Germany*, which is an independent clause. The second part says *with anthropologist Lowell John Bean, she wrote Temalpakh…*, which is also an independent clause. Eliminate any answer that can't correctly connect two independent clauses.

- (A) is correct because it connects the independent clauses with a comma + a coordinating conjunction (*and*), which is acceptable.

- (B) is wrong because a comma without a coordinating conjunction (FANBOYS) can't connect two independent clauses.

- (C) is wrong because a coordinating conjunction (*and*) without a comma can't connect two independent clauses.

- (D) is wrong because some type of punctuation is needed in order to connect two independent clauses.

21. **A** In this Rules question, punctuation is changing in the answer choices. Look for independent clauses. The first part of the sentence says *In 2011, British choreographer and dancer Sarah Michelson considered the space and context of the venue when designing the work she called Devotion*, which is an independent clause. The second part says *sitting in the performers' space, the audience is confronted with a new perspective and urged to identify with the dancers*, which is also an independent clause. Eliminate any answer that can't correctly connect two independent clauses.

- (A) is correct because the period makes each independent clause its own sentence, which is fine.

- (B) is wrong because some type of punctuation is needed in order to connect two independent clauses.

- (C) is wrong because a comma without a coordinating conjunction (FANBOYS) can't connect two independent clauses.

- (D) is wrong because *sitting in the performers' space* is a phrase that shouldn't have a comma within it.

22. **A** This is a Transitions question, so follow the basic approach. Highlight ideas that relate to each other. The preceding sentence states that *She earned her pilot's license,* and this sentence describes another accomplishment: *she and her husband…founded the Sky Ranch Flying Service.* These ideas agree, so a same-direction transition is needed. Make an annotation that says "agree." Eliminate any answer that doesn't match.

- (A) is correct because this sentence is an additional point describing Azellia's accomplishments.

- (B) is wrong because this sentence is not a restatement of the preceding sentence.

- (C) and (D) are wrong because *Nevertheless* and *Still* are opposite-direction transitions.

23. **D** This is a Transitions question, so follow the basic approach. Highlight ideas that relate to each other. The preceding sentence states that he wrote a *play* in *1864,* and this sentence describes a *novel* he wrote in *1870.* Therefore, a time-change transition is needed. Make an annotation that says "time change." Eliminate any answer that doesn't match.

- (A) and (B) are wrong because this sentence doesn't disagree with the preceding sentence.

- (C) is wrong because this sentence isn't an example of a previous idea.

- (D) is correct because *Later* is a time-change transition and describes the event in this sentence as occurring after the event in the preceding sentence.

24. **A** This is a Transitions question, so follow the basic approach. Highlight ideas that relate to each other. The first part of the sentence says *Lemon expressed himself through painting,* then there is a contrast word (*but*), and then it states that *he found that movement through dance* was more effective. The contrast word and the word *found* suggest that over time Lemon changed his focus, so a time-change transition is needed. Make an annotation that says "time-change." Eliminate any answer that doesn't match.

- (A) is correct because *Initially* is a time-change transition and describes his expression through painting as occurring before his expression through dance.

- (B) is wrong because this sentence doesn't describe any effect of the preceding sentence.

- (C) is wrong because this sentence isn't a conclusion based on the preceding sentence.

- (D) is wrong because this sentence doesn't contrast with the preceding sentence.

25. **C** This is a Rhetorical Synthesis question, so follow the basic approach. Highlight the goal(s) stated in the question: *describe what was noteworthy about Algarín's café.* Eliminate any answer that doesn't fulfill this purpose.

- (A) and (D) are wrong because they don't mention something *noteworthy* about the café.

- (B) is wrong because it doesn't mention the café.

- (C) is correct because the bullets state that the café was *noteworthy* for *popularizing slam poetry.*

26. **A** This is a Rhetorical Synthesis question, so follow the basic approach. Highlight the goal(s) stated in the question: *specify the year Alodia was first mentioned in the historical records*. Eliminate any answer that doesn't fulfill this purpose.

- (A) is correct because it specifies *the year Alodia was first mentioned in the historical records*.

- (B), (C), and (D) are wrong because they do not mention the specific year that *Alodia was first mentioned in the historical records*.

27. **C** This is a Rhetorical Synthesis question, so follow the basic approach. Highlight the goal(s) stated in the question: *emphasize a difference between rock operas and conventional operas*. Eliminate any answer that doesn't fulfill this purpose.

- (A) and (B) are wrong because they don't mention *rock operas*.

- (C) is correct because the phrase *Unlike conventional operas* shows a contrast.

- (D) is wrong because it doesn't mention *conventional operas*.

Module 2—Easier

1. **B** This is a Vocabulary question, as it asks for a *logical and precise word or phrase* to fill in the blank. The blank should describe Hadid's building designs, so look for and highlight clues in the passage about these designs. The passage states that Hadid did not adhere, or stick to, *the symmetry of traditional structural elements*. Therefore, a good phrase to enter in the annotation box would be "non-traditional" or "atypical."

- (A) and (D) are wrong because they're the opposite of how Hadid approaches design—her designs don't follow what others might consider traditionally *logical* or *typical*.

- (B) is correct because *unusual* matches "non-traditional."

- (C) is wrong because *straightforward* doesn't match "non-traditional."

2. **D** This is a Vocabulary question, as it asks for a *logical and precise word or phrase* to fill in the blank. The blank should describe something individualized that helps dolphins, so look for and highlight clues in the passage about what the dolphins have that is individualized to each of them. The passage states *Each dolphin has its own whistle sequence*. Therefore, a good phrase to enter in the annotation box would be "sequences" or "patterns."

- (A), (B), and (C) are wrong because *contracts*, *sizes*, and *ornaments* don't match "sequences."

- (D) is correct because *arrangements* matches "sequences."

3. **C** This is a Vocabulary question, as it asks for a *logical and precise word or phrase* to fill in the blank. The blank should describe the interaction between the exhibit and the two generations, so look for and highlight clues in the passage about this interaction. The passage states that the exhibit focused on

exploring the Saar family's history and *tracing how daughters Alison and Lezley expanded their mother Betye's work*. The exhibit, then, explores multiple generations of the Saar family. Therefore, a good phrase to enter in the annotation box would be "connected" or "spanned."

- (A) and (D) are wrong because *disregarded* and *criticized* are the opposite tone of "connected," which is positive.

- (B) is wrong because *adopted* doesn't match "connected."

- (C) is correct because *bridged* matches "connected."

4.   C   This is a Vocabulary question, as it asks for a *logical and precise word or phrase* to fill in the blank. The blank should describe something about accomplished composer Bernard Herrmann, so look for and highlight clues in the passage about this composer. The passage states that Herrmann's *musical works provided the perfect backdrop for Hitchcock's films*. Therefore, a good phrase to enter in the annotation box would be "skill" or "ability."

- (A), (B), and (D) are wrong because *criticisms, arguments*, and *retirement* don't match "skill." Even if it's easy to imagine how criticisms and arguments could potentially help a film director, the passage doesn't discuss anything offered by Herrmann except his musical works.

- (C) is correct because *talent* matches "skill."

5.   C   This is a Purpose question, as it asks for the *function of the underlined portion in the text as a whole*. Read the passage and highlight clues that can explain the role of the underlined sentence. The sentence before explains that a gyre is *a strong ocean current*, and the sentence after explains that *These gyres carry debris along a consistent pathway, leading to significant accumulation of garbage at specific points in the ocean*. Therefore, a good function of the underlined sentence to enter in the annotation box would be "introduce a term that the passage talks about."

- (A) is wrong because the passage never explains the *difference* among canals, rivers, and storm drains.

- (B) is wrong because *Charles Moore's opinion* about his discovery is not given by the passage.

- (C) is correct because it's consistent with the highlighting and annotation.

- (D) is wrong because only the last sentence, not the underlined portion, discusses the discovery by Moore, and the discovery is not described as *intriguing*.

6.   A   This is a Dual Texts question, as it asks what *the author of Text 2* would say about *researchers' claim in Text 1*. Read Text 1 and highlight the researchers' claim, which indicates that *elephants can be altruistic, trying to console other elephants without any direct benefit to themselves*. Then, read Text 2 and highlight what its author says about the same topic. The author states that *However, it is quite likely that the animals are simply congregating following an event that distressed several individuals, with some perhaps showing a delayed reaction to the distressing stimuli and seeking social cohesion as a means of safety*. Therefore, the author of Text 2 does not believe the elephants are necessarily acting

altruistically, or selflessly, as the author thinks they may just be reacting to a stressful situation. Enter "Text 2 disagrees—thinks elephants may just be reacting to stress" into the annotation box.

- (A) is correct because it's consistent with the highlighting and annotated relationship between the passages—the author of Text 2 has given a different reason for the behavior besides altruism.

- (B) is wrong because it goes beyond what the passage can support—it's not known whether the elephants were in an *enclosure*.

- (C) is wrong because it's too extreme of a statement to be supported by the passage—the author of Text 2 does not claim that the elephants were *actively working to benefit themselves*, just that some were possibly showing a *delayed reaction* to a stimulus.

- (D) is wrong because neither Text 1 nor Text 2 clarifies whether it was some or all of the elephants observed that exhibited the trunk-touching behavior from Text 1.

7. **D** This is a Main Idea question, as it asks for the *main idea of the text*. Look for and highlight information that can help identify the main idea. The passage states that *Alvarez invites members of the audience to participate in dance and movement exercises and then create their own collaborative dance*. Since the other sentence gives the background of the company and its collaborative work, the last sentence serves as the main idea. The correct answer should be as consistent as possible with this portion of the passage.

- (A) is wrong because the passage does not claim that Alvarez's goal for having the audience participate is to *illustrate the complexity of the task*.

- (B) is wrong because neither the regions in which the company tours nor the demographics of its collaborators are given by the passage.

- (C) is wrong because it goes beyond what the passage can support—while the company does work with Marjani Forté, it's not known that this is why *Alvarez began* the company.

- (D) is correct because it's consistent with the highlighted portion of the passage.

8. **D** This is a Charts question, as it asks for *data from the table* that will *complete the claim*. Read the title and variables from the table. Then, read the passage and highlight the claim, which should make a statement about *Homo luzonensis* when *compared to several other hominin species*. The correct answer should offer accurate information from the table that completes this comparison.

- (A) is wrong because while *Homo luzonensis* does have a *smaller molar diameter* than the other two hominin species, it is shorter, not *taller*, than either of the other two hominin species.

- (B) and (C) are wrong because they're not consistent with the table—*Homo luzonensis* has a smaller, not a *larger*, molar diameter than the other two hominin species in the table.

- (D) is correct because it's consistent with the table and compares *Homo luzonensis* appropriately to the other two hominin species.

9.   **B**   This is a Charts question, as it asks for *data from the table* that will *complete the statement*. Read the title and variables from the table. Then, read the passage and highlight the statement made regarding the same information, which is that *some objects in the solar system have atmospheres composed of more than 80% nitrogen*. The correct answer should offer accurate information from the table that is an example of this statement.

- (A), (C), and (D) are wrong because Earth's Moon and Mercury are not primarily composed of nitrogen, so the percent of nitrogen in their atmospheres is not given in the chart.

- (B) is correct because it's consistent with the table and the highlighted claim—both Titan and Pluto have *more than 80% nitrogen* in their atmospheres.

10.   **D**   This is a Claims question, as it asks which choice *would most directly support the scholars' claim*. Look for and highlight the claim in the passage, which is that *many scholars believe* that the mechanism discovered *is the world's first computer*. The correct answer should address and be consistent with each aspect of this claim.

- (A), (B), and (C) are wrong because they're each not relevant to the claim—even if other, similar mechanisms were shown to be the *work of inventors,* to *have belonged to* inventors, or to be evidence of *shared ideas* between peoples, none of these findings would specifically support that the mechanism discovered *is the world's first computer*.

- (D) is correct because it's consistent with the highlighted claim—if the device's *primary purpose was to calculate complex mathematical approximations*, this could indeed make it *the world's first computer*.

11.   **A**   This is a Claims question, as it asks which choice *would most directly weaken the team's hypothesis*. Look for and highlight the hypothesis in the passage, which is that the phenomenon of *algae-rich waters becoming more yellow…is the result of human activity, with dams and water runoff altering the composition of the dissolved particles in the water*. The correct answer should offer contradictory data to this hypothesis or an alternative explanation for what was observed.

- (A) is correct because it's consistent with the question task—if *naturally occurring compounds* affected the color of the water, this would *weaken* the hypothesis that the color change occurred due to *human activity*.

- (B) is wrong because it's not relevant to the hypothesis—the hypothesis only relates to normally green, algae-rich water becoming yellow, not mixing *yellow or brown water* with *blue water*.

- (C) is wrong because it would support, not *weaken*, the hypothesis if dams and water runoff do indeed *produce a deeper yellow water color* in the United States.

- (D) is wrong because it's also not relevant to the claim—the frequency with which water types are mixed doesn't directly address the hypothesis. If anything, if water colors *rarely* mix together in nature, this would support the hypothesis that *human activity* may be involved instead.

12. **B** This is a Conclusions question, as it asks what *most logically completes the text*. Look for the main focus of the passage, which is the music of the *Appalachian fiddle musicians, many of whom immigrated from Scotland and Ireland*. Then, highlight the main points made regarding this focus: first, the passage states that *historical recordings of the traditional fiddle music are few and far between*. Then, the passage states that *This has led some historians to dedicate their time to implement safer storage practices for the recordings*. Therefore, these historians are ensuring not only *the security of these valuable sound and video records* but also preserving some of the musicians' culture. The correct answer should be as consistent as possible with this conclusion.

- (A), (C), and (D) are wrong because they go beyond what the passage can support—it's not known from the passage if the historians' work will ensure that there will be *concerts* to attend, will necessarily expand the awareness of fiddle music *beyond the lands of its origin*, or will assist *future* musicians in recording.

- (B) is correct because it's consistent with what the highlighted sentences say about the historians' efforts to preserve recordings of Appalachian fiddle music.

13. **C** This is a Conclusions question, as it asks what *most logically completes the text*. Look for the main focus of the passage, which is the that *the disk that eventually coalesced into the moon must have been primarily solid or liquid particles*. Then, highlight the main points made regarding this focus: first, the passage states that *a disk made primarily of gas would have been vaporized in the collision*. Then, the passage states that *the team set the impact velocity at approximately 15 km/s, leading to the development of a primarily gaseous disk and a very small satellite*. Finally, if *collision velocity depends on the masses of the colliding bodies*, there must have been specific masses involved to produce the collision velocity required to make sure the disk wasn't gaseous. Otherwise, the Moon would not have formed. The correct answer should be as consistent as possible with this conclusion.

- (A) is wrong because it goes beyond what the passage can support—the formation of the *Earth* is not discussed in the passage.

- (B) is wrong because also goes beyond what the passage can support—it's not stated that the *impact velocity* needs to be *slower*, or even faster, than 15 km/s, just that it needs to be different, as 15 km/s formed a gaseous disk, which would vaporize.

- (C) is correct because it's consistent with what the highlighted sentences say about the impact velocity needed—whatever the masses need to be to produce the correct impact velocity, they need to be within some sort of *specific range*, as the impact velocity of 15 km/s did not create the correct type of disk.

- (D) is wrong because it also goes beyond what the passage can support—it's not known from the passage if a *faster* impact velocity leads to a *larger* Moon size.

14. **A**   In this Rules question, verb forms are changing in the answer choices, so it's testing sentence structure. The sentence already contains two main verbs (*allows…and prevents*) for the subject (*This*), so the blank should not be in main verb form and instead should produce a phrase stating what the method *allows aquifers* to do. Eliminate any answer that does not make the phrase clear and correct.

- (A) is correct because *to refill* is what the method *allows aquifers* to do.

- (B), (C), and (D) are wrong because they are in main verb form and do not make the phrase clear and correct.

15. **C**   In this Rules question, punctuation is changing in the answer choices. The punctuation appears after the word *recognized*, but the sentence is stating that the *Critics…have recognized* the book *as one of the pioneering works* in a genre. There is no reason to put punctuation between *recognized* and the title of the book because it's all part of the same idea. Eliminate answers with punctuation.

- (A), (B), and (D) are wrong because there is no reason to use punctuation here.

- (C) is correct because no punctuation should be used here.

16. **A**   In this Rules question, verbs are changing in the answer choices, so it's testing consistency with verbs. Find and highlight the subject, *You*, which is singular, so a singular verb is needed. All of the answers work with a singular subject, so look for a clue regarding tense. This sentence mentions *the previous chapter*. Highlight the word *previous* and write an annotation that says "past." Eliminate any answer not in past tense.

- (A) is correct because it's in past tense.

- (B) and (D) are wrong because they're in future tense.

- (C) is wrong because it's in present tense.

17. **B**   In this Rules question, punctuation is changing in the answer choices. The punctuation appears after the word *learns*, but the sentence is stating that *John Cunliffe…learns about the responsibilities of adulthood*. There is no reason to put punctuation between *learns* and *about* because they are part of the same idea. Eliminate answers with punctuation.

- (A), (C), and (D) are wrong because there is no reason to use punctuation here.

- (B) is correct because no punctuation should be used here.

18. **D**   In this Rules question, pronouns are changing in the answer choices, so it's testing consistency with pronouns. Find and highlight the phrase the pronoun refers back to, *The marble lions*, which is plural, so a plural pronoun is needed. Write an annotation saying "plural." Eliminate any answer that isn't plural or doesn't clearly refer back to *The marble lions*.

- (A) is wrong because *some* doesn't clearly refer back to *The marble lions*.

- (B) and (C) are wrong because they are singular.

- (D) is correct because *they* is plural and is consistent with *The marble lions.*

19. **B** In this Rules question, punctuation is changing in the answer choices. Look for independent clauses. The first part of the sentence says *GMO…foods can contain higher amounts of certain nutrients than non-GMO foods*, which is an independent clause. The second part says *critics of GMO foods claim that the long-term health risks are still unknown*, which is also an independent clause. Eliminate any answer that can't correctly connect two independent clauses.

    - (A) is wrong because some type of punctuation is needed in order to connect two independent clauses.

    - (B) is correct because it connects the independent clauses with a comma + a coordinating conjunction (*but*), which is acceptable.

    - (C) is wrong because a comma without a coordinating conjunction (FANBOYS) can't connect two independent clauses.

    - (D) is wrong because a coordinating conjunction (*but*) without a comma can't connect two independent clauses.

20. **C** In this Rules question, pronouns are changing in the answer choices, so it's testing consistency with pronouns. Find and highlight the word the pronoun refers back to, *Licitars,* which is plural, so a plural pronoun is needed. Write an annotation saying "plural." Eliminate any answer that isn't plural or doesn't clearly refer back to *Licitars.*

    - (A) and (D) are wrong because they don't refer back to a specific thing.

    - (B) is wrong because *this* is singular.

    - (C) is correct because *they* is plural and is consistent with *Licitars.*

21. **B** In this Rules question, verbs are changing in the answer choices, so it's testing consistency with verbs. Find and highlight the subject, *method*, which is singular, so a singular verb is needed. All of the answers work with a singular subject, so look for a clue regarding tense. The sentence is discussing what this method *could be utilized* to do, so because it refers to a hypothetical scenario, the description of what the method would do to *the cells' nuclei* should be in present tense. Highlight *could be utilized* and write an annotation that says "present." Eliminate any answer not in present tense.

    - (A) and (C) are wrong because they are in past tense.

    - (B) is correct because it's in present tense.

    - (D) is wrong because although it is in present tense, *is targeting* would refer to something currently in progress, but the sentence is describing something that could hypothetically happen.

22. **A**   In this Rules question, verbs are changing in the answer choices, so it's testing consistency with verbs. Find and highlight the subject, *Hippocamp*, which is singular, so a singular verb is needed. Write an annotation saying "singular." Eliminate any answer that is not singular.

- (A) is correct because it's singular.

- (B), (C), and (D) are wrong because they are plural.

23. **C**   This is a Transitions question, so follow the basic approach. Highlight ideas that relate to each other. The first part of the sentence says *Spaldin was one of the first researchers to explain why there are so few multiferroics*, and the second part of the sentence explains why Spaldin joined a team *studying bismuth ferrite and its multiferroic characteristics*. These ideas agree, so a same-direction transition is needed. Make an annotation that says "agree." Eliminate any answer that doesn't match.

- (A) is wrong because the second part of the sentence is not a restatement of the first part of the sentence.

- (B) is wrong because it is an opposite-direction transition.

- (C) is correct because the second part of the sentence happened *as a result* of the first part of the sentence.

- (D) is wrong because the second part of the sentence is not stating a similarity to the first part of the sentence.

24. **D**   This is a Transitions question, so follow the basic approach. Highlight ideas that relate to each other. The preceding sentence says *Wildfires…affect the weather in the central United States*, and this sentence explains that the byproducts of wildfires create *an environment more conducive to storms* in this region. These ideas agree, so a same-direction transition is needed. Make an annotation that says "agree." Eliminate any answer that doesn't match.

- (A) is wrong because this sentence provides more details on how wildfires affect the weather rather than offering a second point.

- (B) is wrong because this sentence is continuing with the same topic, not introducing a new, similar topic.

- (C) is wrong because this sentence is not a conclusion based on the previous sentence.

- (D) is correct because this sentence provides details that specify some ways wildfires *affect the weather in the central United States*.

25.   **A**   This is a Transitions question, so follow the basic approach. Highlight ideas that relate to each other. The first sentence provides a general statement about the importance of *The Atlantic menhaden*. The second sentence provides one *important function* of the species, and this sentence offers a second role the menhaden plays. These ideas agree, so make an annotation that says "agree." Eliminate any answer that doesn't match.

- (A) is correct because this sentence is a second function of the menhaden in addition to the function stated in the preceding sentence.

- (B) and (D) are wrong because this sentence provides a second function of the menhaden rather than reinforcing or providing specific details about the previous statement.

- (C) is wrong because this sentence is not an example of the idea in the previous sentence.

26.   **B**   This is a Rhetorical Synthesis question, so follow the basic approach. Highlight the goal(s) stated in the question: *specify how Saturn's rings may have been formed.* Eliminate any answer that doesn't fulfill this purpose.

- (A) is wrong because it states what material the rings were *formed* out of but doesn't specify *how* they came into existence.

- (B) is correct because it provides a theory that would explain how the rings *may have been formed*.

- (C) is wrong because it doesn't offer any specific theory.

- (D) is wrong because it describes Saturn's rings but doesn't *specify how* the rings were *formed*.

27.   **D**   This is a Rhetorical Synthesis question, so follow the basic approach. Highlight the goal(s) stated in the question: *emphasize how harmful the venom of the inland taipan can be.* Eliminate any answer that doesn't fulfill this purpose.

- (A) and (C) are wrong because they mention the venom of the inland taipan but do not *emphasize how harmful* it is.

- (B) is wrong because it mentions that the venom is harmful but does not emphasize *how harmful*.

- (D) is correct because it *emphasizes how harmful* the inland taipan venom can be by specifying how deadly it is to humans.

Module 2—Harder

1. **C** This is a Vocabulary question, as it asks for a *logical and precise word or phrase* to fill in the blank. The blank should describe Noguchi's relationship to the idea of incorporating a range of cultural perspectives into his art pieces, so look for and highlight clues about this relationship. The passage states that Noguchi created his art in part by *studying traditional Japanese pottery and Chinese calligraphy*. This means that incorporating a range of cultural perspectives was something Noguchi aimed to do in his work. Therefore, a good phrase to enter in the annotation box would be "aimed to" or "wanted to."

   • (A), (B), and (D) are wrong because *skeptical*, *unfamiliar*, and *resistant* all suggest either a negative or an uncertain relationship to incorporating a range of cultural perspectives, but this is something Noguchi actively "aimed to" do.

   • (C) is correct because *focused on* matches "aimed to."

2. **D** This is a Vocabulary question, as it asks for a *logical and precise word or phrase* to fill in the blank. The blank should something undertaken, or experienced, by James Jarvis, so look for and highlight clues in the passage about what may have happened to Jarvis. The passage states that Jarvis *goes from expressing ignorance towards the plight of those around him to providing aid and hope to those downtrodden by societal injustices*. Therefore, a good phrase to enter in the annotation box would be "change" or "alteration."

   • (A) and (B) are wrong because *burden* and *precaution* don't match "change."

   • (C) is wrong because *dormancy* (a period of rest) would be the opposite of experiencing "change."

   • (D) is correct because *transformation* matches "change."

3. **B** This is a Vocabulary question, as it asks for a *logical and precise word or phrase* to fill in the blank. The blank should describe the warbling music tones produced by the theremin, so look for and highlight clues in the passage about these tones. The passage states that *the pitch and volume can be altered substantially by minute changes to the position of the musician's hands*. Therefore, a good phrase to enter in the annotation box would be "varied" or "numerous."

   • (A), (C), and (D) are wrong because *neglected*, *commanding*, and *predictable* don't match "varied."

   • (B) is correct because *diverse* matches "varied."

4. **B** This is a Vocabulary question, as it asks for a *logical and precise word or phrase* to fill in the blank. The blank should describe something about the access that Heap utilized, so look for and highlight clues in the passage about this access. The passage states *the rise in personal computers allowed artists greater access to MIDI devices that create electronic music*. Therefore, a good phrase to enter in the annotation box would be "greater" or "improved."

   • (A) and (D) are wrong because *routine* and *expected* imply that the level of access granted to artists is normal, but the passage supports that this is a greater level of access than they used to have.

- (B) is correct because *expanded* matches "greater."

- (C) is wrong because *unstable* doesn't match "greater."

5. **A** This is a Dual Texts question, as it asks for a *statement about brown tree snakes* about which *Adams's team and the author of Text 2 would most likely agree*. Read Text 1 and highlight Adams's team's statement about the snakes, which is that *they observed no brown tree snakes on the island*. Then, read Text 2 and highlight what its author says about the same topic. The author states that *The snakes are well camouflaged, and there were probably individuals hidden during the Adams team's surveys*. Therefore, Adams's team and the author of Text 2 would agree that it's difficult to see brown tree snakes on the island, even if the two groups draw different conclusions from this. Enter "both agree snakes hard to locate" into the annotation box.

   - (A) is correct because it's consistent with the highlighting and annotated relationship between the passages.

   - (B) is wrong because it goes beyond what the passage can support—the snakes' ability to camouflage on *other islands* besides Saipan is not discussed in either passage.

   - (C) is wrong because neither passage claims that *different types of surveys* would be more successful in locating snakes—the author of Text 2 only indicates that *the island must continue to be surveyed*.

   - (D) is wrong because no *other snake species* are mentioned or compared to the brown tree snakes.

6. **D** This is a Main Idea question, as it asks for the *main idea of the text*. Look for and highlight information that can help identify the main idea. The passage states that *Alvarez invites members of the audience to participate in dance and movement exercises and then create their own collaborative dance*. Since the other sentence gives the background of the company and its collaborative work, the last sentence serves as the main idea. The correct answer should be as consistent as possible with this portion of the passage.

   - (A) is wrong because the passage does not claim that Alvarez's goal for having the audience participate is to *illustrate the complexity of the task*.

   - (B) is wrong because neither the regions in which the company tours nor the demographics of its collaborators are given by the passage.

   - (C) is wrong because it goes beyond what the passage can support—while the company does work with Marjani Forté, it's not known that this is why *Alvarez began* the company.

   - (D) is correct because it's consistent with the highlighted portion of the passage.

7. **D** This is a Main Idea question, as it asks for the *main idea of the text*. Look for and highlight information that can help identify the main idea. The passage states that *Each type of study is valuable in different ways*, but *if the results of an interventional and an observational study…are in opposition, there may have been bias in participant selection in one or both of the studies that affected the results produced.* Since the other sentences explain the two types of studies and their benefits, the second sentence and last sentences together serve as the main idea. The correct answer should be as consistent as possible with these portions of the passage.

   • (A) is wrong because it makes too extreme of a statement—conflicting results are not *strong* indicators of an error made by *both* studies but may just indicate a *bias in participant selection in one or both of the studies.*

   • (B) is wrong because the passage does not indicate which of the two study types is more or less *credible* when conflicting data is presented.

   • (C) is wrong because it goes beyond what the passage can support—it is not known if *scientists struggle to reconcile*, or make sense of, the conflicting data once presented with it.

   • (D) is correct because it's consistent with the highlighted portions of the passage—it captures the fact that both types of study have their benefits but either kind can still have bias.

8. **A** This is a Charts question, as it asks for *data from the graph* that will *support Brock and colleagues' reasoning*. Read the title and variables from the table. Then, read the passage and highlight the reasoning, which is that *the unfamiliarity of the loggerhead turtles to the artificial nourishment initially deterred them from nesting at the nourished beach, but that this effect was reduced as the turtles became more acclimated to the nourishment*. The correct answer should offer accurate information from the graph that supports this reasoning.

   • (A) is correct because it's consistent with the graph and the reasoning—the nesting success ratio at the nourished beach initially dropped, but then recovered in 2003, indicating that the turtles may have become more acclimated to, or comfortable with, nesting at the nourished beach.

   • (B) and (D) are wrong because they're consistent with the graph but not relevant to the reasoning—neither references the initial decline and then recovery of the nesting success ratio at the nourished beach.

   • (C) is wrong because it's not consistent with the graph—in 2001, the nesting success ratio at the nourished beach was lower, not *greater*, than the nesting success ratio at the nourished beach.

9. **A** This is a Claims question, as it asks which choice *would be the most effective evidence* to include *in support of this claim*. Look for and highlight the claim in the passage, which is that the NEA's *funds have resulted in a significant increase in the number of non-profit theater companies and symphony orchestras in the United States*. The correct answer should address and be consistent with each aspect of this claim.

   • (A) is correct because it's consistent with the highlighted claim—while it doesn't reference *symphony orchestras*, if the NEA's funding has led to a *six-fold increase in the number of non-profit theater companies*, that would most certainly be a *significant increase*.

- (B), (C), and (D) are wrong because they're each not relevant to the claim—calls for the NEA to be an *independent agency*, the proposal of the NEA being *initially met with skepticism*, and a goal to *enrich the lives of its populace* don't support that NEA funds have actually resulted in a *significant increase in the number of non-profit theater companies and symphony orchestras.*

10. **A** This is a Claims question, as it asks which choice *would most directly support the researchers' conclusion*. Look for and highlight the conclusion in the passage, which is that *very little local precipitation comes from Lake Volta and most of the water that evaporates from the lake is transported elsewhere*. Note and highlight the evidence before this conclusion, which indicates that an average recycling ratio should fall *between 10 and 50%*—this may be important for properly evaluating what the passage considers to be *very little*. The correct answer should address and be consistent with each aspect of this conclusion and its evidence.

    - (A) is correct because it's consistent with the highlighted conclusion and evidence—both 6% and 2% would be well below the average recycling ratio given in the passage.

    - (B) and (D) are wrong because each is the opposite of what is stated in the passage—if Lake Volta or the area around it had *an average recycling ratio between 10% and 50%* or even *greater than 50%*, this would not be *very little* compared to the average recycling ratio given in the passage.

    - (C) is wrong because the passage makes no distinction between the *lake's shoreline* and the area *farther* from the *lake,* and either of these ratios being *above 10%* would be considered *average* rather than *very little.*

11. **C** This is a Charts question, as it asks for *data from the table* that will *complete the text*. Read the title and variables from the table. Then, read the passage and highlight a statement made in the passage regarding the same information, which is that *They found that educating people about the process increased public approval*. Since the incomplete idea explains that *25% of respondents did not know what they thought about CCS at the start of the survey, while at the end, that number decreased to 8%*, the correct answer should offer accurate information from the table that completes this statement by referencing something related to *increased public approval*.

    - (A) is wrong because it's not consistent with the table—only 6%, not 16%, of respondents *strongly* approve of CCS at the end of the survey.

    - (B) and (D) are wrong because they're the opposite of the statement—the statement focuses on how public approval should increase, but each of these answers focuses on disapproval or strong disapproval. Even though the disapprove and strongly disapprove categories drop, this by itself does not mean that public approval has increased, as those respondents could simply have become neutral.

    - (C) is correct because it's consistent with the table and highlighted statement. This answer directly references public approval, which has increased to 32%.

12.   **C**   This is a Conclusions question, as it asks what *most logically completes the text*. Look for the main focus of the passage, which is the *Rapa Nui people*. Then, highlight the main points made regarding this focus: first, the passage states that the Rapa Nui people developed *a pictorial script called Rongorongo, which researchers and linguists have been unable to decipher*. Then, the passage states that *knowledge of the Rapa Nui people has been carried forward over time through archaeological artifacts, customs, and oral traditions*. Therefore, knowledge of the Rapa Nui has been able to be passed on even though researchers and linguists have been unable to decipher their writing system. The correct answer should be as consistent as possible with this conclusion.

- (A) is wrong because it's the opposite of what is stated in the passage—the researchers and linguists *have been unable to decipher* the writing system, meaning they haven't been able to *decode* it.

- (B) is wrong because it goes beyond what the passage can support—the passage doesn't claim that the researchers and linguists' inability to understand the writing system has actually made the research of the culture *more straightforward*.

- (C) is correct because it is consistent with what the highlighted sentences say about the Rapa Nui's writing system and artifacts, customs, and oral traditions.

- (D) is wrong because the passage does not recommend that linguistics research in general should *focus on archaeological artifacts rather than understanding pictorial scripts* just because a single writing system is difficult to decipher.

13.   **B**   This is a Conclusions question, as it asks what *most logically completes the text*. Look for the main focus of the passage, which is that capuchin *monkeys have been found to use stones to open seeds and nuts*. Then, highlight the main points made regarding this focus: first, the passage states that the stones the monkeys used as a hammer were four times heavier than average stones, while the stones used as anvils were over eight times heavier. Then, the passage states that stone tools from 600 to 700 years ago are *similar to the ones used by monkeys today in terms of rock materials and weights, and both tool types had been arranged in small piles to be used again and again*. Therefore, the monkeys have used both hammer and anvil stone tools for a long time and continue to use these tools repeatedly. The correct answer should be as consistent as possible with this conclusion.

- (A), (C), and (D) are wrong because they each go beyond what the passage can support—the two types of stone tools are not compared to the monkeys' *own teeth*, and it's not stated which stone tool is *easier* to use (even if one is lighter than the other) or that monkeys *trade* one tool type but not the other.

- (B) is correct because it's consistent with what the highlighted sentences say about the hammer and anvil stone tools.

14. **B** In this Rules question, verb forms are changing in the answer choices, so it's testing consistency with verbs. Find and highlight the subject, *depiction*, which is singular, so a singular verb is needed. Write an annotation saying "singular." Eliminate any answer that is not singular.

   - (A), (C), and (D) are wrong because they are plural.

   - (B) is correct because it's singular.

15. **A** In this Rules question, punctuation is changing in the answer choices. The part of the sentence that follows the colon is a list of what the sensors do: 1) *monitor wound healing in real time*, 2) *prevent risk of infection*, and 3) *save on healthcare costs*. There should be a comma between these items, so eliminate any answer that doesn't have a comma after the first item.

   - (A) is correct because it has a comma after the first item.

   - (B), (C), and (D) are wrong because they don't have a comma after the first item.

16. **D** In this Rules question, punctuation is changing in the answer choices. The main meaning of the sentence is *Gravity…is significantly weaker than the other three fundamental forces.* The phrase *an attraction that occurs between all objects that have mass* is a describing phrase that has a comma before it, so it must have a comma after it to show that it is Extra Information. Eliminate answers that do not have a comma after the describing phrase.

   - (A), (B), and (C) are wrong because they don't use a comma.

   - (D) is correct because it uses a comma after the Extra Information.

17. **D** In this Rules question, punctuation with a transition is changing in the answer choices. Look for independent clauses. The first part of the sentence says *The technology of search engines has transformed the internet by allowing keywords or questions to be inputted and then generating a list of relevant sources within seconds.* There is an option to add *still* to this independent clause, but this idea isn't a continuation of a previous idea, given that there is no previous idea, so continue reading. The second part of the sentence says *the process of researching each source can be time-consuming in comparison to the more direct answers that an AI chatbot can provide.* This idea builds on the previous idea and presents a comparison, so *still* belongs in the second part of the sentence. Eliminate options with *still* in the first part.

   - (A) and (C) are wrong because the sentence contains two independent clauses, which cannot be connected with commas alone.

   - (B) is wrong because it puts *still* with the first independent clause.

   - (D) is correct because it puts *still* with the second independent clause and puts a semicolon between the two independent clauses.

18. **A** In this Rules question, the subjects of the answers are changing, which suggests it may be testing modifiers. Look for and highlight a modifying phrase: *A research initiative from Daniel Hermens and other Australian scientists.* Whatever is the *research initiative* needs to come immediately after the comma. Eliminate any answer that doesn't start with something that could be a research initiative.

- (A) is correct because *the Longitudinal Adolescent Brain Study* could be a research initiative.

- (B) is wrong because *MRI scans* can't be a research initiative.

- (C) is wrong because *mental health outcomes* can't be a research initiative.

- (D) is wrong because *it* doesn't refer to a research initiative.

19. **D** In this Rules question, punctuation is changing in the answer choices. The blank comes between the subject of the sentence (*Walid Raad*) and its verb (*instituted*). A single punctuation mark can't separate a subject and its verb, so eliminate answers with punctuation.

- (A), (B), and (C) are wrong because a single punctuation mark can't come between a subject and its verb.

- (D) is correct because no punctuation should be used here.

20. **A** In this Rules question, verb forms are changing in the answer choices, so it's testing sentence structure. The main meaning of the sentence is *Ojibwe poet Heid Erdrich…has produced a number of award-winning video-poems.* The phrase between the commas is a describing phrase that gives Extra Information about Erdrich. Therefore, the verb shouldn't be in main verb form and instead should construct a describing phrase. Eliminate any answer that does not correctly form this phrase.

- (A) is correct because it correctly describes the *poet* as *hoping*.

- (B) is wrong because it doesn't provide a clear meaning as to who is hoping.

- (C) and (D) are wrong because they're in main verb form, but that isn't appropriate in a describing phrase.

21. **C** In this Rules question, verbs are changing in the answer choices, so it's testing consistency with verbs. Find and highlight the subject, *Zoonotic diseases,* which is plural, so a plural verb is needed. Write an annotation saying "plural." Eliminate any answer that is not plural.

- (A), (B), and (D) are wrong because they are singular.

- (C) is correct because it's plural.

22. **B** This is a Transitions question, so follow the basic approach. Highlight ideas that relate to each other. The preceding sentence states that *The Atlantic hurricane season officially runs from June 1 to November 30,* and this sentence states that *a recent study found that hurricanes in the Atlantic basin have been trending about five days earlier…suggesting the possibility of a need for a shift in what's considered the*

hurricane season. These ideas disagree, so an opposite-direction transition is needed. Make an annotation that says "disagree." Eliminate any answer that doesn't match.

- (A) and (C) are wrong because they are same-direction transitions.

- (B) is correct because *however* is an opposite-direction transition and presents a new idea that disagrees with the previous idea.

- (D) is wrong because the second sentence doesn't indicate an exception.

23. **C** This is a Transitions question, so follow the basic approach. Highlight ideas that relate to each other. The first part of the sentence states that *Jeanette Epps was the first African American woman to complete the CAVES course,* and the second part of the sentence states that *she became a role model for future female and African American candidates.* These ideas agree, so a same-direction transition is needed. Make an annotation that says "agree." Eliminate any answer that doesn't match.

- (A) is wrong because the second part of the sentence doesn't specify something about the first part.

- (B) and (D) are wrong because they are opposite-direction transitions.

- (C) is correct because *therefore* is a same-direction transition and her being a role model was a result of her accomplishment.

24. **C** This is a Transitions question, so follow the basic approach. Highlight ideas that relate to each other. The preceding sentence describes what *some* do with the Martenitsa, and this sentence describes what others do with it. These ideas disagree, so an opposite-direction transition is needed. Make an annotation that says "disagree." Eliminate any answer that doesn't match.

- (A) is wrong because this sentence doesn't dismiss the previous idea.

- (B) and (D) are wrong because they are same-direction transitions.

- (C) is correct because *alternatively* is an opposite-direction transition and this sentence provides an alternative custom for placing the Martenitsa.

25. **B** This is a Rhetorical Synthesis question, so follow the basic approach. Highlight the goal(s) stated in the question: *emphasize a difference between tropical and temperate deciduous forests.* Eliminate any answer that doesn't fulfill this purpose.

- (A), (C), and (D) are wrong because they don't mention any specific *difference* between the two types of deciduous forests.

- (B) is correct because *whereas* suggests a difference, and it contrasts *variations in temperature* with *variations in rainfall.*

26. **C** This is a Rhetorical Synthesis question, so follow the basic approach. Highlight the goal(s) stated in the question: *explain a possible cause of the Eocene-Oligocene extinction event*. Eliminate any answer that doesn't fulfill this purpose.

- (A) and (B) are wrong because they don't mention *a possible cause*.

- (C) is correct because *may have been the result of* introduces *a possible cause*.

- (D) is wrong because it gives a possible cause of a hypothetical extinction event but doesn't mention the *Eocene-Oligocene extinction* specifically.

27. **A** This is a Rhetorical Synthesis question, so follow the basic approach. Highlight the goal(s) stated in the question: *contrast monoculture farming with polyculture farming*. Eliminate any answer that doesn't fulfill this purpose.

- (A) is correct because *less susceptible to pests* offers a *contrast*.

- (B) is wrong because it only mentions *monoculture farming* and not *polyculture farming*.

- (C) is wrong because it doesn't mention *monoculture farming* or *polyculture farming* by name.

- (D) is wrong because it doesn't mention a *contrast* between *monoculture farming* and *polyculture farming*.

PRACTICE TEST 1—MATH EXPLANATIONS

Module 1

1. **B** The question asks for the value of an expression based on an equation. When a PSAT question asks for the value of an expression, there is usually a straightforward way to solve for the expression without needing to completely isolate the variable. The question asks for the value of $2a$, which is $8a$ divided by 4. Divide both sides of the equation by 4 to get $2a = 10$. The correct answer is (B).

2. **C** The question asks for the equivalent form of an expression. Two of the terms are numbers without a variable, so combine those terms to get $9 - 4 = 5$. Thus, $9 - x^3 - 4 = -x^3 + 5$. The correct answer is (C).

3. **B** The question asks for an equation that represents a specific situation. Translate the information in Bite-Sized Pieces and eliminate after each piece. One piece states that the soup *cools at an average rate of 0.63 degrees Fahrenheit per minute*, and another piece states that m is the number of minutes. Thus, the decrease in temperature can be represented by $-0.63m$. Eliminate (C) and (D) because they do not include this term. Another piece of information states that the *temperature, t, of a bowl of soup is 145 degrees Fahrenheit when the soup is first served*, so the number 145 is the initial temperature and must be part of the equation. Eliminate (A) because it does not include 145. The correct answer is (B).

4. **D**   The question asks for a system of equations that represents a specific situation. Translate the English into math in Bite-Sized Pieces, and eliminate after each piece. One piece of information states that *Daniel weighs d pounds* and *Frank weighs f pounds*, and another piece states that *the combined weight of Daniel and his father, Frank, is 240 pounds*. The total weight in pounds can be represented by $d + f = 240$. Eliminate (B) and (C) because they do not include this equation. The question also states that *Frank weighs 3 times as much as Daniel*. Translate *weighs* as equals and *times* as multiplication to get $f = 3d$. Eliminate (A) because it does not include this equation. The correct answer is (D).

5. **A**   The question asks for a value based on a graph. Specifically, the question asks for the amount of money the child adds to the piggy bank each week. Find a point on the graph and divide the amount of money by the number of weeks to find the money per week. Find 20 on the *x*-axis and move up to the line of the graph, using the mouse pointer or the edge of the scratch paper, and then move left to see that the value on the *y*-axis is 50. Thus, after 20 weeks the child has added 50 dollars to the piggy bank. This is a rate of $\frac{50}{20} = \$2.50$ per week. The correct answer is (A).

6. **B**   The question asks for a measure on a geometric figure. Write out the formula for the area of a rectangle, which is $A = lw$, where A is the area, l is the length, and w is the width. Plug in the given values for the area and length to get $42 = (6)w$. Divide both sides of the equation by 6 to get $7 = w$. The correct answer is (B).

7. **5**   The question asks for a value given an equation. The question gives the value of b as 12, so plug in 12 for b and solve for h. The equation becomes $\frac{1}{2}(12)h = 30$. Simplify the left side of the equation to get $6h = 30$. Divide both sides of the equation by 6 to get $h = 5$. The correct answer is 5.

8. **D**   The question asks for the interpretation of a term in context. Start by reading the final question, which asks for the meaning of 72. Rewrite the equation on the scratch paper. Then label the parts of the equation with the information given and eliminate answers that do not match the labels. The question states that w represents the number of words and m represents the number of minutes spent typing. Rewrite the equation as *number of words* = 72(*number of minutes*). Thus, 72 has something to do with the relationship between the number of words and the number of minutes. Eliminate (A) and (B) because they refer to the number of words only. Compare the remaining answers: the difference is whether the stenographer is typing at a rate of 72 words per minute or $\frac{1}{72}$ words per minute. Since 72 is multiplied by m, the number of minutes, it is the rate per minute. Eliminate (C) because it has the wrong rate. The correct answer is (D).

9. **C** The question asks for the solution to a system of equations. One method is to enter both equations into the built-in graphing calculator, then scroll and zoom as needed to find the point of intersection. Click on the gray dot to see that the coordinates of the point are (4, 5), which is (C).

To solve algebraically, substitute 5 for y in the first equation to get $3x + 5 = 17$. Subtract 5 from both sides of the equation to get $3x = 12$. Divide both sides of the equation by 3 to get $x = 4$. Thus, when $y = 5$, $x = 4$, and the point (4, 5) is the solution to the system of equations.

Using either method, the correct answer is (C).

10. **C** The question asks for an equivalent form of an expression. The first and third terms are perfect squares, so one approach is to factor the perfect squares to get $(12x - 8)(12x - 8)$. Check that (C) is correct by using FOIL—First, Outer, Inner, Last—to expand factored form into standard form: $(12x - 8)(12x - 8) = 144x^2 - 96x - 96x + 64$, which becomes $144x^2 - 192x + 64$. Thus, $(12x - 8)(12x - 8)$ is an equivalent form of $144x^2 - 192x + 64$, and (C) is correct.

There are variables in the answer choices, so another option is to plug in. Plug in a simple number for x, such as $x = 2$. The expression becomes $144(2)^2 - 192(2) + 64$. Simplify the expression to get $144(4) - 384 + 64$, then $576 - 384 + 64$, and finally 256. This is the target value; write it down and circle it. Now plug $x = 2$ into each answer choice and eliminate any that do not match the target value of 256. Choice (A) becomes $[6(2) - 4][6(2) - 4] = (12 - 4)(12 - 4) = (8)(8) = 64$. This does not match the target value, so eliminate (A). Choice (B) becomes $[6(2) + 4][6(2) - 4] = (12 + 4)(12 - 4) = (16)(8) = 128$. Eliminate (B). Choice (C) becomes $[12(2) - 8][12(2) - 8] = (24 - 8)(24 - 8) = (16)(16) = 256$. This matches the target value, so keep (C) but check (D). Choice (D) becomes $[12(2) + 8][12(2) - 8] = (24 + 8)(24 - 8) = (32)(16) = 512$. Eliminate (D), and only (C) is left.

Using either method, the correct answer is (C).

11. **A** The question asks for the median of a data set. The median of a list of numbers is the middle number when the numbers are arranged in order. In lists with an even number of numbers, the median is the mean of the two middle numbers. This list has 6 numbers, so the median will be the average of the two numbers in the middle. The list is already in order, so cross out one number at a time from each end until only the two middle numbers are left, like so: 3̶, 1̶2̶, 15, 21, 2̶6̶, 3̶7̶. To find the mean of 15 and 21, add them and divide by 2: $\dfrac{15 + 21}{2} = \dfrac{36}{2} = 18$. The correct answer is (A).

12. **−4** The question asks for the value of a function. In function notation, the number inside the parentheses is the x-value that goes into the function, or the input, and the value that comes out of the function is the y-value, or the output. The question provides an input value of 25. Plug 25 into the function for x to get $f(25) = \sqrt{25} - 9$. Simplify to get $f(25) = 5 - 9$, and then $f(25) = -4$. The correct answer is −4.

13. **D** The question asks for correct values based on a graph that represents a situation. When given a graph and asked for the table of values, check one point at a time and eliminate answers that contain a point that is not on the graph. Three of the tables include an x-value of 0, so start there. On the graph, when $x = 0$, $y = 0$. Eliminate (A) and (C) because they have the incorrect y-values for this x-value. Compare the remaining answer choices. They both contain the point (6, 60), so there is no need to check that on the graph. The difference is whether $y = -64$ or 64 when $x = 8$. On the graph, when $x = 8$, y is greater than 60, so keep (D). Eliminate (B) because it has the incorrect y-value for this x-value. The correct answer is (D).

14. **C** The question asks for the interpretation of a statement in context. In function notation, the number inside the parentheses is the x-value that goes into the function, or the input, and the value that comes out of the function is the y-value, or the output. The number inside the parentheses, 2, is the x-value, and x represents the number of years. Eliminate (A) because it does not have 2 at all, and eliminate (B) because it states that 2 is a percentage, not the number of years. The question states that the output, $p(x)$, is equal to the estimated value of a photocopier, in dollars, x years after the date of purchase. Thus, the number 4,778 represents the photocopier's estimated value 2 years after the date of purchase. Eliminate (D) because 4,778 is the value after 2 years, not a decrease in estimated value. The correct answer is (C).

15. **5760** The question asks for a measurement and gives conflicting units. The question provides the conversions that 1 day = 24 hours and 1 hour = 60 minutes. Set up proportions one at a time, being sure to match up units. First, convert days to hours with the proportion $\frac{1 \text{ day}}{24 \text{ hours}} = \frac{4 \text{ days}}{x \text{ hours}}$. Cross-multiply to get $(1)(x) = (24)(4)$, which becomes $x = 96$ hours. Next, convert hours to minutes with the proportion $\frac{1 \text{ hour}}{60 \text{ minutes}} = \frac{96 \text{ hours}}{x \text{ minutes}}$. Cross-multiply to get $(1)(x) = (60)(96)$, which becomes $x = 5,760$ minutes. Leave out the comma when entering the answer in the fill-in box. The correct answer is 5760.

16. **B** The question asks for the slope of the line of best fit of a scatterplot. The line is ascending from left to right, so it has a positive slope. Eliminate (A) and (C) because they have negative slopes. Use two points on the line of best fit to calculate the slope of the line using the formula slope $= \frac{y_2 - y_1}{x_2 - x_1}$. The line of best fit passes through a point close to (2, 6) and through another point close to (6, 12). Plug those values into the slope formula to get slope $= \frac{12 - 6}{6 - 2}$, which becomes slope $= \frac{6}{4}$, or slope = 1.5. Eliminate (D) because it is not close to 1.5. The correct answer is (B).

17.   **A**   The question asks for a measure on a geometric figure. Use the Geometry Basic Approach. Start by drawing a right triangle on the scratch paper. Next, label the figure with information from the question. Label one leg with a length of 6 inches and the hypotenuse of the triangle with a length of 8 inches. Next, write out the Pythagorean Theorem, either from memory or after looking it up on the reference sheet. The equation is $a^2 + b^2 = c^2$, where a and b represent the lengths of the legs of the triangle and c is the length of the hypotenuse. Plug in the given values to get $6^2 + b^2 = 8^2$. Square the numbers on both sides of the equation to get $36 + b^2 = 64$. Subtract 36 from both sides of the equation to get $b^2 = 28$. Take the square root of both sides of the equation to get $b \approx 5.292$. Eliminate (B), (C), and (D) because they are too large. To check (A), use a calculator to convert $2\sqrt{7}$ into decimal form, which is approximately 5.292. The correct answer is (A).

18.   **A**   The question asks for an equation in terms of specific variables. The question asks about the relationship among variables and there are variables in the answer choices, so Plugging In is an option. However, that might get messy with three variables, and all of the answer choices have b on the left side of the equation, so the other option is to solve for b. To isolate b, subtract $37a$ from both sides of the equation to get $b = c - 37a$. The correct answer is (A).

19.   **B**   The question asks for the product of the solutions to a quadratic equation. One approach is to enter the equation into the built-in calculator. When graphed, the points where the two vertical lines cross the x-axis, represented by gray dots, are the solutions. Click on each gray dot and write down the x-values: -15.39 and 0.39. Multiply the solutions to get $-15.39 \times 0.39 = -6.0021$. Only (B) is close, so it is correct.

To solve algebraically, the shortcut is to recall that, when a quadratic equation is in the form $ax^2 + bx + c = 0$, the product of the solutions equals $\frac{c}{a}$. In this quadratic, $a = 2$, $b = 30$, and $c = -12$. Plug in the values for a and c to get $\frac{-12}{2} = -6$, or (B).

Using either method, the correct answer is (B).

20.   **108**   The question asks for the value of a function. In function notation, the number inside the parentheses is the x-value that goes into the function, or the input, and the value that comes out of the function is the y-value, or the output. The function in this question also has an unknown constant k. To find the value of the constant k, use the provided input value of 7 and output value of 40. Plug them into the function to get $40 = k(7) - 79$. Add 79 to both sides of the equation to get $119 = 7k$. Divide both sides of the equation by 7 to get $17 = k$. The function now becomes $f(x) = 17x - 79$. Plug the second input value of 11 into the equation for x to get $f(11) = 17(11) - 79$, which becomes $f(11) = 187 - 79$, and then $f(11) = 108$. The correct answer is 108.

21. **B** The question asks for a net percentage decrease. No information is given about the initial value, so plug in. Make the initial value 100 because 100 works well with percentages. Next, translate the information in Bite-Sized Pieces. One piece of information says that the value *decreased by 70% from September 1997 to September 1998*. *Percent* means out of 100, so translate 70% as $\frac{70}{100}$. Take 70% of 100 to get $\frac{70}{100}(100) = 70$. Translate *decreased by* as subtraction to get $100 - 70 = 30$ as the enrollment in September 1998. Another piece of information says that the value *increased by 110% from September 1998 to September 1999*. Take 110% of 30 and add it to 30 to get $30 + \frac{110}{100}(30) = 30 + 33 = 63$ as the enrollment in September 1999.

The question asks for the net percentage decrease from the end of September 1997, when the enrollment was 100, to the end of September 1999, when the enrollment was 63. This is a decrease of $100 - 63 = 37$, which is 37% of 100. The correct answer is (B).

22. **80** The question asks for the value of an expression. When a PSAT question asks for the value of an expression, there is usually a straightforward way to solve for the expression without needing to completely isolate the variable. Start by adding 20 to both sides of the equation to get $x^2 + 2x = 20$. The question asks for the value of $4x^2 + 8x$, so multiply both sides of the equation by 4 to get $4x^2 + 8x = 80$. The correct answer is 80.

Module 2—Easier

1. **A** The question asks for a probability based on a situation. Probability is defined as $\frac{\text{number of outcomes you want}}{\text{number of possible outcomes}}$. Read carefully to find the numbers that make up the probability. The questions states that there are *45 gumballs*, so 45 is the total number of possible outcomes. The question also states that there are *9 watermelon gumballs*. Thus, the number of outcomes that fit the requirements is 9. Therefore, the probability of selecting a watermelon gumball is $\frac{9}{45}$. The correct answer is (A).

2. **D** The question asks for a value based on data in a table. To find *how many patients had their most recent visit to the dentist's office* either one month ago or three months ago, look up the values of both responses from the table and add them together. According to the table, 17 patients had their most recent visit one month ago and 54 patients had their most recent visit three months ago, so $17 + 54 = 71$ patients had their most recent visit either one month ago or three months ago. The correct answer is (D).

3. **B** The question asks for the solution to an equation. To begin to isolate a, add 364 to both sides of the equation to get $7a = 490$. Divide both sides of the equation by 7 to get $a = 70$, which is (B).

Another approach is to plug in the answers. Rewrite the answer choices on the scratch paper and label them "a." Start with (B) and plug in 70 for a in the equation to get $7(70) - 364 = 126$, which becomes $490 - 364 = 126$, and then $126 = 126$, so (B) is correct.

Using either method, the correct answer is (B).

4. **C** The question asks for a value based on a graph. The y-intercept is the point where the graph crosses the y-axis, which happens when $x = 0$. Find $x = 0$ on the graph and move straight up to see that the graph intersects the y-axis approximately halfway between $y = 5$ and $y = 6$. Eliminate (A) and (B) because they contain y-coordinates that are negative, and eliminate (D) because its y-coordinate is 0. Only (C) has a positive y-coordinate, and $\frac{11}{2} = 5.5$, which is halfway between 5 and 6. The correct answer is (C).

5. **5** The question asks for a value given a ratio. To maintain a ratio while changing the values, multiply or divide both parts of the ratio by the same number. A ratio can be written as a fraction, and dividing both the numerator and the denominator of a fraction by 5 is the same as dividing the entire fraction by 1, which does not change the value of the fraction. In this case, $\frac{\frac{35}{5}}{\frac{22}{5}} = \left(\frac{35}{5}\right)\left(\frac{5}{22}\right) = \frac{35}{22}$. Thus, both c and d are divided by 5, and 5 is correct.

Another approach is to plug in. Use the numbers in the ratio and make $c = 35$ and $d = 22$. Next, divide c by 5 to get $\frac{35}{5} = 7$ as the new value of c. The question states that the ratio will remain the same, so set up a proportion: $\frac{35}{22} = \frac{7}{d}$. Solve for the new value of d by cross-multiplying to get $(35)(d) = (22)(7)$, which becomes $35d = 154$. Divide both sides of the equation by 35 to get $d = 4.4$. Finally, to find out what d was divided by, divide the original value of d by the new value of d to get $\frac{22}{4.4} = 5$. Thus, d is divided by 5 when c is divided by 5, and 5 is correct.

Using either method, the correct answer is 5.

6. **140** The question asks for a value based on a percentage. Translate the English to math in Bite-Sized Pieces. *Percent* means out of 100, so translate 50% as $\frac{50}{100}$. Translate *of* as times. Thus, 50% of the 280 grapes translates to $\frac{50}{100}$ (280). Use a calculator or solve by hand to get 140. The correct answer is 140.

7. **C** The question asks for the *x*-coordinate of the solution to a system of equations. One method is to enter both equations into the built-in graphing calculator, then scroll and zoom as needed to find the point of intersection. Click on the gray dot to see that the coordinates of the point are (23, 18). The *x*-value is 23, which is (C).

   To solve algebraically, substitute 18 for *y* in the first equation to get $18 = x - 5$. Add 5 to both sides of the equation to get $x = 23$, which is (C).

   Using either method, the correct answer is (C).

8. **22** The question asks for a measurement and gives conflicting units. To convert feet to fathoms, set up a proportion. Be sure to match up units. The question states that *1 fathom = 6 feet*, so the proportion is $\frac{1 \text{ fathom}}{6 \text{ feet}} = \frac{x \text{ fathoms}}{132 \text{ feet}}$. Cross-multiply to get $(1)(132) = (6)(x)$, which becomes $132 = 6x$. Divide both sides of the equation by 6 to get $x = 22$ feet. The correct answer is 22.

9. **C** The question asks for the value of a function. In function notation, the number inside the parentheses is the *x*-value that goes into the function, or the input, and the value that comes out of the function is the *y*-value, or the output. The question provides an input value, so plug $x = 50$ into the function to get $f(50) = 3(50) - 10$. Simplify to get $f(50) = 150 - 10$, and then $f(50) = 140$. The correct answer is (C).

10. **D** The question asks for the equation that represents a situation. Translate the information in Bite-Sized Pieces and eliminate after each piece. One piece of information says *the robot takes 41.2 seconds to weld one seam*. Since *s* represents the number of seams, multiplying 41.2 by *s*, or 41.2*s*, represents the total time spent welding seams. Eliminate (A), (B), and (C) because they do not include the term 41.2*s*. Choice (D) also correctly translates the time spent drilling *h* holes at 15.5 seconds per hole as 15.5*h*. The correct answer is (D).

11. **A** The question asks for a specific value given a situation. Use the units to determine where to start. The question states that *there are 2,750 trees in an apple orchard* and that *there are 110 trees planted per acre of land*, so look for a way to find a value in acres. Set up a proportion, being sure to match up the units. The proportion is $\frac{110 \text{ trees}}{1 \text{ acre}} = \frac{2,750 \text{ trees}}{x \text{ acres}}$. Cross-multiply to get $(110)(x) = (1)(2,750)$, or $110x = 2,750$. Divide both sides of the equation by 110 to get $x = 25$. The correct answer is (A).

12. **C** The question asks for a value given a ratio. Begin by reading the question to find information about the ratio. The question states that *the ratio of road bikes to mountain bikes is 7 to 3*. Eliminate (A) and (B) because there are more road bikes than mountain bikes, so with 24 mountain bikes, there must be more than 24 road bikes. To solve for the number of road bikes, set up a proportion, being sure to match up the mountain bike and road bike numbers. The proportion is $\frac{7 \text{ road}}{3 \text{ mountain}} = \frac{x \text{ road}}{24 \text{ mountain}}$. Cross-multiply to get $(7)(24) = (3)(x)$, which becomes $168 = 3x$. Divide both sides of the equation by 3 to get $56 = x$. The correct answer is (C).

13. **10** The question asks for a measure on a geometric figure. Use the Geometry Basic Approach. Start by drawing a rectangle, which has two pairs of equal sides and 4 right angles. Next, label the figure with information from the question. The question states that *the length of each of the two longer sides of the rectangle is 22 centimeters*, so label each of the long sides as 22. The perimeter of a geometric figure is the sum of its sides, so label the other two sides as x, then plug in 64 for the perimeter and 22 for each of the long sides to get $22 + 22 + x + x = 64$. Combine like terms to get $44 + 2x = 64$. Subtract 44 from both sides of the equation to get $2x = 20$. Divide both sides of the equation by 2 to get $x = 10$. The correct answer is 10.

14. **C** The question asks for an x-intercept based on a graph. This is the point at which $y = 0$ and the graph intersects the x-axis. Look on the graph for the point at which the y-coordinate equals 0 and the graph touches the x-axis. This point is (2, 0). The correct answer is (C).

15. **A** The question asks for a value based on a graph. First, check the units on each axis of the line graph. The x-axis shows the number of yards of blue fabric, and the y-axis shows the number of yards of red fabric. The question asks how many yards of blue fabric were purchased if 6 yards of red fabric were purchased, so find 6 on the y-axis. Move right from there to where the line crosses the horizontal line for 6, using the mouse pointer or edge of the scratch paper, and then move down from there to the x-axis. The x-value is 2. Thus, 2 yards of blue fabric were purchased when 6 yards of red fabric were purchased. The correct answer is (A).

16. **B** The question asks for a value given a specific situation. Translate the information in Bite-Sized Pieces. One piece of information states that the *pack contains 20 of the 400-mg packets*. The total mass of the 400-mg packets can be represented by 20(400), or 8,000 mg. Another piece of information states that the *total mass of the variety pack is 29,000 mg*. If the total mass of the 400-mg packets is 8,000 mg, the total mass of the 600-mg packets is $29,000 - 8,000 = 21,000$ mg. To find the number of 600-mg packets, divide the total mass of the 600-mg packets by 600 mg to get $\frac{21,000 \text{ mg}}{600 \text{ mg}} = 35$. The correct answer is (B).

17. **D** The question asks for the value of the measure of an angle on a geometric figure. Use the Geometry Basic Approach. Start by drawing a figure on the scratch paper. The question states that the triangle is a right triangle, so mark one of the angles with the right angle symbol, or 90°. An acute angle is an angle with a measure less than 90°, and the question states that *one of the acute angles measures 20°*, so label one of the other angles as 20°. All triangles contain 180°, so the measure of the third angle in the triangle is 180° − 90° − 20° = 70°. The correct answer is (D).

18. **D** The question asks for the slope of a line. The question states that *line b is parallel to line a*, which means they have the same slope. The question gives the equation of line a, so find the slope of that line. First, put the equation of line a into slope-intercept form, $y = mx + b$, in which m is the slope and b is the y-intercept. Divide both sides of the equation by 2 to get $y = \frac{1}{2}x - 12$. In the equation, $m = \frac{1}{2}$, so the slope of line a is $\frac{1}{2}$. The slope of line b is the same as the slope of line a, so the slope of line b is also $\frac{1}{2}$. The correct answer is (D).

19. **A** The question asks for measures on a geometric figure. Use the Geometry Basic Approach. Redraw the figure and the labels. Next, draw another cone and label the radius r_2 and the height h_2. Write out the formula for the volume of a cone, either from memory or after looking it up on the reference sheet. The formula is $V = \frac{1}{3}\pi r^2 h$. No specific values are given for the radius or height of either cylinder, only the relationship between the two volumes, so plug in. Since the dimensions of the second cone are given in terms of the first cone, start by plugging in values for the first cone. Make $r_1 = 2$ and $h_1 = 3$, and label this on the first cone. Plug those values into the volume formula to get $V = \frac{1}{3}\pi(2)^2(3)$, which becomes $V = \frac{1}{3}\pi(4)(3)$, and then $V = 4\pi$. The question states that the volume of the second cone is 100 times the volume of the first cone, so the volume of the second cone is $(4\pi)(100) = 400\pi$. This is the target value; write it down and circle it.

Next, plug $r_1 = 2$ and $h_1 = 3$ into each answer choice, and use the resulting values of r_2 and h_2 in the volume formula. Eliminate any answers that do not match the target value. In (A), $r_2 = 5(2)$, or $r_2 = 10$, and $h_2 = 4(3)$, or $h_2 = 12$. Plug 10 and 12 into the volume formula to get $V = \frac{1}{3}\pi(10)^2(12)$, which becomes $V = \frac{1}{3}\pi(100)(12)$, and then $V = 400\pi$. This matches the target value of 400π, so keep (A). In (B), the height is the same as in (A) and the radius is greater, so the volume will be greater than 400π; eliminate (B). In (C), $r_2 = 4(2)$, or $r_2 = 8$, and $h_2 = 5(3)$, or $h_2 = 15$. Plug 8 and 15 into the volume formula to get $V = \frac{1}{3}\pi(8)^2(15)$, which becomes $V = \frac{1}{3}\pi(64)(15)$, and then $V = 320\pi$.

This does not match the target value, so eliminate (C). In (D), $r_2 = 4(2)$, or $r_2 = 8$, and $h_2 = 25(3)$, or $h_2 = 75$. Plug 8 and 75 into the volume formula to get $V = \frac{1}{3}\pi(8)^2(75)$, which becomes $V \frac{1}{3}\pi(64)(75)$, and then $V = 1,600\pi$. This does not match the target value, so eliminate (D). The correct answer is (A).

20. **550** The question asks for the area of a geometric figure. Use the Geometry Basic Approach. Start by drawing an isosceles triangle, which has two equal angles and two equal corresponding sides. Next, label the figure with information from the question. Label the height as 25 centimeters and the base as 44 centimeters. The drawing should look something like this:

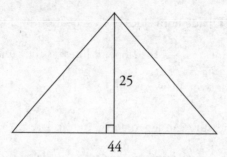

Next, write out the formula for the area of a triangle, either from memory or after looking it up on the reference sheet. The formula is $A = \frac{1}{2}bh$. Plug in the values given in the question to get $A = \frac{1}{2}(44)(25)$. Simplify the right side of the equation to get $A = 550$. The correct answer is 550.

21. **B** The question asks for a range of values given a specific situation. The question states that *according to the triangle inequality theorem, the length of any side of a triangle must be greater than the difference between the lengths of the other two sides.* The question gives two sides of a triangle as 11 and 9. The difference, $11 - 9 = 2$, must be less than the length of the third side, p, or $2 < p$. Eliminate (A) and (D) because they show the third side, p, as less than 2, when the reverse is true. The length of the third side of the triangle, p, must be greater than 2, not 20, so eliminate (C). The correct answer is (B).

22. **1.05** The question asks for a value given a specific situation. The question is about the relationship among variables, so plug in. Make $u = 100$ because 100 works well with percentages. *Percent* means out of 100, so translate 30% as $\frac{30}{100}$. Multiply this by 100 to find 30% of 100: $\frac{30}{100}(100) = 30$. The question states that the *number t is 30% less than the positive number u*, so $t = 100 - 30$, or $t = 70$. The question also states that the *number v is 50% greater than t*, so take 50% of 70 and add it to 70 to get $v = 70 + \frac{50}{100}(70)$, which becomes $v = 70 + 35$, and then $v = 105$. The question asks *how many times the value of u is the number v*, so translate the words into an equation. Translate *how many* as a

variable, such as *x*. Translate *times* as multiplication. Translate *is* as equals. Plug in the values for *u* and *v*, and the equation becomes $(x)(100) = 105$. Divide both sides of the equation by 100 to get $x = 1.05$. The correct answer is 1.05.

Module 2—Harder

1. **5**   The question asks for a value based on a percentage. Translate the English to math in Bite-Sized Pieces. Translate *is* as =. *Percent* means out of 100 and *what* means a variable, such as *x*, so translate *x*% as $\frac{x}{100}$. Translate *of* as times. Thus, *17 is what percent of 340* becomes $17 = \frac{x}{100}(340)$. Multiply both sides of the equation by 100 to get $1,700 = 340x$. Divide both sides of the equation by 340 to get $5 = x$. The correct answer is 5.

2. **B**   The question asks for a value given a specific situation. The question asks for a specific value, and there are numbers in order in the answer choices, so plug in the answers. First, rewrite the answers on the scratch paper and label them "days overdue." Next, start with one of the numbers in the middle and try (B), 15. The question states that *the library charges a fine of $0.21 for each day the book is overdue*. If the book is overdue by 15 days, the charge is $($0.21)(15) = 3.15. The question also states that *there is a fee of $1.85 for each overdue book*. Add this to the other charge to get $$1.85 + $3.15 = 5.00. This matches the total charge given in the question, so stop here. The correct answer is (B).

3. **D**   The question asks for an inequality that models a specific situation. Translate the information in Bite-Sized Pieces and eliminate after each piece. One piece of information says that *the factory produces a minimum of 10,000 units of this part in one week*. Translate *a minimum of 10,000 units* as at least, which is the same as greater than or equal to, or ≥. Eliminate (A) and (C) because the inequality sign is facing the wrong direction. The question also states that *Team A produces the part at an average rate of 725 per day*, and that *a* represents the number of days team A produced the part. Multiplying the number of days that team A produced the part by the average number of parts per day for team A gives the total number of parts produced by team A. Translate this as 725*a*. Eliminate (B) because it does not include this term. Choice (D) correctly translates the number of parts produced by team B over *b* days as 650*b*. The correct answer is (D).

4. **C**   The question asks for a probability based on a situation. Probability is defined as $\frac{\text{number of outcomes you want}}{\text{number of possible outcomes}}$. Read carefully to find the numbers that make up the probability. First, find the total number of lights by adding up the numbers of each type. This is $10 + 45 + 8 + 45 = 108$, so 108 is the *number of possible outcomes*. To find the *number of outcomes you want*, subtract the number of clear lights and the number of multi-colored lights from the total number of lights to get

108 – 10 – 8 = 90. Thus, there are 90 lights that are neither clear nor multi-colored. Therefore, the probability of selecting a light that is neither clear nor multi-colored is $\frac{90}{108}$. This is not an answer choice, so reduce the fraction by dividing both the numerator and denominator by 18 to get $\frac{5}{6}$. The correct answer is (C).

5. **B**   The question asks for a measure on a geometric figure. Use the Geometry Basic Approach. Start by drawing a square on the scratch paper. Next, label the figure with information from the question. Label the area as 5,184 square inches. Next, write out the formula for the area of a square, which is *Area = side²*, or $A = s^2$. Plug in the value for *A* given in the question to get $5,184 = s^2$. Take the positive square root of both sides of the equation to get $72 = s$. The correct answer is (B).

6. **C**   The question asks for the value of a function. In function notation, the number inside the parentheses is the *x*-value that goes into the function, or the input, and the value that comes out of the function is the *y*-value, or the output. The question provides an input value of 330, so plug 330 into the function for *x* to get $f(330) = 330 - 30$. Combine like terms on the right side of the equation to get $f(330) = 300$. The correct answer is (C).

7.   **4.25 or** $\frac{17}{4}$

The question asks for a measurement and gives conflicting units. The question provides the conversion that 1 hour = 3,600 seconds. To convert the escape velocity of Mercury from kilometers per hour to kilometers per second, multiply the rate by the conversion. This becomes $\left(\frac{15,300 \text{ kilometers}}{1 \text{ hour}} \right) \left(\frac{1 \text{ hour}}{3,600 \text{ seconds}} \right) = \frac{15,300}{3,600}$ kilometers per second. Either use a calculator to get the decimal form 4.25 or reduce the fraction one step at a time to get $\frac{17}{4}$. The correct answer is 4.25 or $\frac{17}{4}$.

8.   **5**   The question asks for a value given a ratio. To maintain a ratio while changing the values, multiply or divide both parts of the ratio by the same number. A ratio can be written as a fraction, and dividing both the numerator and the denominator of a fraction by 5 is the same as dividing the entire fraction by 1, which does not change the value of the fraction. In this case, $\frac{\frac{35}{5}}{\frac{22}{5}} = \left(\frac{35}{5} \right) \left(\frac{5}{22} \right) = \frac{35}{22}$. Thus, both *c* and *d* are divided by 5, and 5 is correct.

Another approach is to plug in. Use the numbers in the ratio and make $c = 35$ and $d = 22$. Next, divide c by 5 to get $\frac{35}{5} = 7$ as the new value of c. The question states that the ratio will remain the same, so set up a proportion: $\frac{35}{22} = \frac{7}{d}$. Solve for the new value of d by cross-multiplying to get $(35)(d) = (22)(7)$, which becomes $35d = 154$. Divide both sides of the equation by 35 to get $d = 4.4$. Finally, to find out what d was divided by, divide the original value of d by the new value of d to get $\frac{22}{4.4} = 5$. Thus, d is divided by 5 when c is divided by 5, and 5 is correct.

Using either method, the correct answer is 5.

9. **A** The question asks for the equation that represents a line. One method is to translate the information in Bite-Sized Pieces and eliminate after each piece. The answer choices are all in slope-intercept form, $y = mx + b$, in which m is the slope and b is the y-intercept. Use the two points to calculate the slope of the line using the formula slope $= \frac{y_2 - y_1}{x_2 - x_1}$. Plug in the given values to get slope $= \frac{15 - 17}{1 - 0}$, which becomes slope $= \frac{-2}{1}$, or slope $= -2$. Thus, in slope-intercept form, $m = -2$. Eliminate (B), (C), and (D) because they have the wrong value for m, which leaves (A) as correct.

Another method is to plug in the given points and eliminate any equations that don't work. Start with the point (0, 17), and plug $x = 0$ and $y = 17$ into each answer choice. Choice (A) becomes $17 = -2(0) + 17$, or $17 = 17$. This is true, so keep (A), but check the remaining answers with the first point. Choice (B) becomes $17 = -\frac{1}{2}(0) + 17$, or $17 = 17$. This is also true, so keep (B). Choice (C) becomes $17 = 15(0) - 2$, or $17 = -2$; eliminate (C). Choice (D) becomes $17 = 15(0) - \frac{1}{2}$, or $17 = -\frac{1}{2}$; eliminate (D).

The first point worked in two answers, so try the second point and plug $x = 1$ and $y = 15$ into the remaining answer choices. Choice (A) becomes $15 = -2(1) + 17$, or $15 = 15$. Keep (A). Choice (B) becomes $15 = -\frac{1}{2}(1) + 17$, or $15 = \frac{33}{2}$. Eliminate (B). Only (A) works for both points, so it is correct.

Using either method, the correct answer is (A).

10. **4800** The question asks for a value based on a specific situation. Translate the English to math in Bite-Sized Pieces. First, find the number of seconds it takes jet A to shoot water 64 times by multiplying the number of seconds it takes jet A to shoot water at one interval, 405 seconds, by 64 times. The result is 405(64) = 25,920 seconds. Next, find the number of seconds it takes jet B to shoot water 64 times by multiplying the number of seconds it takes jet B to shoot water at one interval, 330 seconds, by 64 times. The result is 330(64) = 21,120 seconds. The question asks *how much longer*, so find the difference of the two values: 25,920 − 21,120 = 4,800. Leave out the comma when entering the answer in the fill-in box. The correct answer is 4800.

11. **A** The question asks for a value based on a percentage. Translate the English to math in Bite-Sized Pieces. First, find the value of k by multiplying 0.97 by 100 to get $k = 0.97(100)$, or $k = 97$. The question asks for a specific percent, and the answers contain numbers in order, so plug in the answers to see which one results in $k = 97$. Start with (B) and try 9.7%. *Percent* means out of 100, so translate 9.7% as $\frac{9.7}{100}$. Take 9.7% of 100 to get $\frac{9.7}{100}(100) = 9.7$. The question asks for the *percent less*, so subtract 9.7 from 100 to get 100 − 9.7 = 90.3. This does not match the correct value of k, so eliminate (B). Since the percentages in (C) and (D) are greater, they will result in an even smaller value for k; eliminate (C) and (D). To check (A), find 3% of 100 and subtract it from 100 to get $100 − \frac{3}{100}(100) = 100 − 3 = 97$. This matches the correct value of k, so stop here. The correct answer is (A).

12. **D** The question asks for the solution to an equation. The question asks for a specific value and the answers contain numbers in increasing order, so plug in the answers. Start with the easier of the two middle numbers and try (C), 2. Plug $a = 2$ into the equation to get $-\frac{7}{5}(2 − 2) + \frac{3}{2}(2 − 2) = 6$, which becomes $-\frac{7}{5}(0) + \frac{3}{2}(0) = 6$, then 0 + 0 = 6, and finally 0 = 6. This is not true, so eliminate (C). The value on the left side of the equation was too small, so try a larger number. Try (D), and plug $a = 62$ into the equation to get $-\frac{7}{5}(62 − 2) + \frac{3}{2}(62 − 2) = 6$, which becomes $-\frac{7}{5}(60) + \frac{3}{2}(60) = 6$, then −84 + 90 = 6, and finally 6 = 6. This is true, so stop here. The correct answer is (D).

13. **B** The question asks for the slope of a line. Use the two points given in the question to calculate the slope of the line using the formula slope = $\frac{y_2 - y_1}{x_2 - x_1}$. The formula becomes slope = $\frac{0 - (-10)}{\frac{95}{2} - 0}$. Simplify to get slope = $\frac{10}{\frac{95}{2}}$. Divide 10 by $\frac{95}{2}$ to get $\frac{20}{95}$, which reduces to $\frac{4}{19}$. It is also possible to use a calculator to find the decimal form of $\frac{10}{\frac{95}{2}}$ and then use a calculator again to see which answer choice equals the same decimal. Using fractions or decimals, the correct answer is (B).

14. **B** The question asks for the value of the y-coordinate of the solution to a system of equations. One method is to enter both equations into the built-in graphing calculator, then scroll and zoom as needed to find the point of intersection. The graphs intersect at (0, 0), so the y-coordinate is 0, and (B) is correct.

To solve the system for the y-coordinate algebraically, set both equations equal to each other since they are both equal to y. The new equation becomes $-\frac{1}{3}x = -5x$. Multiply both sides of the equation by -3 to get $x = 15x$. Subtract x from both sides of the equation to get $0 = 14x$. Divide both sides of the equation by 14 to get $0 = x$. Be careful: this is the value of x, but the question asks for the value of y. Plug 0 in for x in either equation to get $y = 0$, which is (B).

Using either method, the correct answer is (B).

15. **10** The question asks for a measure on a geometric figure. Use the Geometry Basic Approach. Redraw the figure on the scratch paper, and then label it with information from the question. Label angle JLK as 27° and angle MNO as 17°, and use hash marks to indicate that LM and MO have the same length. The figure should look something like this:

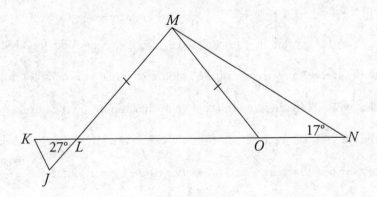

Vertical angles have the same measures, so angle *MLO* is also 27°. When two sides have the same length, the angles opposite them have the same measure. Thus, angles *MLO* and *LOM* have the same measure, 27°. Label angle *LOM* as 27°, and the figure now looks like this.

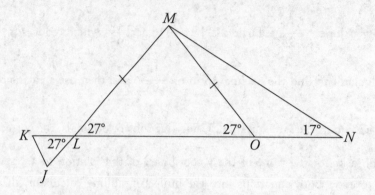

Angles *LOM* and *MON* form a straight line, and any straight line is 180°. Thus, angle *MON* measures 180° − 27° = 153°. Label this on the figure, which now looks like this:

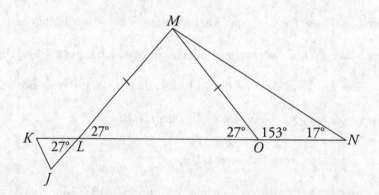

Now that two angles in triangle *MON* are labeled, solve for the third angle. The sum of the angles in any triangle is 180°, so subtract the two known angles to get 180° − 153° − 17° = 10°. Thus, angle

NMO measures 10°. The correct answer is 10.

16. **1975** The question asks for a value in a linear model. Work the question in Bite-Sized Pieces. Start by

determining the average growth rate of the amount of money in the account from the end of week

5 to the end of week 24 by dividing the change in the amount by the number of weeks. To find the

change in the amount, subtract $2,278 from $4,195 to get $1,917. This growth occurred from week

5 to week 24, which is 19 weeks. Thus, the amount grew by an average of $\frac{1,917}{19} \approx \$100.89$ per week.

Use this average rate to determine the growth from week 2 to week 5. The amount at the end of week 5 was $2,278, and it grew at an average rate of $100.89 per week for 3 weeks. Multiply the number of weeks by the average rate to get an increase of (3)($100.89) = $302.67. Subtract this from the amount at the end of week 5 to get $2,278 − $302.67 = $1,975.33 as the amount in the account at the end of week 2. Round $1,975.33 to the nearest dollar to get $1,975. Leave out the comma when entering the answer in the fill-in box. The correct answer is 1975.

17. **C** The question asks for the slope of the line represented by a table. The slope of a line can be found by using the formula slope = $\dfrac{y_2 - y_1}{x_2 - x_1}$. The table shows four pairs of x and y values, which represent four points on the line. Pick any two points and plug them into the slope formula. Using the points $(c - 25, 4)$ and $(c, 0)$, the formula becomes slope = $\dfrac{4 - 0}{c - 25 - c}$, and then slope = $\dfrac{4}{-25}$, or slope = $-\dfrac{4}{25}$. The correct answer is (C).

18. **D** The question asks for the data set with the least mean. To find a mean, or average, use the formula $T = AN$, in which T is the *Total*, A is the *Average*, and N is the *Number of things*. A frequency table has two columns: the left-hand column contains the values, and the right-hand column contains the number of times each value occurs, or its frequency. Start with (A) and add the numbers in the Frequency column to get 3 + 3 + 3 + 3 + 3 = 15. This is the *Number of things*. Find the *Total* by multiplying each value by the number of times it occurs, and add the results. For (A), multiply 5 × 3, 10 × 3, 15 × 3, 20 × 3, and 25 × 3. Add the results to get 15 + 30 + 45 + 60 + 75 = 225. Plug 225 for the *Total* and 15 for the *Number of things* into the average formula to get 225 = (A)(15). Divide both sides of the equation by 15 to get 15 = A.

For (B), the *Number of things* is 3 + 4 + 4 + 4 + 3 = 18. The *Total* is (5)(3) + (10)(4) + (15)(4) + (20)(4) + (25)(3) = 270. The average formula becomes 270 = (A)(18), and 15 = A. For (C), the *Number of things* is 6 + 2 + 2 + 2 + 6 = 18. The *Total* is (5)(6) + (10)(2) + (15)(2) + (20)(2) + (25)(6) = 270. These are the same numbers as (B), so the average will also be 15. For (D), the *Number of things* is 6 + 5 + 4 + 3 + 2 = 20. The *Total* is (5)(6) + (10)(5) + (15)(4) + (20)(3) + (25)(2) = 250. The average formula becomes 250 = (A)(20), and 12.5 = A. The data set shown in (D) has the least mean of the four data sets, which makes (D) correct.

An alternative to calculating all of the values is to look at the distribution of the values in the frequency tables. All four tables have the same values: 5, 10, 15, 20, and 25. In (A), the values are equally distributed. In (B) and (C), the values are distributed symmetrically about the median. Thus, (A), (B), and (C) will all have a mean that is equal to the median, 15, but (D) has a greater number of smaller values than larger values so it will have a mean less than the median. This gives (D) the least mean and makes it correct.

Using either method, the correct answer is (D).

19.   **A**   The question asks for measures on a geometric figure. Use the Geometry Basic Approach. Redraw the figure and the labels. Next, draw another cone and label the radius r_2 and the height h_2. Write out the formula for the volume of a cone, either from memory or after looking it up on the reference sheet. The formula is $V = \frac{1}{3}\pi r^2 h$. No specific values are given for the radius or height of either cylinder, only the relationship between the two volumes, so plug in. Since the dimensions of the second cone are given in terms of the first cone, start by plugging in values for the first cone. Make $r_1 = 2$ and $h_1 = 3$, and label this on the first cone. Plug those values into the volume formula to get $V = \frac{1}{3}\pi(2)^2(3)$, which becomes $V = \frac{1}{3}\pi(4)(3)$, and then $V = 4\pi$. The question states that the volume of the second cone is 100 times the volume of the first cone, so the volume of the second cone is $(4\pi)(100) = 400\pi$. This is the target value; write it down and circle it.

Next, plug $r_1 = 2$ and $h_1 = 3$ into each answer choice, and use the resulting values of r_2 and h_2 in the volume formula. Eliminate any answers that do not match the target value. In (A), $r_2 = 5(2)$, or $r_2 = 10$, and $h_2 = 4(3)$, or $h_2 = 12$. Plug 10 and 12 into the volume formula to get $V = \frac{1}{3}\pi(10)^2(12)$, which becomes $V = \frac{1}{3}\pi(100)(12)$, and then $V = 400\pi$. This matches the target value of 400π, so keep (A). In (B), the height is the same as in (A) and the radius is greater, so the volume will be greater than 400π; eliminate (B). In (C), $r_2 = 4(2)$, or $r_2 = 8$, and $h_2 = 5(3)$, or $h_2 = 15$. Plug 8 and 15 into the volume formula to get $V = \frac{1}{3}\pi(8)^2(15)$, which becomes $V = \frac{1}{3}\pi(64)(15)$, and then $V = 320\pi$.

This does not match the target value, so eliminate (C). In (D), $r_2 = 4(2)$, or $r_2 = 8$, and $h_2 = 25(3)$, or $h_2 = 75$. Plug 8 and 75 into the volume formula to get $V = \frac{1}{3}\pi(8)^2(75)$, which becomes $V = \frac{1}{3}\pi(64)(75)$, and then $V = 1,600\pi$. This does not match the target value, so eliminate (D). The correct answer is (A).

20. **−112** The question asks for the value of a constant in a function. In function notation, the number inside the parentheses is the *x*-value that goes into the function, or the input, and the value that comes out of the function is the *y*-value, or the output. A graph crosses the *x*-axis when *y* = 0, so there is a point at (−56, 0). A graph crosses the *y*-axis when *x* = 0, so there is a point at (0, 114). Thus, the question provides two points on the graph, which are also pairs of input and output values. Try the first point, and plug *x* = −56 and *g*(*x*) = 0 into the function to get $0 = 2c^{-56} - k$. There are still two constants, so it is not possible to solve for *k*. Try the second point, and plug *x* = 0 and *g*(*x*) = 114 into the function to get $114 = 2c^0 - k$. Any value raised to the power of zero is 1, so $c^0 = 1$. The function becomes 114 = 2(1) − *k*, or 114 = 2 − *k*. Add *k* to both sides of the equation to get 114 + *k* = 2. Subtract 114 from both sides of the equation to get *k* = −112. The correct answer is −112.

21. **C** The question asks for an equation that represents the given scenario. Translate the English to math in Bite-Sized Pieces. One piece of information says that *the number of students that chose the 9-ounce slushy was 6 times the number of students t that chose the 12-ounce slushy*. Translate *times* as multiplication, and the number of students who chose the 9-ounce slushy becomes 6*t*. The question also states that there were *4 students who chose the 5-ounce slushy*. Add the number of students who chose the 5-ounce slushy, 4, the number of students who chose the 9-ounce slushy, 6*t*, and the number of students who chose the 12-ounce slushy, *t*, to find the total number of students: 4 + 6*t* + *t*. Combine like terms to get 7*t* + 4. Finally, the question states that the class has 25 students, so set the sum of the number of students equal to 25 to get 7*t* + 4 = 25. This matches an answer choice, so stop here. The correct answer is (C).

22. **D** The question asks for a solution with a variable to a system of equations. Start by entering both equations into the built-in calculator to see that the same line is graphed twice. Since the two equations represent the same line, any point only needs to make one equation true in order to be a solution to the system. Since there are variables in the answer choices, plug in. The points in the answer choices include fractions with both 2 and 5 in the denominator, so make *n* = 10. Start with (A). If *n* = 10, the coordinates of the point are $\left(-\dfrac{3(10)}{5} - 22, \dfrac{3(10)}{5} - 11\right)$. Simplify the coordinates to get (−6 − 22, 6 − 11), and then (−28, −5). Plug these into the second equation for *x* and *y* to get −5(−28) + 3(−5) = −11. Simplify the left side of the equation to get 140 − 15 = −11, and then 125 = −11. This is not true, so eliminate (A).

Next, try (B). If $n = 10$, the coordinates of the point are $\left(\dfrac{10}{2} - 11, \dfrac{10}{2} - 22\right)$. Simplify the coordinates to get $(5 - 11, 5 - 22)$, and then $(-6, -17)$. Plug these into the second equation for x and y to get $-5(-6) + 3(-17) = -11$. Simplify the left side of the equation to get $30 - 51 = -11$, and then $-21 = -11$; eliminate (B). Try (C). If $n = 10$, the coordinates of the point are $\left(10, \dfrac{3(10)}{5} + \dfrac{11}{5}\right)$. Simplify the coordinates to get $\left(10, 6 + \dfrac{11}{5}\right)$, and then $\left(10, \dfrac{41}{5}\right)$. Plug these into the second equation for x and y to get $-5(10) + 3\left(\dfrac{41}{5}\right) = -11$. Simplify the left side of the equation to get $-50 + \dfrac{123}{5} = -11$, and then $-\dfrac{127}{5} = -11$; eliminate (C). Choice (D) is the reverse of (C), so the coordinates of the point are $\left(\dfrac{41}{5}, 10\right)$. Plug these into the second equation for x and y to get $-5\left(\dfrac{41}{5}\right) + 3(10) = -11$. Simplify the left side of the equation to get $-41 + 30 = -11$, and then $-11 = -11$. This is true, so the point in (D) is a solution to the system of equations for any value of n. The correct answer is (D).

Part III
PSAT 8/9 Prep

Chapter 5
Reading and Writing Introduction

Now that you've learned some general strategies for the PSAT 8/9 and taken and analyzed your first test, it is time to dive into some content chapters. This chapter will introduce you to the Reading and Writing section of the PSAT 8/9.

FIND YOUR STRENGTHS AND WEAKNESSES

As you may recall from the Introduction, your PSAT 8/9 is going to have two Reading and Writing modules, each consisting of 27 questions. Of those 54 total verbal questions, 25–33 will be Reading questions and 19–31 will be Writing questions. You'll have 32 minutes for each module, which gives you a little more than a minute for each question.

While College Board jams the topics of Reading and Writing into the same section, you may have recognized that they really represent two different sets of skills. The Reading questions ask you to either answer a question about a passage you have read (such as what its main idea is or why the author included a certain piece of information) or choose an answer that completes the passage based on the inferences that can be made. On the other hand, the Writing questions will ask you to choose the best construction of a sentence based on such aspects as punctuation, grammar, and style. These questions will also ask you to connect ideas with transitions or to fit certain rhetorical goals.

This distinction is important because you may find that you are stronger at Reading or stronger at Writing. Recognizing your strengths and weaknesses will help you follow POOD most effectively, and as you practice it will allow you to identify what areas you need to focus on during your study time.

THE LESSER OF TWO (OR THREE) EVILS

We think you'll find it most helpful to think of each Reading and Writing module as having three parts, displayed visually below.

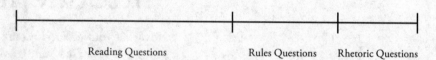

Reading Questions   Rules Questions   Rhetoric Questions

This is the same order and rough proportion of questions you will see in each module. (It's worth keeping in mind that the Reading actually has two parts according to College Board. However, there isn't a strong difference in the types of questions you'll see in both parts, so we don't think you need to notice when the section switches. See the Reading lesson for more on that.) If you are stronger or faster at Writing questions, you may find that it makes more sense for you to start about halfway through the section where those questions start. Of course, if Reading questions are easier for you, it's fine to start at the beginning of the module. Either way, it's helpful to be able to recognize these three categories of questions so that you'll notice when the module switches from one to the next and be able to apply the right set of steps to each question type. Let's take a look at the characteristics of each category.

Reading Questions

Any question with text in the form of a poem or a work of fiction is going to be in the Reading portion. The same is true for dual texts (which have a Text 1 and a Text 2), passages that involve graphs, and questions that ask you to fill in the blank with the most appropriate word. The rest of the Reading questions will generally ask you for the meaning or purpose of some or all of the passage.

Rules Questions

It should be easy to spot when the module switches from Reading questions to Rules questions. That's because all Rules questions ask the same thing: *Which choice completes the text so that it conforms to the conventions of Standard English?* Only Rules questions ask this, so if you're planning to start with the Rules questions, you can skip to about the middle of the section and click ahead until you see the first one with that question. It's worth noting that Rules questions will be some of the fastest ones for many students, as you typically only need to read a single sentence and will be tested on basic punctuation and grammar rules, rather than comprehension.

Rhetoric Questions

Once again, it should be easy to spot when the Rules questions end. That's because the rest of the questions, Rhetoric questions, will not ask the standard question you saw above for Rules questions. If you want to start with these questions, go about three-quarters of the way into the section and continue until you stop seeing the question about the conventions of Standard English. Furthermore, Rhetoric questions come in only two formats. The first involves transition words, and the second has bullet points instead of a passage. So, these should be relatively easy to identify by looking for those two unique attributes, but you will learn more about these distinctions in later chapters.

As you prepare for the PSAT 8/9, try to identify which of these three categories makes sense for you to begin with. It's best to start with the category in which you will be able to get the questions right quickly and easily.

COMMON QUESTION TYPES

It is also useful to consider how common a question type is, meaning how frequently it comes up on the Digital SAT. Since the Reading and Writing questions fall neatly into distinct categories, we've marked each category in the RW chapters with how commonly it is tested. While your strengths and weaknesses largely determine where you focus your prep time, knowing that a question comes up often is another indicator that you want to do your best to master that question type. So, look out for the indicators of whether each RW question type is common, moderately common, or uncommon.

STARTING OFF ON THE RIGHT SIDE...OF THE SCREEN

As you saw earlier in this introduction, it's the question, rather than the passage, that will give you a clue as to what category of question you are dealing with. Once you've established that, you'll be able to execute the appropriate strategy for that specific type of question. To that end, we've developed a basic approach for all Reading and Writing questions:

Reading and Writing Basic Approach

1.   Read the question.
2.   Identify the question type.
3.   Follow the basic approach for that question type.

As we discussed earlier, you are free (and encouraged!) to start with the types of questions at which you excel and to leave for last the ones you struggle with most or that you expect to take the most time. For each question, skip over the passage initially and go straight to the question. That will help you to confirm whether it is a Reading question, Rules question, or Rhetoric question. In some cases, such as with most Reading questions, reading the question first will also give you an idea of what you need to find in the passage, which will allow you to do double duty as you read: you can already start to look out for what the question will be asking you about as you read the passage.

In the chapters that follow, we'll show you our basic approach for each type of question that we expect you to see on the Reading and Writing section. Once you have learned and practiced these approaches, you'll know exactly what to do once you identify the type of question you are looking at. It's worth noting that we have put the verbal chapters in the same order that we expect the questions to be in for both modules of the Reading and Writing section, so you can use them as a guide for approximately where each question type will appear. Let's dive in!

Chapter 6
Reading Comprehension

Reading questions will account for just over half of the 54 RW questions and will always appear before the Writing questions in each of the two RW modules. The Reading questions will ask you to perform many different tasks, including selecting the best vocabulary word to fill in a blank, understanding the function of portions of the passage, comparing two passages, finding the main idea of a passage, determining which answer would best support an argument, and completing the passage based on data from tables and graphs. Each passage will range from 25 to 150 words and be accompanied by just a single question, so efficiency will be of the essence. The purpose of this chapter is to introduce you to how the Reading and Writing Basic Approach can be adapted to each of the Reading question types. This will help you streamline how you take the test and keep you focused on what information you need in order to get your points.

PSAT 8/9 READING: CRACKING THE PASSAGES

Answering Reading questions is exactly like taking an open-book test: all of the information that you could be asked about is right in front of you, so you never have to worry about any history, literature, or chemistry that you may (or may not) have learned in school. Of course, you will use the passage to answer the question, but your *primary* goal is to find the information that helps answer the question, not to understand every last word of the passage perfectly. What you need is a way to get in and get out of this section with as little stress and as many points as possible.

To put it another way, think of the process you go through when planning a trip. You start by selecting where you most want to visit before you plan anything else, and then you find the best route to your destination. The PSAT 8/9 Reading questions are the same: for each of them, your first job is to understand the specific question you are answering, then to locate the specific evidence in the passage that either provides a direct answer to the question or offers support as to what the answer to the question should be.

Your Mission

Identify what you are being asked to do for each question and locate the answer or support in the passage as efficiently as possible. Get as many points as you can.

Okay…so how do you get those points? Let's start with the instructions for the Reading and Writing section as a whole.

DIRECTIONS

The questions in this section address a number of important reading and writing skills. Each question includes one or more passages, which may include a table or graph. Read each passage and question carefully, and then choose the best answer to the question based on the passage(s).

All questions in the section are multiple-choice with four answer choices. Each question has a single best answer.

Notice that the directions clearly state the correct answer is based on the passage(s). This is great news! You do not have to rely on your outside knowledge here. All College Board cares about is whether you can read a passage and understand it well enough to answer some questions about it. Unlike in Math or the Writing questions, there are no formulas to memorize, no comma rules to learn. You just need to know how to efficiently process the passage, the question, and the answer choices in order to maximize your score.

Your POOD and the Reading Questions

You will get one question with its passage (or occasionally, with two passages) on screen at a time. While it's tempting to do the questions in the order they appear, you will sometimes be confronted with a question or passage that seems difficult or confusing to you for one reason or another. In that situation, skip the question for now or Mark and Move if you already started working on it and think you'll be able to get it later. You can always come back to any questions you skipped or marked later after you've tackled every question you knew how to do for certain.

How do you decide which ones to do and which ones to skip? Consider these concepts:

- **Topic:** You may be able to tell from glancing at the passage whether it is about science, history, the arts, or another topic area. If you have significant topic-based strengths and weaknesses, use that knowledge to decide your POOD.
- **Literature:** Literature-based passages will contain a blurb, which will, at minimum, introduce the author and title. This will help you quickly decide when to do these passages. You'll also spot poems quickly, and your strengths and weaknesses will tell you when to do those.
- **Question Type:** In this lesson, you'll learn how to identify the different types of questions as well as the order they come in. Determine which ones will be fastest and easiest for you and start with those.

Don't forget: On any questions that you decide to skip permanently or won't have time for, fill in a random answer—you have nothing to lose!

BASIC APPROACH FOR THE READING QUESTIONS

To tackle the Reading questions, we'll expand on the Reading and Writing Basic Approach that you learned previously. No matter what type of question you are confronted with, you will follow the same five basic steps. We'll adapt these steps for each question type as we go through this chapter.

1. **Read the Question**. As with all Reading and Writing questions, you need to first understand what you are being asked to do before you dive into the passage.

2. **Identify the Question Type**. Each question has a phrase that indicates a very specific task that you are being asked to accomplish for that question. This also affects how you will adapt the rest of the approach and is, lastly, a chance to apply your POOD, marking and using LOTD on question types you'd rather deal with later or not at all.

3. **Read the Passage(s)**. Read the passages(s) thoroughly, keeping the question task in mind. Remember that you are looking for an answer to the question, or at the very least, evidence that can help answer the question. You don't need to memorize, or even understand, every detail!

4. **Highlight What Can Help (and Annotate if Needed)**. Within the passage, you'll want to highlight a phrase or sentence that can help answer the question. It could be a direct answer to the question or a piece of information that the question wants you to do something with. On certain question types, such as Vocabulary or Purpose, you'll also make an annotation that will help you nail the correct answer.

5. **Use POE**. Eliminate anything that isn't consistent with your highlighting (and annotation if you made one). Don't necessarily try to find the right answer immediately, because there is a good chance you won't see anything that you like. If you can eliminate answers that you know are wrong, though, you'll be closer to the right answer. If you can't eliminate three answers with your annotation, use the POE criteria (which we'll talk about on the next page).

Where the Money Is

A reporter once asked notorious thief Willie Sutton why he robbed banks. Legend has it that his answer was, "Because that's where the money is." While reading comprehension is safer and slightly more productive than larceny, the same principle applies. Concentrate on the questions and answer choices because that's where the points are. The passage is just a place for College Board to stash facts and details. You'll find them when you need to. Think of the Reading questions as an open-book test. The correct answer is correct because the passage says so, not because of any deep understanding or interpretation of the story.

Before we see these steps in action, we should revisit POE. You saw earlier in this book how POE, or Process of Elimination, is an effective way to earn points on multiple-choice questions. On Reading, there are very specific types of traps. If you catch them, your accuracy will improve dramatically!

POE Criteria

On most of the easy and medium questions, you'll be able to eliminate three of the four answers simply by using your highlighting and annotation. On other, harder questions, your highlighting and annotation may help you get rid of one or two answers, and then you'll need to consider the remaining answers a little more carefully. If you're down to two answers, and they both seem to make sense, you're probably down to the right answer and a trap answer. Luckily, there are some common traps that College Board will set for you, and knowing them can help you figure out which is the trap answer and which is the right answer. Here are the main types of traps you will see:

When to use the POE Criteria?
Use these criteria if you have multiple answers remaining after comparing the answers to what you highlighted/annotated in the passage.

- **Opposite:** These answer choices use a single word or phrase that make the answer convey a tone, viewpoint, or meaning not intended by the author. This can include using a word such as "not" in the answer or using a negative vocabulary word when the tone of the passage was positive.
- **Extreme Language:** These answers look just about perfect except for a word or phrase that goes too far beyond what the passage can support. This also includes answers that could be called insulting or offensive to a person or a group.
- **Recycled Language:** These answer choices repeat exact words and phrases from the passage but use those words and phrases incorrectly. They often establish relationships between the words and phrases that do not exist in the passage.
- **Right Answer, Wrong Question:** These answer choices are true based on the passage, but they don't answer the question asked. They can also miss the author's purpose in including information and focus on the content of the information instead.
- **Beyond the Text:** These answers might initially look good because they make sense or seem logical based on outside reasoning, but they lack support within the passage itself.
- **Half-Right:** These answers address part but not all of the question task. They can also have one half of the answer address the question perfectly and the other half contain at least one of the traps mentioned previously.

QUESTION TYPES AND FORMATS

Now that you know the steps of the Basic Approach, let's consider the different types of questions you'll be answering. It's not important that you can identify the question types by the names we give them. But it is extremely important that you can read a question and know how to respond. Is the question asking you what the author says, why the author included something, what a particular word means, which answer best supports a claim, etc.? The next section of this chapter will help you decode those question types and formats. Your score will depend on your ability to figure out if a question is asking you what, why, how, or which. Luckily, you can understand what you are being asked by learning and adapting the Basic Approach to each of the question types.

Question Types and Formats

- Vocabulary
- Purpose
- Dual Texts
- Retrieval

- Main Idea
- Claims
- Charts
- Conclusions

COMMON

VOCABULARY

The first group of questions you will see will ask you to choose an appropriate vocabulary word to fill in a blank or determine what the meaning of a word is in the context of the paragraph it's in. The PSAT 8/9 tests a blend of common words with multiple meanings and slightly more advanced vocabulary words, but the important thing to remember is that the context of the sentence(s) surrounding the word will provide a clue that you can highlight. This will allow you to annotate, or write down, your own word for the blank, which will help your POE.

Despite a lack of formal instruction in weaving, Maori artist Te Aue Davis was not _____ when asked to contribute to *Te Mahutonga,* a cloak intended to be worn by the flag bearer of New Zealand's Olympic team. Having worked on her family's cloaks as a child, Davis found the tactile process of weaving intimately connected to her identity and took on the important task gladly.

---

1 ☐ Mark for Review

Which choice completes the text with the most logical and precise word or phrase?

Ⓐ devastated

Ⓑ prepared

Ⓒ intimidated

Ⓓ enthused

Here's How To Crack It

If you **read the question** and see "most logical and precise word or phrase," you can **identify the question type** as a **Vocabulary** question.

As you **read the passage,** look for something you can **highlight** to help understand what word should go in the blank, making sure to note the word *not* before the blank. The passage states that *Despite a lack of formal instruction in weaving,* Te Aue Davis *took on the important task gladly.* A good word to enter into your **annotation** box based on this highlighting would be that Davis was *not* "nervous" or "afraid."

Use POE! Choice (A), *devastated,* is **Extreme Language**—just because Davis lacked formal instruction in weaving does not support that she'd be devastated, or overwhelmed with grief, at being asked to contribute to something. Eliminate (A). Choice (B), *prepared,* is a **Beyond the Text** trap—it's logical that someone without a formal education may not be prepared to work on such an important project, but the passage does not state that the offer took Davis by surprise. Eliminate (B). Choice (C), *intimidated,* is a good match for "nervous" or "afraid." Keep (C). Choice (D), *enthused,* is the **Opposite** of what's stated in the passage—since Davis *took on the important task gladly,* it would be wrong to say she was not enthused, or excited. Eliminate (D). The correct answer is (C).

VOCABULARY (*The Second Format*)

The Basic Approach for Vocabulary works equally well even if a word is provided instead of a blank—you'll highlight a clue in the passage and then write down your own word, treating the word given as if it weren't there. Do not give in to the temptation to simply answer the question without following all of the steps. It's very common for College Board to include 1–2 Could Be True traps on each Vocabulary question, so thinking too much can make you jump to those traps. Read, highlight, and annotate on vocabulary questions, and you will be trap, and stress, free!

The following text has been adapted from the 1900 short story "The Wrong Black Bag" by Angelo Lewis. Mr. Quelch is a middle-aged man married to a woman very unlike himself.

He himself was of a meek and <u>retiring</u> disposition. Mrs. Quelch, on the other hand, was a woman of stern and decided temperament, with strong views upon most subjects.

---

2   ☐ Mark for Review

As used in the text, what does the word "retiring" most nearly mean?

(A) Elderly

(B) Reserved

(C) Unemployed

(D) Exhausted

Here's How To Crack It

If you **read the question** and see "most nearly mean," you can **identify the question type** as a **Vocabulary** question.

As you **read the passage,** treat "retiring" as if it were a blank and look for something you can **highlight** to help understand what similar word could take its place. The passage states that *Mrs. Quelch…was a woman of stern and decided temperament, with strong views.* Because of the phrases *unlike himself* and *on the other hand*, Mr. Quelch should have opposite personality traits of Mrs. Quelch. A good word to enter into your **annotation** box based on this highlighting would be "quiet" or "timid."

Use POE! Choice (A), *Elderly,* is a **Recycled Language** trap—while people may retire from work as they become older, that is not how the word *retiring* is being used in the passage. Eliminate (A). Choice (B), *Reserved,* is a good match for "quiet" or "timid." Keep (B). Choice (C), *Unemployed,* is another **Recycled Language** trap—like (A), it is using *retiring* incorrectly. Eliminate (C). Choice (D), *Exhausted,* is a **Beyond the Text** trap—while it's easy to imagine Mr. Quelch feeling exhausted by Mrs. Quelch's strong personality, the passage offers no support for this relationship between the two. Eliminate (D). The correct answer is (B).

VOCABULARY (*Try it out!*)

Use all of the skills you've learned to this point on this Vocabulary question.

For poet and essayist Leigh Hunt, being _____ was critical to his success. Because Hunt was willing to publicly criticize some of the most powerful political figures in nineteenth-century England, many of his contemporaries respected his resolve and Hunt gained considerable prominence.

3 ⬚ Mark for Review

Which choice completes the text with the most logical and precise word or phrase?

(A) courageous

(B) literate

(C) talented

(D) agreeable

Here's How To Crack It

If you **read the question** and see "most logical and precise word or phrase," you can **identify the question type** as a **Vocabulary** question.

As you **read the passage,** look for something you can **highlight** to help understand what word should go in the blank. The passage states that *Hunt was willing to publicly criticize some of the most powerful political figures* and that *many of his contemporaries respected his resolve.* Therefore, what Hunt did was both something others may not have been willing to do and something he was respected for. A good word to enter into your **annotation** box based on this highlighting would be "bold" or "brave."

Use POE! Choice (A), *courageous* is a good match for "bold" or "brave." Keep (A). Choice (B), *literate*, is a **Beyond the Text** trap—as a poet and essayist, it's safe to say Hunt was literate, but the second sentence doesn't focus on his level of reading and writing ability. Eliminate (B). Choice (C), *talented*, is also **Beyond the Text**—while it's logical that Hunt was probably a talented poet and essayist, none of the passage supports exactly how good he was at either skill. Eliminate (C). Choice (D), *agreeable*, is the **Opposite** of what Hunt did—he was *willing to publicly criticize* people, not be friendly or pleasant to them. Eliminate (D). The correct answer is (A).

One last thing: if you do well enough on your first Reading and Writing module, the harder second Reading and Writing module will likely test some more difficult words than those you've seen here. You may need to start brushing up on some vocabulary as you continue to prepare for the PSAT 8/9 in order to keep your score progressing. As you work your way through this book, whenever you come across a word that you don't know, add it to a word list. Continue adding new words and definitions, and study the list to keep improving your score.

PURPOSE

The next group of questions you may see ask you why the author wrote the passage or how a sentence functions in the passage. The PSAT 8/9 isn't looking for any outside reasoning on these questions, as it's not possible to know why any author does anything without asking them! Instead, you're being asked for the *most likely, best supported* reason that the passage or sentence was written or included. Highlight main ideas in the passage or connecting ideas between sentences and annotate when needed. Lastly, don't forget the power of using POE—some answers will contain words or phrases that simply don't match what happened in the passage regardless of what the author's purpose was.

Utilizing advances in robotic technology, researchers at the University of Graz in Austria have successfully integrated temperature sensors and actuators in a hive of approximately 4,000 honeybees, gathering data on the bees' spatial and temporal fluctuations. This biohybrid technology adjusts to the hive's movements and could conceivably allow for the manipulation of the bees' environment through, for example, adjusting temperature to help pollinators optimize reproduction rates. According to the University of Graz researchers, their work illustrates how robotic devices and living creatures can co-exist in the face of changing climate conditions.

4 ☐ Mark for Review

Which choice best states the main purpose of the text?

(A) To discuss how research on the effects of climate change on honeybees' habitats led to technological breakthroughs that reach beyond the field of biology

(B) To assess a presentation stating that biohybrid technology could create more sustainable beehives that would be invulnerable to environmental manipulation

(C) To outline the exhaustive process of integrating new technology with traditional conservation efforts of beekeepers

(D) To present a brief overview of how one specific technological intervention could address a potential issue

Here's How To Crack It

If you **read the question** and see "main purpose of the text," you can **identify the question type** as a **Purpose** question.

As you **read the passage,** look for something you can **highlight** to help understand why the passage was written. At the end of the passage, the University of Graz researchers claim that *their work illustrates how robotic devices and living creatures can co-exist in the face of changing climate conditions,* which explains the importance of the biohybrid technology utilized by the team. Write in your **annotation** box that the purpose of the passage is to "explain why biohybrid technology might be useful" and look for an answer that is as consistent as possible with this purpose.

Use POE! Choice (A) is **Recycled Language**—while the end of the claim does mention *changing climate conditions*, no actual *research on the effects of climate change* is conducted in the passage. Eliminate (A). Choice (B) is **Extreme Language**—first, the passage doesn't claim that biohybrid technology can *create* beehives, and second, it doesn't claim that any beehives would be *invulnerable*, or totally protected, from the environment. Eliminate (B). Choice (C) goes **Beyond the Text**—the process isn't described as *exhaustive*, or extremely thorough, nor are *traditional conservation efforts of beekeepers* mentioned, even if it seems logical that the technology would help beekeepers. Eliminate (C). Choice (D) is consistent with the highlight and the annotation. The *one specific technological innovation* could be the *biohybrid technology* and the *potential issue* could be *changing climate conditions*. Keep (D). The correct answer is (D).

PURPOSE (Sentence Function)

The same approach can be used when a question asks how a sentence functions in the passage. Generally, if you focus on the sentences before and/or after the indicated sentence, you'll be able to highlight connections between ideas that keep the passage flowing. From this logical flow, you'll be able to annotate the role that the indicated sentence performs.

MODERATELY COMMON

<u>A new study challenges prior research about "generalized reciprocity," or people's tendency to help someone else when unable to repay their original benefactor.</u> According to an experiment by Ashley Harrell and Anna S. Greenleaf, when people are of lesser means than an individual who has done them a financial kindness, the receiver's tendency to "pay it forward" to another individual is lower compared to instances in which the giver and receiver have a more balanced distribution of resources. Harrell and Greenleaf believe this new research more accurately reflects real-world situations, in which individuals rarely have equal access to wealth.

5 ☐ Mark for Review

Which of the following best describes the function of the first sentence in the overall structure of the text?

(A) It suggests a reason that Harrell and Greenleaf's experiment is relevant to daily life.

(B) It describes the way in which the current study differs from prior work on the topic.

(C) It explains a previously held belief and indicates that the belief may not be without opposition.

(D) It introduces a definition of generalized reciprocity which Harrell and Greenleaf's work disproves.

Here's How To Crack It

If you **read the question** and see "function of the _____ sentence," you can **identify the question type** as a **Purpose** question.

As you **read the passage,** look for something you can **highlight** to help understand why the first sentence was included. The passage mentions that *the receiver's tendency to "pay it forward" to another individual is lower compared to instances in which the giver and receiver have a more balanced distribution of resources,* but the first sentence indicates that prior research stated that people tended to *help someone else when unable to repay their original benefactor.* In other words, the rest of the passage indicates that people don't always opt to help someone else if the gap in resources between themselves and the original giver is large enough. Write in your **annotation** box that the function of the sentence here is to "explain what people thought and that it might be wrong."

Use POE! Choice (A) is **Right Answer, Wrong Question**—it describes what happens in the last sentence, not the first sentence. Eliminate (A). Choice (B) goes **Beyond the Text**—the first sentence only mentions that there is a new study, not in what way it's different from prior research. Eliminate (B). Choice (C) is consistent with the annotation and highlighting. It mentions the *previously held belief* and saying that a *new study challenges* the belief means *the belief may not be without opposition.* Keep (C). Choice (D) is **Extreme Language**—Harrell and Greenleaf's work show that people don't always exhibit generalized reciprocity, but nothing they found *disproves* the definition itself. Eliminate (D). The correct answer is (C).

One last thing: you can also be asked for the overall structure of the passage. Don't panic! You are still being asked for the purpose of the passage as a whole. Once you write down what the purpose is, the correct answer will describe what the author did in the passage to accomplish that goal. An example of one of these questions is included in the drill for this chapter.

DUAL TEXTS

MODERATELY COMMON

The next question type you may see will offer you two passages rather than one and asks how someone from one passage would respond to another one or to find some agreement or disagreement between the passages. These can seem intimidating at first, but all you are looking for is a single idea mentioned in the first text that is commented upon by the second. It will be pretty obvious when you are faced with a Dual Texts question (after all, there will be two passages!), so we won't need to **Identify the Question Type.** Instead, you'll slightly modify the Reading Basic Approach to focus on what you need in order to understand the link between these passages!

Dual Texts Basic Approach

1. Read and understand the question.
2. Read the first passage and highlight the claim or a main idea.
3. Read the second passage and highlight what is said about the same idea.
4. Determine and annotate the relationship between the passages.
5. Use POE and eliminate answers that are inconsistent with one or both passages.

Text 1

Neuroscientist Antti Revonsuo suggested that humans dream in order to simulate dangerous situations and practice their responses. Revonsuo based this theory on the fact that dreaming is a limited simulation of daily life that doesn't include many mundane daily tasks. Traumatic experiences tend to stimulate the process of dreaming, and the dreams appear hyperrealistic. Furthermore, Revonsuo emphasizes that practicing skills in dreams enhances their use in the real world and the fact that dreaming is innate implies it is an inherited ability developed through evolution.

Text 2

Psychiatrists J. Allen Hobson and Robert McCarley propose that dreams do not have any deeper purpose; they are merely random interpretations and combinations of things the brain processed throughout the day. As visualized by neuroimaging, the brain is extremely active during REM sleep. This activity represents the cerebral cortex combining emotions and sensations experienced throughout the day with memories previously experienced to create simulations of events that may or may not have occurred in the individual's life.

---

6   🔖 Mark for Review

Based on the texts, how would Hobson and McCarley (Text 2) most likely respond to Revonsuo's theory (Text 1)?

(A) They would argue that neuroimaging disproves the fact that dreaming is an evolutionary development.

(B) They would claim that not everyone experiences traumatic events in their lives.

(C) They would suggest that Revonsuo experiment with the types of skills being practiced in dreams.

(D) They would encourage Revonsuo to consider an alternate explanation for an experience that humans have when they sleep.

Here's How To Crack It

When you **read and understand the question,** you can see that it's asking for Revonsuo's theory from Text 1 and how Hobson and McCarley in Text 2 would respond to that theory.

As you **read the first passage,** look to **highlight** Revonsuo's theory. *Revonsuo suggested that humans dream in order to simulate dangerous situations and practice their responses.* As you **read the second passage,** look for something you can **highlight** related to this theory. Text 2 states that *dreams do not have any deeper purpose; they are merely random interpretations and combinations of things the brain processed throughout the day.*

Write in your **annotation** box that Hobson and McCarley would reply by saying "dreams just random interpretations—no deep purpose." The correct answer will be as consistent as possible with this annotation without going to an extreme.

Use POE! Choice (A) is **Extreme Language**—Text 2 doesn't claim that Hobson and McCarley's neuroimaging work *disproves* Revonsuo's theory. Hobson and McCarley's interpretation of what neuroimaging showed is only a proposal, not firm evidence against Revonsuo's theory. Eliminate (A). Choice (B) goes **Beyond the Text**—even if it's true that *not everyone experiences traumatic events*, this is not a point argued by Hobson and McCarley. Eliminate (B). Choice (C) is **Recycled Language**—only Text 1 mentions *skills*, and the scientists in Text 2 don't *suggest* that Revonsuo perform any type of *experiment*. Eliminate (C). Choice (D) is consistent with the highlighting and annotated relationship between the passages. Since Hobson and McCarley disagree with Revonsuo's theory, it's logical that they might encourage him to *consider an alternate explanation* for why people dream. Keep (D). The correct answer is (D).

DUAL TEXTS (*Try it out!*)

Use all of the skills you've learned to this point on this Dual Texts question.

Text 1

The traditional understanding of how social insects such as termites and cockroaches protect their colonies maintains that they rely on both physical and chemical defense systems. When a potential intruder is spotted, all colony members will cause vibrations within their nests, essentially "sounding the alarm" to signal others about the possible danger. Termites and cockroaches may also emit pheromones through glands located in their abdominal regions as a part of the alert.

Text 2

In a 2023 study, David Sillam-Dusses and his team noted that members of the termite family Neoisoptera have evolved their defense systems away from the colony-wide alarm systems used by most other social insects. For the Neoisoptera termites, the task of defending the colony is performed only by designated adult "fighter" termites, allowing the juveniles to seek safety. This diversity of roles enables these termites to establish habitats that other social insects may find inhospitable.

7 ☐ Mark for Review

Based on the text, how would Sillam-Dusses and his team (Text 2) most likely respond to the "sounding the alarm" concept presented in Text 1?

(A) By conceding that while the idea is integral to orders of social insects, the distinct physical signatures of diverse habitats make comparisons inaccurate

(B) By noting that the concept applies to some insect species, but is too narrow to adequately account for the defensive behavior of all social insects

(C) By disregarding the idea that behaviors demonstrated by termites could share any commonalities with colonies of other social insects such as cockroaches

(D) By acknowledging the accuracy of the concept but faulting it for being dismissive in its understanding of how insect species interact

Here's How To Crack It

When you **read and understand the question,** you can see that it's asking how Sillam-Dusses and his team from Text 2 would respond to the "sounding the alarm" concept in Text 1.

As you **read the first passage,** look to **highlight** the "sounding the alarm" concept. When faced with a threat, *all colony members will cause vibrations within their nests* and *may also emit pheromones* to warn the colony of the danger. As you **read the second passage,** look for something you can **highlight** related to this concept. Text 2 states for a certain family of termites, *the task of defending the colony is performed only by designated adult "fighter" termites.*

Write in your **annotation** box that Sillam-Dusses and his team would reply by saying "some species sound the alarm, others designate defenders." The correct answer will be as consistent as possible with this annotation without going to an extreme.

Use POE! Choice (A) is **Recycled Language**—*diversity* and *habitat*s are being taken from the end of Text 2 and combined together to make an unsupported answer. Eliminate (A). Choice (B) is consistent with the highlighting and annotated relationship between the passages. Sillam-Dusses and his team admit that *colony-wide alarm systems* are *used by most other social insects*, but they've found a family of termites that does something different. Keep (B). Choice (C) is **Extreme Language**—just because Text 2 cites a termite family that defends its colonies differently does not mean that Sillam-Dusses is *disregarding* any possible similarities between termites and cockroaches. Eliminate (C). Choice (D) is **Half-Right**—while the first half is accurate, to say that Text 1 is being *dismissive* of understanding how insect species interact is **Extreme Language**. Eliminate (D). The correct answer is (B).

RETRIEVAL

The next groups of questions you may see mark a shift in the Reading and Writing section. Up until this point, the questions have all been about structure—the right vocabulary word for a blank, the reason something was included, how one passage relates to another, etc. Starting with Retrieval and Main Idea questions, you'll be focusing on what the passage actually says rather than why the author included something or how someone would respond. This means that many times, you'll be able to go right to using POE once you highlight something in the passage. As we move forward through this chapter, we will still mention when you should be annotating.

MODERATELY COMMON

The following text has been adapted from E. Nesbit's 1907 novel *The Enchanted Castle.*

The Princess went first, and Kathleen carried her shining train; then came Jimmy, and Gerald came last. They were all quite sure that they had walked right into the middle of a fairy-tale, and they were the more ready to believe it because they were so tired and hungry. They were, in fact, so hungry and tired that they hardly noticed where they were going, or observed the beauties of the formal gardens through which the pink-silk Princess was leading them. They were in a sort of dream, from which they only partially awakened to find themselves in a big hall, with suits of armor and old flags round the walls, the skins of beasts on the floor, and heavy oak tables and benches ranged along it.

---

8 ☐ Mark for Review

According to the text, what is true about Kathleen, Jimmy, and Gerald?

(A) They are distracted by their current physical condition.

(B) They are much more practical than they appear.

(C) They have difficulty believing in magic when hungry.

(D) Their observation skills are much sharper than those of the Princess.

Here's How To Crack It

If you **read the question** and see "according to the text" or "based on the text," you can **identify the question type** as a **Retrieval** question. It's not looking for anything fancy—it wants to know exactly what the passage says about Kathleen, Jimmy, and Gerald and which answer says the same thing using slightly different words.

As you **read the passage,** look for what you can **highlight** about Kathleen, Jimmy, and Gerald. The passage states that *They were, in fact, so hungry and tired that they hardly noticed where they were going.* The other sentences continue or echo this description of the three children, so it's pretty safe to highlight this sentence and look for a consistent idea among the answer choices.

Use POE! Choice (A) is consistent with the highlighting—*their current physical condition* could be that they are *hungry and tired,* and this is certainly distracting them. Keep (A). Choice (B) goes **Beyond the Text**—while the children are currently distracted from their surroundings, there's no evidence in the passage that indicates they might actually be very *practical,* or logical, people. Eliminate (B). Choice (C) is **Recycled Language** as it misuses the words *fairy-tale, dream,* and *hungry* from the passage to create a claim about the children's beliefs that isn't supported by the text. Eliminate (C). Choice (D) is also **Recycled Language**—it misuses the word *Princess* from the passage, and additionally, the children's *observation skills* are not described as sharp, but rather that they are missing things around them. Eliminate (D). The correct answer is (A).

One last thing: you can also be asked why something happens in the passage. Why something happens is not a Purpose question—it's still Retrieval because it actually wants to know what reason the author gave for something occurring in the passage. You only need to find and highlight that reason, and you're ready to use POE. An example of one of these questions is included in the drill for this chapter.

MAIN IDEA

Often mixed together with Retrieval questions, Main Idea questions also want to know what the author said. The difference is that Main Idea questions are looking for the single sentence or idea that is the main focus of the passage rather than a detail about a character or thing. This should be the sentence or idea that all of the other sentences and ideas are connected to. Many times, this will be the first or last sentence of the paragraph, but College Board can place the main idea anywhere. As you read, ask yourself, "Which sentence does all of the other sentences build to or build off of?"

MODERATELY COMMON

By 1940, the fundamental precepts of Darwin's theory of natural selection, that the strongest and fittest complex organisms survive to pass on their superior DNA to their offspring, were widely accepted. Scientists debated whether simpler organisms such as bacteria—whose DNA is a single chromosome—obey the same process. In 1943, scientists Max Delbrick and Salvador Luria conducted an experiment in which they exposed select groups of bacteria in separate culture tubes to a wide variety of diseases and hazards. In what was a surprise to the research team, the offspring of the bacteria that survived the initial experiments exhibited adaptations to the diseases and hazards that allowed those bacterial lineages to continue to thrive in their cultures.

---

9 ☐ Mark for Review

Which choice best states the main idea of the text?

(A) Darwin's theory of natural selection was not thoroughly accepted and confirmed until the work done by Delbrick and Luria in 1943.

(B) Delbrick and Luria argued that Darwin's theory of natural selection did not apply to simple organisms such as bacteria.

(C) The results of Delbrick and Luria's experiment conflicted with the assumptions of the greater scientific community.

(D) Delbrick and Luria observed that bacteria were not an exception to Darwin's theory of natural selection but actually conformed to its precepts.

Here's How To Crack It

If you **read the question** and see "main idea," you can **identify the question type** as a **Main Idea** question. It's looking for the sentence that all of the other sentences are building up to or support.

As you **read the passage,** look for a main idea that you can **highlight**. While the first three sentences explain the background regarding Darwin's theory and the debate surrounding whether bacteria follow the theory, only the last sentence offers the results of the experiment, addressing both the theory and the debate. So, highlight the last sentence: the correct answer should be consistent with as many aspects of this idea as possible.

Use POE! Choice (A) is **Extreme Language**—the passage doesn't imply that that Delbrick and Luria's work *confirmed* Darwin's theory; it only demonstrated that the theory may be applicable to bacteria. Eliminate (A). Choice (B) is the **Opposite** of what happens in the passage—Delbrick and Luria showed that Darwin's theory may indeed apply to bacteria. Eliminate (B). Choice (C) goes **Beyond the Text**—while the results of the experiment were a *surprise* to the research team, it's not stated what *the greater scientific community* assumed. Eliminate (C). Choice (D) is consistent with the highlighting—it's a paraphrase of what the last sentence states. Keep (D). The correct answer is (D).

CLAIMS

The next group of questions you will see ask which answer would best illustrate, support, or weaken a claim made by the author or someone in the passage. Note that these questions are often interspersed with the next question type, **Charts**, but luckily, the skills you need for these two question types are similar. As with Retrieval and Main Idea questions, your main job here will be to identify the claim made by the author in the passage without any regard to the structure or purpose of the passage. However, you'll need to perform the exact task required by the question and keep a razor-sharp eye as you use POE: it only takes one word or phrase to make an answer do the opposite of what was intended!

Gustave Flaubert's 1862 novel *Salammbô* presents a tragic love story between Matho, the leader of a rebellion, and *Salammbô*, the daughter of the city's leader. Throughout the novel, negative emotions and experiences are portrayed as opportunities to display strength of character: _____

10 🔖 Mark for Review

Which quotation from *Salammbô* most effectively illustrates the claim?

(A) "We have all been vanquished! Each one supports his own misfortune!"

(B) "I have still three thousand Carians, twelve hundred slingers and archers, whole cohorts!

(C) "In their extremity of terror all became brave."

(D) "He had not the strength to finish, and Hamilcar stopped quite amazed at such grief."

Here's How To Crack It

If you **read the question** and see the phrase "illustrates the claim," you can **identify the question type** as a **Claims** question.

When a Claims question asks you to illustrate a claim, the passage will be fairly short with a single claim. So, **read the passage** and **highlight** the claim: the correct answer must be a quotation from *Salammbô* that shows that *negative emotions and experiences are portrayed as opportunities to display strength of character.*

Use POE! Choice (A) is **Half-Right**—while being *vanquished* would certainly be a negative experience, stating that *Each one supports his own misfortune* indicates a negative reaction to the situation, which would be the **Opposite** of showing *strength of character*. Eliminate (A). Choice (B) goes **Beyond the Text**—while stating that someone still has troops left could indicate that there was a negative experience such as a battle, this statement alone wouldn't show *strength of character*. Eliminate (B). Choice (C) is consistent with the highlighted claim—if a group of people showed bravery in the face of extreme terror, this would echo each part of the claim. Keep (C). Choice (D) is also the **Opposite** of the claim—a character going through a negative experience such as grief and being unable to continue his efforts would not show *strength of character*. Eliminate (D). The correct answer is (C).

CLAIMS (*Poetry*)

UNCOMMON

While poetry can be tested on Purpose, Retrieval, and Main Idea questions, Claims questions are where you will most often see poetry. The nice thing about it showing up on Claims questions is that you don't need to read and attempt to understand an entire poem. Instead, just like the previous question, your main job is to understand the claim in the question stem and then read through the couplets in the answer choices extremely carefully, eliminating answers that only address part of the claim or miss it entirely.

"Paul Revere's Ride" is an 1860 poem by Henry Wadsworth Longfellow that recounts Revere's actions in support of the rebels during the American Revolution. The poem indicates that both the physicality and goal of Revere's ride were worthy of attention from others: _____

---

11 🔖 Mark for Review

Which quotation from "Paul Revere's Ride" most effectively illustrates the claim?

(A) "A hurry of hoofs in a village-street, / A shape in the moonlight, a bulk in the dark, / And beneath from the pebbles, in passing, a spark / Struck out by a steed that flies fearless and fleet."

(B) "In the hour of darkness and peril and need, / The people will waken and listen to hear / The hurrying hoof-beats of that steed, / And the midnight message of Paul Revere."

(C) "And the meeting-house windows, blank and bare, / Gaze at him with a spectral glare, / As if they already stood aghast / At the bloody work they would look upon."

(D) "And one was safe and asleep in his bed / Who at the bridge would be first to fall, / Who that day would be lying dead, / Pierced by a British musket-ball."

Here's How To Crack It

If you **read the question** and see the phrase "illustrates the claim," you can **identify the question type** as a **Claims** question.

As you **read the passage**, **highlight** the claim: *the physicality and goal of Revere's ride were worthy of attention from others*. The correct answer should be as consistent as possible with each aspect of this claim. It doesn't matter that the answers are excerpts from a poem rather than from a story—they should be treated the exact same way.

Use POE! Choice (A) is **Half-Right**—while the *physicality* of the ride, particularly the horse itself, is described in great detail, there's no mention of the ride's goal or that either was *worthy of attention from others.* Eliminate (A). Choice (B) is consistent with the highlighted claim—not only will *people waken and listen to hear the hoof-beats* of Revere's horse, they'll listen to and hear Revere's *midnight message* in *the hour of darkness and peril and need.* Keep (B). Choice (C) is irrelevant to the claim—describing windows as if they'll be *aghast,* or shocked, at the battles to come does not address any aspect of the claim. Eliminate (C). Choice (D) goes **Beyond the Text**—it focuses things that happened during the battles of the American Revolution but is irrelevant to the claim itself. Eliminate (D). The correct answer is (B).

CLAIMS (*Try it out!*)

Use all of the skills you've learned to this point on this Claims question. Note that this question is asking you to support the claim and is accompanied by significantly more text. Don't panic: since the question wants you to support a hypothesis, find and highlight that hypothesis and then make sure the answer is as consistent with what you highlighted as possible!

In the growing field of nanotechnology, research has focused on generating electricity through evaporation, but the nanoparticles used in this system require large surface areas to generate sufficient electrical charges. Additionally, the microorganisms that create these nanoparticles require consistent sources of food in order to maintain a continuous particle output. A research team led by Ziaomeng Liu hypothesized that reducing the thickness of the biofilm, a substance placed between the specialized mesh electrodes that are necessary to capture energy from the microorganisms, may reduce the number of microorganisms needed for the system to operate and in turn reduce both the surface area and food resources required. If this is successful, possible applications include generating electricity sufficient to operate a portable device from the perspiration on a person's forearm.

12 ☐ Mark for Review

Which finding, if true, would most directly support the team's hypothesis?

(A) Thinner biofilms have been shown to make more efficient use of the electricity generated by microorganisms than thicker ones.

(B) Specialized mesh electrodes are appropriate conductors for generating electricity through evaporation.

(C) Technological advances in portable electronic devices have allowed these devices to charge their batteries more easily.

(D) Advancements in nanotechnology now demand thicker biofilm layers between mesh electrodes in order to capture the energy produced by nanoparticles.

Here's How To Crack It

If you **read the question** and see the phrases "support _____'s hypothesis," you can **identify the question type** as a **Claims** question. The question could also use words such as claim, argument, prediction, assertion, suggestion, etc., in place of "hypothesis."

As you **read the passage**, **highlight** the hypothesis: *reducing the thickness of the biofilm…may reduce the number of microorganisms needed for the system to operate and in turn reduce both the surface area and food resources required.* The correct answer should be as consistent as possible with each aspect of this hypothesis. Don't be distracted by how technical or professional the answers sound—the correct answer must stay on topic.

Use POE! Choice (A) is consistent with the highlighted hypothesis—if a thinner biofilm *makes more efficient use of the electricity* generated by the system, this is consistent with *reducing the thickness of the biofilm* improving how the system operates. Keep (A). Choice (B) is **Recycled Language**—it joins *specialized mesh electrodes* and *generating electricity through evaporation* from completely different parts of the passage to create an unsupported connection between these ideas. Eliminate (B). Choice (C) is irrelevant to the claim—while more efficient battery charging is certainly good for the operation of the devices themselves, the claim made by the team is specifically about *reducing the thickness of the biofilm*. Eliminate (C). Choice (D) is the **Opposite** of the question task—if *thicker* biofilm layers were now demanded or required, this would weaken, not support, the team's hypothesis regarding *reducing the thickness of the biofilm*. Eliminate (D). The correct answer is (A).

One last thing: These questions can also ask you to weaken or undermine a claim or hypothesis. When confronted with weaken or undermine, you will still highlight the claim and then look for an answer that contradicts as much as possible without introducing anything irrelevant to the claim (like battery charging!). An example of one of these questions is included in the drill for this chapter.

CHARTS

MODERATELY COMMON

As mentioned before, Charts questions are interspersed with Claims questions, and you won't necessarily see both on the same module. The biggest difference here is that you'll be reading some information from a table or graph in addition to the passage. As with Dual Texts, it will be pretty clear when you are asked a Charts question, so we'll once again modify the Reading Basic Approach slightly to make sure you catch everything needed to earn these points!

Charts Basic Approach

1. Read and understand the question.
2. Read the title, key/legend, variables, and units in the chart.
3. Read the passage and look for the same information you saw in the chart.
4. Highlight the claim or conclusion made regarding that same information.
5. Use POE and eliminate answers that are inconsistent with the chart, the passage, or both.

Performance of Participants on a Memory Test Before and After Receiving Deep-Brain Stimulation

Participant	Score on Memory Test on Day 1	Score on Memory Test on Day 2
1	74%	81%
2	62%	63%
3	55%	75%
4	55%	47%
5	31%	52%

To assess the effect of brain stimulation on memory, Itzhak Fried and his research team provided deep-brain stimulation to participants while they were in non-REM sleep (a period when the brain is thought to be solidifying memories). The five participants (all of whom had been previously diagnosed with conditions known to impede the performance of memory) completed a memory test on two consecutive days, receiving deep-brain stimulation while sleeping the night in between the two days. Fried and his colleagues claim that the majority of participants performed better on the memory tests after receiving the treatment.

13 🔖 Mark for Review

Which choice best describes data from the table that support Fried and his team's claim?

A) The highest score on the memory test on Day 1 was 74% for Participant 1, while the lowest score on the memory test on Day 1 was 31% for Participant 5.

B) Day 1 memory test scores included 62% for Participant 2 and 55% for Participant 4 but were not the highest Day 1 memory test scores.

C) None of the Day 2 memory test scores were below 47%, and four of the five participants improved their memory test score from Day 1 to Day 2.

D) Day 1 and Day 2 memory scores are shown for each participant, but no information about the specific nature of their conditions is given.

Here's How To Crack It

As you **read and understand the question**, you'll notice the phrase "data from the table" along with "support _____'s claim," which together indicate that this is a **Charts** question. You are looking for Fried and his team's claim regarding the information in the table.

As you **read the title and variables in each column of the table**, you'll want to note that the table shows five participants and their memory scores on two separate days of testing. As you **read the passage,** look for a claim Fried and his team make regarding these terms specifically. **Highlight** the last sentence, which states that *the majority of participants performed better on the memory tests after receiving the treatment.* The answer should be as consistent as possible with this claim.

Use POE! Choice (A) is not relevant to the claim—it focuses on Day 1 scores only, and the claim is related to improvements on Day 2, which is *after receiving the treatment.* Eliminate (A). Choice (B) is also irrelevant to the claim for the same reason—note that neither (A) nor (B) contradicts the data in the table; they simply don't mention improvements from Day 1 to Day 2 as they should. Eliminate (B). Choice (C) is consistent with the claim and the table—it references improvements from Day 1 to Day 2, particularly in the second half of the answer. Keep (C). Choice (D) again describes the content of the table accurately but is irrelevant to the claim as it does not specifically mention that the scores mostly improved from Day 1 to Day 2. Eliminate (D). The correct answer is (C).

CHARTS (*Text Completions*)

Charts questions can also ask you to complete an example or statement made by the passage. Following the Charts Basic Approach is critical because you are looking for what the passage and chart say about the exact same data. Above all else, the answer you choose must be consistent with the data in the table or graph and be relevant to the sentence that you are completing.

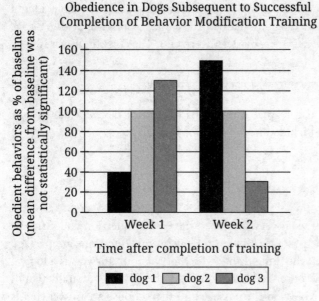

Obedience in Dogs Subsequent to Successful Completion of Behavior Modification Training

Obedient behaviors as % of baseline (mean difference from baseline was not statistically significant)

Time after completion of training

■ dog 1 □ dog 2 ■ dog 3

Some research suggests that the positive effects of obedience training for dogs are short-lived: dogs revert to their previous behavioral patterns once the training ends. Dogs may be obedient with their trainers and successfully complete a behavior modification program, but these improvements soon disappear once their owners take over. In a study of dogs' levels of obedience, a researcher recorded dogs' obedient behaviors (as a percentage of a previously established baseline) after their training programs ended. He concluded that the positive effects of obedience training may not disappear after the program ends, offering as evidence the fact that the dogs in the study _____.

14 🔖 Mark for Review

Which choice most effectively uses data from the table to complete the example?

Ⓐ showed no significant differences between levels of obedience one week after training and two weeks after training.

Ⓑ did not demonstrate a higher percentage of obedience during the second week after completion of the training than during the first week.

Ⓒ showed no significant differences in obedience levels in relation to one another.

Ⓓ did not consistently demonstrate a decrease in obedience percentage in the weeks following behavior modification training.

Here's How To Crack It

As you read and understand the question, you'll notice the phrase "data from the graph" along with "complete the text," which together indicate that this is a **Charts** question. You are looking for a statement or argument in the passage that the data from the graph will be consistent with and complete appropriately.

As you **read the title, variables, and key in the graph,** you'll want to note that graph shows three dogs and their obedience level as a percentage of the baseline across two weeks. As you read the passage, look for a statement or argument regarding this information. **Highlight** the last sentence, which states that the researcher *concluded that the positive effects of obedience training may not disappear after the program ends*. The answer should offer evidence of this argument while remaining consistent with the graph.

Use POE! Choice (A) is the **Opposite** of what's shown in the graph—Dogs 1 and 3 most certainly displayed *differences between levels of obedience* from Week 1 to Week 2. Eliminate (A). Choice (B) is not only the **Opposite** of what happened with Dog 1, but it also goes against the argument made by the researcher. Eliminate (B). Choice (C) is also the **Opposite** of the graph—each dog demonstrated a different obedience level from each of the other two dogs in both weeks. Eliminate (C). Choice (D) is consistent with the highlighted argument and the graph. Dog 1 actually improved its obedience level and Dog 2 remained the same, so neither of these dogs consistently demonstrated a *decrease in obedience percentage*. Keep (D). The correct answer is (D).

———————————◯———————————

One last thing: Charts questions can also feature line graphs instead of tables or bar graphs. An example of one of these questions is included in the drill for this chapter.

CONCLUSIONS

The last question type you will see is very similar to the Charts question you just saw: it will ask you to complete the passage. However, Conclusions questions are passage only and are always asking you the same thing: which of the four answers is a logical conclusion based on all of the other sentences given in the passage? Usually, you'll need to highlight two separate ideas in the passage and then choose an answer that is consistent with both of them.

———————————◯———————————

Travel during the time of the Roman civilization (753 BCE to 476 CE) was initially limited to those of means such as military leaders and wealthy aristocrats. Following military conquests, victorious generals would often conduct a "tour" of Roman cities to be properly acknowledged by Roman citizenry, and wealthy individuals traveled for personal leisure, such as attending the Olympic Games in Greece or visiting the Great Pyramids in Egypt. (These locations were seen as "exotic" by Roman travelers.) Eventually, the expansion of the Roman road system and improved navigational tools for ships reduced the difficulty in arranging for personal travel, implying that during the later years of the Roman civilization, _____

15 🔖 Mark for Review

Which choice most logically completes the text?

Ⓐ Roman citizens without goods to trade were unlikely to be allowed to travel.

Ⓑ average citizens may have had opportunities for travel previously only afforded to aristocrats and members of the military.

Ⓒ the military offensives of Roman generals were effective in seizing foreign lands for future travel.

Ⓓ the number of methods by which one could visit Greece and Egypt reduced sharply after 476 CE.

Here's How To Crack It

If you **read the question** and see "which choice most logically completes the text," you can **identify the question type** as Conclusions: this will almost always be the exact prompt you will see on these questions.

As you **read the passage,** look for a main focus. While the passage focuses on several different reasons for Roman travel, it expands on the last one, *leisure.* You should **highlight** the main points made about leisure: initially, *only upper-class aristocrats had the means required to travel for leisure.* Then, *the expansion of the Roman road system and improved navigational tools for ships reduced the difficulty in arranging for personal travel.* Therefore, a reasonable conclusion would be that the reduction in difficulty in arranging for personal travel may have allowed for non-aristocrats to travel for leisure (you can enter something like "now, regular people could travel too" into your **annotation** box if that will help).

Use POE! Choice (A) is the **Opposite** of what's stated in the passage—the end of the passage implies that many different types of people may be able to travel, not just those with *goods to trade.* Eliminate (A). Choice (B) is consistent with the highlighted ideas about leisure—it's at least possible that *average citizens* may be able to travel now due to the improvements to the roads and navigational tools for the sea. Keep (B). Choice (C) goes **Beyond the Text**—while *seizing foreign lands* may mean one could travel to those lands someday, the passage does not indicate that this actually happened, only that the generals took a victory "tour" of Roman cities. Eliminate (C). Choice (D) also goes **Beyond the Text**—the passage doesn't discuss what happens after the Roman civilization ends in *476 CE,* only what happens during the *later* part of it. Eliminate (D). The correct answer is (B).

CONCLUSIONS (*Try it Out!*)

Conclusions questions are pretty common and it's almost a guarantee you'll see at least one of them on each module you complete. Use all of the skills you've learned to this point on this Conclusions question.

Pungmul is a Korean folk music style that combines singing, drumming, and dancing into one performance and was used heavily during the Joseon dynasty (1392–1897 CE). Many scholars claim that the term *nongak* (meaning "farmers' music") was introduced during the early twentieth century Japanese occupation of Korea in an attempt to reduce the popularity of *pungmul.* Despite the initial success of these efforts, *pungmul* regained popularity in the 1970s when Western-style concert halls and Western music became popular in Korea, thereby casting doubt on the idea that _____

16 ☐ Mark for Review

Which choice most logically completes the text?

(A) the attempt to introduce a new term permanently affected the popularity of a musical style.

(B) the term *nongak* had any initial effect on the popularity of *pungmul* at all.

(C) Western-style concert halls had a positive influence on the revival of *pungmul.*

(D) music was a critical aspect of Korean society and culture.

Here's How To Crack It

If you **read the question** and see "which choice most logically completes the text," you can **identify the question type** as Conclusions: this will almost always be the exact prompt you will see on these questions.

As you **read the passage,** look for a main focus. The passage focuses on *pungmul* and a bit about its history. You should **highlight** the main points made about *pungmul*: a term was introduced in the early twentieth century *in an attempt to reduce the popularity of pungmul*. The passage goes on to say that *Despite the initial success of these efforts, pungmul regained popularity in the 1970s.* Therefore, a reasonable conclusion would be that while the popularity of *pungmul* was reduced for a while, it eventually recovered. (You can enter something like "popularity only reduced temporarily" into your **annotation** box if that will help.) Keep in mind that the question says the evidence should cast doubt on, or contradict, the correct answer.

Use POE! Choice (A) is consistent with the highlighted ideas about *pungmul*—because the passage indicates that the popularity of *pungmul* was reduced only temporarily, this would cast doubt on the idea that its popularity was affected *permanently*. Keep (A). Choice (B) is the **Opposite** of the passage—the new term for *pungmul* did reduce the music style's popularity at first, so the term did have an initial effect. Eliminate (B). Choice (C) is also the **Opposite** of the passage—*Western-style dance halls* contributed to *pungmul* regaining popularity, so they did have a positive influence on its revival. Eliminate (C). Choice (D) is **Extreme Language**—just because *pungmul* was popular at different times does not mean that music is or is not a *critical* aspect of Korean culture. Eliminate (D). The correct answer is (A).

———————◯———————

One last thing: These questions may seem intimidating, but even if you struggle to find the correct ideas to highlight, just focus on eliminating answers that introduce ideas that were not discussed in the passage or are inconsistent with the passage's arguments.

Reading Drill

Time: 10 minutes. Below, you'll find an assessment featuring one of each of the eight question types you've learned in this chapter in the common order in which they would typically appear on a Reading module. Use all of the skills you've learned and be ready for some of the different question variations that we promised you earlier in the chapter. Answers can be found in Part IV.

---

1 ▢ Mark for Review

In 2016, the simple act of helping his mother install a yard sign earned police officer Jeffrey Heffernan a demotion for showing political favoritism. The demotion led to a lawsuit, and *Heffernan v. City of Paterson* made it all the way to the United States Supreme Court. The _____ case came to an end when the Court ruled in favor of Heffernan, bringing an end to a truly odd sequence of events.

Which choice completes the text with the most logical and precise word or phrase?

(A) critical

(B) unprejudiced

(C) trivial

(D) unusual

---

2 ▢ Mark for Review

German dermatologist Alfred Blaschko observed that some patients' skin displays distinctive patterns of patches or streaks that he believed were formed during embryo development. One possible cause of these "Blaschko's lines" was later determined to be *chimerism*—a condition wherein one has cells from two different sources, and consequently two distinct sets of DNA. Blaschko's 1901 findings paved the way for scientists to identify and study chimerism decades later, which has profound implications for the reliability of modern DNA testing.

Which choice best describes the overall structure of the text?

(A) It explains how a scientific phenomenon was discovered, and then explains the significance of that phenomenon.

(B) It describes the methodology of a scientific experiment, and then forms a hypothesis based on the findings of that experiment.

(C) It analyzes procedures used by some scientists, and then rejects that methodology in favor of an arguably superior alternative.

(D) It shows how the medical community arrived at a conclusion, and then shows how that conclusion was later disproved.

3 ☐ Mark for Review

Text 1

In an experiment on the moral development of children, researchers instructed three-year-olds not to select any yellow toys, providing alternatives in other colors instead. Over time, the children learned to reject yellow toys with no prompting. When later asked why, the children frequently responded that yellow was "bad," suggesting that these toddlers had adopted what they believed to be the "morality" of the adult experimenters.

Text 2

A common belief among psychologists is that children are born with some instinctual understanding of right and wrong. While children will naturally avoid situations that are inherently unpleasant or frightening and therefore may seemingly make good moral choices to avoid these situations, they require adult influences and instruction to otherwise conform their behavior to moral norms. A toddler might, with no adult present, control his impulse to take another child's toy, but only out of fear of punishment, not from any independent moral conclusion that stealing is wrong.

Based on the texts, how would the author of Text 2 most likely respond to the underlined portion of Text 1?

Ⓐ By noting that even adults can be influenced by others to adopt a questionable moral code

Ⓑ By suggesting that the children were simply exercising their innate fear of yellow toys rather than exhibiting a sense of learned morality

Ⓒ By asserting that, while the children's choices may appear moral, they were an attempt to avoid negative consequences

Ⓓ By arguing that older children can grasp complex issues of morality and behave accordingly

4 ☐ Mark for Review

Gwo ka refers to both a family of hand drums and the music played by these drums. Gwo ka's originated from the vocal technique bouladjèl, which was initially used by seventeenth century Guadeloupeans to imitate drums in their traditionally African songs and dances. Gwo ka emerged when French influence on Guadeloupe led to the incorporation of two hand drums into bouladjèl performances. Today, additional instruments such as a wider variety of drums and even the electric bass can be used in gwo ka music, but the same fundamental seven drum beats that defined the genre are still part of each composition.

What does the text indicate about the development of gwo ka?

Ⓐ Gwo ka would have stayed in its traditional form if there had not been French influence on Guadeloupe.

Ⓑ Gwo ka is indistinguishable from traditional bouladjèl performances.

Ⓒ Gwo ka united multiple cultures through a celebration of diverse musical styles.

Ⓓ Modern gwo ka has expanded beyond the hand drum but still bears similarities to traditional gwo ka.

5 ☐ Mark for Review

The Johnstown Inclined Plane was completed in 1891 in Pennsylvania, allowing passengers to travel nearly 900 feet up or down a 71% grade hill in under two minutes. This funicular, or mountain railway, was inspired by a devastating flood in 1889 during which it had been difficult to evacuate residents of Johnstown, which lies at bottom of a valley. After the railway's completion, citizens were able to be evacuated safely and efficiently in similar floods in both 1936 and 1977. The Inclined Plane also helped economically, as easy access to hillside communities facilitated both more frequent tourism and local commerce.

Which choice best states the main idea of the text?

(A) The creation of the Johnstown Inclined Plane in the late nineteenth century inspired others to create similar mountain railways.

(B) The completion of the Johnstown Inclined Plane in the late nineteenth century provided multiple benefits to those who lived nearby.

(C) The convenience of the Johnstown Inclined Plane in the late nineteenth century made it the only practical way to visit the valley.

(D) The popularity of the Johnstown Inclined Plane in the late nineteenth century sparked the founding of more hillside communities.

6 ☐ Mark for Review

Although the term "mineral" is used to indicate a compound of inorganic matter, mineralogists debate whether or not the definition as currently constituted adequately covers biogenic—that is, created by living organisms—minerals such as calcite. H. A. Lowenstam and Brian Skinner have contributed to this debate by applying high-resolution genetics and spectroscopy to more closely examine the relationship between minerals and organisms. Lowenstam and Skinner concluded that minerals created by living organisms should not be classified as wholly inorganic.

Which finding about calcite, if true, would most directly support Lowenstam and Skinner's conclusion?

(A) It is marked by streaks that could have been created by organic or inorganic matter.

(B) Its size and structure imply that it is unlikely to have been formed by either immense pressure or water accumulation.

(C) Its spectroscopic analysis demonstrates that it contains remnants of organic matter that were integral to its formation.

(D) Its physical composition is consistent with formation processes often observed in inorganic matter.

7 ⎙ Mark for Review

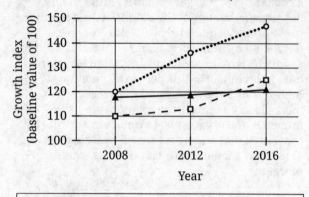

Plastic and Rubber Production, 2008–2016

Legend: total productivity, combined inputs, real outputs

Plastic and rubber production saw an increase in the later 2000s, but multiple factors must be considered to measure the actual performance of an industry. The most important of these is total productivity. Total productivity is calculated by dividing the real outputs (the value of the produced goods) by the combined inputs (labor, cost to produce the goods, emery required, etc.) The US Bureau of Labor Management tracked the production statistics of the plastics and rubber industry over an eight-year period, measuring growth in each category on an index with a baseline value of 100. It is commonly believed that the cost of combined inputs and value of real outputs correlate: for example, _____

Which choice most effectively uses data from the graph to complete the example?

Ⓐ the growth index increased from 2008 to 2012 for both combined inputs and real outputs.

Ⓑ the rise in real outputs slowed from 2012 to 2016.

Ⓒ total productivity and real outputs were higher than combined inputs in 2008.

Ⓓ the growth index for combined inputs was lower than 120 in 2008.

8 ⎙ Mark for Review

One explanation for why humans have phobias is that they are essentially learned behaviors that result from unpleasant experiences with certain objects or situations, especially in early childhood. In categorizing an object or situation as a phobia, the human mind seeks to protect itself from future exposure to the negative emotions brought on by that particular trigger. But some psychologists are quick to point out that strong phobic responses can also develop from objects or situations that an individual has never encountered. These phobias are called unconscious fears as the conscious mind has had no exposure to them. For instance, even though many lifelong city dwellers may have never encountered a snake, they may nonetheless have a severe fear of such a reptile. These observations suggest that _____

Which choice most logically completes the text?

Ⓐ unconscious fears are the result of the mind's natural tendency to develop strong phobic responses.

Ⓑ phobias may be caused by other methods besides exposure, depending on the circumstances.

Ⓒ people with unconscious fears tend to have had unpleasant experiences with the objects of their phobias.

Ⓓ people with no unconscious fears are unlikely to develop phobias in the future.

Summary

o The Reading questions on the PSAT 8/9 make up just over 50 percent of your Reading and Writing Section score.

o Reading questions are presented in order of difficulty (which resets with each question type), but because some question types may appear once, twice, or not at all on each module, it's important to rely on your POOD to pick up the points you can get; don't forget to guess on the rest!

o Reading is an open-book test! Use that to your advantage by focusing only on the text you need to get each point.

o After you read the passage, highlight the phrase or sentence that most addresses the question task. Annotate if you need to—sometimes, writing down a word or phrase will help you use POE more effectively.

o If you have more than one answer left after you eliminate the ones that don't match what you high-lighted and annotated, compare the remaining answers to see if any of them are **Opposite; Extreme Language; Recycled Language; Right Answer, Wrong Question; Beyond the Text;** or **Half-Right**.

o Tackle Dual Texts questions using the Dual Texts Basic Approach. Highlight the information, claim, or theory that both passages make a comment on and annotate the relationship between the passages.

o Tackle Charts questions using the Charts Basic Approach. Highlight the statement or claim in the pas-sage that uses as much terminology in the chart as possible. Always familiarize yourself with the chart first before reading any of the passage.

o Practice, practice, practice—with eight question types, most of which have 2–3 different formats, it can feel at first like it's too much to keep track of. But the more you use the Reading Basic Approach and see that it is the same steps every single time, the more comfortable you will be no matter what the PSAT 8/9 throws at you!

o Remember most of all to not let a question bog you down. If you find yourself stuck or running low on time, Mark and Move and skip around to questions with which you feel most comfortable. Make sure to enter an answer for every question, even those you decide not to try at all.

Question Types Review Chart		
Type	**Question Word**	**Common Question Phrasing**
Vocabulary	What?	• Which choice completes the text with the most logical or precise word or phrase? • As used in the text, what does the word X most nearly mean?
Purpose	Why or How?	• Which choice best describes the function of the X sentence in the overall structure of the text? • Which choice best states the main purpose of the text? • Which choice best describes the overall structure of the text?
Dual Texts	How?	• Based on the texts, how would X (Text 2) most likely respond to X (Text 1)?
Retrieval	What?	• According to/based on the text, what is true about X? • According to the text, why did X happen? • Based on the text, how does X respond to Y?
Main Idea	What?	• What is the main idea of the text?
Claims	Which?	• Which quotation from the poem most effectively illustrates the claim? • Which quotation from X most effectively illustrates X's claim? • Which statement/finding, if true, would most directly/strongly support X's claim/hypothesis/argument/prediction? • Which finding, if true, would most directly weaken/undermine X's claim/hypothesis/argument?
Charts	Which?	• Which choice most effectively uses data from the table/graph to complete the text/statement/example? • Which choice most effectively uses data from the table/graph to illustrate the claim? • Which choice best describes data from the table/in the graph that support X's suggestion/claim/hypothesis/conclusion?
Conclusions	Which?	• Which choice most logically completes the text?

Chapter 7
Rules Questions:
Introduction

After the Reading portion of each RW module, you'll see a set of questions that we call Rules questions. These questions test various punctuation and grammar topics, and rather than being grouped by topic the way the Reading questions are, these ones are in order of difficulty only. This means you'll see a mix of topics, and you may notice the questions getting harder from the first Rules question to the last one. In this chapter, you'll learn our basic approach for all Rules questions and how to identify when each topic is tested.

KNOW THE RULES TO FOLLOW

You've probably wondered at some point whether people are responsible for following laws that they don't know exist. Couldn't someone go to court and say, "Your Honor, I didn't know it was illegal to sing the national anthem incorrectly in Massachusetts!"? Of course, if we allowed this defense, every troublemaker would simply lie and pretend to be ignorant of whatever law has just been broken. As a result, we're all responsible for knowing the rules of our country, state, and local governments, even the ones that sound a little wacky (don't try to stop anyone from putting up a clothesline in Vermont).

Likewise, when it comes to the PSAT 8/9, if you want to score well on the Writing portion of the RW module, you won't be able to plead to College Board that you never learned grammar in school or that you didn't know that commas and semicolons aren't interchangeable. The good news is that the rules that are tested on the PSAT 8/9 are as good as laws. Learn them, follow them, and you won't metaphorically go to jail (get a low RW score, in this case). You won't be asked to choose an answer that merely seems, feels, or looks right. The right answer will be the one that follows the rules, and the three wrong answers will not.

In the real world, there are dozens or possibly even hundreds of rules that good writers follow (and sometimes break). Although you probably don't have to think about it now, at some point you learned to begin a sentence with a capital letter, end with a period, spell each word correctly, put the words in the correct order, and so on. You might assume that the PSAT 8/9 could test you on any of the countless writing rules, but in fact, only a small handful of these rules appear on the test. For instance, the PSAT 8/9 will never test you on capitalization, spelling, frequently confused words (like "effect" and "affect"), or being concise.

Instead of reading each passage and "proofreading" (looking for any possible errors), if you learn the relatively short list of rules that are actually tested, you'll save yourself a great deal of time and effort. In the following chapters, you'll learn every rule that could possibly be tested on the PSAT 8/9.

GIVE YOURSELF A HEAD START

Learning the grammar and punctuation rules is only one part (though it's a big one!) of being successful on Rules questions. As we discussed in the RW Introduction, the pacing strategy you use will play a big role in how many questions you are able to get right in the amount of time that you have. In addition, whenever you decide to do the Rules questions (which for most people should be relatively early on), you want to be able to get them right as efficiently as possible. Of course, the more comfortable you are with the punctuation and grammar rules, the faster you'll complete these questions. In addition, though, there's a strategy you can use for all Rules questions that will help you apply those rules more quickly:

> For all Rules questions, look at the answers to see what's changing and determine what topic is being tested.

Remember, you can easily spot Rules questions by their question stem: *Which choice completes the text so that it conforms to the conventions of Standard English?* But this question doesn't tell you whether the topic is verb tense, commas, or any other rule that is tested. Looking at the answers is key in identifying what topic is being tested, and that goes a long way toward getting you the correct answer in the shortest amount of time. If you see pronouns changing in the answer choices, then you know you don't need to waste time thinking about the punctuation and only need to look for the word the pronoun refers back to (more on that later). On the other hand, if only punctuation is changing in the answer choices, then you don't need to consider how the words could be rewritten, because you don't have the option to do that.

Just like how knowing what the question is asking allows you to focus on what you need for Reading questions, knowing what's changing in the answers before you read the passage on Rules questions lets you know what you do and do not need to consider as you're reading. In fact, you don't always need to read the entire passage for Rules questions. If the question is testing punctuation within a single sentence, you probably don't need to read the surrounding sentences at all. That's just one more way our strategy helps you save time!

Let's take a look at the basic approach for Rules questions:

Rules Questions Basic Approach

1. Look at the answers to see what's changing.
2. Apply the rules associated with that topic.
3. Use Process of Elimination.

Of course, you haven't learned any of the rules yet (at least not from us). But once you have worked through the next two chapters of this book, you should be able to identify what's being tested on each Rules question based on what's changing in the answers, apply the rules you've learned, and get the correct answer every time.

LET THE ANSWER COME TO YOU

You've already learned about the importance of Process of Elimination several times in this book. It's just as helpful for Rules questions as it is for Reading. Here's why: College Board may not write a sentence the way you'd like to write it. For example, you might think that a period should be used in a certain spot, but College Board might choose to use a semicolon instead. If you are looking for the answer with a period, you could make a mistake (pick an answer with a period without realizing it makes some other type of error) or waste time because what you are looking for doesn't appear in the answers. As you know from your own writing, there are often many different correct ways a sentence can be written and punctuated. Instead of looking for a specific word, phrasing, or punctuation mark, use the on-screen Answer Eliminator to cross off answers that do not follow the rules and choose the remaining answer that doesn't break any rule.

In the following drill, we've put answers to Rules questions without showing you the passage, so you won't actually be able to answer these questions. Try to identify what is changing in the answer choices. Don't worry if your answer isn't very specific—once you learn the punctuation and grammar rules and see more example questions, you'll have a better idea of what rule is being tested in each question. You'll see the full version of each question later, as you make your way through the next two chapters.

What's Changing in the Answers Exercise

1 ☐ Mark for Review

A was inspiring

B inspires

C have inspired

D has inspired

What's changing in the answers?

_____

2 ☐ Mark for Review

A its

B it's

C their

D they're

What's changing in the answers?

_____

3 ☐ Mark for Review

(A) found, on

(B) found on

(C) found. On

(D) found on:

What's changing in the answers?

_____

4 ☐ Mark for Review

(A) could cows survive on only one variety of grain.

(B) cows could survive on only one variety of grain.

(C) cows could survive on only one variety of grain?

(D) could cows survive on only one variety of grain?

What's changing in the answers?

_____

Answers to What's Changing in the Answers Exercise

1. verbs
2. pronouns and apostrophes
3. punctuation
4. punctuation (period versus question mark) and wording

Summary

o   Rules questions are not grouped by topic. They go from easy to hard regardless of topic.

o   Rules questions test a specific set of punctuation and grammar topics.

o   The topics are based on rules that you can learn and follow.

o   When you know you are dealing with a Rules question, look at the answers to see what's changing. This will allow you to get an idea of what topic you're being tested on before you read.

o   Use Process of Elimination to remove answers that don't follow the rules, rather than looking for something specific in the answers that may not be there.

Chapter 8
Rules Questions: Punctuation

Many of the Rules questions involve punctuation. In this chapter, you'll learn how punctuation and sentence structure can be tested on the PSAT 8/9 and the rules that will get you the correct answer every time.

FUN-CTUATION

If you have any feelings about punctuation, we suspect they might be described as confusion, dread, or apathy (a word that here means "not caring about punctuation at all"). We all know about ending a sentence with a period (or in some cases an exclamation mark or a question mark), but what about commas? How do you know whether a comma is needed or not? And what's up with those other weird punctuation marks like semicolons and colons? By the end of this lesson, you'll know the answer to all of these questions and much more. You might even start to find punctuation questions a little…fun! Okay, it's hard to describe anything about the PSAT 8/9 as "fun," but at the very least, we can say that these questions can become very easy. That's because College Board tests just a handful of rules over and over. As you learned in the Rules Introduction, there is not an unlimited list of topics for College Board to choose from. You only need to know the rules that are actually tested.

In the real world, there are many more ways punctuation is used that aren't tested on the PSAT 8/9. In fact, there are plenty of gray areas when it comes to punctuation. Have you ever written an email and debated whether to end a sentence with a period or with an exclamation mark? That's because either one can be acceptable, and the choice is a matter of personal preference as well as the tone you want to convey. There are lots of cases like this in the real world, where multiple ways of punctuating can be equally correct. The good news is that none of those gray areas are tested on the PSAT 8/9. If you find yourself wanting to pick one answer over another because it just *seems* better or *feels* right, you probably haven't learned the rules well enough.

GET ON WITH IT. GET ON WITH IT? GET ON WITH IT!

So, what are those rules? Let's start with how a sentence is constructed, which should be familiar to you. You are probably already aware that "running down the street" is not a complete sentence, but "she runs down the street" is. What's the difference? First off, the second one contains a subject, "she." In the second example, we know who did the running (it's okay that we don't know who "she" is—there's still someone doing the action), whereas in the first one there isn't any subject for the verb.

> Every complete sentence must contain a subject and a verb.

In some cases, a sentence needs more than just a subject and a verb. For instance, "the monkeys are" isn't a complete sentence. It has a subject (*monkeys*) and a verb (*are*), but it's missing the rest of the idea—what exactly the monkeys *are*. That being said, in the vast majority of cases, identifying whether an idea has a subject and a verb will be enough to tell you whether it's a complete sentence.

There's another reason that our first example ("running down the street") isn't a complete sentence. We know that it's missing a subject, but even if we add a subject, it still doesn't work: "she running down the street." That's because although it has a verb (*running*), that verb isn't in the right form to be **the** verb in the sentence—what we would call the main verb. It's tricky to define what a main verb looks like because there are many ways main verbs can appear, but when it comes to the PSAT 8/9, all you need to know is what verb forms can't be main verbs. Here's the rule:

> Any verb in the *-ing* or "to" form can't be the main verb in a sentence.

Even if you have never been told this rule before, you may find it quite obvious in the context of a sentence. Here are some examples:

> People <u>to listen</u> to music
>
> People <u>listening</u> to music
>
> People <u>listen</u> to music
>
> People <u>will listen</u> to music
>
> People <u>listened</u> to music

The first two examples aren't complete sentences because their verbs aren't in main verb form. The remaining three examples could be complete sentences (just add a period) because they each contain a subject and a verb in the correct form.

Now let's see how College Board tests this rule.

While attending a show with her brother, American poet Lorna Dee Cervantes was asked to participate; she chose to read from her poem "Refugee Ship," which depicts the dilemma of being a Chicano person torn between two cultures. As a result, Cervantes _____ much attention for her work, including features in numerous newspapers and magazines.

1 ☐ Mark for Review

Which choice completes the text so that it conforms to the conventions of Standard English?

- (A) having gained
- (B) to gain
- (C) gained
- (D) gaining

Here's How to Crack It

First identify the question category, which is Rules because it has the standard Rules question. Next, look at the answers to see what's being tested. Verbs are changing in the answers, so some verb topic is being tested. Find and highlight the subject of the verb: *Cervantes*. Look to see whether there is a main verb for that subject. There isn't, so the blank needs to provide the main verb. Eliminate any answers that aren't in main verb form. Choices (A) and (D) are both *-ing* verbs, so eliminate them. Choice (B) is a "to" verb, so it must be eliminated as well. Therefore, the answer has to be (C).

When you looked at the answers on the last question, you might have assumed that the question was testing tense. That might be the most obvious verb topic, but it's only one of three verb topics that College Board tests. We'll go over verb tense and another one, subject-verb agreement, in the next chapter. Here, though, the rule being tested is **verb form**. Although this obviously isn't a punctuation topic, it relates to whether something is a complete sentence or not, which affects the punctuation that can be used. It's in this chapter because for verb form you will need the same type of skills that you will need for punctuation questions, since they also relate to the structure of the sentence.

> ### How to Spot Verb Form
>
> The answers will contain verbs, including one or more *-ing* or "to" verbs.

Note that verbs such as "was driving" or "were listening" don't count as *-ing* verbs because the first part of the verb is in main verb form.

When verb form is being tested, the *-ing* or the "to" form can be correct, but only when the sentence already contains a main verb, since these verbs can't be the main verb in a sentence.

If you found the last question pretty easy, you'll be glad to see that the next topic may be just as simple. As you already know, every sentence must end with punctuation, namely a period, a question mark, or an exclamation mark. This next topic tests your understanding of when to use these end-of-sentence symbols.

Begun in 1907, the single-grain experiment escalated the advancement of modern nutritional science. In order to move forward with certain plans for agriculture, the team needed to explore an essential question: How _____

2 ☐ Mark for Review

Which choice completes the text so that it conforms to the conventions of Standard English?

(A) could cows survive on only one variety of grain.

(B) cows could survive on only one variety of grain.

(C) cows could survive on only one variety of grain?

(D) could cows survive on only one variety of grain?

Here's How to Crack It

If you know you are looking at a Rules question, then you know to look at the answers to see what's changing. In this case, it's the punctuation at the end of the sentence—periods versus question marks—and some slight variations in the word order at the beginning. The punctuation is likely the easier place to start, so look for a clue in the passage that will let you know whether you are dealing with a question or a statement. The sentence gives a very significant clue indeed: it says *the team needed to explore an essential question.* Highlight this phrase. The phrase is followed by a colon, so that *question* is what should come after. Therefore, the part that fills in the blank should be followed by a question mark. That means you can eliminate (A) and (B) using the Answer Eliminator. Next, compare (C) and (D). Choice (C) reads as *How cows could survive on only one variety of grain?*, which isn't a complete sentence. Therefore, (D) must be the answer.

If you're unsure why (C) doesn't work and (D) does, it's because the word order must be altered for questions. With statements, normally the subject comes before the verb—in this case, the subject is *cows* and the verb is *could survive.* So, (C) follows the structure of a statement, but it's supposed to be a question, so (C) doesn't work. With a question, the verb—or part of it, in this case—actually comes before the subject.

This topic should be easy to identify:

> **How to Spot Question versus Statement**
>
> The answers will contain phrases that end with periods, question marks, and occasionally an exclamation mark. The order of the words will slightly change as well.

You may be wondering about exclamation marks. Does College Board really test how excited the sentences should sound? The answer is...not really. While we have seen exclamation marks show up on this type of question (very rarely), when they have appeared, the phrase ending with an exclamation mark wasn't phrased correctly, much like (C) in question 2. We don't think you'll be asked to choose solely between a period and an exclamation mark since there isn't a strict rule about when to use one over the other.

For "question versus statement" questions, look for and highlight a clue in the passage that tells you whether the blank needs to be a question or a statement. Keep in mind that a question asks for information, while a statement gives information.

Let's take a look at another, more common way the PSAT 8/9 can test "end of sentence" punctuation.

In 1962, American biologist Rachel Carson published an influential book, *Silent Spring*, which warned about the dangers of pesticide _____ book sparked a nationwide debate about the use of chemicals in agriculture and helped to catalyze the modern environmental movement.

3 ☐ Mark for Review

Which choice completes the text so that it conforms to the conventions of Standard English?

(A) use. Her

(B) use her

(C) use, her

(D) use and her

Here's How to Crack It

After establishing that this is a Rules question, look to see what's changing in the answers. This time, it's the punctuation between *use* and *her*. Notice that (A) gives the option to use a period, separating this into two individual sentences. Read the full passage and determine whether that would work. The first part says *In 1962, American biologist Rachel Carson published an influential book, Silent Spring, which warned about the dangers of pesticide use.* This could be a sentence. The second part says *her book sparked a nationwide debate about the use of chemicals in agriculture and helped to catalyze the modern environmental movement.* This could also be its own sentence. Therefore, (A) works! Soon you will learn why (B), (C), and (D) can't work. For now, it's enough to understand that since these are both complete sentences on their own, they can be separated into two sentences. Therefore, (A) is the correct answer.

> You will need to read the words in the answers to judge whether something is a complete sentence. Ignore anything that doesn't appear in all four answer choices, like *and* in (D).

Believe it or not, even though the passage from the last question contained two complete sentences, there are other ways to punctuate these words besides making them two separate sentences. Here are some examples, all of which the PSAT 8/9 considers correctly punctuated and equally acceptable:

> In 1962, American biologist Rachel Carson published an influential book, Silent Spring, which warned about the dangers of pesticide <u>use; her</u> book sparked a nationwide debate about the use of chemicals in agriculture and helped to catalyze the modern environmental movement.

> In 1962, American biologist Rachel Carson published an influential book, Silent Spring, which warned about the dangers of pesticide <u>use: her</u> book sparked a nationwide debate about the use of chemicals in agriculture and helped to catalyze the modern environmental movement.

> In 1962, American biologist Rachel Carson published an influential book, Silent Spring, which warned about the dangers of pesticide <u>use, and her</u> book sparked a nationwide debate about the use of chemicals in agriculture and helped to catalyze the modern environmental movement.

Notice that none of those options appeared in the answer choices in question 3 since College Board decided to use a period and make two separate sentences. That's why your goal should be to eliminate the wrong answers to get the options down to the only one that can work, rather than look for a specific type of punctuation that may not actually appear in the answers.

> College Board will NEVER give you two punctuation options that are equally acceptable.

In the examples above, you can see that these two "complete sentences" can actually form a single sentence when they are connected with a semicolon, a colon, or a comma + *and*. In this case, we'll call each part of the sentence an *independent clause*. This is just another way of saying "complete sentence" that makes it less confusing when the two independent clauses are put together into the same sentence. You don't need to know this term for the test, but we'll be using it in the rest of this chapter. It should be pretty easy to remember because "independent" means that the clause can make a complete sentence on its own.

Besides separating the independent clauses into two sentences, both ending with a period, as you saw in question 3, here are some other ways two independent clauses can be punctuated:

Two independent clauses can be joined with…	Two independent clauses can NEVER be joined with…
• A semicolon, anytime ; • A comma plus an appropriate coordinating conjunction (FANBOYS) • A colon, if the second part of the sentence explains the first in some way :	• A comma without a coordinating conjunction • A coordinating conjunction without a comma • No punctuation to separate the independent clauses

As this chart implies, a semicolon can always be used to connect two independent clauses, at least when it comes to the PSAT 8/9. It functions just like a period, so both halves of the sentence must be independent clauses.

You can also use a comma + FANBOYS to link two independent clauses. FANBOYS stands for **F**or, **A**nd, **N**or, **B**ut, **O**r, **Y**et, **S**o. These are also known as coordinating conjunctions. Let's be clear, though—it's not just the comma or just the FANBOYS word. You must use both a comma and a FANBOYS word to connect two independent clauses. Of course, the specific word matters as well. For example, you can't use *but* if the two halves of the sentence don't contrast with each other. We don't expect this to be tested on the PSAT 8/9, however.

Lastly, a colon can be used when there are two independent clauses. A colon always signifies that the part after the colon will explain the first part of the sentence in some way. We'll talk more about colons later, but for now, understand that they represent another valid way to link two independent clauses.

It's just as important to understand how *not* to connect two independent clauses. Most questions with two independent clauses will have one of the options from the left column of the chart as the correct answer and all three of the options from the right column as the three wrong answers. So, if you can recognize these wrong answers, you'll be able to quickly eliminate them as soon as you realize you're dealing with two independent clauses. The rule is that two independent clauses can never be connected with a comma by itself, with a FANBOYS word by itself (remember, you need both!), or without any punctuation at all.

Now that we know the rules, let's see some examples of how this topic is tested.

National Women's History Month was first observed in the United States in 1987, after being designated by Congress the previous _____ this month-long observance serves to recognize and celebrate the contributions of women throughout history to the development and advancement of society.

Which choice completes the text so that it conforms to the conventions of Standard English?

- (A) year and
- (B) year,
- (C) year;
- (D) year

Here's How to Crack It

First, identify from the question that this falls under Rules. In that case, look to see what's changing in the answer choices: punctuation, including a semicolon and a FANBOYS word (*and*). This is a good sign that the question may be testing how to connect two parts of a sentence, so you want to look for independent clauses. Read up until the punctuation (ignore *and* since it's only in one answer choice): *National Women's History Month was first observed in the United States in 1987, after being designated by Congress the previous year.* That could be a sentence, so it's an independent clause. The second part of the sentence says *this month-long observance serves to recognize and celebrate the contributions of women throughout history to the development and advancement of society,* which is also an independent clause.

Therefore, the sentence contains two independent clauses. Eliminate any answers that can't connect two independent clauses: (A)—just the FANBOYS word, (B)—just a comma, and (D)—no punctuation. Thus, the correct answer has to be (C). Remember, there are other plausible ways of connecting these ideas, but there will be only one answer that follows the rules! Eliminate the wrong ones and you'll be left with the right one.

Cowboys relied on the chuckwagon to satisfy hearty appetites brought on by a life of wrangling cattle. Chuckwagons were open for breakfast and _____ lunch was traditionally eaten on the hoof from the cowboys' saddle bags as they rode through the Old West on horseback.

Which choice completes the text so that it conforms to the conventions of Standard English?

- (A) dinner
- (B) dinner, but
- (C) dinner but
- (D) dinner,

Here's How to Crack It

After identifying from the question that this is Rules, look at the answers to see what's changing. The only punctuation change involves commas, but there are also options with the FAN-BOYS word *but*, which suggests that this question could involve how to connect ideas. Look for independent clauses. The first part of the sentence says *Chuckwagons were open for breakfast and dinner,* which is an independent clause. The second part says *lunch was traditionally eaten on the hoof from the cowboys' saddle bags as they rode through the Old West on horseback,* which is also an independent clause. Therefore, (A), (C), and (D) can all be eliminated because they aren't possible ways to connect independent clauses. See how quick and easy that can be?

A group of neurobiologists led by Marco Gallio at Northwestern University conducted a study on fruit flies to investigate how hot temperatures induce _____ when neurons in the hot temperature circuit in the fruit fly's brain are activated, cells that promote midday sleepiness are also activated.

Which choice completes the text so that it conforms to the conventions of Standard English?

- (A) sleepiness:
- (B) sleepiness
- (C) sleepiness while
- (D) sleepiness,

Here's How to Crack It

You guessed it—confirm that this is Rules and look to see what's changing in the answers. In this case, the only answer that gives a big clue is (A). Colons relate to connecting ideas within a sentence, so that will let us know to look for independent clauses. The first part of the sentence says *A group of neurobiologists led by Marco Gallio at Northwestern University conducted a study on fruit flies to investigate how hot temperatures induce sleepiness,* which is an independent clause. The second part says *when neurons in the hot temperature circuit in the fruit fly's brain are activated, cells that promote midday sleepiness are also activated,* which is also an independent clause. Therefore, the sentence once again contains two independent clauses, so you can eliminate (B), which has no punctuation, and (D), which has only a comma, because those aren't valid ways to connect two independent clauses. Although we haven't yet gone over words like *while,* you may be able to identify that this is a contrast word. Do the two ideas contrast? No, they agree, so eliminate (C). Thus, (A) is the correct answer.

Many students wouldn't have wanted to pick (A) in question 6. That's why it's so important to know the rules. College Board considers this question to be harder than questions 3, 4, or 5. But if you know the rules from the chart on page 188, this question is equally easy for you, and it can be done quickly as well. Although you may not use many colons in your own writing, it's important to know that a colon is a valid way of connecting two independent clauses when the second one expands on the first, as it does here. As always, though, POE gets us there.

There is one more thing to know about colons. While a colon *can* connect two independent clauses, it doesn't have to. The second part of the sentence doesn't have to be an independent clause: it could be a list or a definition based on the first part of the sentence. Here's the rule:

> The part before the colon must be an independent clause. The part after the colon can be but doesn't have to be.

Let's see another example of a question that involves colons.

Hypothesized to form beneath the surface of giant ice planets, diamond rain, a type of precipitation composed of hydrogen and carbon, has been observed in an experiment that mimicked the conditions of the cores of such planets. To create the model for those laboratory conditions, the researchers selected two planets that the appropriate temperatures and pressures were _____ Neptune and Uranus.

7   🔖 Mark for Review

Which choice completes the text so that it conforms to the conventions of Standard English?

(A) found, on

(B) found on

(C) found. On

(D) found on:

Here's How to Crack It

This is Rules, based on the question, so look at the answer choices to see that punctuation is changing. Choice (C) puts a period after *found*, so check whether this could be two separate sentences. Right away you might realize that the second part, *On Neptune and Uranus,* can't be its own sentence because it doesn't have a subject or a verb, so eliminate (C).

Next, notice that (D) uses a colon, so see whether that could work. The first part of the sentence then says *To create the model for those laboratory conditions, the researchers selected two planets that the appropriate temperatures and pressures were found on.* That's an independent clause, so this meets one requirement for using a colon. Does the second part of the sentence elaborate on the first? Yes! It lists what the *two planets* were. Thus, this is an appropriate use of a colon, and the answer is (D).

As for (A), you don't want to put a comma between *found* and *on* because *found on* is part of the same thought in this sentence. Choice (B) doesn't work because this makes the whole sentence into a single idea, which ends up making the whole thing not a complete sentence.

When you see periods, semicolons, and/or colons in the answers, that's your sign to look for independent clauses and see whether any of these options would work.

COMMON

How to Spot Connecting Independent Clauses

The answers will contain one or more of the following: a period, a semicolon, a colon, a comma + FANBOYS.

One more related topic has to do with **dependent clauses**. A dependent clause is what it sounds like: a clause that can't stand on its own. It *depends* on an independent clause in order to form a complete sentence. Here are some examples of dependent clauses:

while we ate sandwiches

because we ran out of peanut butter

though I don't like onions

when you eat a peanut butter and onion sandwich

Notice that each of these begins with a transition word, which we've underlined. The rest of the clause, after the underlined word, would be an independent clause since it contains a subject and a verb. So, a dependent clause is like an independent clause but with one of these words tacked onto the front. Let's see how we can make a sentence with these:

While we ate sandwiches, we debated whether straws have one hole or two.

We had to stop by the store because we ran out of peanut butter.

I could eat peanut butter with a spoon, though I don't like onions.

When you eat a peanut butter and onion sandwich, you won't be too happy about it.

As you can see, it's possible for a dependent clause to go either before or after the independent clause. If the dependent clause comes first, it should be followed by a comma. If the dependent clause comes second, a comma should be used if there is a contrast (like the third example above). If there isn't a contrast and the dependent clause comes second in the sentence, there usually isn't a comma (like the second example above), but this is somewhat of a gray area, so we think College Board won't test this.

While they may look very different from one _____ and sapphires are both varieties of corundum—a mineral form of aluminum oxide in which the color is determined by the presence of different kinds of transition metal impurities.

8 Mark for Review

Which choice completes the text so that it conforms to the conventions of Standard English?

(A) another; rubies

(B) another. Rubies

(C) another, rubies

(D) another rubies

Here's How to Crack It

The question tells us that this is Rules, so look to see what's changing in the answers. There is a semicolon and a period, so look for independent clauses. The first part of the sentence says *While they may look very different from one another*. This isn't an independent clause—it couldn't be its own sentence. That eliminates (A) and (B) because both a semicolon and a period are used to connect two independent clauses. If you recognize that this is a dependent clause, since it begins with *While*, then you can identify that there should be a comma after the dependent clause. Thus, eliminate (D) and choose (C).

> If both a semicolon and a period appear in the answers, neither could be correct because they perform the same function.

Dependent clauses aren't tested often, but they occasionally show up on the test. They'll look like the independent clause questions that we just went over, so keep an eye out for dependent clauses in those questions as well.

Before moving on, try the following exercise to review the rules you just learned.

Connecting Clauses Exercise

Instructions: Mark whether each combination is possible or not possible. Answers are on page 204.

		Possible	Not Possible
1.	Independent Clause; Independent Clause.	_____	_____
2.	Independent Clause, Independent Clause.	_____	_____
3.	Independent Clause. Independent Clause.	_____	_____
4.	Independent Clause: Independent Clause.	_____	_____
5.	Independent Clause **and** Independent Clause.	_____	_____
6.	Independent Clause Independent Clause.	_____	_____
7.	Independent Clause, **but** Independent Clause.	_____	_____
8.	Independent Clause: List.	_____	_____
9.	Non-Independent Clause: List.	_____	_____
10.	Dependent Clause, Independent Clause.	_____	_____
11.	Independent Clause, Dependent Clause.	_____	_____
12.	Independent Clause; Dependent Clause.	_____	_____

Next we'll take a look at a few more punctuation topics that could be tested.

EVEN MORE FUN-CTUATION

To illustrate this next rule, we're going to begin with a very basic sentence:

Rahul Viswanathan described the book as dull.

There's nothing wrong with this sentence, but we might have some questions. Who's Rahul, and why should we care about his opinion? And what book are we talking about anyway? Let's add some additional information:

Literary critic Rahul Viswanathan described the book, a 500-page explanation of the machines used in early textile factories, as dull.

Now we know a bit more. The phrase *Literary critic* is a title or label for Rahul (so we now know that his opinion might actually be worth listening to). Notice that we don't put any punctuation before or after his name. You can think of this title or label like an adjective. When you write "the purple sock," you don't put a comma between "purple" and "sock," so don't put any punctuation here either.

> Titles or labels before names don't get punctuation.

We also added a describing phrase set off by commas. This describing phrase tells us a little more about the book. We do need to set it off from the rest of the sentence with punctuation, though—either with two commas, as we did in the example, or with two dashes (two parentheses can also be used in some cases). We call these describing phrases **Extra Information**. They aren't absolutely essential to the meaning of the sentence, so we need to separate them with matching punctuation before and after. Extra Information won't always be in this form, but it's worth noting that describing phrases beginning with "a"/"an" or "the" are always Extra.

> Extra Information should be separated from the rest of the sentence with either commas or dashes, both before and after.

Obviously, if the Extra phrase comes at the beginning or end of the sentence, it will only have one comma or dash. Let's see an example of how this topic could appear on the test.

Pearl S. Buck was an American novelist and teacher who spent most of her life in China. Her novel *The Good Earth,* a historical fiction novel about life in a Chinese village in the early 20th _____ drew upon Buck's own observations of village life while living in Zhenjiang, China.

---

9 ☐ Mark for Review

Which choice completes the text so that it conforms to the conventions of Standard English?

(A) century;

(B) century,

(C) century

(D) century—

Here's How to Crack It

Note that this is a Rules question, so look to see what's changing in the answers. In this case, there is a semicolon, so check whether there are two independent clauses. Neither side of the semicolon is an independent clause, so eliminate (A). Next, note that (D) has a dash. This is a good clue that the question could be testing describing phrases. Identify that the subject of the sentence is *novel* and the verb is *drew*. In between the subject and the verb is a phrase set off by a comma: *a historical fiction novel about life in a Chinese village in the early 20th century.* Because this phrase has a comma before it, it must have a second comma after it to show that it is Extra. Thus, the answer has to be (B).

It's worth noting that you can never have a single punctuation mark between a subject and its verb—that wouldn't be a complete sentence. The original sentence has this, which suggests that a second punctuation mark is needed to show that the phrase is Extra. And since the phrase has a comma before, it must have a second comma after—and not a dash. If it had had a dash before, it would need to have another dash after.

Sometimes there are describing phrases that *are* essential to the sentence's meaning. We call these phrases **Specifying Information.** In fact, you saw this in the previous example:

> Literary critic <u>Rahul Viswanathan</u> described the book, *a 500-page explanation of the machines used in early textile factories,* as dull.

The critic's name is Specifying Information. If we remove his name from the sentence, it reads *Literary critic described the book...*, which doesn't work because *Literary critic* doesn't refer to a specific person and can't be the subject of the sentence. His name specifies which literary critic we're talking about, so that's why it's Specifying Information. Specifying Information isn't separated by any punctuation and is essential to the meaning of the sentence.

If you see this rule tested and you need to determine whether a phrase is Specifying or Extra, try removing the phrase from the sentence. If the sentence still has the same meaning and still works without the phrase, it's Extra and should be set off with punctuation. If the sentence changes its meaning or doesn't work without the phrase, it's Specifying and shouldn't be separated with punctuation.

How to Spot Extra/Specifying Information

One or more answers will contain a dash, or only commas will change in the answers, but they will move around a specific phrase.

Try the following exercise to practice determining whether a phrase is Specifying (and therefore shouldn't have punctuation) or Extra (and should have punctuation). But keep in mind that many questions, like question 9, won't require you to decide because there will be a clue in the sentence.

Describing Phrases Exercise

Instructions: Determine whether the bolded phrase is Specifying or Extra and write your answer on the line. If it's Extra, add punctuation. Answers are on page 204.

1. The person **who wrote the book we just read** spoke in my English class. _____

2. We recently watched the movie ***Back to the Future.*** _____

3. The play **a drama about the Cold War** was a bit long. _____

4. Eating pizza **with pineapple** is considered controversial. _____

5. **Running around** the kids almost bumped into each other. _____

6. Cryptozoology **the study of mythical creatures** has been called a pseudoscience. _____

The next punctuation topic is Lists. You are most likely familiar with how to write a basic list. Here's an example:

> *My favorite singers are Taylor Swift, Olivia Rodrigo, and SZA.*

Because this is a list of three or more items, the list is separated by commas. Additionally, this type of list needs to have the word *and* or sometimes the word *or* before the last item in the list. If this type of basic list is tested on the PSAT 8/9, just follow those simple rules. However, sometimes College Board might throw a more difficult type of list at you. Let's see an example:

> *My favorite singers are Taylor Swift, who was born in Pennsylvania; Olivia Rodrigo, who was born in California; and SZA, who was born in Missouri.*

In this case, we're adding an additional detail about each singer, and that detail is Extra Information, so it needs to be separated with a comma. However, if we were to just add those additional commas, the list could be confusing because it could look like the additional details are part of the list. Instead, we use semicolons to visually separate the list items from each other, and the commas are used within the list items. Remember, semicolons are normally used only when the sentence contains two independent clauses. This is a second, separate use of semicolons. Keep in mind that the semicolons here are being used as a visual separation—they don't perform a structural function like they normally do.

> College Board doesn't test whether there should be a comma before the *and* or *or* near the end of a list.

Let's see how the PSAT 8/9 could test lists.

In 2012, the National Museum of Women in the Arts, the first museum dedicated wholly to artworks created by women, featured the exhibition *Royalists to Romantics: Women Artists from the Louvre, Versailles, and Other French National Collections*, which included pieces such as *Portrait of a Woman*, by Adélaïde Labille-Guiard, from _____ by Angélique Mongez, from 1841; and *Portrait of Jean-Baptiste Deburau*, by Arsène Trouvé, from 1832.

10 ☐ Mark for Review

Which choice completes the text so that it conforms to the conventions of Standard English?

(A) 1787; *Mars and Venus*

(B) 1787, *Mars and Venus*,

(C) 1787; *Mars and Venus*,

(D) 1787, *Mars and Venus*:

Here's How to Crack It

The question type tells us that this is Rules, so look for what's changing in the answers. In this case, the answers have commas and semicolons in different positions. We know that semicolons are usually used to link independent clauses, but if you look at the last part of the sentence, you may notice that the original sentence already has a semicolon and the part after it (*and Portrait of Jean-Baptiste Deburau, by Arsène Trouvé, from 1832*) isn't an independent clause. This suggests that the question must be testing lists with semicolons.

In that case, you want to highlight a complete list item, such as the last one, which begins after the word *and*. Then, write an annotation of what appears in that item. In this case, there's a title, then a comma, then a person's name, then another comma, then a year. So, write an annotation saying "title – comma – name – comma – year." Use this to do Process of Elimination beginning at the start of the first item. The sentence contains the title, a comma, a name, a second comma, and then the beginning of the year. That's it for each item, so after the year there should be a semicolon, since this item is finished and we're moving on to the second list item. Eliminate (B) and (D) because they don't have a semicolon after the year. Next, do it again with the second item. The answer contains the title, and according to our annotation, the title should be followed by a comma. This eliminates (A), so the answer has to be (C).

As you can see, questions involving complex lists can be tricky. Using this strategy should help a lot. It's worth noting that in some cases the list items may not be parallel. For instance, only one item could contain a comma (in which case the list items are still separated with semicolons). If that happens, you'll just have to use Process of Elimination and be careful.

How to Spot Lists

The answers will likely contain commas and semicolons. The original sentence will have the word *and* or *or* toward the end, especially after a comma or a semicolon.

We have one more punctuation topic to go over, and the good news is, in a way, you already know the rules for it. That's because this last topic is "no punctuation." Sometimes, College Board will give you the option to put punctuation in a place that simply has no reason for punctuation. In that case, pick the answer without punctuation. It's a perfectly legitimate option, but be sure to first go through the rules from this lesson to ensure that there isn't a reason to use punctuation.

If there isn't a reason to use punctuation, don't use any!

Puerto Rican scholar and activist Miriam Jiménez Román and her husband Juan Flores co-edited the *Afro-Latin@ Studies Reader: History and Culture in the United States*, a collection _____ memoirs, interviews, essays, short stories, and poetry that was an important contribution to the field of Afro-Latino studies.

11 ☐ Mark for Review

Which choice completes the text so that it conforms to the conventions of Standard English?

Ⓐ of:

Ⓑ of

Ⓒ of—

Ⓓ of,

Here's How to Crack It

Use the question to identify that we're dealing with Rules. That means you need to look at the answers to see what's changing. In this case, there are a few different punctuation symbols, and there's no clear indication of what topic is being tested. Try reading the sentence to see whether it may involve connecting independent clauses, describing phrases, or another punctuation topic from this lesson.

When you read the sentence, you will probably notice that we don't want to put any punctuation here: "a collection of memoirs" is a phrase that should be kept together, not split up. It's also possible to go through the rules for colons, dashes, and commas to see whether any of these symbols can be used. There isn't any rule that applies in order to use any of these, so (A), (C), and (D) can be eliminated, and the answer must be (B), the "no punctuation" option.

A NOTE ABOUT IDENTIFYING QUESTION TYPES

Throughout this lesson, we have given you some tips for how to identify when each punctuation topic is being tested. Knowing whether you should look for independent clauses, a list, or a describing phrase can make you more efficient at answering these questions. That being said, there are cases in which you may look at the answers and not be sure which punctuation topic is being tested. In that case, just read the sentence to determine what the topic is. The tips in this chapter should help a lot, but they won't cover every single way a question can be tested.

A NOTE ABOUT SCRATCH PAPER AND ONLINE TOOLS

You may have noticed that we aren't advising you to highlight or annotate for many punctuation questions. Remember, you can't highlight in the answer choices, so if you wanted to do something like highlight independent clauses, you wouldn't necessarily be able to do that because you would need one or more words from the answers. That being said, if you find any additional highlighting and annotating to be helpful, we certainly wouldn't discourage you from using those tools. Furthermore, while we aren't promoting the use of scratch paper on RW because we think the online tools are sufficient, if you prefer to use pencil and paper, go right ahead. Learning the rules is nonnegotiable, but do what works for you when it comes to the methods you use to apply them.

CONCLUSION

You have now learned all of the punctuation rules that could be tested on the PSAT 8/9 (except for apostrophes, which will be covered in the next lesson). On the following drill, see if you can identify the rules being tested based on what you see in the answers. You won't be able to every time, but in many cases you should at least be able to come up with a good guess for what the punctuation topic is when you see punctuation changing in the answer choices. Remember, punctuation on the PSAT 8/9 is completely rule-based. Make it your goal to master the rules from this chapter and use them every time. When you are eliminating answers or choosing a correct answer, ask yourself what the reason is based on these rules.

Punctuation Drill

Time: 12 minutes. Note that these questions have been placed in order of difficulty, as they will appear on the test, although on the test they will be interspersed with grammar questions. Check your answers in Part IV.

---

1 ☐ Mark for Review

Scientists have recently discovered the fossilized remains of a giant ancestor of the otter. This otter would have lived around the same time as one of humans' earliest ancestors, australopithecines, and, unlike modern otters, does not appear to have been aquatic. Geochemist Kevin Uno and his team analyzed the fossilized tooth enamel to determine what food sources _____ The team found that land-based animals, rather than aquatic ones, made up the otter's diet.

Which choice completes the text so that it conforms to the conventions of Standard English?

(A) the otter likely ate?

(B) the otter likely ate.

(C) did the otter likely eat?

(D) did the otter likely eat.

---

2 ☐ Mark for Review

American educator Laura Owens blends old-fashioned and contemporary techniques to create large works based on historical artifacts. One of her most famous pieces portrays newspaper stereoplates from World War II that she found under the siding of her home, _____ traditional oil painting with modern digital image editing.

Which choice completes the text so that it conforms to the conventions of Standard English?

(A) combines

(B) combining

(C) combined

(D) to combine

---

3 ☐ Mark for Review

Althing, Iceland's parliament, traces its roots back to 930 CE. In medieval Iceland, the island's free male residents would meet at a designated outdoor assembly place to settle legal _____ approve new laws, and listen to a speaker recite a list of all existing laws from memory.

Which choice completes the text so that it conforms to the conventions of Standard English?

(A) disputes:

(B) disputes,

(C) disputes;

(D) disputes

4 ☐ Mark for Review

Soil acidification, the reduction of soil pH, can occur due to natural causes, such as the breakdown of rock surfaces by lichen and _____ it can also be caused by human activities, such as pollution and agriculture.

Which choice completes the text so that it conforms to the conventions of Standard English?

(A) algae. Though

(B) algae, though

(C) algae; though

(D) algae: though

5 ☐ Mark for Review

In the late 19th century in western Europe, plover eggs were a luxurious food _____ and fetched high prices during nesting season.

Which choice completes the text so that it conforms to the conventions of Standard English?

(A) item:

(B) item,

(C) item

(D) item;

6 ☐ Mark for Review

Since 2015, Sea Shepherd Conservation Society has been working to protect the vaquita marina, the world's most endangered marine mammal, through Operation Milagro, a campaign aimed at removing illegal gillnets in the Upper Gulf of California, where the vaquitas are _____ these efforts, the vaquita population continues to decline, and there are currently estimated to be fewer than 20 individuals left.

Which choice completes the text so that it conforms to the conventions of Standard English?

(A) found, despite

(B) found despite

(C) found. Despite

(D) found but despite

7 ☐ Mark for Review

While running the experimental school Visva-Bharati University, which blended Indian and Western traditions, Bengali writer Rabindranath Tagore continued his writing career, bringing Bengali literature to the world through multiple works—*Gitanjali* (*Song Offerings*), *Gora* (*Fair-Faced*) and *Ghare-Baire* (*The Home and the* _____ that explored love, politics, and philosophy.

Which choice completes the text so that it conforms to the conventions of Standard English?

(A) *World*)

(B) *World*,)

(C) *World*)—

(D) *World*),

8 ☐ Mark for Review

The denomination effect, proposed in 2009 by business and marketing professors Priya Raghubir and Joydeep Srivastava, states that consumers are less likely to spend money in larger cash denominations than in smaller ones, even when the dollar amounts are _____ this theory was developed over the course of three studies, including one in which participants were given different denominations of currency and presented with the option to use that currency to buy candy.

Which choice completes the text so that it conforms to the conventions of Standard English?

(A) equivalent and

(B) equivalent

(C) equivalent,

(D) equivalent;

9 ☐ Mark for Review

The Kansas City preventive patrol experiment, conducted over a one-year period in the early 1970s and designed to determine the effects of adjusting the number of visible police on patrol, yielded some surprising _____ changing the level of patrol did not significantly affect the frequency of certain crimes (such as robberies, burglaries, and vandalism), the rate at which crimes were reported, or fear of crime.

Which choice completes the text so that it conforms to the conventions of Standard English?

(A) findings,

(B) findings but

(C) findings:

(D) findings

10 ☐ Mark for Review

Zero waste is a movement that focuses on repurposing or reusing all products to achieve waste prevention. Zero waste goes beyond reducing, reusing, and _____ it also looks at how distribution and production systems can be restructured to reduce waste.

Which choice completes the text so that it conforms to the conventions of Standard English?

(A) recycling, however;

(B) recycling; however,

(C) recycling, however,

(D) recycling however,

Answers to Connecting Clauses Exercise

1. **Possible**—a semicolon is used to connect two independent clauses.
2. **Not possible**—a comma by itself can never connect two independent clauses.
3. **Possible**—independent clauses can stand on their own as sentences.
4. **Possible**—a colon can link two independent clauses if the second one elaborates on the first.
5. **Not possible**—a FANBOYS word without a comma can't connect two independent clauses.
6. **Not possible**—it's never allowed to put two independent clauses together without any punctuation.
7. **Possible**—a comma + FANBOYS can connect two independent clauses.
8. **Possible**—a colon can be used when the first part is an independent clause and the second part is a list that expands on that clause.
9. **Not possible**—a colon can only be used when the first part is an independent clause. Plus, every sentence must have at least one independent clause.
10. **Possible**—when a dependent clause comes before an independent clause, a comma should be used.
11. **Possible**—when a dependent clause comes after an independent clause, a comma is often used.
12. **Not possible**—a semicolon links two independent clauses, so it can't be used with a dependent clause.

Answers to Describing Phrases Exercise

1. **Specifying**—without the phrase, the sentence says *The person spoke in my English class,* which loses the original meaning.
2. **Specifying**—without the phrase, the sentence says *We recently watched the movie.* Since there isn't only one movie in existence, this doesn't work. You can also think of *the movie* as a label for the movie name, and labels don't get punctuation.
3. **Extra**—this phrase should be separated by commas, dashes, or parentheses on both sides. Phrases starting with *a* or *the* are always Extra.
4. **Specifying**—without the phrase, the sentence says *Eating pizza is considered controversial,* which isn't the sentence's original meaning.
5. **Extra**—the sentence works without this phrase, and this phrase should be followed by a comma to separate this introductory information from the rest of the sentence so that it doesn't sound like it says "Running around the kids."
6. **Extra**—the phrase should be separated with commas, dashes, or parentheses on both sides. Phrases starting with *a* or *the* are always Extra.

Summary

o   Punctuation on the PSAT 8/9 involves a limited range of topics and is based around specific rules that you can learn and use on the test.

o   When verb form is tested, find and highlight the subject. Look for a main verb. If there isn't one, the blank must provide the main verb.

o   For question versus statement, highlight a clue in the passage that tells you whether the sentence with the blank should be a question (asking for information) or a statement (giving information).

o   Two independent clauses can each end with a period and be separate sentences. They can also be in the same sentence if they are connected with a semicolon, a colon, or a comma + FANBOYS.

o   FANBOYS stands for For, And, Nor, But, Or, Yet, So.

o   Two independent clauses can never be connected with just a comma, just a FANBOYS word, or no punctuation at all.

o   For colons, the second part of the sentence doesn't have to be an independent clause, but the first part does.

o   A dependent clause has a subject and a verb but starts with a transition word that makes the clause not a complete sentence. Dependent clauses are usually connected to independent clauses with a comma.

o   Specifying Information is essential to the meaning of the sentence and isn't separated with punctuation. Extra Information can be removed without changing the meaning of the sentence, and it's set off with commas, dashes, or parentheses.

o   A basic list uses commas between the list items. If one or more list items contains a comma within it, then the list items will be separated with semicolons instead. If the items are in a matching pattern, highlight a complete item and annotate what it includes.

o   All punctuation on the PSAT 8/9 is rule-based. Don't pick an answer with punctuation if you don't have a rule-based reason to use that punctuation. The option without punctuation is sometimes correct.

Chapter 9
Rules Questions: Grammar

Besides punctuation, Rules questions also test grammar. In this chapter, you'll learn to recognize and correctly answer all of the types of grammar questions that could appear on the PSAT 8/9.

THE WORDS CHANGE, BUT THE SONG REMAINS THE SAME

In the last chapter, we looked at what to do when the PSAT 8/9 is testing punctuation. In this chapter, we're going to look at what to do when the PSAT 8/9 is testing the parts of speech—mainly verbs, nouns, and pronouns.

Our basic strategy, however, has remained the same. As we saw in the previous chapter, when faced with a PSAT 8/9 Rules question, you should always

> Check what's changing in the answer choices and use POE.

Remember that the grammar questions and punctuation questions will be mixed up together in the Rules portion, organized from easy to hard.

As you will notice, throughout this chapter, we talk a lot about certain parts of speech, but we don't really use a lot of grammar terms. That's because we find that on the PSAT 8/9 grammar questions, there is really one main idea to keep in mind: **consistency**. Correct answers must be consistent with the rest of the sentence and the passage as a whole.

Let's look at some examples of how consistency relates to the grammar topics you can expect to see on the test.

VERBS

Mathematician John Nash's contributions to the field of economic theory _____ numerous games, or strategic simulations, that are meant to enrich our understanding of individuals' decision-making and interactions in various real-world spheres such as law, business, and political conflict.

1 ☐ Mark for Review

Which choice completes the text so that it conforms to the conventions of Standard English?

- Ⓐ was inspiring
- Ⓑ inspires
- Ⓒ have inspired
- Ⓓ has inspired

Here's How to Crack It

First, identify the question type. Since the question mentions Standard English, this is a Rules question. Next, look at the answers to determine the topic. The answers contain verbs, so this question is testing consistency with verbs.

As you saw on the verb form topic in the previous lesson, when you see verbs changing in the answer choices, the first thing to check is the subject of that verb. Look for and highlight the one-word subject—who or what is doing the action. Who or what has inspired *numerous games*? It might look like the subject is *economic theory* since that comes right before the verb. Or you might think the subject is *John Nash* since that's the person discussed in the sentence. However, the subject is actually *contributions*. It's his *contributions* that have inspired games. It's all about the meaning of the sentence—the sentence isn't saying that Nash himself inspired games and definitely not that *the field of economic theory* inspired games.

> The subject will almost always come before the verb, but it may not be right before. Watch out for describing phrases or other phrases in between.

After highlighting the subject, *contributions*, write an annotation saying "plural" because this word is plural. Since the subject is plural, the verb must also be plural in order to be consistent. Therefore, (A), (B), and (D) have to be eliminated because they're all singular. So, (C) must be the correct answer.

Thus, when you see verbs changing in the answer choices, check the subject first. Subjects and verbs need to be consistent with each other. You might assume that the question is testing tense when you see verbs, but as with this question, typically only one answer will agree with the subject when the question is testing subject-verb agreement. Therefore, our strategy saves you a lot of time since you don't have to consider tense on this type of question.

One more tip: if you're not sure whether a verb is singular or plural, try putting "they" (plural) and "it" (singular) before the verb to see which one agrees with it (for example, you would say "it inspires" and not "they inspires," so "inspires" is singular).

How to Spot Subject-Verb Agreement

The answers will contain verbs, and whether the verbs are singular or plural will vary (look for verbs that end in *-s* and those that don't, or differences such as "is"/"are" or "has"/"have"). It's likely that three answers will be plural and one will be singular, or vice versa.

MODERATELY COMMON

Try the following exercise to practice this topic further.

Subject-Verb Agreement Exercise

Instructions: Circle the subject of the underlined verb. Answers are on page 218.

1. The school down the street <u>has</u> three stories.

2. The new game, which came out last week, <u>seems</u> impossible to beat.

3. The dog chasing the cat <u>barked</u> loudly.

4. Musicians from the orchestra <u>will judge</u> our performances.

5. Nobody, especially not me, <u>wants</u> to take a field trip to the cactus garden in August.

Of course, sometimes tense will be tested. Let's see an example.

———————————————○———————————————

According to the legends of native Andean peoples, the first discoverer of the medication quinine was a feverish Andean man who was lost in the jungle. Suffering from malaria, he _____ from a pool of water at the base of a cinchona tree. His disease was cured, and he was able to pass on the knowledge of the tree's medicinal properties.

2 🔖 Mark for Review

Which choice completes the text so that it conforms to the conventions of Standard English?

(A) drank

(B) will drink

(C) has drunk

(D) was drinking

Here's How to Crack It

Identify the question type first. The question reveals that this falls under the Rules category, so look at the answers to see what's changing. Verbs are changing in the answer choices, so this is a grammar question testing consistency of verbs. The subject is *he*, so highlight that word. All of the answers work with that subject, so this question is testing tense, not subject-verb agreement.

Look for clues in the passage to determine whether past, present, or future tense is needed. The passage is about *the first discoverer of the medication quinine* and all of the verbs in the passage (*was*, several times) are in past tense, so some form of past tense should be used. Highlight the clues in the passage and make an annotation saying "past." Then, eliminate (B) because it's in future tense. Compare the remaining options. Choice (C), *has drunk*, would suggest that this person is still alive, which doesn't seem to be the case, plus it's not consistent with *was*, so eliminate (C). Choice (D) is past tense, but this tense describes an event in progress. The passage isn't saying that the man "was drinking" when something else happened, so eliminate (D). Choice (A), *drank*, is consistent with the other past tense verbs in the passage, and it's the correct answer.

How to Spot Tense

The answers will contain verbs, all of which agree with the subject and produce a structurally correct sentence.

MODERATELY COMMON

Note that verb form and subject-verb agreement questions will also have changes in tense. That's why you don't want to look for a question to have different tenses in the answer choices to know when tense is being tested. Instead, look for the features of verb form and subject-verb agreement questions—if those aren't there, then the question must be testing tense.

Verb Tense Exercise

Instructions: Highlight a clue in the sentence and circle the correct verb to match the tense that the clue indicates. Answers are on page 218.

1. People today rarely {leave | left | will leave} their homes without their cell phones.

2. Next week, the school {hosts | hosted | will host} a dance for the eighth graders.

3. I {see | saw | will see} that movie many years ago.

4. The friends {relaxed | were relaxing | relax} outside when the sky suddenly darkened.

5. Even if you {watch | watched | have watched} ten YouTube videos about World War II already, you will still need to take World History.

As you can see, verbs are all about consistency.

> When you see verbs changing in the answer choices, make sure those verbs are:
>
> - CONSISTENT with their subjects
> - CONSISTENT with other verbs in the sentence and surrounding sentences

Consistency applies across the grammar questions. Let's see another topic in which the idea of Consistency might help us.

PRONOUNS

What are pronouns? Pronouns are words that stand in for nouns. They make writing less repetitive because they prevent us from having to use the same nouns over and over. On the PSAT 8/9, you'll be tested on which pronoun agrees with the noun (or sometimes another pronoun) that it is referring back to. Let's see an example.

A group of researchers from Washington State University and Pacific Northwest National Laboratory created nanoparticles from shellfish remains and added them to cement samples. The resulting samples were up to 40% stronger, and it took an hour longer for _____ to set, making the reinforced concrete ideal for construction projects requiring long transport of materials.

3   🔖 Mark for Review

Which choice completes the text so that it conforms to the conventions of Standard English?

- (A) one
- (B) those
- (C) it
- (D) them

Here's How to Crack It

Start by identifying the question type: Rules. Next, look at the answers to determine what topic is being tested. Since pronouns are changing in the answer choices, the question is testing consistency with pronouns.

Since a pronoun refers back to a noun or another pronoun, determine who or what *took an hour longer...to set*. The sentence is about *The resulting samples*, so highlight the word *samples* and write an annotation saying "plural." Since the blank refers back to the *samples*, the pronoun must also be plural. Eliminate (A) and (C), which are both singular. Choice (B) is plural, but *those* isn't as clear as *them,* so eliminate (B) and choose (D), which is the best way to refer back to the *samples.*

A less common way that pronouns can be tested is with apostrophes. Let's see an example.

French and German scientists discovered that *Parhyale hawaiensis,* a species of shrimp-like crustacean, can regrow _____ legs if those legs are severed; the new legs are almost perfect replicas of the original limbs.

4 ☐ Mark for Review

Which choice completes the text so that it conforms to the conventions of Standard English?

(A) its

(B) it's

(C) their

(D) they're

Here's How to Crack It

Begin by identifying the category of question. Since it mentions Standard English, it's a Rules question. Next, look to see what's changing in the answer choices: pronouns. Therefore, the question is testing consistency of pronouns.

Identify who or what the pronoun refers back to. The sentence is talking about *Parhyale hawaiensis,* which it describes as *a species*, so the species should be referred back to using a singular pronoun. Highlight the name of the species and annotate "singular." Then, go to the answers. Choices (C) and (D) can be eliminated right away because they're plural. Compare (A) and (B). Choice (B), *it's*, means "it is." Do you want to say "it is legs?" No, you are trying to say that the legs belong to the crustacean. Therefore, (B) is wrong and (A) is right. The word *its* is the proper spelling of the possessive form of "it."

Here are the rules to keep in mind for pronoun questions:

Pronoun Rules

On the PSAT 8/9, "it" is always singular and "they" is always plural.

It's means "it is." *Its* means "belonging to it." *They're* means "they are." *Their* means "belonging to them."

Although you will often see pronouns such as *some*, *one*, *those*, *this*, and *you* on pronoun questions, they aren't likely to be correct. The correct answer is almost certainly going to be some form of *it* or *they*. Keep in mind that while in the real world we may refer to an individual or a company, for example, as "they," this pronoun should only be used to refer back to plural nouns on the PSAT 8/9.

How to Spot Pronouns

The answers will contain pronouns. They may contain apostrophes as well.

NOUNS

You just saw how apostrophes can be tested on pronoun questions. You'll also see apostrophes tested in a second, slightly more common way: with nouns. As you may recall from school, apostrophes on nouns are used to show possession. Here are some examples:

> *the toy belonging to the baby → the baby's toy*
>
> *the idea of the students → the students' idea*
>
> *the stories that people have → people's stories*

As you can see, when the noun is singular, like *baby*, you add an apostrophe + *s* to show possession. When the noun is plural and ends with -*s*, like *students*, you keep it plural and add the apostrophe after. And for irregular plurals like *people* (plural nouns that don't end in -*s*), they just get the usual apostrophe + *s*. Finally, keep in mind that only possessive nouns need apostrophes. In the third example, *stories* is plural, but it doesn't get an apostrophe because it's not possessive.

Let's see how College Board could test these rules.

American sculptor and architect Maya Lin is best known for her minimalistic yet poignant stone memorials. Consisting solely of _____ carved in black granite, the Vietnam Veterans Memorial was controversial at the time of construction but is now recognized as a solemn site of remembrance and as a model for other American monuments.

5 ☐ Mark for Review

Which choice completes the text so that it conforms to the conventions of Standard English?

- Ⓐ soldiers names
- Ⓑ soldier's names
- Ⓒ soldiers' names
- Ⓓ soldiers' names'

Here's How to Crack It

Use the question to identify that this is Rules. Then, look at the answers to see that apostrophes with nouns are changing. Read the sentence and start by determining whether the first noun is possessive. Do the soldiers possess anything? Yes, it's "their" names, so the first word should be possessive. Eliminate (A) because it's not possessive since it doesn't have an apostrophe at all. Next, determine whether the second word should be possessive. Do the names possess anything? No, it's saying that the memorial consists of names. There is nothing belonging to the names, so the second word shouldn't be possessive. Eliminate (D) because the apostrophe on the second word makes it incorrectly possessive.

Next, compare (B) and (C). You'll have to determine the appropriate placement for the apostrophe in the first word. Choice (B) is referring to a single soldier, while (C) is a plural possessive. If the sentence were referring to just one soldier, it would need to say "a soldier" or "the soldier," but it doesn't, so it must be *soldiers*, plural. This eliminates (B), so the answer must be (C).

> Only nouns can be possessed. A noun can't be possessive if the word after it isn't also a noun.

It's worth noting that in many cases you won't need to decide how the possessive is written (like what we had to do in choosing between (B) and (C) in question 5). That's why it's best to start with whether each noun is possessive or not and hold off on deciding exactly where the apostrophe should go.

UNCOMMON

How to Spot Nouns

The answers will contain a single noun or a phrase with multiple nouns. They will have apostrophes in different places.

MODIFIERS

Let's take a look at a type of question that students often have difficulty with.

The densest objects in the observable universe, _____ because they no longer produce enough energy to overcome the immense force of gravity acting on their matter.

6   ▢ Mark for Review

Which choice completes the text so that it conforms to the conventions of Standard English?

- (A) neutron stars' formation occurs when supergiant stars collapse

- (B) neutron stars are formed when supergiant stars collapse

- (C) the collapse of supergiant stars forms neutron stars

- (D) astrophysicists explain the formation of neutron stars as occurring when supergiant stars collapse

Here's How to Crack It

Look at the question to determine the category: Rules. Next, look at the answers to see what's changing. You'll probably notice right away that the beginnings of the answers (which you could call the subjects) are changing. Or, you might say that the order of the words changes. This is a big clue that the question could be testing modifiers—that's because this is the *only* question type on the PSAT 8/9 that looks like this. So while the phrasing of the answers might not necessarily tell you what's being tested, if you're familiar with the test, you'll know that modifiers are almost certainly the topic because no other question type looks like this in the answers.

What you want to do is look for a modifier, a describing phrase that often comes at the beginning of a sentence, followed by a comma. Did you spot it? At the beginning, the sentence says *The densest objects in the observable universe.* Highlight that phrase. What is it describing? Take a look at the subjects in the answers and use POE.

Choice (A) may look like its subject is *neutron stars,* but be careful. It's referring to those stars' *formation.* Could their *formation* be referred to as *objects*? No, so eliminate (A). Now, (B) should look pretty good because *neutron stars* could be *The densest objects in the observable universe.* Keep that one, but let's check the other options just in case. Choice (C) says the *collapse,* which couldn't be *objects,* so that option is out. Then, (D) starts with *astrophysicists,* who aren't *objects* (and it wouldn't be very polite to call them dense!). So, the answer must be (B). It's the only one that starts with something that could logically be called *objects.*

> Modifiers can appear elsewhere in a sentence, but College Board almost always puts them at the beginning of the sentence with a comma after.

For modifier questions, the toughest part is identifying the error. Once you've spotted it, all you need to do is eliminate answers that don't match with what the phrase is intended to describe.

Note that on modifier questions you may not even need to read the whole answer choice or the rest of the sentence. All that matters for these questions is whether the person or thing at the beginning of the answer choice could be described by the modifier. Only one answer will do that correctly.

How to Spot Modifiers

The answers will start with different subjects, or you may notice that the answers say something similar but have the words in a different order.

Modifiers Exercise

Instructions: Each sentence contains a modifier error. Highlight the modifier. Draw an arrow to what it is currently describing and circle what it is supposed to be describing. Answers are on page 218.

1. Screaming too loudly, the singer had to ask a few of the fans to quiet down.

2. With no fur and pink skin, I find the naked mole-rat strange to look at.

3. Printed in an incredibly small font, we struggled to read the assignment.

4. As high school students, the college-level exam was too challenging for them.

5. Don't play that song at the party that's over 10 minutes long.

> ## Consistency
>
> - When verbs are changing in the answer choices, make sure those verbs are consistent with their subjects and with other verbs.
>
> - When pronouns are changing in the answer choices, make sure those pronouns are consistent with the nouns or other pronouns that they refer back to.
>
> - When the subjects are changing in the answer choices, look for a modifier. The modifier must come as close as possible to the person or thing it's describing.

As we have seen in this chapter, when the PSAT 8/9 is testing grammar (i.e., any time the words are changing in the answer choices), make sure that those words are **consistent** with the rest of the sentence and passage.

Answers to Subject-Verb Agreement Exercise
1. school
2. game
3. dog
4. Musicians
5. Nobody

Answers to Verb Tense Exercise
1. **Clue:** today. **Answer:** leave
2. **Clue:** Next week. **Answer:** will host
3. **Clue:** many years ago. **Answer:** saw
4. **Clue:** when the sky suddenly darkened. **Answer:** were relaxing
5. **Clue:** already. **Answer:** have watched

Answers to Modifiers Exercise
1. **Modifier:** *Screaming too loudly.* It currently describes *the singer*, but it should describe *a few of the fans*.
2. **Modifier:** *With no fur and pink skin.* It currently describes *I*, but it should describe *the naked mole-rat*.
3. **Modifier:** *Printed in an incredibly small font.* It currently describes *we*, but it should describe *the assignment*.
4. **Modifier:** *As high school students.* It currently describes *the college-level exam*, but it should describe *them*.
5. **Modifier:** *that's over 10 minutes long.* It currently describes *the party*, but it should describe *that song*.

Grammar Drill

Time: 12 minutes. Note that these questions have been placed in order of difficulty, as they will appear on the test, although on the test they will be interspersed with punctuation questions. Check your answers in Part IV.

1 ▢ Mark for Review

With the goal of displaying how mundane and boring traditionally-considered-feminine household chores can be, Ghada Amer created a series of embroidered pieces showing women providing childcare, cooking, and cleaning. These pieces _____ well-known for exhibiting a new way to present art on canvases.

Which choice completes the text so that it conforms to the conventions of Standard English?

- (A) has been
- (B) is
- (C) are
- (D) was

2 ▢ Mark for Review

Founded in Mexico City in 1986 by Enrique Norten, the architecture firm TEN Arquitectos has grown to include over 70 members. The architects work on a wide variety of structures; _____ worked on residential and industrial buildings, landscapes, and cultural artifacts.

Which choice completes the text so that it conforms to the conventions of Standard English?

- (A) it has
- (B) he or she has
- (C) they have
- (D) any have

3 ▢ Mark for Review

200 million years ago, the Earth's continents existed as a single supercontinent, Pangaea, which broke up when the Atlantic Ocean formed due to the motion of tectonic plates. According to geophysicist Chuan Huang, over the next several hundred million years, the Atlantic Ocean _____ to expand until the Pacific Ocean disappears and a new supercontinent is created.

Which choice completes the text so that it conforms to the conventions of Standard English?

- (A) continued
- (B) will continue
- (C) has continued
- (D) is continuing

4 ▢ Mark for Review

During a pilgrimage through North Africa, Mansa Musa, the ruler of the Mali Empire in the 14th century, gave away enormous amounts of wealth. One of the _____ generosity was that the price of gold in Egypt dropped significantly and did not recover for twelve years.

Which choice completes the text so that it conforms to the conventions of Standard English?

- (A) effect's of the kings
- (B) effects of the kings
- (C) effect's of the king's
- (D) effects of the king's

5 ☐ Mark for Review

In an attempt to draw attention from listeners, many audio engineers have increased the volume of recordings as part of a trend known as the loudness war. Such recordings are often criticized because _____ sound quality is reduced in order to achieve greater volume.

Which choice completes the text so that it conforms to the conventions of Standard English?

- (A) its
- (B) it's
- (C) their
- (D) they're

6 ☐ Mark for Review

The first movies, produced in the late 19th century, displayed the novelty of a moving picture and were composed of single shots rather than _____ cut together to create a narrative as seen in modern film.

Which choice completes the text so that it conforms to the conventions of Standard English?

- (A) sequence's of scenes
- (B) sequences of scene's
- (C) sequence's of scene's
- (D) sequences of scenes

7 ☐ Mark for Review

Spark plugs emit across a small gap a bolt of electricity that _____ the fuel and air mixture in the combustion chamber, producing the power needed to put the pistons of an engine in motion.

Which choice completes the text so that it conforms to the conventions of Standard English?

- (A) was igniting
- (B) would ignite
- (C) ignites
- (D) ignited

8 ☐ Mark for Review

Considered the first organisms to have produced oxygen, _____ produce 20% of the oxygen in the Earth's atmosphere.

Which choice completes the text so that it conforms to the conventions of Standard English?

- (A) cyanobacteria's antennae harvest light for oxygenic photosynthesis and
- (B) the oxygenic photosynthesis requires light harvested by antennae of cyanobacteria, which
- (C) the antennae of cyanobacteria harvest light for oxygenic photosynthesis and
- (D) cyanobacteria use antennae to harvest light for oxygenic photosynthesis and

9 ☐ Mark for Review

The social contract theory states that a government's legitimacy to rule over its citizens _____ derived from the consent of the governed rather than from any external source.

Which choice completes the text so that it conforms to the conventions of Standard English?

(A) is

(B) were

(C) are

(D) have been

10 ☐ Mark for Review

Belarusian poet Valzhyna Mort studied at the State University of Linguistics in Minsk, Belarus, and American University in Washington, DC. Known for live performances of her poetry, _____

Which choice completes the text so that it conforms to the conventions of Standard English?

(A) *Poets & Writers* magazine has featured Mort on its cover.

(B) the cover of *Poets & Writers* has featured Mort.

(C) the magazine *Poets & Writers*'s cover has featured Mort.

(D) Mort has been featured on the cover of *Poets & Writers* magazine.

Summary

○ Grammar questions are all about consistency.

○ When verbs are changing in the answer choices, highlight the subject and annotate whether it's singular or plural. Eliminate answers that don't agree.

○ If the question isn't testing verb form or subject-verb agreement, it's testing tense. Look for clues about whether past, present, or future tense is needed and make an annotation, then use POE.

○ When pronouns are changing in the answer choices, highlight the word the pronoun refers back to and annotate whether it's singular or plural, then use POE.

○ When apostrophes with nouns are changing in the answers, consider whether each noun possesses anything and use POE.

○ When the order of the words or the subjects change in the answers, the question is testing modifiers. Look for and highlight a modifying phrase, then eliminate answers that start with something the modifying phrase cannot describe.

Chapter 10
Rhetoric
Questions

After all of the Rules questions, you'll see the last category of RW questions, which we call Rhetoric. You'll see Transitions questions, from easy to hard, and then Rhetorical Synthesis questions, from easy to hard. In this lesson, you'll learn how to approach both types of questions that fall into this category.

The last portion of each Reading and Writing module will include two types of questions: Transitions and Rhetorical Synthesis, in that order. We call these Rhetoric questions because they relate to the purpose or quality of the writing. These questions will not test your understanding of the rule-based punctuation and grammar topics. In fact, for these questions, all four answer choices will be or will produce complete sentences that are grammatically correct. Instead, you will need to consider the *content* of the writing and how the answers fulfill certain meaning-related or rhetorical goals. Let's take a look at the first type of question in this category.

A SMOOTH TRANSITION

Transition questions will be easy to spot. Let's look at an example.

Botanical historians theorize that ancient peoples in India first cultivated the bean plant known as true indigo (*Indigofera tinctoria*), the original source of indigo dye. Though Europeans initially resisted the import of the dye, as it was in direct competition with their own deep blue dye extracted from the woad plant (*Isatis tinctoria*), they eventually embraced indigo as the less expensive and more durable option. Today, indigo finds application in various spheres of everyday life. _____ indigo is the dye used to give blue jeans their iconic hue.

1 ☐ Mark for Review

Which choice completes the text with the most logical transition?

(A) Additionally,

(B) For example,

(C) Nevertheless,

(D) Likewise,

Like the question above, all transition questions will ask you the same thing: *Which choice completes the text with the most logical transition?* As soon as you see that question, you'll know you're dealing with a transition question. Let's take a look at the basic approach for transition questions and apply it to this one.

Transition Questions Basic Approach

1. Read the passage and highlight any ideas that support or contradict each other.
2. Make an annotation indicating whether the ideas surrounding the blank agree, disagree, or involve a time change.
3. Eliminate any answers that go the wrong direction. Then, use POE on any remaining options.

Here's How to Crack It

First, read the passage. For Transitions questions, the most important sentences will usually be the one with the blank and the sentence before (but use the surrounding sentences as needed). You want to look for something that this sentence and the one before have in common. They both mention *indigo*. The previous sentence says that *indigo finds application in various spheres of everyday life*, and this sentence says *indigo is the dye used to give blue jeans their iconic hue*. Highlight both of these phrases. They agree with each other, as the second one gives an everyday application of indigo, so write an annotation saying "agree."

Next, eliminate any opposite-direction transitions since you are looking to continue in the same direction. That means (C) is out because *Nevertheless* is an opposite-direction transition. The remaining answers are same-direction transitions, so next eliminate any that don't match the relationship between the sentences. *Additionally* is used to add another point, but this sentence isn't an additional point—it's emphasizing the point from the sentence before. Eliminate (A). *For example* is a good match because this sentence is giving an example of how indigo is used in *everyday life*, so keep (B). *Likewise* is used to provide a second example of something or to discuss another, separate thing that is similar to the last thing discussed. That isn't the case here because we're still talking about the same topic, so eliminate (D). Therefore, the answer has to be (B).

If you look at the sentence with the blank and recognize that it's an example, feel free to write down "example" in the annotation box in addition to "agree." Writing "agree," "disagree," or "time change" is all that is needed, but if you can identify more about the specific relationship, it's fine to write that down as well. Just be sure to check all four answers.

Let's try another example.

A *fest noz*, or night party, is a Breton traditional festival of dance and music. Celebrated for many years in the Brittany region of France, this festival became less popular in the mid-twentieth century. _____ the tradition was revived in the 1970s and now has gained international recognition.

---

2 ⬜ Mark for Review

Which choice completes the text with the most logical transition?

- (A) Likewise,
- (B) Moreover,
- (C) However,
- (D) Thus,

Here's How to Crack It

Start by highlighting ideas that relate to each other. The sentence before states that *this festival became less popular in the mid-twentieth century*. The sentence with the blank says it *was revived in the 1970s and now has gained international recognition*. These ideas disagree, so write that in an annotation. Next, eliminate any same-direction transitions: (A), (B), and (D). Choice (C) is the only opposite-direction transition, so it has to be the answer.

Let's try one more.

Jacopo Peri was a 16th-century Italian singer, instrumentalist, and composer. He is credited with creating what is considered the very first instance of opera, *Dafne*, in 1597. Peri composed the music, now mostly lost, as part of a production that was intended to be reminiscent of ancient Greek drama, which Peri believed was far superior to the art of his time. _____ in 1600, he wrote *Euridice*, the earliest opera that has survived, based on the myth of Orpheus, which would later serve as inspiration for Jacques Offenbach's *Orpheus in the Underworld*.

---

3 ☐ Mark for Review

Which choice completes the text with the most logical transition?

(A) Consequently,

(B) However,

(C) Specifically,

(D) Subsequently,

Here's How to Crack It

First, highlight any phrases that draw a connection. The second sentence states that Peri created *Dafne* in 1595, and the next sentence provides some details about it. Then, this sentence says that he wrote *Euridice* in 1600. Since this event happened later, the transition that should be used here is probably going to be a time-change transition. Thus, write "time change" in the annotation box and use POE. It's a good idea to consider all of the answer choices since there can be overlap with time changes and other types of transitions.

Choice (A) doesn't work because *Consequently* means "as a result." The passage doesn't draw any type of cause-and-effect relationship between the 1597 work and the 1600 work, so eliminate (A). *However* doesn't work because these ideas don't disagree. Choice (C) can also be eliminated because this sentence definitely isn't providing more specific information based on the sentence before. *Subsequently* is a time-change transition that means "after that" or "next," so it's a good match. Choice (D) is the correct answer.

READY, SET...SYNTHESIZE

Now let's move on to the other type of question in the Rhetoric category, the one that will appear at the very end of each verbal module: Rhetorical Synthesis. The word *synthesize* means "put together," so these questions are asking you to put together two or more bullet points in order to fulfill a certain rhetorical goal. Let's see an example.

While researching a topic, a student has taken the following notes:

- Xuan paper is a type of paper that originated in ancient China and is used for calligraphy and painting.

- Shengxuan, or "Raw Xuan," paper is not specially processed.

- This paper easily absorbs water, which causes the ink to blur.

- Shuxuan, or "Ripe Xuan," paper has potassium alum added to it.

- This paper has a stiffer texture and absorbs water less easily.

4 ☐ Mark for Review

The student wants to emphasize the differences between Shengxuan and Shuxuan paper. Which choice most effectively uses relevant information from the notes to accomplish this goal?

(A) While Shengxuan is not specially processed and easily absorbs water, Shuxuan contains potassium alum and absorbs water less easily.

(B) One type of Xuan paper has potassium alum added to it.

(C) Shuxuan paper has potassium alum added to it, resulting in a stiffer texture.

(D) Both Shengxuan and Shuxuan are types of Chinese Xuan paper.

Here's How to Crack It

First, identify the type of question. Rhetorical Synthesis questions are extremely easy to identify: they are the only question type to use bullet points instead of a paragraph. Then, like with all Reading and Writing questions, determine what the question is asking. Rhetorical Synthesis questions always contain the same question: *Which choice most effectively uses relevant information from the notes to accomplish this goal?* The key part to notice is *this goal*. You MUST read the sentence before the question to determine what the goal is.

Here, the stated goal is to *emphasize the differences between Shengxuan and Shuxuan paper*. Now, your impulse might be to read the bullet points to identify differences. However, we've found that you probably don't need to do this. Instead, highlight the task or tasks of the question and then go straight to the answer choices and eliminate anything that doesn't completely fulfill the task.

In this case, highlight *emphasize the differences between Shengxuan and Shuxuan paper* and make a mental note of what this means we're looking for. The answer must mention these two types of paper as well as *differences* between them. Any answer that doesn't do both of these things can be eliminated. Let's go to POE.

Choice (A) mentions both paper types and uses a contrast word, *While*, so keep it. Choice (B) doesn't mention either type of paper by name, so it can't work. Choice (C) mentions only one paper type, so that definitely can't be right. Choice (D) mentions both paper types, but there's no contrast or anything about *differences*. Thus, (A) must be the right answer. Note that you really didn't need to understand anything about these two types of paper or even what the differences are, as stated in (A). Choice (A) was the only answer that mentioned both things and used a contrast word. Most of the time, Rhetorical Synthesis questions are as simple as that!

Of course, all of this information is stated in the notes. But you didn't need to read them in order to get the answer, so don't waste your time!

———————————◯———————————

Here's the basic approach for these questions:

Rhetorical Synthesis Basic Approach

1. Read the question and highlight each goal that is mentioned.
2. Eliminate any answer choice that does not completely fulfill the goal or goals.
3. Read the bullet points to confirm the answer if needed.

It's very unlikely that you will see an answer choice that is inconsistent with what is stated in the bullet points. That is, you won't see the kind of wrong answers that you will see on the Reading questions—ones that could be arrived at through misreading or making assumptions. Instead, the wrong answers will simply not completely fulfill the goal or goals stated in the question. This is why you can save yourself some time by not reading the bullet points first; you generally won't need to prove that the information is supported. It's also worth remembering that these questions do NOT test you on punctuation, grammar, style, being concise, or any other Rules topics. Focus on the content of the sentence in each answer choice and how well it does or does not fulfill the goal or goals.

Let's try another one.

While researching a topic, a student has taken the following notes:

- Sea turtles dig holes in the sand on beaches in order to make nests for their eggs.
- Studying sea turtle nests can be limited to observing events on the surface of the sand.
- Making observations in the underground nests is difficult, but researchers are trying out new tools.
- TurtleSense is a new system that can be used to make observations in the nests.
- The system can measure temperature and motion within sea turtle nests.
- This information can be used to detect developmental activity patterns and possibly to predict when the turtles will emerge from a nest.

5 🔖 Mark for Review

The student wants to explain an advantage of TurtleSense. Which choice most effectively uses relevant information from the notes to accomplish this goal?

(A) Sea turtle nests can be observed using a system called TurtleSense, which measures motion and temperature.

(B) TurtleSense can be used as another way to make observations of sea turtle nests.

(C) TurtleSense, which can measure temperature and motion, can be used in the underground nests where it is more difficult to make observations.

(D) Researchers can make observations of sea turtles above the sand, but underground nests are more difficult to observe.

Here's How to Crack It

Once you've established that you're dealing with a Rhetorical Synthesis question, highlight the goal or goals in the question. Here, you should highlight *explain an advantage of TurtleSense*. The correct answer should be about *TurtleSense* (whatever that is) and provide an *advantage* (something good about it). Move on to POE.

Choice (A) mentions *TurtleSense*, but nothing described here is stated as being an *advantage*, so eliminate it. The same for (B). Choice (C) includes some of the same information as (A) and (B) but takes it a step further: by stating that TurtleSense can be used *where it is more difficult to make observations*, this answer actually provides an *advantage* of TurtleSense. Keep (C). Choice (D) doesn't mention *TurtleSense* at all, so it can't be right. This means the answer must be (C).

Let's try one more.

While researching a topic, a student has taken the following notes:

- The *tar* is an instrument from Azerbaijan.
- It is a long-necked string instrument.
- Its body is made from mulberry wood.
- Its neck is made from nut wood.
- Its tuning pegs are made from pear wood.

6 🔖 Mark for Review

The student wants to list the materials used to make a *tar* to an audience familiar with the instrument. Which choice most effectively uses relevant information from the notes to accomplish this goal?

(A) An instrument from Azerbaijan, the *tar* is made from a variety of woods.

(B) The *tar* is a long-necked stringed instrument made from mulberry wood, nut wood, and pear wood.

(C) The neck of a *tar* (a long-necked stringed instrument from Azerbaijan) is made from nut wood.

(D) The *tar* is made from a variety of woods: the body is made from mulberry wood; the neck, nut wood; and the tuning pegs, pear wood.

Here's How to Crack It

Identify that this is a Rhetorical Synthesis question, and then highlight the goal or goals in the question. In this case, you should highlight *list the materials used to make a tar to an audience familiar with the instrument*. Sometimes Rhetorical Synthesis questions may specify whether the audience is familiar or unfamiliar with something. If the audience is unfamiliar, the answer should explain who or what the person or thing is. If the audience is familiar, the answer should not do that. In this case, the answer needs to *list the materials used to make a tar*, and because the audience is *familiar with the instrument*, the answer shouldn't explain what a *tar* is. Let's go to POE.

Choice (A) explains what a *tar* is, which it shouldn't do because the audience is familiar. Furthermore, it doesn't *list the materials used* to make one. Eliminate (A). Be careful with (B). It does *list the materials*, but notice that it also describes what a *tar* is. The audience is *familiar with the instrument*, so the answer shouldn't do this. Eliminate (B). Choice (C) also explains what a *tar* is, so it's out. Choice (D) lists the materials and doesn't bother to explain what a *tar* is, since the audience is familiar with it. That's exactly what we wanted, so (D) is the answer.

CONCLUSION

While the term Rhetoric might have sounded scary initially, we hope you're feeling more confident now that you know how to approach the two types of questions in this category. Remember, you choose the order of questions—practice Rhetoric questions on the following drill and use the results to help determine when to attempt them.

Take a Breather
You've made it through the entire Reading and Writing section! Next up is Math, so feel free to take a break before diving in. Grab a snack, relax with a book, go for a walk—anything that will help you refresh before reviewing more content. Remember that study breaks can make you more productive, so don't deprive yourself of some needed relaxation time.

Rhetoric Questions Drill

Time: 12 minutes. Note that these questions have been placed in order of difficulty for each of the two question types, as they will appear on the test. Check your answers in Part IV.

---

1 ☐ Mark for Review

A whale fall occurs when a whale dies and its body sinks to the ocean floor, providing nourishment through multiple stages of decomposition. _____ scavengers, such as hagfish and sleeper sharks, eat the soft tissue. Second, animals inhabit the whale's bones and nearby sediments. Third, bacteria break down fat in the bones, releasing nutrients for mussels, clams, limpets, and sea snails.

Which choice completes the text with the most logical transition?

- Ⓐ Furthermore,
- Ⓑ First,
- Ⓒ Later,
- Ⓓ Additionally,

---

2 ☐ Mark for Review

Jeong Seon, a 17th-century Korean painter, broke with tradition by depicting landscapes that were realistic rather than imagined. _____ one of his most famous works, *Geumgang jeondo*, or "General view of Mt. Geumgangsan," was painted while the artist was facing the mountain and captures the details of the peaks.

Which choice completes the text with the most logical transition?

- Ⓐ Regardless,
- Ⓑ Nevertheless,
- Ⓒ For example,
- Ⓓ Additionally,

3 🔖 Mark for Review

The ancient art of lost-wax casting is a laborious process for making metal sculptures. First, a model of the object to be cast in metal is formed from wax. Next, a material such as plaster or clay is placed around the model and fired, melting the wax and leaving a ceramic mold with a hollow space inside. _____ molten metal is poured inside the mold, solidifying into the shape of the original wax model.

Which choice completes the text with the most logical transition?

(A) Therefore,

(B) Specifically,

(C) In conclusion,

(D) Finally,

4 🔖 Mark for Review

Climate change negatively affects birds' breeding season by reducing the availability of food. _____ birds living in old growth forests, which have large trees and cooler microclimates, are protected from the negative impacts. Researchers found that the forests provide plentiful food for the birds during their breeding season.

Which choice completes the text with the most logical transition?

(A) Therefore,

(B) For instance,

(C) However,

(D) In addition,

5 🔖 Mark for Review

Indonesia, an island nation in the Pacific Ring of Fire, has a long history of destructive volcanic eruptions. The underground heat of volcanoes can, however, be harvested to generate geothermal energy. _____ Indonesia was an early adopter of geothermal power plant technology and today ranks second in the world in the production of this type of renewable energy.

Which choice completes the text with the most logical transition?

(A) Consequently,

(B) In other words,

(C) That is,

(D) In sum,

6 ☐ Mark for Review

While researching a topic, a student has taken the following notes:

- Murasaki Shikibu was a well-known Japanese novelist.
- She was born in 973 in Heian-kyō, Japan.
- She is best known for writing what is considered the first novel.
- *The Tale of Genji* is a novel about Hikaru Genji, the son of an emperor.
- The novel explores the lives and romances of members of the aristocratic society.

The student wants to introduce Murasaki Shikibu and her novel. Which choice most effectively uses relevant information from the notes to accomplish this goal?

Ⓐ The lives and romances of members of the aristocratic society are explored in the novel *The Tale of Genji* by Murasaki Shikibu.

Ⓑ Japanese novelist Murasaki Shikibu wrote *The Tale of Genji*, considered the first novel ever written.

Ⓒ Japanese writer Murasaki Shikibu was born in 973.

Ⓓ *The Tale of Genji*, written by Murasaki Shikibu, is about Hikaru Genji.

7 ☐ Mark for Review

While researching a topic, a student has taken the following notes:

- Turbofan engines and turboprop engines are both used in commercial airplanes.
- Turbofan engines are the most efficient jet engines at airspeeds near the speed of sound.
- Large commercial airliners travel at airspeeds near the speed of sound and use turbofan engines.
- Turboprop engines are more efficient than turbofan engines at airspeeds significantly below the speed of sound.
- Many regional commuter airliners use turboprop engines.

The student wants to specify a reason that some commercial airplanes use turbofan engines. Which choice most effectively uses relevant information from the notes to accomplish this goal?

Ⓐ Turbofan engines and turboprop engines are used in different kinds of airliners and are most efficient at different airspeeds.

Ⓑ Since large commercial airliners travel at airspeeds near the speed of sound, they use turbofan engines, which are the most efficient jet engines at those airspeeds.

Ⓒ Turbofan engines are less efficient than other kinds of engines at airspeeds significantly below the speed of sound, so many regional commuter airliners do not use them.

Ⓓ Large commercial airliners use turbofan engines, while many regional commuter airliners use turboprop engines.

8 ☐ Mark for Review

While researching a topic, a student has taken the following notes:

- During the Harlem Renaissance in the 1920s and 1930s, Augusta Savage was a sculptor, teacher, and advocate for equal rights.
- She opened her own studio, Savage Studio of Arts and Crafts, and was also the director of the Harlem Community Art Center.
- She was commissioned to produce a work of art for the 1939 New York World's Fair.
- She was the only Black woman to receive a commission for that event.
- Her sculpture, *The Harp*, also known as *Lift Every Voice and Sing*, was based on a poem by James Weldon and Rosamond Johnson.
- Unfortunately, the piece was destroyed at the end of the fair.

The student wants to emphasize the uniqueness of Savage's accomplishment. Which choice most effectively uses relevant information from the notes to accomplish this goal?

Ⓐ Savage was the only Black woman commissioned for an art piece for the 1939 New York World's Fair.

Ⓑ The sculpture Savage created based on a poem was destroyed at the end of the 1939 World's Fair.

Ⓒ During the Harlem Renaissance, Savage opened her own studio and was the director of the Harlem Community Art Center.

Ⓓ Savage's artwork, *The Harp*, was a sculpture commissioned for the 1939 New York World's Fair.

9 ☐ Mark for Review

While researching a topic, a student has taken the following notes:

- Mawsynram, India, has been reported as the wettest place in the world by the *Guinness Book of World Records*.
- The rainfall in Mawsynram has been recorded as 12,393 mm per year.
- This rainfall is concentrated during the monsoon season from May to September.
- López de Micay, Colombia, has been reported as the wettest place in the world by IDEAM, the Colombian weather service.
- IDEAM has recorded the rainfall in López de Micay as 12,892 mm per year.
- This rainfall is relatively evenly distributed throughout the year.

The student wants to emphasize a difference between the yearly rainfall in two places. Which choice most effectively uses relevant information from the notes to accomplish this goal?

Ⓐ The rainfall in Mawsynram, India, is concentrated during the monsoon season from May to September, while the rainfall in López de Micay, Colombia, is relatively evenly distributed throughout the year.

Ⓑ Mawsynram, India, and López de Micay, Colombia have each been reported as the wettest place in the world, and both places have recorded a rainfall of over 12,000 mm per year.

Ⓒ López de Micay, Colombia, has been reported as the wettest place in the world by IDEAM, the Colombian weather service, but other sources disagree.

Ⓓ Mawsynram, India, has been reported as the wettest place in the world by the *Guinness Book of World Records*, with a yearly rainfall of 12,393 mm per year.

10 ☐ Mark for Review

While researching a topic, a student has taken the following notes:

- Antonio Stradivari was an Italian violinmaker who lived in the 1600s and 1700s.

- Scientists have spent decades researching why violins created by Stradivari seem to sound better than modern instruments.

- A group of analytical chemists led by Chiaramaria Stani discovered a protein-based layer in between the wood and varnish of a Stradivari violin.

- This layer may change the wood's natural resonance.

- Changing the resonance of the wood affects the sound of the violin.

The student wants to explain recent research results for an audience familiar with Stradivari's violins. Which choice most effectively uses relevant information from the notes to accomplish this goal?

Ⓐ Italian violinmaker Antonio Stradivari, who lived in the 1600s and 1700s, created violins that seem to sound better than modern instruments.

Ⓑ A group of analytical chemists led by Chiaramaria Stani discovered a protein-based layer in between the wood and varnish of a Stradivari violin that may change the wood's natural resonance and, in turn, affect the sound of the violin.

Ⓒ Scientists, such as the group of analytical chemists led by Chiaramaria Stani, have spent decades researching why violins created by Stradivari seem to sound better than modern instruments.

Ⓓ The discovery made by a group of analytical chemists led by Chiaramaria Stani may help explain why the violins made by Italian violinmaker Antonio Stradivari, who lived in the 1600s and 1700s, seem to sound better than modern instruments.

Summary

- o Rhetoric questions relate to the meaning of the passage and the answer choice. They don't test punctuation or grammar.

- o Transition questions are organized from easy to hard.

- o Highlight ideas in the passage that relate to each other, specifically near the blank and in the surrounding sentences (usually the sentence just before the one with the blank).

- o Annotate whether those ideas agree, disagree, or involve a time change.

- o Eliminate based on the direction of the answers and then use POE for anything that remains.

- o Rhetorical Synthesis questions are organized from easy to hard.

- o Don't read the bullet points unless you need to.

- o Highlight the goal(s) stated in the question and go straight to POE.

- o Eliminate any answer that doesn't completely fulfill the goal(s). Don't consider the construction of the answer choice—all that matters is whether it fulfills the goal(s).

Chapter 11
Math Basics

Although we'll show you which mathematical concepts are most important to know for the PSAT 8/9, this book relies on your knowledge of basic math concepts. If you're a little rusty, this chapter is for you. Read on for a review of the math basics you'll need to know before you continue.

HOW TO CONQUER PSAT 8/9 MATH

So, what do you need to do? There are three important steps:

1. **Know the basic content.** Obviously you do need to know the basics of arithmetic, algebra, and geometry. We'll cover what you need to know in this chapter.
2. **Learn some PSAT 8/9-specific problem-solving skills.** Since these basic concepts appear in ways you're probably not used to from math class, you need to prepare yourself with a set of test-specific problem-solving skills designed to help you answer PSAT 8/9 Math questions. We'll cover the most important ones in the next chapter.
3. **Have a sound overall testing strategy.** This means knowing what to do with difficult questions and having a plan to pace yourself to get the maximum number of points in the time allotted. Be sure to read carefully the material in Chapter 2 to make sure you're using the strategy that will get you the greatest number of points in the time you have.

KNOW THE STRUCTURE

The Math section of the Digital PSAT 8/9 is split into two modules. Each module contains 22 questions, of which 14–16 are multiple-choice questions and the rest are student-produced response questions (SPR), meaning that you fill in your own answer instead of choosing from four answers. Questions on the second module are, on average, easier or harder based on performance on the first module. Each module has two "pre-test" questions that do not count toward your score, but they are not identified, so treat every question as if it counts.

The Math section is further broken down by question type and content area, as follows.

By Question Type	
70% Problem Solving	15–16 questions per module
30% Word Problems	6–7 questions per module

By Content Area	
42.5% Algebra	8–9 questions per module
20% Advanced Math	4–5 questions per module
25% Problem-Solving & Data Analysis	5–6 questions per module
12.5% Geometry and Trigonometry	2–3 questions per module

(PERSONAL) ORDER OF DIFFICULTY

The questions on each module in the Math section of the Digital PSAT 8/9 have a loose order of difficulty. You may notice the questions getting harder as the section progresses. More important than any question format, math content, or official order of difficulty is your own Personal Order of Difficulty. Though the last questions of each module are likely to be the hardest, use your own personal strengths and weaknesses to decide which questions to do and which to skip.

USING THE ONLINE TOOLS AND SCRATCH PAPER

Online Tools

Several of the on-screen features of the Digital PSAT 8/9 will be useful on the Math section.

- Mark for review tool to mark questions to come back to later
- Built-in calculator, which can be accessed at any time
- Reference sheet with common math formulas, which can be accessed at any time
- The annotate tool is NOT available on the Math section, so you will not be able to underline or highlight parts of the question.

Scratch Paper

The proctor at the test center will hand out three sheets of scratch paper, and you can use your own pen or pencil. Plan ahead about how to use the scratch paper in combination with what's on the screen.

Use the Tools Effectively!

Online Tools
- Eliminate wrong answers
- Work steps on the calculator
- Look up geometry formulas

Scratch Paper
- Rewrite key parts of the question
- Write out every calculation
- Redraw geometric figures and label them
- Rewrite answer choices as needed

USING YOUR CALCULATOR

You are allowed to use a calculator on all Math questions on the PSAT 8/9, and you should definitely do so. You can use any graphing, scientific, or plain old four-function calculator, **provided that it doesn't have a keyboard**.

The Calculator Guide in your Online Student Tools will show you how to get the most out of the built-in calculator. Refer to it as you work through the Math chapters in this book.

There is a built-in Desmos calculator that you can click open on the screen at any time. Even if you plan to use your own calculator, there are many things that the built-in calculator can do more easily. To make the most of the built-in calculator, you need to practice with it. Download the Bluebook app from College Board website, where you can do untimed practice to get used to the built-in calculator. It will make many questions, especially ones dealing with functions and graphs, easier than they would be by hand.

There are a few simple rules to remember when dealing with your calculator:

1. Use the calculator you're most comfortable with. You definitely don't want to be trying to find the right button on test day. Ideally, you should be practicing with the same calculator you'll use on test day.
2. Change or charge your batteries the week before the test. If they run out during the test, you can use the built-in Desmos calculator instead.
3. Be sure to hit the "clear" or "on/off" button after each calculation to reset the calculator after an operation. A common mistake to make when using your calculator is to forget to clear your last result.
4. Your calculator is very good at calculating, but watch out for mis-keying information. (If you type the wrong numbers in, you'll get the wrong result.) Check each number on the display as you key it in.
5. For the most part, you'll use your calculator for the basic operations of addition, subtraction, multiplication, and division; the ability to convert fractions to decimals, and vice versa; and the ability to do square roots and exponents. Don't forget, though, that it likely has handy buttons for things like sine, cosine, and absolute value, should you encounter those on the test.
6. Then, there's one really big, important rule whenever you think about using your calculator:

Not sure whether your calculator is acceptable? Check College Board's website for a list of approved calculators.

> A calculator can't think; it can only calculate.

What does this mean? It means that a calculator can't think through a question for you. You have to do the work of understanding and setting up the problem correctly to make sure you know what the right calculation will be to get the answer. Only then can you use the calculator to calculate the answer.

So, use your paper and pencil to practice your problem-solving skills on all Math questions. You should always be sure to set up the question on your scratch paper—writing it down is still the best method—which will help you catch any errors you might make and allow you to pick up where you left off if you lose focus. Then, move quickly to your calculator or the built-in calculator to chug your way through the calculations, and be careful to enter each number and operator correctly. Remember, using your calculator is already saving you time on these questions—don't rush and lose the advantage that it gives you.

Drill 1

DEFINITIONS

One of the reasons that good math students often don't get the score they expect on the PSAT 8/9 is that they've forgotten one or more of these definitions—or they read too fast and skip over these "little" words. Be sure you know them cold and watch out for them!

Match the words with their definitions, and then come up with some examples. Answers can be found in Part IV.

1. integers

2. positive numbers

3. negative numbers

4. even numbers

5. odd numbers

6. factors

7. multiples

8. prime numbers

9. distinct

10. digit

a. numbers that a certain number can be divided by, leaving no remainder
    Examples: _____

b. integers that cannot be divided evenly by 2
    Examples: _____

c. numbers that have no fractional or decimal parts
    Examples: _____

d. numbers that are greater than zero
    Examples: _____

e. having a different value
    Examples: _____

f. integers that can be divided by 2 evenly (with no remainder)
    Examples: _____

g. numbers that are less than zero
    Examples: _____

h. numbers that have exactly two distinct factors: themselves and 1
    Examples: _____

i. numbers that can be divided by a certain number with no remainder
    Examples: _____

j. a numerical symbol from 0 through 9 that fills a place in a number
    Examples: _____

11. consecutive numbers

12. divisible

13. remainder

14. sum

15. product

16. difference

17. quotient

18. absolute value

k. the result of addition
    Examples: _____

l. a whole number left over after division
    Examples: _____

m. the result of subtraction
    Examples:_____

n. can be divided with no remainder
    Examples: _____

o. a number's distance from zero; always a
    positive value or 0
    Examples: _____

p. numbers in sequential order
    Examples: _____

q. the result of division
    Examples: _____

r. the result of multiplication
    Examples: _____

EXPONENTS

Exponents are just shorthand for multiplication. Instead of writing $3 \times 3 \times 3 \times 3$, you can write 3^4. Thus, you can handle exponents by expanding them out if necessary.

$$y^2 \times y^3 = y \times y \times y \times y \times y = y^5$$

$$\frac{y^4}{y^2} = \frac{y \times y \times y \times y}{y \times y} = \frac{\cancel{y} \times \cancel{y} \times y \times y}{\cancel{y} \times \cancel{y}} = y \times y = y^2$$

$$(y^2)^3 = (y \times y)^3 = (y \times y)(y \times y)(y \times y) = y^6$$

However, you can also multiply and divide exponents that have the same base using a shortcut called MADSPM. MADSPM also helps you remember how to deal with raising exponents to another power. Let's see the breakdown:

- **MA** means when you see a **Multiplication** sign between like bases, **Add** the exponents. So, $y^2 \times y^3 = y^{2+3} = y^5$.

- **DS** means when you see a **Division** sign (or fraction), **Subtract** the exponents. So, $\frac{y^5}{y^2} = y^{5-2} = y^3$.

- **PM** means when you see a base with an exponent raised to a **Power**, **Multiply** the exponents. So, $(y^2)^3 = y^{2\times3} = y^6$. (This is really easy to confuse with multiplication, so watch out!)

Here are some additional rules to remember about exponents:

- Anything to the zero power equals 1: $3^0 = 1$. Mathematicians argue about whether 0^0 is 1 or is undefined, but that won't come up on the PSAT 8/9.
- Anything to the first power equals itself: $3^1 = 3$.
- 1 to any power equals 1: $1^{3876} = 1$.
- A **negative exponent** means to take the reciprocal of what would be the result if the negative weren't there: $2^{-2} = \frac{1}{2^2} = \frac{1}{4}$.

- A **fractional exponent** has two parts (like any other fraction): the numerator is the power the base is raised to, and the denominator is the root of the base. For example, $8^{\frac{2}{3}} = \sqrt[3]{8^2} = \sqrt[3]{64} = 4$.

> **Warning**
> The rules for multiplying and dividing exponents do not apply to addition or subtraction:
> $2^2 + 2^3 = 12$
> $(2 \times 2) + (2 \times 2 \times 2) = 12$
> It does not equal 2^5 or 32.

Drill 2

Time: 7 minutes. Answers can be found in Part IV.

a. $3^3 \times 3^2 =$ _____

b. $\dfrac{3^3}{3^2} =$ _____

c. $\left(3^3\right)^2 =$ _____

d. $x^6 \times x^2 =$ _____

e. $\dfrac{x^6}{x^2} =$ _____

f. $\left(x^6\right)^2 =$ _____

---

1 ▢ Mark for Review

If $t^3 = -8$, what is the value of t^2?

Ⓐ -4

Ⓑ -2

Ⓒ 2

Ⓓ 4

---

2 ▢ Mark for Review

If $a + b = 8$, what is the value of $3^a 3^b$?

Ⓐ 3^8

Ⓑ 3^{16}

Ⓒ 9^8

Ⓓ 9^{16}

---

3 ▢ Mark for Review

$$(np^{-2}q^3)(n^5p^3q^2)$$

Which of the following expressions is equivalent to the given expression, where n, p, and q are positive?

Ⓐ $n^3p^{-4}q^8$

Ⓑ $n^4p^{-2}q^{10}$

Ⓒ $n^5p^{-6}q^6$

Ⓓ n^6pq^5

---

4 ▢ Mark for Review

Which of the following is equivalent to $x^{\frac{2}{3}}$?

Ⓐ $\dfrac{x^2}{x^3}$

Ⓑ $\sqrt[3]{x^2}$

Ⓒ $\dfrac{x^2}{3}$

Ⓓ $\sqrt{x^3}$

EQUATIONS AND INEQUALITIES

An **equation** is a statement that contains an equals sign, such as $3x + 5 = 17$.

To solve an equation, you must get the variable x alone on one side of the equals sign and everything else on the other side.

The first step is to put all of the variables on one side of the equation and all of the numbers on the other side, using addition and subtraction. As long as you perform the same operation on both sides of the equals sign, you aren't changing the value of the variable.

Then you can divide both sides of the equation by the *coefficient,* which is the number in front of the variable. If that number is a fraction, you can multiply everything by its reciprocal.

For example,

$$3x + 5 = 17$$
$$\underline{\quad -5 \quad -5 \quad}$$ Subtract 5 from each side.
$$3x \quad = \quad 12$$
$$\underline{\div 3 \qquad \div 3}$$ Divide each side by 3.
$$x \quad = \quad 4$$

Always remember this rule of equations:

> Whatever you do to one side of the equation, you must also do to the other side.

The example above was fairly simple. The PSAT 8/9 may test this idea with more complex equations and formulas, though. Just keep trying to isolate the variable in question by undoing the operations that have been done to it. Here's an example.

1   🔖 Mark for Review

$$9x = 2y - z$$

The given expression relates the variables x, y, and z. Which equation correctly expresses y in terms of x and z?

Ⓐ $y = \dfrac{9x + z}{2}$

Ⓑ $y = \dfrac{9}{2}x + z$

Ⓒ $y = 18x + z$

Ⓓ $y = 2(9x + z)$

Here's How to Crack It

The question asks for one variable in terms of two other variables. To isolate y, start by undoing the subtraction on the right side of the equation by performing the opposite operation. Add z to both sides of the equation to get $9x + z = 2y$. Next, undo the multiplication on the right side of the equation by performing the opposite operation. Divide both sides of the equation by 2 to get $y = \dfrac{9x + z}{2}$. The correct answer is (A).

An **inequality** is any statement with one of these signs:

<	(less than)
>	(greater than)
≤	(less than or equal to)
≥	(greater than or equal to)

You can solve inequalities in the same way you solve equations, with one exception: whenever you multiply or divide an inequality by a negative value, you must change the direction of the sign: for example, > becomes <, and ≤ becomes ≥.

For example,

$$3x + 5 > 17$$

$$\underline{-5 \quad -5} \quad \text{Subtract 5 from each side.}$$

$$3x \quad > 12$$

$$\underline{\div 3 \qquad \div 3} \quad \text{Divide each side by 3.}$$

$$x \quad > \quad 4$$

In this case, we didn't multiply or divide by a negative value, so the direction of the sign didn't change. However, if we were to divide by a negative value, we would need to change the direction of the sign.

$$-4x + 3 > 15$$

$$\underline{-3 \quad -3} \quad \text{Subtract 3 from each side.}$$

$$-4x \quad > 12$$

$$\underline{\div -4 \qquad \div -4} \quad \text{Divide each side by } -4.$$

$$x \quad < -3$$

Try the kind of inequality question you might see on the PSAT 8/9 with this knowledge in mind.

---

2 🔖 Mark for Review

$$2x - 6 \leq -8$$

Which of the following is equivalent to the given inequality?

(A) $x \leq -7$

(B) $x \geq -7$

(C) $x \leq -1$

(D) $x \geq -1$

Here's How to Crack It

The question asks for an equivalent inequality. The answer choices all have x on the left side of the inequality, so isolate x. Start by adding 6 to both sides of the inequality to get $2x \leq -2$. Next, divide both sides of the inequality by 2 to get $x \leq -1$. Because 2 is positive, do not switch the sign when dividing. The correct answer is (C).

―――――――――○―――――――――

ABSOLUTE VALUES

Absolute value is just a measure of the distance between a number and 0. Since distances are always positive, the absolute value of a number is also always positive. The absolute value of a number is written as $|x|$.

When solving for the value of a variable inside the absolute value bars, it is important to remember that the variable could be either positive or negative. For example, if $|x| = 2$, then $x = 2$ or $x = -2$ since both 2 and -2 are a distance of 2 from 0.

Here's an example.

―――――――――○―――――――――

PSAT 8/9 Smoke and Mirrors

When you're asked to solve an equation involving an absolute value, it is very likely that the correct answer will be the negative result. Why? Because the test-writers know that you are less likely to think about the negative result!

3 ☐ Mark for Review

$$|2x - 3| = 5$$

Which of the following is a possible solution to the given equation?

Ⓐ −4

Ⓑ −1

Ⓒ 0

Ⓓ 1

Here's How to Crack It

The question asks for a possible solution to an equation with an absolute value. With an absolute value, the value inside the absolute value bars can be either positive or negative, so this equation has two possible solutions. To find one solution, either set $2x - 3$ equal to 5 or set $2x - 3$ equal to -5, and solve for x. When $2x - 3 = 5$, add 3 to both sides of the equation to get

$2x = 8$, and then divide both sides of the equation by 2 to get $x = 4$. Be careful: -4 is an answer choice, but x is positive 4. Keep going and find the other solution. When $2x - 3 = -5$, add 3 to both sides of the equation to get $2x = -2$, and then divide both sides of the equation by 2 to get $x = -1$. The correct answer is (B).

SIMULTANEOUS EQUATIONS

Simultaneous equations occur when you have two or more equations at the same time. Occasionally, all you have to do is stack the equations and then add or subtract them, so try that first. Sometimes, it won't get you exactly what you want, but it will get you close to it.

---

4 ⬜ Mark for Review

$$-x + y = 5$$
$$x + 2y = 13$$

The solution to the given system of equations is (x, y). What is the value of y?

(A) 1

(B) 6

(C) 8

(D) 18

Here's How to Crack It

The question asks for the y-value in the solution to a system of equations. The equations contain x with opposite signs, so find the y-value by stacking and adding the two equations, which will make the x terms disappear.

$$
\begin{array}{r}
-x + y = 5 \\
+ \underline{(x + 2y = 13)} \\
3y = 18
\end{array}
$$

Divide both sides of the resulting equation by 3 to get $y = 6$, which is (B).

It is also possible to enter both equations into the built-in calculator, then scroll and zoom as needed to find the point of intersection. Click on the gray dot to see that the coordinates of the point are (1, 6). The value of y is 6, which is (B).

Using either method, the correct answer is (B).

———————————————○———————————————

WRITING YOUR OWN EQUATIONS

For the most part, we've been looking at solving equations given to you in questions. Sometimes, however, you'll be required to create one of your own. The PSAT 8/9 Math section tests not only your math skills but also, and possibly even more important to your score improvement, your reading skills. On word problems, it is imperative that you read the question carefully and translate the words in the question into math.

ENGLISH	MATH EQUIVALENTS
is, are, were, did, does, costs	=
what (or any unknown value)	*any variable (x, y, b)*
more, sum	+
less, difference	−
of, times, product	× (*multiply*)
ratio, quotient, out of, per	÷ (*divide*)

Sometimes you'll be asked to take a word problem and create equations or inequalities from that information. Usually, they will not ask you to solve these equations/inequalities, so if you are able to locate and translate the information in the question, you have a good shot at getting the correct answer. Always start with the most straightforward piece of information. What is the most straightforward piece of information? Well, that's up to you to decide. Consider the following question.

5 ☐ Mark for Review

A volunteer is distributing water bottles during a marathon. She starts with 700 bottles of water and distributes an average of 70 bottles each hour. Which of the following equations represents the relationship between the remaining number of water bottles, w, and the amount of time, h, in hours, that the volunteer spends distributing water bottles?

(A) $w = 10h$

(B) $w = 700h - 70$

(C) $w = 700 - 70h$

(D) $w = 700 + 70h$

Here's How to Crack It

The question asks for an equation that represents a specific situation. Translate the information given in the question one piece at a time. One piece of information says that the volunteer *distributes an average of 70 bottles each hour*, and another piece says that h represents the time in hours. The number of water bottles distributed per hour times the number of hours gives the total number of water bottles distributed and translates to $70h$. Eliminate (A) and (B) because they do not include this term. Compare the remaining answers: the difference between (C) and (D) is whether $70h$ is subtracted from or added to 700. When the volunteer distributes water bottles, she has fewer left than she started with, so $70h$ should be subtracted from the starting number of 700. Eliminate (D) because it adds instead of subtracts. The correct answer is (C).

USE YOUR TOOLS!

We showed you in the introduction how important it is to utilize the online tools and scratch paper frequently and effectively. This question is a great example. You worked the question one piece at a time and eliminated answers as you went. Use your scratch paper to rewrite parts of the question and translate them into math, and then use the Answer Eliminator tool to eliminate answers that don't match that piece. Take a look below at an example of what your screen and scratch paper should look like at the end of a question like this.

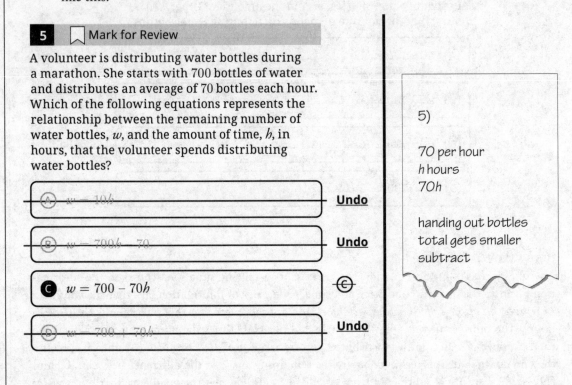

5 ☐ Mark for Review

A volunteer is distributing water bottles during a marathon. She starts with 700 bottles of water and distributes an average of 70 bottles each hour. Which of the following equations represents the relationship between the remaining number of water bottles, w, and the amount of time, h, in hours, that the volunteer spends distributing water bottles?

A. $w = 70h$ Undo

B. $w = 700h - 70$ Undo

C. $w = 700 - 70h$ ⊖

D. $w = 700 + 70h$ Undo

5)

70 per hour
h hours
$70h$

handing out bottles
total gets smaller
subtract

Drill 3

Time: 12 minutes. Answers can be found in Part IV.

---

1 ▢ Mark for Review

The number x is 8 less than three times the number y. Which of the following equations represents the relationship between x and y?

(A) $x = \frac{y-8}{3}$

(B) $x = 3y - 8$

(C) $x = 3y + 8$

(D) $x = 8 - 3y$

---

2 ▢ Mark for Review

$$16a + 20b > 12$$

Which of the following inequalities is equivalent to the given inequality?

(A) $a + b > -24$

(B) $4a + 5b > 3$

(C) $4a + 5b > 12$

(D) $8a + 10b > 24$

---

3 ▢ Mark for Review

$$4x - 15y = 7$$
$$2x - 15y = 11$$

The solution to the given system of equations is (x, y). What is the value of x?

(A) -2

(B) -1

(C) 4

(D) 6

---

4 ▢ Mark for Review

What is the positive solution to the equation $4|x - 1| = 24$?

▢

---

5 ⬚ Mark for Review

A sports memorabilia store sells two types of cards: r rare cards for $20 each and c common cards for $2 each. A collector purchases 40 cards for a total of $296. Which of the following systems of equations represents this situation?

(A) $20c + 2r = 40$
$r + c = 296$

(B) $20c + 2r = 296$
$r + c = 40$

(C) $20r + 2c = 40$
$r + c = 296$

(D) $20r + 2c = 296$
$r + c = 40$

6 ⬚ Mark for Review

$$8(2 - x) = 10 - 5(x + 3)$$

What value of x is the solution to the given equation?

(A) 1

(B) $\frac{21}{13}$

(C) 7

(D) $\frac{17}{2}$

7 ⬚ Mark for Review

A cat consumed greater than 290 calories and fewer than 340 calories every day for one week. The cat consumed a total of c calories for the week. Which of the following inequalities represents all possible values of c?

(A) $290 < c < 340$

(B) $2{,}030 < c < 2{,}080$

(C) $2{,}030 < c < 2{,}380$

(D) $2{,}330 < c < 2{,}380$

8 ⬚ Mark for Review

A bakery sells only two types of cakes: funnel cakes and ice cream cakes. One funnel cake costs $27, and one ice cream cake costs $45. On a certain day, the bakery sold 26 funnel cakes and made a total of $1,332. How many ice cream cakes did the bakery sell on that day?

⬚

THE COORDINATE PLANE

You will definitely see some questions about the coordinate plane, or *xy*-plane, on the PSAT 8/9. Let's start by covering the basics here. You'll see more advanced concepts in the Advanced Math chapter. So, let's just review:

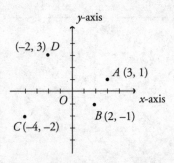

The *x*-axis is the horizontal axis, and the *y*-axis is the vertical axis. Points are given on the coordinate plane with the *x*-coordinate first. Positive *x*-values go to the right, and negative ones go to the left; positive *y*-values go up, and negative ones go down. So, point *A* (3, 1) is 3 points to the right on the *x*-axis and 1 point up from the *y*-axis. Point *B* (2, –1) is 2 points to the right on the *x*-axis and 1 point down from the *y*-axis.

Slope is a measure of the steepness of a line in the coordinate plane. On some slope questions, you need to recognize only whether the slope is positive, negative, or zero. A line that goes up and to the right has a positive slope; a line that goes down and to the right has a negative slope, and a flat line has a slope of 0. In the figure below, ℓ_1 has a positive slope, ℓ_2 has a slope of 0, and ℓ_3 has a negative slope.

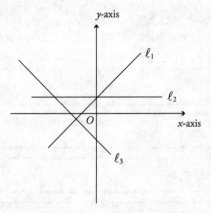

If you do need to calculate the slope, and the graph is drawn for you, here's how: slope = $\dfrac{y_2 - y_1}{x_2 - x_1}$. The *slope* of a line is equal to $\dfrac{rise}{run}$. To find the slope, take any two points on the line and count off or calculate the distance you need to get from one of these points to the other.

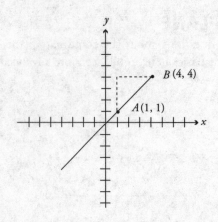

In the graph above, to get from point A to point B, we count up (rise) 3 units, and count over (run) 3 units. Therefore, the slope is $\dfrac{rise}{run} = \dfrac{3}{3} = 1$. Always remember to check whether the slope is positive or negative when you use $\dfrac{rise}{run}$.

If you're not given a figure and you can't draw one easily using the points given, you can find the slope by plugging the coordinates you know into the slope formula. Just remember to plug the numbers into the formula carefully!

Here's an example.

---

1 🔖 Mark for Review

Line l contains the points $(-2, 2)$ and $(4, 8)$. What is the slope of line l?

Ⓐ -1

Ⓑ 0

Ⓒ 1

Ⓓ 2

Here's How to Crack It

The question asks for the slope of a line and gives two points. Use $\dfrac{rise}{run}$ to find the slope, being sure to start with the same point for both. Plug the values into the equation slope = $\dfrac{y_2 - y_1}{x_2 - x_1}$ to get slope = $\dfrac{2 - 8}{-2 - 4}$. Simplify to get slope = $\dfrac{-6}{-6}$, and then slope = 1. The correct answer is (C).

The equation of a line can take multiple forms. One is known as **standard form**. In this form, $Ax + By = C$, the slope is $-\dfrac{A}{B}$ and the y-intercept is $\dfrac{C}{B}$. Knowing these shortcuts can help you avoid having to convert a linear equation into the more common form known as **slope-intercept form**. A slope-intercept equation takes the form $y = mx + b$, where m is the slope and b is the y-intercept.

Knowing how to find the slope is useful for solving questions about perpendicular and parallel lines. **Perpendicular lines** have slopes that are negative reciprocals of one another. **Parallel lines** have the same slope and no solutions. You may also be given two equations that have infinitely many solutions.

Take a look at an example.

---

2 ☐ Mark for Review

$$15x - 12y = 63$$
$$ay + 5x = 21$$

The given system of equations has infinitely many solutions. If a is a constant, what is the value of a?

(A) -12

(B) -4

(C) -3

(D) 3

> **To Infinity…and Beyond!**
> When given two equations with infinitely many solutions, find a way to make them equal. The equations represent the same line.

Here's How to Crack It

The question asks for the value of a constant in a system of equations. The question states that the system has infinitely many solutions, so the two equations represent the same line. The first equation is in standard form, $Ax + By = C$, but the second is not. The test-writers are trying to confuse you, but avoid that by putting the second equation in the same form. Switch the two terms on the left side of the second equation to get $5x + ay = 21$.

Next, find the slope of each line. When a linear equation is in standard form, slope $= -\dfrac{A}{B}$. In the first equation, $A = 15$ and $B = -12$, so slope $= -\dfrac{15}{-12}$, which reduces to slope $= \dfrac{5}{4}$. In the second equation, $A = 5$ and $B = a$, so slope $= -\dfrac{5}{a}$. Since the two equations have the same slope, set the two slopes equal to each other to get $\dfrac{5}{4} = -\dfrac{5}{a}$. To solve for a, cross-multiply to get $(5)(a) = (4)(-5)$, or $5a = -20$. Divide both sides of this equation by 5 to get $a = -4$. The correct answer is (B).

Let's look at a question for which slope-intercept form is useful.

---

3 ☐ Mark for Review

$$y = \frac{1}{3}x + 6$$

The graph of the given equation in the xy-plane crosses the y-axis at $(0, b)$. What is the value of b?

(A) $\dfrac{1}{6}$

(B) $\dfrac{1}{3}$

(C) 3

(D) 6

Here's How to Crack It

The question asks for the y-coordinate of the point where a line crosses the y-axis. This is also known as the y-intercept. The equation is already in slope-intercept form, $y = mx + b$, where m is the slope and b is the y-intercept. Since 6 in the equation is where b goes in slope-intercept form, b is the y-intercept, and $b = 6$. The correct answer is (D).

To find the **point of intersection** of two lines, find a way to set them equal and solve for one of the variables. If the equations are already in $y = mx + b$ form, set the $mx + b$ part of the two equations equal and solve for x. If the question asks for the value of y, plug the value of x back into either equation to solve for y. It may also be possible to plug in the answers (see Chapter 12 for more on this). The built-in graphing calculator can also be extremely useful: often, you can enter both equations and then scroll and zoom as needed to see the point of intersection, which is represented by a gray dot. Click on the gray dot to show the coordinates of the point. These skills will also help find the point(s) of intersection between a line and a parabola.

Here's a question for which the built-in calculator and solving algebraically both work.

> **4** ☐ Mark for Review
>
> $$y = 5x - 5$$
> $$y = 3x + 3$$
>
> The solution to the given system of equations is (x, y). What is the value of y?
>
> ☐

Here's How to Crack It

The question asks for the y-coordinate of the solution to a system of equations. One approach is to use the built-in calculator. Enter both equations, and two lines will appear in the graphing area. If the point of intersection isn't visible, zoom by using your mouse scroll wheel or the + and – buttons in the upper right of the graphing area. You can also click and drag in the graphing area to move things around. After doing that, it might be necessary to click on one of the lines or one of the equations to make the dots show up again. Click on the gray dot where the two lines intersect. The dot turns black, and the coordinates (4, 15) appear. The question asks for the value of y, which is 15.

To solve algebraically, set the right sides of the equations equal to each other because they are both equal to y. This becomes $5x - 5 = 3x + 3$. Subtract $3x$ from both sides of the equation to get $2x - 5 = 3$, and then add 5 to both sides of the equation to get $2x = 8$. Finally, divide both sides of the equation by 2 to get $x = 4$. Be careful! You've done a lot of work to find the value of x, but the question asks for the value of y. Plug $x = 4$ into the first equation to get $y = 5(4) - 5$, which becomes $y = 20 - 5$, and then $y = 15$.

Using either method, the correct answer is 15.

───────────────○───────────────

The built-in calculator can save time and avoid mistakes like stopping when you solve for x. The test-writers give you this useful tool, so take advantage of it!

Drill 4

Time: 12 minutes. Answers can be found in Part IV.

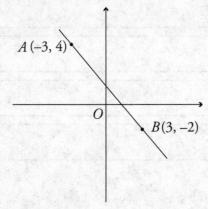

a. What is the change in *y* (rise?)

_____

b. What is the change in *x* (run)?

_____

c. What is the slope of the line above?

_____

(Remember, the line is going down to the right, so it must have a negative slope.)

d. What would be the slope of a line parallel to *AB*? _____

e. What would be the slope of a line perpendicular to *AB*? _____

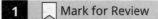

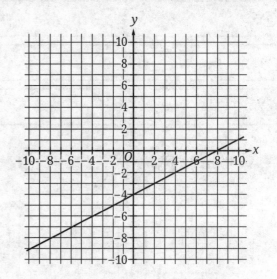

What is the *y*-intercept of the graph shown?

Ⓐ (0, −8)

Ⓑ (0, −4)

Ⓒ (0, 4)

Ⓓ (0, 8)

2 ☐ Mark for Review

The x-intercept of the graph of $y = -\frac{1}{2}x + 4$ in the xy-plane is $(x, 0)$. What is the value of x?

(A) −2

(B) 2

(C) 4

(D) 8

3 ☐ Mark for Review

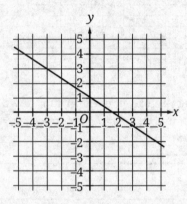

The line shown in the xy-plane contains the point $\left(\frac{3}{2}, 0\right)$. Which of the following could be the equation of the line?

(A) $y = -2x + 1$

(B) $y = -\frac{3}{2}x + 2$

(C) $y = -\frac{2}{3}x + 1$

(D) $y = -\frac{2}{3}x + 2$

4 ☐ Mark for Review

In the xy-plane, line m passes through the points $(3, 1)$ and $(0, 7)$. If line n is parallel to line m, what is the slope of line n?

(A) −2

(B) $-\frac{1}{2}$

(C) $\frac{1}{2}$

(D) 2

5 ☐ Mark for Review

$$3x - 6y = 15$$
$$x - 2y = 10$$

At how many points do the graphs of the given equations intersect in the xy-plane?

(A) Exactly one

(B) Exactly two

(C) Infinitely many

(D) Zero

6 Mark for Review

$$x - \frac{y}{5} = 2$$
$$24x + 2y = 82$$

If (x, y) is a solution to the given system of equations, what is the value of x?

7 Mark for Review

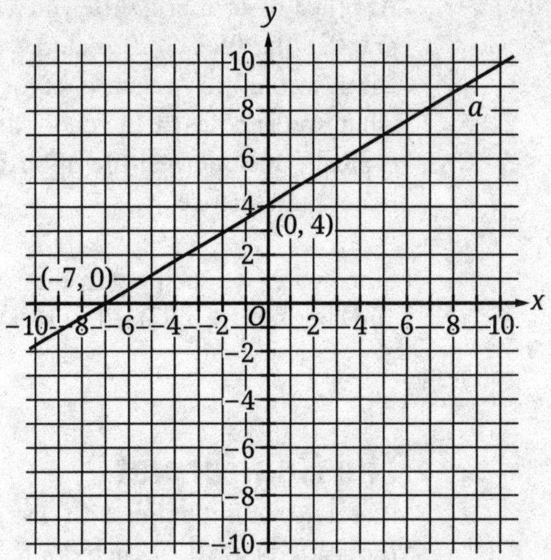

Line a graphed in the xy-plane is shown. Line b (not shown) is perpendicular to line a. Which of the following could be the equation of line b?

Ⓐ $y = -\frac{7}{4}x - 2$

Ⓑ $y = -\frac{4}{7}x + 4$

Ⓒ $y = \frac{4}{7}x + 3$

Ⓓ $y = \frac{7}{4}x - 6$

CHARTS AND GRAPHS

Another basic math skill you will need for the PSAT 8/9 is the ability to read charts and graphs. The PSAT 8/9 includes charts, graphs, and tables throughout the test (not just in the Math section) to present data for students to analyze. The test-writers believe this better reflects what students learn in school and need to understand in the real world. The situations will typically include real-life applications, such as finance and business situations, social science issues, and science.

Since you'll be seeing graphics throughout the test, let's look at the types you may encounter and the skills you'll need to be familiar with when you work with charts and graphs.

The Scatterplot

A scatterplot is a graph with distinct data points, each representing one piece of information. On the scatterplot below, each dot represents the number of televisions sold at a certain price point.

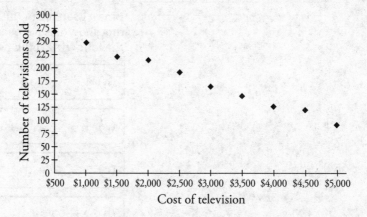

Here's How to Read It

To find the cost of a television when a certain number of televisions are sold, start at the number of televisions sold on the vertical axis and imagine a horizontal line to the right until you hit a data point. You can't draw on the figures on the Digital PSAT 8/9, but you can move the mouse pointer to the right starting from the number on the vertical axis. Once you hit a point, trace with the mouse pointer a straight line down from it to the horizontal axis and read the number the line hits. To determine the number of televisions sold when they cost a certain amount, reverse the steps—start at the bottom, trace up until you hit a point, and then move left until you intersect the vertical axis. You can also hold your scratch paper up to the screen and use it as a ruler.

The Line Graph

A line graph is similar to a scatterplot in that it shows different data points that relate the two variables. The difference with a line graph, though, is that the points have been connected to create a continuous line.

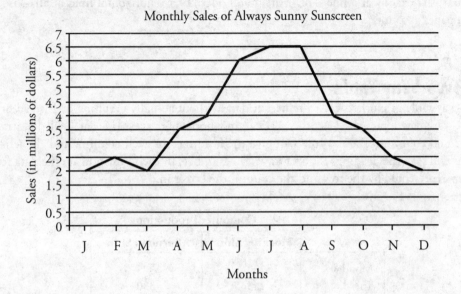

Monthly Sales of Always Sunny Sunscreen

Here's How to Read It

Reading a line graph is very similar to reading a scatterplot. Start at the axis that represents the data given and trace a straight line with the mouse pointer up or to the right until you intersect the graph line. Then move left or down until you hit the other axis. For example, in February, indicated by an F on the horizontal axis, Always Sunny Sunscreen had 2.5 million in sales. Make sure to notice the units on each axis. If February sales were only $2.50, rather than $2.5 million, then this company wouldn't be doing very well!

The Bar Graph (or Histogram)

Instead of showing a variety of different data points, a bar graph will show how many items belong to a particular category. If the variable at the bottom is given in ranges, instead of distinct items, the graph is called a histogram, but you read it the same way.

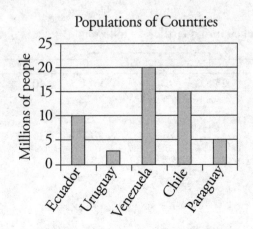

Populations of Countries

Here's How to Read It

The height of each bar corresponds to a value on the vertical axis. In this case, the bar above Chile hits the line that intersects with 15 on the vertical axis, so there are 15 million people in Chile. Again, watch the units to make sure you know what the numbers on the axes represent. On this graph, horizontal lines are drawn at 5-unit intervals, making the graph easier to read. If the bar isn't exactly at a line—or if the graph doesn't have horizontal lines at all—use your scratch paper as a ruler.

The Two-Way Table

A two-way table is another way to represent data without actually graphing it. Instead of having the variables represented on the vertical and horizontal axes, the data will be arranged in rows and columns. The top row will give the headings for each column, and the left-most column will give the headings for each row. The numbers in each box indicate the data for the category represented by the row and the column the box is in.

	Computer Production	
	Morning Shift	**Afternoon Shift**
Monday	200	375
Tuesday	245	330
Wednesday	255	340
Thursday	250	315
Friday	225	360

Here's How to Read It

If you wanted to see the number of computers produced on Tuesday morning, you could start in the Morning Shift column and look down until you found the number in the row that says "Tuesday," or you could start in the row for Tuesday and look to the right until you found the Morning Shift column. Either way, the result is 245. Some tables will give you totals in the bottom row and/or the right-most column, but sometimes you will need to find the totals yourself by adding up all the numbers in each row or in each column. More complicated tables will have more categories listed in rows and/or columns, or the tables may even contain extraneous information.

The Box Plot

A box plot shows data broken into quartiles, as follows:

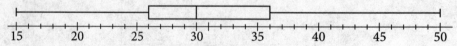

Here's How to Read It

Here is what all the parts of the box plot represent.

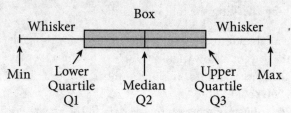

The line in the middle of the box shows the median value of the data, which is 30 in the example above. The "whiskers," which give this figure the alternate name "box-and-whisker plot," represent the highest value in the list with the end of the whisker on the right and the lowest value with the end of the whisker on the left. Thus, the minimum value of this data set is 15, and the maximum is 50. Then the data between the median and these minimum and maximum values is broken into two parts on each side, creating four "quartiles." The median of the lower half of the data is the Q1 value on the left side of the box, at about 26, and the median of the upper half of the data is the Q3 value on the right side of the box, at about 36.

The Stem-and-Leaf Plot

A stem-and-leaf plot shows data according to a common first digit.

```
2 | 0 1 7
3 | 2 2 4
4 | 0 1 5 7 7 8
5 | 1 1 4 5 5 7 9
6 | 2 5 8 8 9
7 | 0
```

A book club took a survey of the age, in years, of its members. The data is shown in the stem-and-leaf plot above.

Here's How to Read It

The numbers on the left of the vertical line are the initial digit of each age, and the numbers to the right of the vertical line are the following digits corresponding to the given first digit. This means that the ages of the members of the book club are 20, 21, 27, 32, 32, 34, etc. Questions using stem-and-leaf plots often ask for things like the range of the data, the median of the data, or the probability of selecting a certain number. We will look at all those statistical measures in the Math Techniques chapter.

From a stem-and-leaf plot or a box plot, you can determine the median and range of the set of data. It is also possible to calculate the mode and mean from a stem-and-leaf plot and the interquartile range from a box plot.

Figure Facts

Every time you encounter a figure or graphic on the PSAT 8/9, you should make sure you understand how to read it by checking the following things:

- What are the variables for each axis or the headings for the table?
- What units are used for each variable?
- Are there any key pieces of information (numbers, for example) in the legend of the chart that you should note?
- What type of relationship is shown by the data in the chart? For instance, if the chart includes curves that show an upward slope, then the graph exhibits a *positive association*, while curves that show a downward slope exhibit a *negative association*.
- You can use the mouse pointer or the edge of your scratch paper to make sure you are locating the correct data in the graph.

FILL-INS: THE BASICS

You will see 10–12 questions in the Math section of the PSAT 8/9 that ask you to enter your own numerical answer in a box rather than answer a multiple-choice question. The test-writers call these Student-Produced Response questions, but we're going to keep things simple and call them fill-ins.

The only difficulty with fill-ins is getting used to the way in which you are asked to answer the question. For each fill-in question, you will have a box like this:

To enter your answer, click inside the box and start typing. The numbers you enter will automatically appear left to right, and the computer will show a preview of your answer, so you can make sure it looks right.

The fill-in instructions appear on the left side of the screen for every fill-in question. You can click in the center and drag left to shrink the fill-in instructions and focus on the question.

You don't want to have to spend time re-reading the instructions every time, so here is some additional information about entering a fill-in answer:

1. There is space to enter 5 characters if the answer is positive and 6 characters— including the negative sign—if the answer is negative.

2. You can enter your answer as either a fraction or a decimal. For example, .5, 0.5, and 1/2 are all acceptable answers. Use the forward slash for fractions.

3. If your answer is a fraction, it must fit within the space. Do not try to enter something like $\dfrac{200}{500}$ as a fraction: either reduce it or convert it to a decimal.

4. Fractions do not need to be in the lowest reduced form. As long as it fits, it's fine.

5. You cannot fill in mixed numbers. Convert all mixed numbers to ordinary fractions or decimals. If your answer is $2\dfrac{1}{2}$, you must convert it to 5/2 or 2.5. If you enter 21/2, the computer will read your answer as $\dfrac{21}{2}$.

6. You do not need to type the comma for numbers longer than three digits, such as 4,200. In fact, the computer will not allow it.

7. The computer also will not allow symbols such as %, $, or π. Additionally, square roots, units, and variables cannot be entered.

8. If your answer is a decimal that will not fit in the space provided, either enter as many digits as will fit or round the last digit. The fraction $-\dfrac{2}{3}$ can be entered in decimal form as −0.666, −0.667, −.6666, or −.6667.

9. Some questions will have more than one right answer. Any correct answer you enter will count as correct; do not try to enter multiple answers.

Drill 5

Time: 12 minutes. Answers can be found in Part IV.

1 ☐ Mark for Review

	Enrolled in Chemistry	Enrolled in Physics	Enrolled in Biology
11th grade	62	36	75
12th grade	24	54	18

The table shows the numbers of 11th grade students and 12th grade students enrolled in three different science classes. Each student is enrolled in only one science class. What percent of students enrolled in Physics are in 11th grade?

(A) 20%

(B) 30%

(C) 40%

(D) 50%

2 ☐ Mark for Review

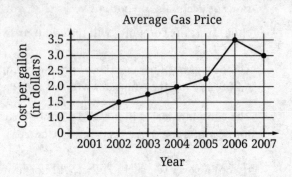

The average cost of a gallon of gas from 2001 to 2007 is displayed in the line graph. According to the graph, how much more did a gallon of gas cost in 2007 than in 2003?

(A) $1.00

(B) $1.25

(C) $1.75

(D) $3.00

3 ☐ Mark for Review

The scatterplot shows the relationship between two variables, x and y. A line of best fit is also shown.

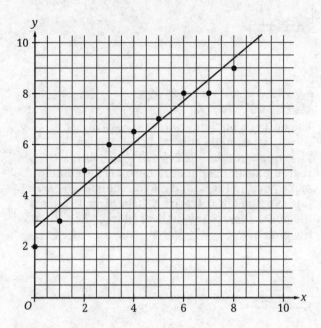

Which of the following equations best represents the line of best fit shown?

Ⓐ $y = -0.75x - 2.75$

Ⓑ $y = -0.75x + 2.75$

Ⓒ $y = 0.75x - 2.75$

Ⓓ $y = 0.75x + 2.75$

4 ☐ Mark for Review

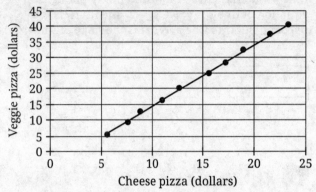

The scatterplot shows the prices, in dollars, of a cheese pizza and a veggie pizza for ten different pizzerias. A line of best fit is also shown. According to the line of best fit, which of the following is the closest to the price, in dollars, of a cheese pizza at the pizzeria that charges $15 for a veggie pizza?

Ⓐ 5

Ⓑ 10

Ⓒ 15

Ⓓ 25

5 ☐ Mark for Review

Line p and line q are graphed in the xy-plane. The equation of line p is $y = -3x - 2$, and line q is perpendicular to line p. What is the slope of line q?

6 ☐ Mark for Review

$$y = -8x + 24$$
$$y = -2x + 6$$

The solution to the given system of equations is (x, y). What is the value of x?

7 ☐ Mark for Review

If $5x^2 = 125$, what is one possible value of $5x$?

8 ☐ Mark for Review

The host of a birthday party makes a punch consisting of apple juice and cherry juice. The equation $1.9a + 2.2c = 13.9$ models the ingredients in the punch, where a is the volume of apple juice, in liters, and c is the volume of cherry juice, in liters. If there are 5 liters of apple juice in the punch, how many liters of cherry juice are in the punch?

Summary

o   Each Math module is arranged in a loose order of difficulty, which can make it easier to spot the less difficult questions. However, remember that the test-writers' idea of "easier" questions is not necessarily the same as your idea. Let your Personal Order of Difficulty be your guide.

o   Write on your scratch paper to set up your work, and then use your calculator or the built-in calculator to figure out solutions. And remember to type carefully—a calculator won't check for mistakes.

o   Review basic definitions again before the test to make sure you don't get stuck on the "little words."

o   When you have to manipulate exponents, remember the MADSPM rules.

o   To solve equations for a variable, isolate the variable. Make sure you perform the same operations on both sides of the equation.

o   Inequalities can be worked just like equations until you have to multiply or divide by a negative number. Then you need to flip the inequality sign.

o   The absolute value of a number is the positive distance from zero, or practically, making the thing inside the | | sign positive. Everything inside the | | is equal to the positive and the negative value of the expression to which it is equal.

o   To solve simultaneous equations, simply add or subtract the equations. When the simultaneous equation question asks for a single variable and addition and subtraction don't work, try to make something disappear. Multiply the equations by a constant to make the coefficient(s) of the variable(s) you want go to zero when the equations are added or subtracted.

o   When writing a system of equations, start with the most straightforward piece of information.

o   You can also use the equations or inequalities in the answer choices to help you narrow down the possibilities. Eliminate any answers in which an equation or inequality doesn't match a piece of information in the question.

o   Parallel lines have the same slope and no solutions. If two lines have the same slope and infinitely many solutions, they are the same line. Perpendicular lines have slopes that are negative reciprocals of each other.

o   When you encounter charts, carefully check the chart for information you should note, and use the mouse pointer or edge of your scratch paper to locate information.

o   When answering fill-in questions, don't bother reducing fractions or rounding decimals if they fit in the allotted space. Check the answer preview on the screen before moving on.

Chapter 12
Math Techniques

In the previous chapter, we mentioned that one of the keys to doing well on the PSAT 8/9 is to have a set of test-specific problem-solving skills. This chapter discusses some powerful strategies, which—though you may not use them in school—are specifically designed to get you points on the PSAT 8/9. Learn them well!

PLUGGING IN

One of the most powerful problem-solving skills on the PSAT 8/9 is a technique we call Plugging In. Plugging In will turn nasty algebra questions into simple arithmetic and help you through the particularly twisted problems that you'll often see on the PSAT 8/9. There are several varieties of Plugging In, each suited to a different kind of question.

Plugging In Your Own Numbers

The problem with doing algebra is that it's just too easy to make a mistake.

> Whenever you see a question with variables in the answer choices, use Plugging In.

Start by picking a number for the variable in the question (or for more than one variable, if necessary), solve the problem using your number, and then see which answer choice gives you the correct answer.

Take a look at the following question.

---

1 ☐ Mark for Review

Which expression is equivalent to $x^2 + 15x - 54$?

Ⓐ $(x - 9)(x + 6)$

Ⓑ $(x - 3)(x + 18)$

Ⓒ $(x + 3)(x - 18)$

Ⓓ $(x + 9)(x - 6)$

Here's How to Crack It

The question asks for an expression that is equivalent to the given expression. You may already know how to factor quadratics, and we'll go over that topic in the Advanced Math chapter. However, you don't need to do that here because plugging in your own number works just as well, if not better. When two expressions are equivalent, they will always equal each other no matter what value the variable has. That means you can make the variable equal anything you want, and the correct answer will always be equivalent to the given expression.

Keep the math simple and use a small number, such as 2. Plug $x = 2$ into the expression in the question, and it becomes $2^2 + 15(2) - 54$. Simplify the expression to get $4 + 30 - 54$, and then -20. This is the target value; write it down on your scratch paper and circle it.

Now plug $x = 2$ into each answer choice and eliminate any answer that does not equal your target value of -20.

A) $(2 - 9)(2 + 6) = (-7)(8) = -56$ Not -20; eliminate!

B) $(2 - 3)(2 + 18) = (-1)(20) = -20$ Is -20; keep!

C) $(2 + 3)(2 - 18) = (5)(-16) = -80$ Not -20; eliminate!

D) $(2 + 9)(2 - 6) = (11)(-4) = -44$ Not -20; eliminate!

Notice that all of the wrong answers include factors of 54, but they either don't add to 15 or have the wrong signs. When you use real numbers instead of variables, you are much less likely to make that kind of mistake. Here, you did some arithmetic instead of algebra and got (B) as the correct answer.

Use Your Tools!

Plugging In offers a fantastic opportunity to make full use of the online tools and your scratch paper. See all those notes above that helped find the target value and check each answer choice? Those go on your scratch paper. Instead of writing down "eliminate," use the Answer Eliminator tool on the screen.

Plugging In is such a great technique because it turns hard algebra questions into medium and sometimes even easy arithmetic questions. Remember this when you're thinking of your POOD and looking for questions to do among the hard ones; if you see variables in the answers, there's a good chance it's one to try.

Don't worry too much about what numbers you choose to plug in; just plug in easy numbers (small numbers like 2, 5, or 10 or numbers that make the arithmetic easy, like 100 if you're looking for a percent). Also, be sure your numbers fit the conditions of the questions (for example, if they say $x \leq 11$, don't plug in 12).

Also, be sure to check all four answers. Once in a while, the numbers you plug in work for more than one answer. In those cases, pick a new number or numbers, get a new target value, and plug into the remaining answers until you are down to one.

Now let's try one with two variables.

2 ☐ Mark for Review

If $\frac{y}{3} = 6x$, which of the following is equivalent to x in terms of y?

(A) $\frac{y}{18}$

(B) $\frac{y}{2}$

(C) y

(D) $2y$

When to Plug In
- phrases like "in terms of" or "equivalent form" in the question
- variables in the question and/or answer choices

Here's How to Crack It

The question asks for one variable in terms of another. Like "equivalent expression," the phrase "in terms of" means that you're dealing with the relationship between numbers or variables.

Seeing variables in the answer choices is also a clue to plug in your own number or numbers.

The right side of the equation looks simpler, so start with x. Pick a small number to make the math easy, and plug in $x = 2$. The equation becomes $\frac{y}{3} = 6(2)$, and then $\frac{y}{3} = 12$. To solve for y, multiply both sides of the equation by 3 to get $y = 36$.

The question asks for the value of x in terms of y, so plug $y = 36$ into each answer choice and eliminate any that do not equal 2. Once again, use your scratch paper to keep track of things.

A) $\frac{36}{18} = 2$ Is 2; keep!

B) $\frac{36}{2} = 18$ Not 2; eliminate!

C) 36   Not 2; eliminate!

D) 2(36) = 72   Not 2; eliminate!

Only (A) works, so it's the answer!

As you can see, Plugging In can turn messy algebra questions into more straightforward arithmetic questions. Here are the steps to follow.

Plugging In

1. When you see *in terms of* or *equivalent* and there are variables in the answer choices, you can plug in.
2. Pick your own number(s) for the variable(s) in the question.
3. Do the necessary math to find the answer to the question, which is the target number. Circle the target number.
4. Use POE to eliminate every answer that doesn't match the target number.

OTHER TIMES TO PLUG IN

Plugging In isn't just for problem-solving questions! Approximately 30% of the Math questions on the PSAT 8/9 are word problems. The test-writers like to use "real world" contexts to make things look more complicated. The strategies we've already discussed and will discuss later in this book work on problem-solving questions *and* word problems. Look for chances to do things like plug in your own numbers throughout the math modules on the PSAT 8/9.

Additionally, questions that ask you to interpret something within the context of a word problem are good opportunities to plug in. Using real numbers can help you see how things fit together rather than trying to figure it out conceptually.

Finally, you might see a question that doesn't contain a variable but is about the relationship between values. If one value is given as a fraction, percent, or proportion of another, try plugging in.

Here's an example of plugging in on a word problem.

---○---

> We'll cover rates in more detail later in this chapter.

3 🔖 Mark for Review

One box of cookies costs n dollars. At this rate, how much will 4 boxes of cookies cost?

(A) $\frac{n}{4}$

(B) $\frac{4}{n}$

(C) $4n$

(D) $n + 4$

Here's How to Crack It

The question asks for a value given a specific situation. The answer might seem obvious, but notice how all of the answer choices are some combination of n and 4. It's easy to think you know what the answer should look like and fall for a trap answer. You don't want to miss a pretty easy question by going too fast and doing too much in your head, so plug in and use your scratch paper instead.

Make $n = 8$ to make it easy to divide by 4 in (A). If one box of cookies costs $8, 4 boxes of cookies will cost $(8)(4) = 32$ dollars. This is the target value; write it down and circle it.

Next, plug $n = 8$ into the answer choices and eliminate any that do not equal 32.

A) $\frac{8}{4} = 2$ Not 32; eliminate!

B) $\frac{4}{8} = \frac{1}{2}$ Not 32; eliminate!

C) $4(8) = 32$ Is 32; keep!

D) $8 + 4 = 12$ Not 32; eliminate!

Yes, (C) is for cookie, but in this case it's also the correct answer!

---○---

Drill 1

Time: 9 minutes. Answers can be found in Part IV.

---

1 ☐ Mark for Review

$$y^2 - 8y + 2$$

Which of the following is equivalent to the given expression?

Ⓐ $(y - 4)^2 - 14$

Ⓑ $(y - 4)^2 + 14$

Ⓒ $(y + 4)^2 - 14$

Ⓓ $(y + 4)^2 + 14$

---

2 ☐ Mark for Review

A certain type of square nametag comes in one size for adults and one size for children. The side length of a child-sized nametag is one-third the side length of an adult-sized nametag. The area of an adult-sized nametag is how many times the area of a child-sized nametag?

Ⓐ 3

Ⓑ 9

Ⓒ 27

Ⓓ 81

---

3 ☐ Mark for Review

John and Joan went to lunch together and split the cost of lunch equally. The total cost of John's lunch was d dollars, and the total cost of Joan's lunch was $4 less than the total cost of John's lunch. Which of the following expressions gives the amount, in dollars, that each person paid?

Ⓐ $\dfrac{d}{2} - 4$

Ⓑ $d - 2$

Ⓒ $2d - 2$

Ⓓ $2d - 4$

---

4 ☐ Mark for Review

A local badminton club charges a monthly membership fee of $25, and each hour of play costs $2.50. Which of the following equations represents this situation, where h is the number of hours played and c represents the total monthly cost?

Ⓐ $c = 2.50h + 25$

Ⓑ $c = 2.50h + 27.50$

Ⓒ $c = 25h + 2.50$

Ⓓ $c = 27.50h$

---

5 Mark for Review

Abigail creates a pricing plan for her job as a piano teacher. She charges a one-time registration fee to every student in order to begin lessons. The equation $C = 40h + 100$ represents the total amount, C, in dollars, that Abigail charges for h hours of lessons. Which of the following is the best interpretation of the number 100 in this context?

(A) The hourly rate for lessons, in dollars

(B) The amount of the registration fee, in dollars

(C) The total amount, in dollars, Abigail charges for a one-hour lesson

(D) The total amount, in dollars, Abigail charges for 40 hours of lessons

6 Mark for Review

A construction worker is digging a hole. The equation $d = 1.8t + 4.5$ represents the depth, d, in meters, that the construction worker has reached t minutes after beginning to dig. Which of the following is the best interpretation of the number 1.8 in this context?

(A) The time it takes the construction worker to dig to a depth of 4.5 meters

(B) The depth, in meters, of the hole when the construction worker started to dig

(C) The depth, in meters, of the hole 4.5 minutes after the construction worker started to dig

(D) The depth, in meters, that the construction worker digs each minute

PLUGGING IN THE ANSWERS (PITA)

You can also plug in when the answer provided to a question is an actual value, such as 2, 4, 10, or 20. Why would you want to do a lot of complicated algebra to solve a question when the answer is right there on the screen? All you have to do is figure out *which* choice it is.

How can you tell which is the correct answer? Try every choice *until you find the one that works.* Even if this means you have to try all four choices, PITA is still a fast and reliable means of getting the right answer.

If you work strategically, however, you almost never need to try all four answers. If the question asks for either the greatest or the least answer, start there. Otherwise, start with one of the middle answer choices. If that answer works, you're done. If the answer you started with was too big, try a smaller answer. If the answer you started with was too small, try a bigger answer. You can almost always find the answer in two or three tries this way. Let's try PITA on the following question.

---

1 ▢ Mark for Review

$$3\left(\frac{x}{2}+1\right)=9$$

What is the solution to the given equation?

(A) 2

(B) $\frac{8}{3}$

(C) 3

(D) 4

Here's How to Crack It

The question asks for the solution to an equation. This probably looks a lot like something from the previous chapter where you would have solved the equation algebraically. That would work here, but the fraction and parentheses mean there are many ways to make a mistake and get the wrong answer. Instead, take advantage of the multiple-choice format! One of the four numbers in the answers *has* to be the solution to the equation, so plug in the answers until one of them works.

A solution to an equation is a value that makes the equation true, so the correct answer is the value of x that, when plugged into the equation, will result in the two sides of the equation being equal. First, rewrite the answers on your scratch paper and label them with what the question is asking for: x. Notice that the answers go in order. If you start with one of the numbers in the middle and it doesn't work, you might be able to figure out whether you need a larger or smaller number. Choice (B) looks messy with the fraction, so start with (C), 3. Plug 3 into the equation for x to get $3\left(\dfrac{3}{2} + 1\right) = 9$. Now that you're dealing with numbers and arithmetic instead of variables and algebra, you can use a calculator. Follow the order of operations and calculate $\dfrac{3}{2}$ + 1 first. It equals 2.5. Multiply that by 3 to get 7.5. The equation becomes 7.5 = 9, which is not true. Eliminate (C).

One Answer
Only one of the numbers in the answer choices can be the specific value that the question asked for. Once you plug in an answer choice that works, STOP. You don't need to try the rest.

The result on the left side of the equation was too small, so use a larger value for x and try (D), 4. Plug 4 into the equation for x to get $3\left(\dfrac{4}{2} + 1\right) = 9$. Either use a calculator again or continue solving on paper to get 3(2 + 1) = 9, which becomes 3(3) = 9, and then 9 = 9. This is true, so stop here. The correct answer is (D).

Neat, huh? If the question asks for the solution to a system of equations instead of just one equation, you can do the same thing. Here's an example.

2　🔖 Mark for Review

$$2x + 3y = -9$$
$$x - y = -2$$

Which of the following ordered pairs (x, y) is the solution to the given system of equations?

Ⓐ $(-3, -1)$

Ⓑ $(-1, -3)$

Ⓒ $(1, 3)$

Ⓓ $(3, 1)$

Here's How to Crack It

The question asks for the solution to a system of equations. The question asks for a specific point and the answers contain points, one of which must be the solution to the system, so plug in the answers. Rewrite the answer choices on your scratch paper and label them "(x, y)." Starting in the middle might not help as much with points, so start with some easy numbers and try (C). Plug $x = 1$ and $y = 3$ into the simpler second equation to get $1 - 3 = -2$, or $-2 = -2$. This is true, so try the same point in the first equation. Plug $x = 1$ and $y = 3$ into the first equation to get $2(1) + 3(3) = -9$, which becomes $2 + 9 = -9$, and then $11 = -9$. This is not true, so eliminate (C).

Choice (D) will not work in the first equation because the sum of two positive values can never equal -9, so also eliminate (D). Try (B) next, and plug $x = -1$ and $y = -3$ into the second equation to get $-1 - (-3) = -2$, which becomes $-1 + 3 = -2$, and then $2 = -2$. This is not true, so eliminate (B).

Only (A) is left, so stop here and pick it. If you had tried (A) before you were down to one answer choice, you would have discovered that it works: the second equation becomes $-3 - (-1) = -2$, then $-3 + 1 = -2$, and finally $-2 = -2$. The first equation becomes $2(-3) + 3(-1) = -9$, then $-6 + (-3) = -9$, and finally $-9 = -9$. Thus, the point in (A) works in both equations, so it is a solution to the system of equations. The correct answer is (A).

———————○———————

What about word problems? Just like plugging in your own numbers, PITA works on problem-solving questions and word problems. When the question asks for a specific value and the answer choices are numbers, plug in those answers!

Try using PITA on the following word problem.

———————○———————

3 ▢ Mark for Review

In May of 1937, Amelia Earhart attempted to circumnavigate the globe. According to flight logs, the first stage of the trip was 110 nautical miles less than the second stage of the trip, and the two stages combined totaled 676 nautical miles. How many nautical miles was the first stage of the trip?

Ⓐ 249

Ⓑ 283

Ⓒ 327

Ⓓ 390

PITA = Plugging In the Answers
Don't try to solve problems like this by writing equations and solving for *x* or *y*. Plugging In the Answers lets you use arithmetic instead of algebra, so you're less likely to make errors.

Here's How to Crack It

The question asks for a value given a specific situation. The question asks for a specific value and the answers contain numbers in order, so plug in the answers. Rewrite the answer choices on your scratch paper and label them "first stage." Next, start with an answer in the middle and try (B), 283. The question states that *the two stages combined totaled 676 nautical miles*. If the first stage was 283 nautical miles, the second stage was 676 – 283 = 393 nautical miles. The question also states that *the first stage of the trip was 110 nautical miles less than the second stage of the trip*. If the second stage was 393 nautical miles, the first stage was 393 – 110 = 283 nautical miles. In both cases, the first stage was 283 nautical miles. The correct answer is (B).

Use Your Tools!

Be sure to let your scratch paper and the Answer Eliminator tool help on PITA questions. Rewrite the answers in order to try them out one by one. Label what the answers represent: one of them is the answer to the question. Then label each step along the way and check whether the result matches the information in the question. If it doesn't, cross out that answer on the screen. Here's what your screen and scratch paper should look like after finishing the previous question.

3 🔖 Mark for Review

In May of 1937, Amelia Earhart attempted to circumnavigate the globe. According to flight logs, the first stage of the trip was 110 nautical miles less than the second stage of the trip, and the two stages combined totaled 676 nautical miles. How many nautical miles was the first stage of the trip?

Ⓐ 249

Ⓑ 283

Ⓒ 327

Ⓓ 390

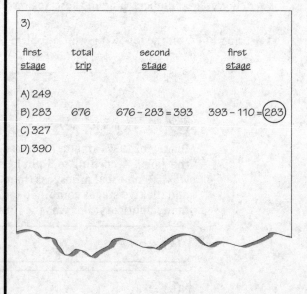

3)

first stage	total trip	second stage	first stage
A) 249			
B) 283	676	676 – 283 = 393	393 – 110 = (283)
C) 327			
D) 390			

Plugging In the Answers (PITA)

When to Use PITA

- When the question asks for a specific amount
- When there are numbers in the answer choices
- When you are tempted to write your own equation

PITA Pointers

- Keep your work neatly organized on your scratch paper
- Start with one of the middle values and work through the problem
- Eliminate answers that are too big or too small
- When one answer works, stop! That's the correct answer.

Drill 2

Time: 9 minutes. Answers can be found in Part IV.

1 ☐ Mark for Review

If 4 less than the product of b and 6 is 44, what is the value of b?

- Ⓐ 4
- Ⓑ 6
- Ⓒ 8
- Ⓓ 14

2 ☐ Mark for Review

$$\frac{x-4}{28} = \frac{1}{4}$$

Which of the following is the solution to the given equation?

- Ⓐ 6
- Ⓑ 7
- Ⓒ 10
- Ⓓ 11

3 ☐ Mark for Review

$$\frac{7}{4}(x+8) < 56$$

Which of the following is a solution to the given inequality?

- Ⓐ 20
- Ⓑ 24
- Ⓒ 32
- Ⓓ 40

4 ☐ Mark for Review

Which of the following is a solution to the equation $3 + 2x = x^2 - 5$?

- Ⓐ −4
- Ⓑ −2
- Ⓒ 1
- Ⓓ 5

5 ☐ Mark for Review

A community garden produced 295 tomatoes, and the gardeners are preserving all of the tomatoes in jars that hold either 3 tomatoes each or 5 tomatoes each. If the gardeners fill 55 jars with 3 tomatoes each, how many jars can they fill with 5 tomatoes each?

Ⓐ 26

Ⓑ 33

Ⓒ 59

Ⓓ 130

6 ☐ Mark for Review

In the expression $x^2 + cx - 8$, c is an integer constant. If the expression can be rewritten as $(x - c)(x + 4)$, what is the value of c?

Ⓐ −4

Ⓑ −2

Ⓒ 2

Ⓓ 4

DATA ANALYSIS

The PSAT 8/9 has questions that ask you to work with concepts such as averages, percentages, and unit conversions. Luckily, The Princeton Review has you covered! The rest of this chapter will give you techniques and strategies to help you tackle these questions.

Averages and *T = AN*

When a PSAT 8/9 question asks for the mean of a list of numbers or a data set, write down the average formula: *Total = Average × Number of things*, or *T = AN*. One benefit of this formula is that it spells a word (tan), so it's easy to memorize. The other benefit is that you can fill in any information the question gives you and solve for what you need.

Let's try this example.

---

1 ☐ Mark for Review

12.0, 12.5, 13.0, 13.5, 14.0

The volumes, in milliliters, of five water bottles are shown. What is the mean volume, in milliliters, of the five bottles?

(A) 2.0

(B) 12.0

(C) 13.0

(D) 14.0

Total
When calculating averages, always find the total. It's the one piece of information that PSAT 8/9 loves to withhold.

Here's How to Crack It

The question asks for the mean of a list of numbers. Write down the average formula: *Total = Average × Number of things*, or *T = AN*. The question states that there are five water bottles, so the *Number of things* is 5. The question asks for the mean, or average, so find the total by adding the 5 numbers to get $12.0 + 12.5 + 13.0 + 13.5 + 14.0 = 65$. Plug the *Total* of 65 and the *Number of things* of 5 into the average formula to get $65 = (A)(5)$. Divide both sides of the equation by 5 to get $13 = A$. The correct answer is (C).

Median

Another statistical concept that you might see on the PSAT 8/9 is median.

The **median** of a group of numbers is the number in the middle, just as the "median" is the large divider in the middle of a road. To find the median, here's what you do:

- First, put the elements in the group in numerical order from lowest to highest.
- If the number of elements in the group is *odd*, find the number in the middle. That's the median.
- If you have an *even* number of elements in the group, find the two numbers in the middle and calculate their average (arithmetic mean).

Try this on the following question.

> **Finding a Median**
> To find the median of a set containing an even number of items, take the average of the two middle numbers after putting the numbers in order.

---

2 ☐ Mark for Review

Runs scored	Frequency
0	1
1	3
2	4
3	0
4	3
5	2
6	2

The frequency table displays the number of runs scored by a baseball team over 15 games. Based on the data, what was the median number of runs scored?

(A) 2

(B) 3

(C) 3.5

(D) 4

Here's How to Crack It

The question asks for the median of data shown in a frequency table. A frequency table has two columns: the left-hand column contains the values, and the right-hand column contains the number of times each value occurs, or its frequency. It would take a while to write out all 15 numbers and then find the middle number, so a better approach is to divide 15 by 2 to get 7.5. Is the median the 7th number in the list or the 8th number? Well, there are 8 – 1 = 7 numbers to the left of the 8th number, and there are 15 – 8 = 7 numbers to the right of the 8th number, so the median is the 8th number. Always round up after dividing by 2 when there is an odd number of numbers in the list.

Now, use the right-hand column of the frequency table to find the 8th number. Add the frequencies until you get to 8. The team scored 0 runs 1 time and 1 run 3 times, so those are the first 1 + 3 = 4 numbers. Keep going: the team scored 2 runs 4 times, so that gets you to 4 + 4 = 8. Thus, the 8th number is 2, and 2 is the median. The correct answer is (A).

Range

Mean and median relate to the center of a data set. One way the PSAT 8/9 could test the spread of a data set is with range. The **range** of a list of numbers is the difference between the greatest number in the list and the least number in the list. For the list 4, 5, 5, 6, 7, 8, 9, 10, 20, the greatest number is 20 and the least is 4, so the range is 20 – 4 = 16.

Let's look at a question.

---

3   🔖 Mark for Review

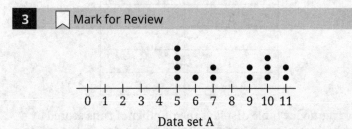

Data set A

The dot plot shown represents the data in data set A. Data set B is created by adding a value of 3 to data set A. Which of the following correctly compares the ranges of data sets A and B?

(A) The range of data set A is equal to the range of data set B.

(B) The range of data set A is less than the range of data set B.

(C) The range of data set A is greater than the range of data set B.

(D) There is not enough information to compare the ranges of the two data sets.

Here's How to Crack It

The question asks for a comparison of the ranges of two data sets. The range of a list of numbers is the difference between the greatest number and the least number. Start by finding the range of data set A. The greatest number with at least one dot on the dot plot is 11, and the least number is 5, so the range of data set A is 11 − 5 = 6. Data set B has the same greatest number, 11, but the least number is now 3, so the range is 11 − 3 = 8. Thus, the range of data set A, 6, is less than the range of data set B, 8. The correct answer is (B).

PROBABILITY

Probability refers to the chance that an event will happen, and it is given as a percent or a fractional value between 0 and 1, inclusive. A probability of 0 means that the event will never happen; a probability of 1 means that it is certain to happen.

$$\text{Probability} = \frac{\text{number of outcomes you want}}{\text{number of possible outcomes}}$$

For instance, if you have a die with faces numbered 1 to 6, what is the chance of rolling a 2? There is one face with the number 2 on it, out of 6 total faces. Therefore, the probability of rolling a 2 is $\frac{1}{6}$.

What is the chance of rolling an even number on one roll of this die? There are 3 faces of the die with an even number (the sides numbered 2, 4, and 6) out of a total of 6 faces. Therefore, the probability of rolling an even number is $\frac{3}{6}$, or $\frac{1}{2}$.

Let's look at how this concept will be tested on the PSAT 8/9.

4 ▢ Mark for Review

Number of cars owned in lifetime	Number of people
0	25
1–2	110
3–4	120
More than 4	45

The table shows the results of a survey of 300 people who were asked how many cars they had owned in their lifetimes. If one person is selected at random, what is the probability that the person has owned 3–4 cars?

(A) $\frac{2}{25}$

(B) $\frac{3}{20}$

(C) $\frac{1}{5}$

(D) $\frac{2}{5}$

Here's How to Crack It

The question asks for a probability based on survey data in a table. Probability is defined as $\frac{\text{number of outcomes you want}}{\text{number of possible outcomes}}$. Look up the appropriate numbers in the table. The table shows the survey results of *300 people*, and the question states that *one person is selected at random*, so 300 is the *number of possible outcomes*. The question asks about people who *owned 3–4 cars*, so find 3–4 in the left-hand column. The corresponding number of people in the right-hand column is 120, so this is the *number of outcomes you want*. Therefore, the probability that the person selected has owned 3–4 cars is $\frac{120}{300}$. This is not an answer choice, so either work with the fraction or use a calculator to work with decimals. To reduce the fraction, divide both the numerator and the denominator by 10 to get $\frac{12}{30}$, then divide both the numerator and the denominator by 6 to get $\frac{2}{5}$. To use a calculator, enter 120 ÷ 300 to get 0.4. Enter each answer choice into the calculator, and see that 2 ÷ 5 is also 0.4. The correct answer is (D).

PROPORTIONS

Proportions occur when two variables increase together or decrease together. These questions generally ask you to make a conversion (such as from ounces to pounds) or to compare two sets of information and find a missing piece. For example, a proportion question may ask you to figure out the amount of time it will take to travel 300 miles at a rate of 50 miles per hour.

> To answer proportion questions, just set up two equal fractions. One will have all the information you know, and the other will have a missing piece that you're trying to figure out.

$$\frac{50 \text{ miles}}{1 \text{ hour}} = \frac{300 \text{ miles}}{x \text{ hours}}$$

Be sure to label the parts of your proportion so you'll know you have the right information in the right place; the same units should be in the numerator on both sides of the equals sign, and the same units should be in the denominator on both sides of the equals sign. Notice how using a setup like this helps us keep track of the information we have and to find the information we're looking for, so we can use Bite-Sized Pieces to work through the question.

Now we can cross-multiply and then solve for x: $50x = 300$, so $x = 6$ hours.

> **Formula for Proportions**
>
> $$\frac{x_1}{y_1} = \frac{x_2}{y_2}$$

Let's try the following question.

---◯---

5 ▢ Mark for Review

A full water jug in an office contains 3,785 milliliters of water. What is the water jug's volume, in liters? (1 liter = 1,000 milliliters)

▭

Here's How to Crack It

The question asks for a measurement in different units. The question provides the conversion that 1 liter = 1,000 milliliters. Set up a proportion, being sure to match up units, and use x for the unknown value. The proportion is $\dfrac{1 \text{ liter}}{1,000 \text{ milliliters}} = \dfrac{x \text{ liters}}{3,785 \text{ milliliters}}$. Cross-multiply to get $(1)(3,785) = (1,000)(x)$, or $3,785 = 1,000x$. Divide both sides of the equation by 1,000 to get $3.785 = x$. There is space in the fill-in box for five characters when the answer is positive, so enter the entire number. The correct answer is 3.785.

——————⚬——————

RATES

Rate is a concept related to averages. Cars travel at an average speed. Work gets done at an average rate. Questions about rate might also require you to convert units, so read carefully and use your scratch paper. Setting up a proportion is often the best way to solve these questions, but be sure to match up the units! You can use x or the variable of your choice for unknown values.

Let's look at an example of a PSAT 8/9 rate question.

——————⚬——————

6 ▢ Mark for Review

A continuous reaction produces carbon dioxide at a rate of 0.02 pounds per minute. After 15 minutes, approximately how many <u>grams</u> of carbon dioxide have been produced?
(1 pound = 453.6 grams)

(A) 9.1

(B) 30.2

(C) 68.0

(D) 136.1

Here's How to Crack It

The question asks for a value given a rate and conflicting units. Work the question in Bite-Sized Pieces. First, calculate how many pounds of carbon dioxide are produced in 15 minutes. Set up a proportion, being sure to match up units. The proportion is $\frac{0.02 \text{ pounds}}{1 \text{ minute}} = \frac{x \text{ pounds}}{15 \text{ minutes}}$. Cross-multiply to get $(0.02)(15) = (1)(x)$, or $0.3 = x$. Thus, 0.3 pounds are produced in 15 minutes. Next, convert 0.3 pounds to grams by setting up another proportion. This proportion is $\frac{1 \text{ pound}}{453.6 \text{ grams}} = \frac{0.3 \text{ pounds}}{x \text{ grams}}$. Cross-multiply to get $(1)(x) = (453.6)(0.3)$, or $x = 136.08$ grams of carbon dioxide produced in 15 minutes. The question asks for an approximate value, and 136.1 is closest to 136.08. The correct answer is (D).

RATIOS

Ratios are about relationships between numbers. Whereas a fraction is a relationship between a part and a whole, a ratio is about the relationship between parts. So, for example, if there were 3 boys and 7 girls in a room, the fraction of boys in the room would be $\frac{3}{10}$. But the ratio of boys to girls would be 3:7 or $\frac{3}{7}$. Notice that if you add up the parts, you get the whole: $7 + 3 = 10$.

Ratio questions usually aren't difficult to identify. The question will tell you that there is a "ratio" of one thing to another, such as a 2:3 ratio of boys to girls in a club. Often, a ratio can be treated like a proportion, which means you need to be consistent about which part of the ratio goes in the numerator and which part goes in the denominator. To do so, divide the first part of the ratio by the second and compare the resulting values.

> $\text{Fraction} = \frac{\text{part}}{\text{whole}}$
>
> $\text{Ratio} = \frac{\text{part}}{\text{part}}$

> **Filling In**
> A ratio is usually expressed as 2:3 or 2 to 3, but on a fill-in question, enter it as 2/3.

Try this one.

---○---

7 🔖 Mark for Review

A bakery's specialty flour is a mixture of almond flour and coconut flour. The ratio of almond flour to coconut flour is 7:38 by volume. If the bakery uses 152 cups of coconut flour for the specialty flour in one day, what is the volume, in cups, of almond flour used for the specialty flour in the same day?

Ⓐ 4

Ⓑ 28

Ⓒ 114

Ⓓ 152

Here's How to Crack It

The question asks for a value given a ratio. Begin by reading the question to find information about the ratio. The question states that *the ratio of almond flour to coconut flour is 7:38.* Eliminate (D) because there is more coconut flour than almond flour, so with 152 cups of coconut flour, there must be fewer than 152 cups of almond flour. To solve for the number of cups of almond flour, set up a proportion, being sure to match up the two types of flour. The proportion is $\frac{7 \text{ cups of almond flour}}{38 \text{ cups of coconut flour}} = \frac{x \text{ cups of almond flour}}{152 \text{ cups of coconut flour}}$. Cross-multiply to get $(7)(152) = (38)(x)$, which becomes $1{,}064 = 38x$. Divide both sides of the equation by 38 to get $28 = x$. The correct answer is (B).

---○---

PERCENTS

Percent just means "divided by 100." So, 20 percent = $\dfrac{20}{100} = \dfrac{1}{5}$, or 0.2.

Likewise, 400 percent = $\dfrac{400}{100} = \dfrac{4}{1} = 4$.

Any percent question can be translated into algebra—just use the following rules:

percent	÷ 100
of	×
what	x (or any variable)
is, are, equals	=

Take a look at some examples of phrases you might have to translate on the PSAT:

8 percent of 10		$\dfrac{8}{100}(10) = 0.8$
10 percent of 80		$\dfrac{10}{100}(80) = 8$
5 is what percent of 80?	becomes	$5 = \dfrac{x}{100} \times 80$
5 is 80 percent of what number?		$5 = \dfrac{80}{100}x$
What percent of 5 is 80?		$\dfrac{x}{100} \times 5 = 80$

Even on more complicated questions, translating the English into math will help you get questions about percents correct. Keep an eye out for chances to use some of the other PSAT 8/9 skills you've learned in this book, as well.

Try a question.

---

8   ▢ Mark for Review

If a quantity c is decreased by 35%, which of the following is equivalent to the resulting value?

Ⓐ $0.35c$

Ⓑ $0.65c$

Ⓒ $35c$

Ⓓ $65c$

Here's How to Crack It

The question asks for a value based on a percentage. Translate the English to math in Bite-Sized Pieces. The question doesn't provide a value for c, so plug in your own number. Make $c = 100$ because 100 works well with percent questions. *Percent* means out of 100, and *of* means multiplication, so translate 35% of 100 as $\frac{35}{100}$ (100) = 35. See why 100 was a good choice? The question states that c *is decreased by 35%*, so subtract 35 from the starting value of 100 to get $100 - 35 = 65$. This is the target value; write it down and circle it.

Next, plug $c = 100$ into the answer choices and eliminate any that do not equal 65. Choice (A) becomes 0.35(100) = 35. This does not match the target value, so eliminate (A). Choice (B) becomes 0.65(100) = 65. This matches the target value, so keep (B), but check the remaining answers just in case. Choice (C) becomes 35(100) = 3,500; eliminate (C). Choice (D) will be even larger than (C), so also eliminate (D). The correct answer is (B).

Drill 3

Time: 15 minutes. Answers can be found in Part IV.

a. If a student earns test scores of 70, 90, 95, and 105, what is the mean score for those four tests? _____

b. If a student has a mean score of 80 on 4 tests, what is the total of the scores received on those tests? _____

c. If a student has a mean of 60 on tests, with a total of 360, how many tests has the student taken? _____

d. If the mean of 2, 8, and x is 6, what is the value of x? _____

  2, 3, 3, 4, 6, 8, 10, 12
e. What is the median of the group of numbers above? _____

f. What is the range of the group of numbers above? _____

g. What percent of 5 is 6? _____

h. 60 percent of 90 is the same as 50 percent of what number? _____

i. One hogshead is equal to 64 gallons. How many hogsheads are equal to 96 gallons? _____

---

1 ☐ Mark for Review

	County A	County B	County C	County D	County E
Maximum elevation	239	289	329	240	195
Minimum elevation	132	153	196	119	122

The table shows the minimum and maximum elevations, in meters, of five counties in a certain state. What is the mean maximum elevation, in meters, of the five counties shown?

Ⓐ 114.0

Ⓑ 144.4

Ⓒ 240.0

Ⓓ 258.4

---

2 ☐ Mark for Review

A random sample of 200 widgets was tested from the 5,913 widgets produced by a factory one day. If 41 of the tested widgets were defective, approximately how many widgets produced by the factory that day would be expected to be defective?

Ⓐ 1,200

Ⓑ 2,200

Ⓒ 3,000

Ⓓ 4,700

3 ☐ Mark for Review

Rating	Frequency
☆☆☆☆	14
☆☆☆	31
☆☆	12
☆	18

A video game company asked a focus group with 75 people to rate a new video game on a scale of one star to four stars. The results are summarized in the frequency table. If one member of the focus group is selected at random, what is the probability that the focus group member did <u>not</u> give the game a three-star rating?

Ⓐ $\frac{7}{75}$

Ⓑ $\frac{31}{75}$

Ⓒ $\frac{44}{75}$

Ⓓ $\frac{61}{75}$

4 ☐ Mark for Review

An annual interest rate of 5 percent is paid to a certificate of deposit (CD) account. If the account has a balance of $4,200.00 after one year, what was the balance of the account before the annual interest was paid?

Ⓐ $3,750

Ⓑ $3,990

Ⓒ $4,000

Ⓓ $4,410

5 ☐ Mark for Review

A distance runner preparing for a meet runs at a rate of 1 mile every 7 minutes. What is the runner's pace in kilometers per hour? (1 mile ≈ 1.61 kilometers)

Ⓐ 0.19

Ⓑ 5.32

Ⓒ 11.27

Ⓓ 13.80

6 ☐ Mark for Review

	Daily Temperature (°F)
Sunday	44
Monday	54
Tuesday	52
Wednesday	58
Thursday	54
Friday	56
Saturday	60

The table displays the temperature each day for a week in a certain town in mid-April. What was the median temperature during the week shown, in degrees Fahrenheit?

Ⓐ 53

Ⓑ 54

Ⓒ 55

Ⓓ 58

7 ☐ Mark for Review

The ratio of x to y is 4 to 3, and the ratio of x to z is 1 to 2. What is the ratio of y to z?

- (A) 3 to 8
- (B) 2 to 3
- (C) 3 to 2
- (D) 8 to 3

8 ☐ Mark for Review

The value of a certain stock decreased by 20% from the beginning of 2020 to the beginning of 2021. The value then increased by 15% from the beginning of 2021 to the beginning of 2022. What was the net percentage decrease in the value of the stock from the beginning of 2020 to the beginning of 2022?

- (A) 5%
- (B) 8%
- (C) 23%
- (D) 35%

Summary

o   The test is full of opportunities to use arithmetic instead of algebra—just look for your chances to use Plugging In and Plugging In the Answers (PITA).

o   If a question has *in terms of* or variables in the answer choices, it's a Plugging In question. Plug in your own number, do the math, find the target number, and use POE to get down to one correct answer.

o   If a question doesn't have variables but asks for a fraction or a percent of an unknown number, you can also plug in. Just substitute your own number for the unknown and take the rest of the question step by step.

o   If a question has an unknown and asks for a specific amount, making you feel like you have to write an equation, try PITA instead.

o   When a question asks about the mean, use $T = AN$, plug in the values given in the question, and solve for what you need.

o   The median is the middle value in a list of numbers in order. If there is an even number of elements, the median is the average of the two middle values.

o   The range is the difference between the greatest and least values in a list of numbers.

o   Probability is a fractional value between 0 and 1 (inclusive), and it is equal to the number of outcomes the question is asking for divided by the total number of possible outcomes. It can also be expressed as a percent.

o   A proportion means that the values both increase or both decrease. The formula is $\dfrac{x_1}{y_1} = \dfrac{x_2}{y_2}$.

o   Rates are similar to proportions and often deal with distance, work, and time.

o   Percent simply means "out of 100." Many percent questions can be tackled by translating English to math.

o   Set up ratios like fractions. Take care to put the first term of the ratio in the numerator and the second term in the denominator.

o   Sometimes you'll need to treat ratios like fractions or decimals. Use your calculator to turn the numbers into the easiest form to work the question.

Chapter 13
Advanced Math

There will be 4 or 5 questions on each Math module of the PSAT 8/9 that test what College Board calls "Advanced Math." This category includes topics such as functions and quadratics. If you've learned these topics already in school, great! You'll have a step up on the PSAT 8/9. If not, fear not—this chapter will give you the foundation needed for tackling these questions on the PSAT 8/9.

FUNCTIONS

In the Math Basics chapter, we looked at some concepts related to the xy-plane. Here, we will look at some more complicated topics involving functions and graphs. The functions on the PSAT 8/9 mostly look like this:

$$f(x) = x^2 + 6x + 24$$

Most questions of this type will give you a specific value to plug in for x and then ask you to find the value of the function. Each function is just a set of instructions that tells you what to do to x—or the number you plug in for x—in order to find the corresponding value for $f(x)$ (a fancy name for y). Just plug your information into that equation and follow the instructions.

Let's try an easy one.

> **Just Follow the Instructions**
> Functions are like recipes. Each one is just a set of directions for you to follow. College Board provides the ingredients and you work your magic.

---

1 🔖 Mark for Review

The function f is defined by $f(x) = x + 4$. What is the value of $f(9)$?

(A) 4

(B) 5

(C) 9

(D) 13

Here's How to Crack It

The question asks for the value of a function. In function notation, the number inside the parentheses is the x-value that goes into the function, or the input, and the value that comes out of the function is the y-value, or the output. The question provides an input value of 9, so plug $x = 9$ into the function to get $f(9) = 9 + 4$, which becomes $f(9) = 13$. The correct answer is (D).

> **Fundamental facts about functions**
> $f(x) = y$
> x is the input
> y is the output

Did you notice that you plugged in on the previous question? That's what you'll do whenever a question gives you the equation of a function and an input value, or x. You don't even have to come up with your own number! Other times, a PSAT 8/9 question will give you the equation of a function and an output value, or y. In that case, you will use one of the other skills you learned earlier in this book and plug in the answers.

Here's an example.

---

2 ☐ Mark for Review

$$f(x) = 3x^2 + 3$$

The function f is defined by the given equation. For which of the following values of x does $f(x) = 15$?

Ⓐ 2

Ⓑ 3

Ⓒ 6

Ⓓ 678

Here's How to Crack It

The question asks for a value given a function. Think about input (x) and output (y), and determine which one the question gave you. Since $f(x) = y$, the question is telling you that $y = 15$. That's the output value, and the answer choices have possible input values, so plug in the answers. Rewrite the answer choices on your scratch paper, and label them "x." Start with one of the middle numbers and try (B), 3. Plug 3 into the function for x to get $f(3) = 3(3)^2 + 3$. Simplify the right side of the equation to get $f(3) = 3(9) + 3$, then $f(3) = 27 + 3$, and finally $f(3) = 30$. This is not 15, so eliminate (B). The result was too large, so also eliminate (C) and (D). Choice (A) works because when $x = 2$, the function becomes $f(2) = 3(2)^2 + 3$, which simplifies to $f(2) = 3(4) + 3$, then $f(2) = 12 + 3$, and finally $f(2) = 15$. It is also possible to set the equation equal to 15 and solve for x, and this will be the best approach on fill-in questions because there are no answers to plug in. Using either method, the correct answer is (A).

Sometimes the PSAT 8/9 will use a word problem to describe a function, and then ask you to "build a function" that describes that real-world situation.

Try one of those.

---

3 🔖 Mark for Review

A company rents out a vacation home for periods ranging from 7 days to 21 days. The company charges $165 per day plus a booking fee of $100. Which of the following functions best represents the total cost, C, to rent the vacation home for d days, where $7 \leq d \leq 21$?

Ⓐ $C(d) = 100d + 165$

Ⓑ $C(d) = 165d + 100$

Ⓒ $C(d) = 165(d + 100)$

Ⓓ $C(d) = 265d$

Here's How to Crack It

The question asks for a function that models a specific situation. Translate the information in Bite-Sized Pieces and eliminate after every piece. One piece of information says that *The company charges $165 per day*. Since d represents the number of days, multiplying 165 by d, or $165d$, represents the total of the daily fees. Eliminate (A) and (D) because they do not include the term $165d$. The question also states that the company charges *a booking fee of $100*. This fee is only charged once, so it should not be multiplied by anything. Eliminate (C) because it multiplies 100 by 165. The correct answer is (B).

What's the Point?

Functions are closely related to graphs. Each pair of input and output values is an (x, y) point on the line, parabola, or other graph generated by a function. Because $f(x) = y$, an equation can be written either way: $f(x) = 3x + 2$ and $y = 3x + 2$ are the same line. You already know how to work with linear equations from the Math Basics chapter, and you'll use the same skills when the equation uses function notation.

Take a look at this example.

---○---

4	🔖 Mark for Review

For linear function h, $h(0) = 2$ and $h(15) = 7$. When $h(x)$ is graphed in the xy-plane, what is the slope of the line?

_____

Here's How to Crack It

The question asks for the slope of a line. The question uses function notation, so think about input and output. The question provides two pairs of input and output values: when $x = 0$, $y = 2$, and when $x = 15$, $y = 7$. Thus, the line contains points at $(0, 2)$ and $(15, 7)$. Use these two points to calculate the slope of the line using the formula slope = $\frac{y_2 - y_1}{x_2 - x_1}$. Plug in the values to get slope = $\frac{7 - 2}{15 - 0}$. Simplify the fraction to get slope = $\frac{5}{15}$. This fraction fits in the fill-in box, so stop here. The reduced form of the fraction, $\frac{1}{3}$, or the decimal form, .3333, would also be accepted as correct. The correct answer is $\frac{5}{15}$ or equivalent forms.

---○---

The PSAT 8/9 will also relate points and functions by using tables, and plugging in will come in handy once again. If the question has a table and the answers have functions, plug pairs of values from the table into the answer choices and eliminate functions that don't work. If the question has a function and the answers have tables of values, plug in x-values from the answers and eliminate answers that have the wrong y-value.

Here's one with a table in the question.

_____ ◯ _____

5 🔖 Mark for Review

x	0	1	2	3	4
$f(x)$	2	−2	−6	−10	−14

The table shows five values of x and their corresponding values of $f(x)$ for linear function f. Which of the following equations defines $f(x)$?

Ⓐ $f(x) = -4x + 2$

Ⓑ $f(x) = -3x + 1$

Ⓒ $f(x) = -2x + 2$

Ⓓ $f(x) = 4x - 2$

Here's How to Crack It

The question asks for the function that represents values given in a table. The table includes five input and output values, and the correct equation must work for every pair of values. Plug in values from the table and eliminate functions that don't work. Because 0 and 1 are likely to make more than one answer work, try the third column of the table and plug $x = 2$ and $f(x) = -6$ into the answer choices. Choice (A) becomes $-6 = -4(2) + 2$, then $-6 = -8 + 2$, and finally $-6 = -6$. This is true, so keep (A), but check the remaining answers with this pair of values. Choice (B) becomes $-6 = -3(2) + 1$, then $-6 = -6 + 1$, and finally $-6 = -5$. This is not true, so eliminate (B). Choice (C) becomes $-6 = -2(2) + 2$, then $-6 = -4 + 2$, and finally $-6 = -2$; eliminate (C). Choice (D) becomes $-6 = 4(2) - 2$, then $-6 = 8 - 2$, and finally $-6 = 6$; eliminate (D). The correct answer is (A).

_____ ◯ _____

Drill 1

Time: 10 minutes. Answers can be found in Part IV.

---

1 ▢ Mark for Review

$$f(x) = |7x - 4|$$

The function f is defined by the given equation. What is the value of $f(-3)$?

Ⓐ −25

Ⓑ 1

Ⓒ 17

Ⓓ 25

---

2 ▢ Mark for Review

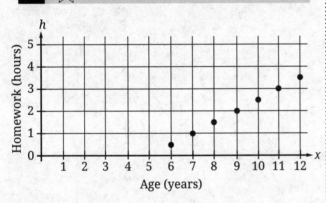

Age (years)

The scatterplot shows the number of hours, h, that a child spent on homework in relation to her age, x, in years. Which of the following equations best models the data shown, where $6 \le x \le 12$?

Ⓐ $h(x) = -2.5x - 0.5$

Ⓑ $h(x) = -0.5x - 2.5$

Ⓒ $h(x) = 0.5x - 2.5$

Ⓓ $h(x) = 2.5x - 0.5$

---

3 ▢ Mark for Review

$$g(x) = -\frac{1}{3}x + 9$$

The function g is defined by the given equation. For what value of x does $g(x) = 3$?

---

4 ▢ Mark for Review

In the xy-plane, the point (–2, 6) lies on the graph of the function $f(x) = 2x^2 + kx + 18$. What is the value of k?

---

5 ▢ Mark for Review

A student is reading a book for class. The number of pages the student has left to read can be modeled by the function $f(x) = 252 - 47x$, where x is the number of days after the book was assigned. Which of the following is the best interpretation of the number 252 in this context?

Ⓐ The student will finish reading the book in 252 days.

Ⓑ The book contains 252 pages.

Ⓒ The student reads 252 pages per day.

Ⓓ The student reads 252 pages every 47 days.

6 ☐ Mark for Review

$$f(x) = 2x^2 - 2$$

For the given function f, which table gives four values of x and their corresponding values of $f(x)$?

Ⓐ

x	$f(x)$
-1	0
0	-2
1	0
2	6

Ⓑ

x	$f(x)$
-1	-4
0	-2
1	0
2	14

Ⓒ

x	$f(x)$
-1	2
0	0
1	2
2	8

Ⓓ

x	$f(x)$
-1	0
0	0
1	0
2	2

7 ☐ Mark for Review

The function $m(x) = 300(1.06)^x$ gives the total money, m, in dollars, in an interest-generating savings account x months after the account was opened. What is the best interpretation of the statement "$m(0)$ is equal to 300" in this context?

Ⓐ The account had a value of $0 when it was opened.

Ⓑ The account will have a value of $0 when it has been open for 300 months.

Ⓒ The account had a value of $300 when it was opened.

Ⓓ The account will have a value of $300 when it has been open for 300 months.

QUADRATIC EQUATIONS

Ah, quadratics. You're likely to see several questions on the PSAT 8/9 that require you to expand, factor, or solve quadratics. You may even need to find the vertex of a parabola or the points of intersection of a quadratic and a line. So, let's review, starting with the basics.

Expanding

You may be asked to expand an expression simply by multiplying it out. When working with an expression of the form $(x + 3)(x + 4)$, multiply it out using the following rule:

> FOIL = First Outer Inner Last

Start with the *first* term in each set of parentheses: $x \times x = x^2$.

Now do the two *outer* terms: $x \times 4 = 4x$.

Next, the two *inner* terms: $3 \times x = 3x$.

Finally, the *last* term in each set of parentheses: $3 \times 4 = 12$.

Add them all together, and we get $x^2 + 4x + 3x + 12$, or $x^2 + 7x + 12$.

Factoring

If you ever see an expression of the form $x^2 + 7x + 12$ on the PSAT 8/9, there is a good chance that factoring it will be the key to cracking it.

The key to factoring is figuring out what pair of numbers will multiply to give you the constant term (12, in this case) and add up to the coefficient of the x term (7, in this case).

Let's try an example:

$$x^2 + 7x + 12$$

Step 1: Draw two sets of parentheses next to each other and fill an x into the left side of each. That's what gives us our x^2 term.

$$(x \quad)(x \quad)$$

Step 2: 12 can be factored a number of ways: 1×12, 2×6, or 3×4. Which of these adds up to 7? 3 and 4, so place a 3 on the right side of one set of parentheses and a 4 in the other.

$$(x \quad 3)(x \quad 4)$$

Step 3: Now we need to figure out what the correct signs should be. They should both be positive in this case, because that will sum to 7 and multiply to 12, so fill plus signs into each parentheses.

$$(x + 3)(x + 4)$$

If you want to double-check your work, try expanding out $(x + 3)(x + 4)$ using FOIL and you'll get the original expression.

Now try the following question.

———————————○———————————

1   ⬚ Mark for Review

The expression $x^2 - 4x - 32$ can be rewritten as $(x - 8)(x + k)$, where k is a constant. What is the value of k?

⬚

Here's How to Crack It

The question asks for the value of a constant in a quadratic. Normally, you would need to factor the entire quadratic. In this case, however, three parts of the factored form are already filled in, and you only need to find the fourth part. Think about FOIL, and start with the Last terms: $(-8)(k) = -32$. Divide both sides of the equation by -8 to get $k = 4$. To check, work with the Outer and Inner terms. The factored form quadratic is now $(x - 8)(x + 4)$, so the Outer terms become $(x)(4)$, or $4x$, and the Inner terms become $(-8)(x)$, or $-8x$. Combine the x-terms to get $4x + (-8x)$, which becomes $4x - 8x$, and then $-4x$. This matches the middle term of the original quadratic, so everything is equivalent when $k = 4$. The correct answer is 4.

———————————○———————————

Solving Quadratic Equations

Sometimes you'll want to factor to solve an equation. In this case, there will be two possible values for x, called the roots of the equation. To solve for x, use the following steps:

Step 1: Make sure that the equation is set equal to zero.
Step 2: Factor the equation.
Step 3: Set each parenthetical expression equal to zero. So, if you have $(x + 2)(x - 7) = 0$, you get $(x + 2) = 0$ and $(x - 7) = 0$. When you solve for each, you get $x = -2$ and $x = 7$. Therefore, -2 and 7 are the solutions or roots of the equation.

Try the following question.

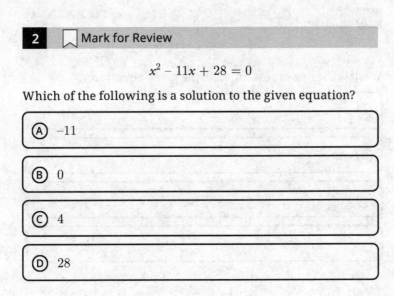

2 ⬚ Mark for Review

$$x^2 - 11x + 28 = 0$$

Which of the following is a solution to the given equation?

(A) -11

(B) 0

(C) 4

(D) 28

Here's How to Crack It

The question asks for the solution to a quadratic. This quadratic is already equal to zero, so it's time to start factoring. Find two numbers that multiply to 28 and add to -11. These are -7 and -4, so the factors are $(x - 7)$ and $(x - 4)$. Set each factor equal to zero and solve for x. When $x - 7 = 0$, add 7 to both sides of the equation to get $x = 7$. When $x - 4 = 0$, add 4 to both sides of the equation to get $x = 4$. Only 4 is an answer choice, so (C) is correct.

There's another way to crack this question. When a question asks for a specific value and the answer choices have numbers in order, you can plug in the answers (PITA). Rewrite the answer choices on your scratch paper and label them "x." Start with one of the numbers in the middle and try (B), 0. Plug $x = 0$ into the equation to get $0^2 - 11(0) + 28 = 0$, which becomes $0 - 0 + 28 = 0$, and then $28 = 0$. This is not true, so eliminate (B). Try (C) next, and plug $x = 4$ into the equation to get $4^2 - 11(4) + 28 = 0$, which becomes $16 - 44 + 28 = 0$, and then $0 = 0$. This is true, so 4 is a solution to the equation and (C) is correct.

Using either method, the correct answer is (C).

PITA is a good idea whenever the question asks for a solution and has numbers in the answer choices, but it's a *great* idea when the quadratic is difficult to factor. When there is a coefficient on the x^2-term, the numbers are large or awkward (such as fractions or decimals), or the quadratic doesn't factor cleanly, you will be glad you know how to plug in the answers.

The built-in calculator can also be used to find the solutions to a quadratic, and you might be surprised at just how useful this tool can be. Try using the built-in calculator yourself on the following question, and then we'll explain some of the details.

Here's a question with a quadratic that is harder to factor.

---

3   ☐ Mark for Review

$$3x^2 - 10x - 8 = 0$$

What is the negative solution to the given equation?

Ⓐ -10

Ⓑ -4

Ⓒ $-\dfrac{8}{3}$

Ⓓ $-\dfrac{2}{3}$

Here's How to Crack It

The question asks for the negative solution to a quadratic. The quadratic is difficult to factor, so one option is to plug in the answers. Even that might be time-consuming with fractions, so utilize the most efficient approach: the built-in calculator. First, click the calculator icon in the upper right to open the calculator, and then click Expand in the upper right of the calculator to make it easier to see the graphing area. Next, enter the equation into the first entry field on the left, either by typing it or by opening the on-screen keyboard with the icon in the lower left. The graphing area on the right shows something that might look a little strange.

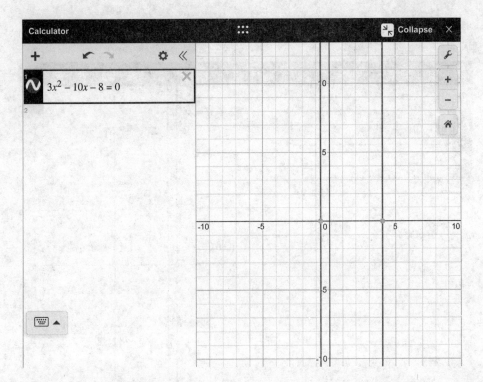

The two vertical lines represent the solutions to the equation. If you prefer to see a parabola, delete the "= 0" part of the equation. The next screenshot has both versions so you can see that they intersect the *x*-axis at the same two points.

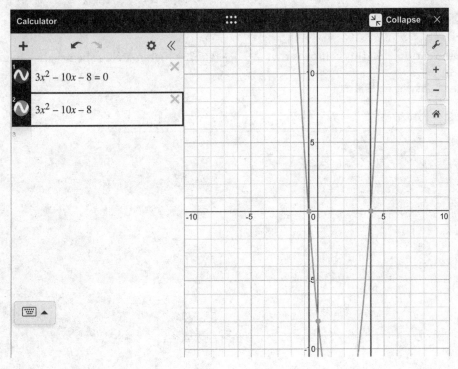

Click on the gray dots at the solutions, and they turn black and show you the coordinates of the points.

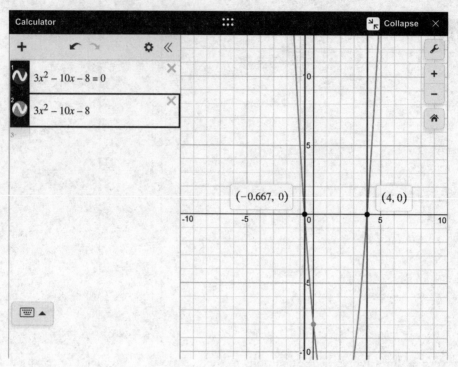

The solutions are at (−0.667, 0) and (4, 0). Notice that 4 is the positive solution, so (B) is a trap answer. Enter $-\dfrac{2}{3}$ in the built-in calculator, and the decimal form will appear in the lower right of the entry field. This confirms that $-\dfrac{2}{3} = -0.667$, which matches the negative solution. The correct answer is (D).

○

Forms of Quadratics

When graphed in the *xy*-plane, quadratics form a parabola. The PSAT 8/9 will ask questions using three different forms of the equation for a parabola.

The **standard form** of a parabola equation is as follows:

$$y = ax^2 + bx + c$$

In the standard form of a parabola, the value of *a* tells whether a parabola opens upward or downward (if *a* is positive, the parabola opens upward, and if *a* is negative, the parabola opens downward).

The **factored form** of a parabola equation is as follows:

$$y = a(x - s)(x - t)$$

In the factored form, *s* and *t* are the *x*-intercepts.

We discussed factoring quadratics a few pages back. The result of factoring a parabolic equation is the factored form.

The **vertex form** of a parabola equation is as follows:

$$y = a(x - h)^2 + k$$

In the vertex form, the point (h, k) is the vertex of the parabola.

It is definitely helpful to know the three forms of a quadratic equation, what they show, and how to convert one to another. However, the built-in graphing calculator will show the same graph no matter which form the equation is in, or even if it's in a different form entirely. Know the rules, but also know when to ignore them and let the built-in calculator do your work for you.

Take a look at this one.

---

4 ☐ Mark for Review

$$4x^2 + 1 = 25 - 4x$$

What is the product of the solutions to the given equation?

Ⓐ −6

Ⓑ 1

Ⓒ 6

Ⓓ 25

Here's How to Crack It

The question asks for the product of the solutions to a quadratic equation. One method is to put the quadratic into standard form. When a quadratic is in standard form, $ax^2 + bx + c = 0$, the product of the solutions equals $\frac{c}{a}$. Add $4x$ to both sides of the equation to get $4x^2 + 4x + 1 = 25$, and then subtract 25 from both sides of the equation to get $4x^2 + 4x - 24 = 0$. Now that the quadratic is in standard form, $c = -24$ and $a = 4$, so the product of the solutions is $\frac{-24}{4}$, or −6, which is (A).

That got the correct answer, but it took a few steps and there are trap answers lying in wait, such as getting a sign wrong and picking (C) instead of (A). The safer and more efficient method is to use the built-in calculator. Enter the equation as written into an entry field. The points where the two vertical lines cross the x-axis, represented by gray dots, are the solutions. Click on each gray dot and write down the x-values: −2 and 3. Multiply the solutions to get $(-2)(3) = -6$, which is (A)

Using either method, the correct answer is (A).

The previous question asked for the product of the solutions, which removes PITA as an option. The same will be true when the question asks for the sum of the solutions, so learn the shortcuts for both. When a quadratic is in standard form, $ax^2 + bx + c = 0$, the sum of the solutions equals $-\dfrac{b}{a}$ and the product of the solutions equals $\dfrac{c}{a}$, as seen in the previous question. Memorize these shortcuts in case you encounter a question like this that can't be solved with the built-in calculator.

Words Squared

Sometimes, quadratic equations will be tested with word problems or data. Let's look at a word problem with a quadratic equation.

5　　🔖 Mark for Review

A biologist studying the population of birds on an island finds that the equation $P = -0.2w^2 + 10w + 120$ can be used to model the number of birds in the population, P, at w weeks since the study began. After how many weeks was the population of birds at its maximum number?

Ⓐ　0

Ⓑ　25

Ⓒ　60

Ⓓ　120

Here's How to Crack It

The question asks for a maximum value given a quadratic that models a specific situation. The graph of a quadratic is a parabola, and a parabola reaches its minimum or maximum value at its vertex, so the question is asking about the vertex of the parabola. Factoring the quadratic would get messy, but there is an algebraic shortcut. When a quadratic is in standard form, $ax^2 + bx + c$, the x-coordinate of the vertex can be found using the equation $h = -\dfrac{b}{2a}$, where (h, k) is the vertex. In this case, $b = 10$ and $a = -0.2$, so $h = -\dfrac{10}{2(-0.2)}$, which becomes $h = -\dfrac{10}{-0.4}$, and then $h = 25$, which is (B).

Even with this shortcut, that was pretty complicated. A better approach would be to save time and mental energy by using the built-in calculator. There are a couple of quirks to be aware of. First, the built-in calculator only shows a graph with x and y, so change w to x and P to y before entering the equation. Enter the equation as usual, and you will see that, unless you had resized the graphing area on a previous question, there is only a small piece of the graph showing, and the vertex is nowhere to be seen.

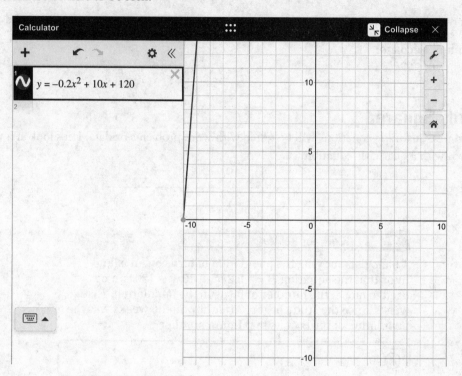

You can use the + and − buttons in the upper right, the scroll wheel on your mouse, or the track pad on your computer to make the area larger or smaller. You can also click and drag in the graphing area to move things around. If at some point you want to recenter everything to its default setting, click on the icon of a house that appears in the upper right.

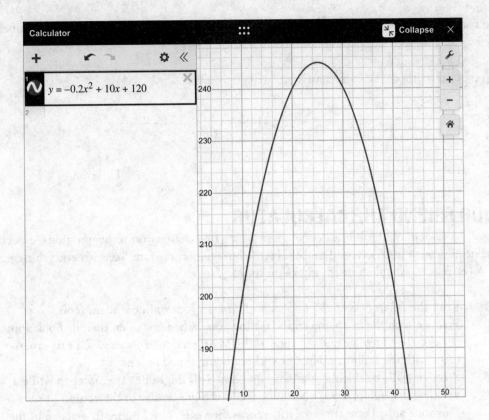

Once you do that, you can see the vertex, but there's no gray dot. Click on the graph or on the equation in the entry field to bring back the gray dots. Then click on the gray dot at the vertex to see that the coordinates are (25, 245).

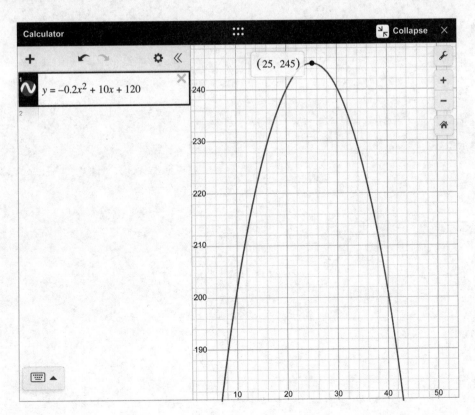

The *x*-axis represents the number of weeks, so the population reaches its maximum number 25 weeks after the study began, and (B) is correct.

Using either method, the correct answer is (B).

YOUR FRIEND THE CALCULATOR

As you have seen, the built-in calculator can be a game changer on some questions, especially ones dealing with functions and graphs. Here's how to become familiar with everything it can do so you're ready to take full advantage on test day.

1. Read the *Digital PSAT 8/9 Calculator Guide* in your online student tools.
2. Practice with the calculator in the testing app. When you open the Bluebook app, click on Test Preview and advance to the Math section. This way, you can experiment with the built-in calculator without being timed or scored.
3. Practice with the calculator at Desmos.com. This might be easier to open while working through practice questions, and it is quite similar to the version in the Bluebook app. There are some differences, however, so it's better to practice in the testing app as much as possible.
4. Use it while working through this book, practice tests, and any other prep that you do.

Drill 2

Time: 10 minutes. Answers can be found in Part IV.

---

1 🔖 Mark for Review

$$f(x) = x^2 + 8x + 23$$

The function f is defined by the given equation. The graph of $f(x)$ in the xy-plane reaches its minimum at (a, b). What is the value of a?

_____

---

2 🔖 Mark for Review

$$625x^2 - 144$$

Which of the following expressions is equivalent to the given expression?

(A) $(25x - 12)(25x - 12)$

(B) $(25x - 36)(125x - 4)$

(C) $(25x - 12)(25x + 12)$

(D) $(25x - 36)(125x + 4)$

---

3 🔖 Mark for Review

$$x^2 - 20x + 75 = 0$$

What is the sum of the solutions to the given equation?

(A) -20

(B) -10

(C) 10

(D) 20

---

4 🔖 Mark for Review

$$y = -x^2 + 2x + 1$$
$$y - 4 = -2$$

The given system of equations has one solution at (x, y). What is the value of x?

_____

5 ☐ Mark for Review

When $x^2 + 2x + 4$ is subtracted from $3x^2 - 4x + 27$, the result can be written in the form $ax^2 + by + c$, where a, b, and c are constants. What is the value of $b + c$?

6 ☐ Mark for Review

$$(ax - b)(ax - b) = 25x^2 - 40x + 16$$

In the given equation, a and b are constants. Which of the following could be the value of a?

Ⓐ 4

Ⓑ 5

Ⓒ 16

Ⓓ 25

7 ☐ Mark for Review

$$y = x^2 - 2x - 6$$
$$y = -5x + 4$$

The graphs of the equations in the given system of equations intersect at the point (x, y). What is a possible value of x?

Ⓐ −6

Ⓑ −2

Ⓒ 2

Ⓓ 5

Summary

o   Given a function, you plug in an x-value (input) and get a y-value (output).

o   Look for ways to use Plugging In and PITA on function questions.

o   When a word problem asks for a function that represents or models are situation, work in Bite-Sized Pieces and use POE.

o   For questions about the graphs of functions, remember that $f(x) = y$.

o   If a graph contains labeled (x, y) points or a table provides pairs of x and $f(x)$ values, plug those values into the equations in the answer choices and eliminate any that aren't true.

o   To find a point of intersection, either use the built-in calculator or set the equations equal to each other and solve.

o   When solving quadratic equations, you may need to use FOIL or factor to get the equation into the easiest form for the question task.

o   Know the three forms of a quadratic equation and how to convert an equation in one form into another form.

o   When a quadratic is in standard form, $ax^2 + bx + c = 0$, there are three shortcuts to know:

   • The sum of the solutions is $-\dfrac{b}{a}$.

   • The product of the solutions is $\dfrac{c}{a}$.

   • The x-coordinate of the vertex is $-\dfrac{b}{2a}$.

o   Use the built-in calculator as often as possible for questions about functions, quadratics, and graphs. Practice with it *a lot* before test day.

Chapter 14
Geometry

Between four and six questions on the PSAT 8/9 Math section will be about geometry. While there are many topics in these categories that could be tested, each one will only appear once or twice on the test. Everything you've learned so far, such as PITA and POE, will often work on geometry questions. Spend time on this chapter only after you have mastered the topics and techniques in the previous three chapters.

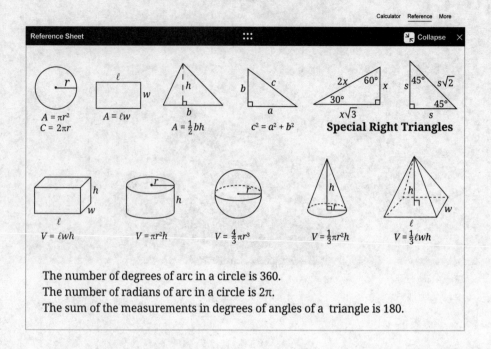

Calculator Reference More

The number of degrees of arc in a circle is 360.
The number of radians of arc in a circle is 2π.
The sum of the measurements in degrees of angles of a triangle is 180.

You can access the reference sheet above at any point during the Math section by clicking **Reference** in the upper right corner of the screen. Once you look up the information you need, click the **X** to return to the question. You can also click **Collapse** to shrink the reference window in order to see the formulas and the question at the same time or **Expand** to make it full size.

GEOMETRY

Lines and Angles

Common sense might tell you what a line is, but for this test you are going to have to learn the particulars of a line and a line segment.

A **line** continues on in each direction forever. You need only two points to form a line, but that line does not end at those points. A straight line has 180° on each side.

A **line segment** is a line with two distinct endpoints. It requires two points, and it is the length from one point to the other. A line segment has 180°. Geometric figures are made up of connected line segments.

Whenever you have angles on a line, remember *the rule of 180*: The angles on any line must add up to 180. These angles are called *supplementary angles*. In the figure below, what is the value of x? We know that $2x + x$ must add up to 180, so we know that $3x = 180$. This makes $x = 60$.

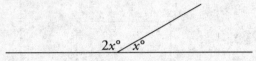

Note: Figure not drawn to scale.

If two lines cross each other, they make *vertical angles*—that is, angles opposite each other when two lines intersect. These angles will always have the same measure. In the figure below, z and x are vertical angles, and y and the 130° angle are vertical angles. Also, we know that z must equal 50, since $130 + z$ must equal 180. We know that y is 130, since it is across from the 130° angle. We also know that x is 50, since it is across from z.

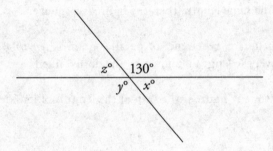

Any time you have two parallel lines and a line that crosses them, you have two kinds of angles: big angles and small angles. All of the big angles have the same measure, and all of the small angles have the same measure. In the following figure, angles a, d, e, and h all have the same measure; angles b, c, f, and g also all have the same measure. The sum of the measure of any big angle plus any small angle equals 180°.

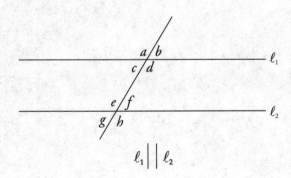

Four-Sided Figures

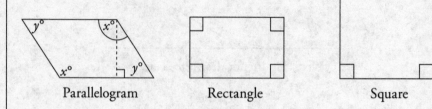

Parallelogram   Rectangle   Square

A figure with two sets of parallel sides is a **parallelogram**. In a parallelogram, the opposite angles are equal, and any adjacent angles add up to 180°. (In the left-hand figure above, $x + y = 180°$.) Opposite sides are also equal. The sum of all angles of a parallelogram is 360°.

If all of the angles are also right angles, then the figure is a **rectangle**. And if all of the sides are the same length, then the figure is a **square**.

The *area* of a square, rectangle, or parallelogram is *length* × *width*. (In the parallelogram above, the length is shown by the dotted line.)

The *perimeter* of any figure is the sum of the lengths of its sides.

Drill 1

Time: 6 minutes. Answers can be found in Part IV.

---

1 ☐ Mark for Review

What is the area, in square inches, of a square with a side length of 26 inches?

(A) 52

(B) 104

(C) 338

(D) 676

---

2 ☐ Mark for Review

A rectangle has a length of 15 centimeters and a width of 30 centimeters. What is the perimeter of the rectangle?

(A) 45

(B) 60

(C) 90

(D) 450

---

3 ☐ Mark for Review

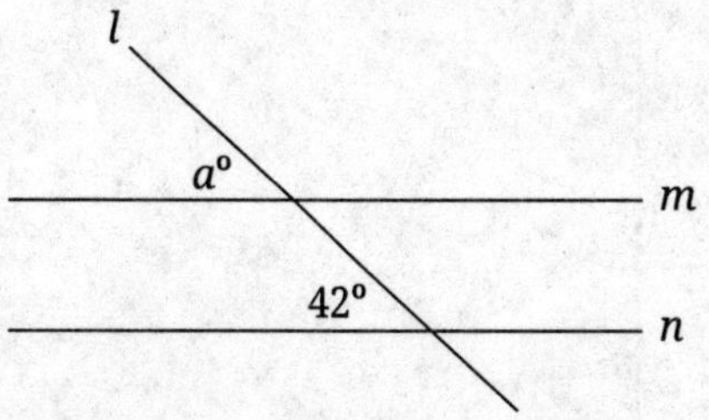

Note: Figure not drawn to scale.

In the figure shown, line *l* intersects parallel lines *m* and *n*. What is the value of *a*?

(A) 42

(B) 48

(C) 138

(D) 142

---

4 ☐ Mark for Review

The area of a certain rectangle is given by the equation $72 = (2w)(w)$. What is the value of w?

TRIANGLES

The sum of the angles inside a triangle must be equal to 180°. This means that if you know two of the angles in a triangle, you can always solve for the third. Since you know that two of the angles in the following figure are 90° and 60°, you can solve for the third angle, which must be 30°. (Note: The little square in the bottom corner of the triangle indicates a right angle, which is 90°.)

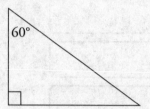

An **isosceles triangle** has two sides that are equal. Angles that are opposite equal sides must be equal. The figure below is an isosceles triangle. Since $AB = BC$, you know that angles x and y are equal. And since their sum must be 150° (to make a total of 180° when you add the last angle), they each must be 75°.

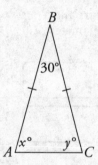

The **area** of a triangle is $\frac{1}{2}$ *base* × *height*. Note that the height is always perpendicular to the base.

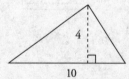

$$\text{Area} = \frac{1}{2} \times 10 \times 4 = 20 \qquad \text{Area} = \frac{1}{2} \times 6 \times 4 = 12$$

An **equilateral triangle** has all three sides equal and all of its angles equal to 60°.

Here's a typical example of a one kind of triangle question you might see on the PSAT 8/9.

1	🔖 Mark for Review

Two sides of an equilateral triangle have a combined length of 110 meters. What is the perimeter, in inches, of the triangle?

_____

Here's How to Crack It

The question asks for the perimeter of an equilateral triangle. Start by drawing a figure on your scratch paper. An equilateral triangle has equal sides and equal angles, so the figure should look something like this:

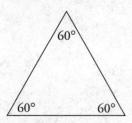

Look for more information in the question that you can make use of. If two of the equal sides have a combined length of 110 meters, each side has a length of $\frac{110}{2} = 55$ meters. All three sides of an equilateral triangle have the same length, so label each side on the figure 55.

Being Aggressive on Geometry Questions

The most important problem-solving technique for tackling PSAT 8/9 geometry is to learn to be aggressive. This means that, whenever you have a diagram, ask yourself, *What else do I know?* Write everything you can think of on your scratch paper. You may not see right away why it's important, but write it down anyway. Chances are good that you will be making progress toward the answer without even knowing it.

The PSAT 8/9 is also fond of disguising familiar figures within more complex shapes by extending lines, overlapping figures, or combining several basic shapes. So be on the lookout for the basic figures hidden in complicated shapes.

The figure now looks like this:

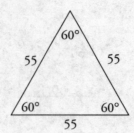

The perimeter of any geometric figure is the sum of the lengths of its sides, so add up the three sides to get 55 + 55 + 55 = 165. Since the sides are all the same length, it is also possible to multiply one side length by 3 to get 55(3) = 165. The correct answer is 165.

The Pythagorean Theorem

Whenever you have a right triangle, you can use the Pythagorean Theorem. The theorem says that the sum of the squares of the legs of the triangle (the sides that form the right angle) will equal the square of the hypotenuse (the side opposite the right angle).

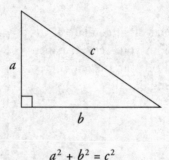

$$a^2 + b^2 = c^2$$

Try the following example.

2	🔖 Mark for Review

The length of the hypotenuse of a certain right triangle is $6\sqrt{13}$. If one of the legs has length 18, what is the length of the other leg?

Ⓐ $\sqrt{42}$

Ⓑ 12

Ⓒ 18

Ⓓ $12\sqrt{13}$

Here's How to Crack It

The question asks for a measure on a geometric figure. Start by drawing a right triangle on your scratch paper, and then label it with information from the question. Label the hypotenuse $6\sqrt{13}$, and label one of the other sides 18. Next, write out the Pythagorean Theorem, either from memory or after looking it up on the reference sheet: $a^2 + b^2 = c^2$. Fill in the given side lengths to get $a^2 + 18^2 = \left(6\sqrt{13}\right)^2$. Use a calculator to get $a^2 + 324 = 468$. Subtract 324 from both sides of the equation to get $a^2 = 144$. When dealing with geometry, only the positive root matters (a length on a figure can't be negative), so take the positive square root of both sides of the equation to get $a = 12$. The correct answer is (B).

Similar Triangles

Similar triangles have the same shape, but they are not necessarily the same size. Having the same shape means that the angles of the triangles are identical and that the corresponding sides have the same ratio. Look at the following two similar triangles:

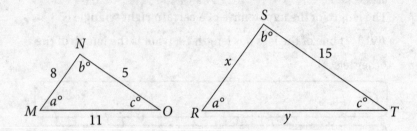

These two triangles both have the same set of angles, but they aren't the same size. Whenever this is true, the sides of one triangle are proportional to those of the other. Notice that sides $\overline{NO}$ and $\overline{ST}$ are both opposite the angle that is $a°$. These are called corresponding sides, because they correspond to the same angle. So, the lengths of $\overline{NO}$ and $\overline{ST}$ are proportional to each other. In order to figure out the lengths of the other sides, set up a proportion: $\dfrac{MN}{RS} = \dfrac{NO}{ST}$.

Now fill in the information that you know: $\dfrac{8}{x} = \dfrac{5}{15}$. Cross-multiply and you find that $x = 24$.

You could also figure out the length of y: $\dfrac{NO}{ST} = \dfrac{MO}{RT}$. So, $\dfrac{5}{15} = \dfrac{11}{y}$, and $y = 33$. Whenever you have to deal with sides of similar triangles, just set up a proportion.

Drill 2

Time: 6 minutes. Answers can be found in Part IV.

1 ⬚ Mark for Review

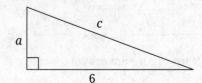

Note: Figure not drawn to scale.

Which of the following equations expresses a in terms of c?

(A) $a = \sqrt{c - 6}$

(B) $a = \sqrt{c^2 - 36}$

(C) $a = c - 6$

(D) $a = c^2 - 36$

2 ⬚ Mark for Review

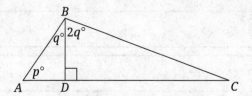

Note: Figure not drawn to scale.

In the figure shown, angle BCD measures 20°. What is the value of p?

(A) 50

(B) 55

(C) 60

(D) 70

3 ☐ Mark for Review

Triangle ABC is similar to triangle $A'B'C'$, where A, B, and C correspond to A', B', and C', respectively. The measure of angle B is 60°, the measure of angle C is 105°, and the length of each side of $A'B'C'$ is five times the length of each corresponding side of ABC. What is the measure of angle A'?

(A) 15

(B) 45

(C) 75

(D) 165

4 ☐ Mark for Review

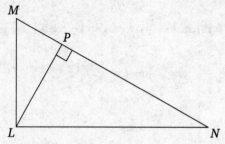

Note: Figure not drawn to scale.

In the figure shown, the measure of angle LNP is equal to the measure of angle MLP. If $MP = 8$ and the length of $\overline{LN}$ is twice the length of $\overline{LM}$, what is the length of $\overline{LP}$?

(A) 4

(B) 8

(C) 16

(D) 32

VOLUME

Volume questions on the PSAT 8/9 can seem intimidating at times. The PSAT 8/9 sometimes gives you questions featuring unusual shapes such as pyramids and spheres. Luckily, the reference sheet contains all the formulas you will ever need for volume questions on the PSAT 8/9. Remember to click it open whenever you need a geometry formula that you don't have memorized.

Let's look at an example.

---

1   🔖 Mark for Review

A pool in the shape of a rectangular prism has a depth of 3 meters and a volume of 288 cubic meters. If the pool is 4 meters longer than it is wide, what is the width of the pool, in meters?

(A) 8

(B) 12

(C) 24

(D) 44

Here's How to Crack It

The question asks for a measure on a geometric figure. Start by drawing a rectangular prism on your scratch paper as best as possible. It doesn't have to be perfect, and you can use the one on the reference sheet to guide you. The depth of the pool is the same thing as the height of the rectangular prism, so label the height 3. Next, write down the formula for the volume of a rectangular prism, either from memory or after looking it up on the reference sheet. The formula is $V = lwh$.

The question gives the relationship between the length and the width, and the answer choices have numbers in order, so plug in the answers. Rewrite the answer choices on your scratch paper and label them "width." Start with one of the middle numbers and try (B), 12. The question states that *the pool is 4 meters longer than it is wide*, so the length is 12 + 4 = 16 when the width is 12. Plug in these values and the values given in the question for the volume and height to get 288 = (16)(12)(3). Simplify the right side of the equation to get 288 = 576. This is not true, so eliminate (B). The result on the right side of the equation was too large, so also eliminate (C) and (D). Choice (A) works because, when the width is 8, the length is 8 + 4 = 12. This makes the volume formula 288 = (12)(8)(3), or 288 = 288, which is true. The correct answer is (A).

PLUGGING IN ON GEOMETRY

As you saw on the previous question, plugging in the answers (PITA) works on geometry questions too! The question asked for a specific value and the answers had numbers in order, both of which are clues that you can use PITA. You can also plug in your own numbers on some geometry questions. The clues to look for are a question about relative values and answer choices with variables.

Here's an example.

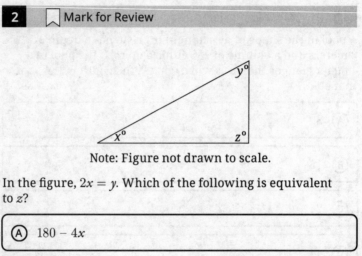

Note: Figure not drawn to scale.

In the figure, $2x = y$. Which of the following is equivalent to z?

(A) $180 - 4x$

(B) $180 - 3x$

(C) $180 + x$

(D) $180 + 2x$

Here's How to Crack It

The question asks for an equivalent expression. The question asks about the relationship among variables, and there are variables in the answer choices, so plug in. Make $x = 30$, which makes $y = 2(30)$, or $y = 60$. All triangles contain 180°, so $z = 180 - 30 - 60$, or $z = 90$. This is the target value; write it down and circle it.

Next, plug $x = 30$ into each answer choice, and eliminate any that do not equal the target value. Choice (A) becomes $180 - 4(30)$, then $180 - 120$, and finally 60. This does not match the target value of 90, so eliminate (A). Choice (B) becomes $180 - 3(30)$, then $180 - 90$, and finally 90. This matches the target value, so keep (B), but check the remaining answers just in case. Choice (C) becomes $180 + 30$, or 210; eliminate (C). Choice (D) will be even bigger, so also eliminate (D), which leaves (B).

We got a little lucky to get $z = 90$ because that matches the figure. Keep in mind, however, that the figures are not drawn to scale, and you don't need to worry about picking numbers that match the figure precisely. For example, if $x = 20$, $y = 40$, $z = 120$, and (B) becomes $180 - 3(20) = 120$. Or if $x = 50$, $y = 100$, $z = 30$, and (B) becomes $180 - 3(50) = 30$. No matter what value you plug in for x, (B) will always have the same value as z. That's why plugging in works so well on questions about the relationship among variables.

The correct answer is (B).

Drill 3

Time: 6 minutes. Answers can be found in Part IV.

---

1 ☐ Mark for Review

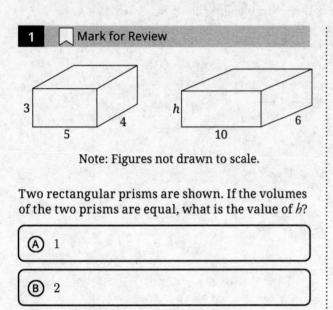

3

5   4

h

10   6

Note: Figures not drawn to scale.

Two rectangular prisms are shown. If the volumes of the two prisms are equal, what is the value of *h*?

(A) 1

(B) 2

(C) 5

(D) 8

---

2 ☐ Mark for Review

The area of a certain triangle is 21 square centimeters. If the height of the triangle is 1 centimeter longer than the base of the triangle, which of the following is the length, in centimeters, of the height of the triangle?

(A) 4

(B) 5

(C) 6

(D) 7

---

3 ☐ Mark for Review

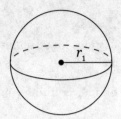

The figure shown is a sphere with a radius of r_1. A second sphere (not shown) has a radius of r_2. If the volume of the second sphere is 8 times the volume of the first sphere, which of the following represents the radius of the second sphere, r_2 in terms of r_1?

Ⓐ $r_2 = \frac{1}{2}r_1$

Ⓑ $r_2 = 2r_1$

Ⓒ $r_2 = 6r_1$

Ⓓ $r_2 = 8r_1$

4 ☐ Mark for Review

Two square garden plots are next to each other. Each side of plot A is 4 feet longer than each side of plot B. The area of plot A is 64 square feet greater than the area of plot B. What is the length of one side of plot B, in feet?

Ⓐ 6

Ⓑ 8

Ⓒ 10

Ⓓ 16

Summary

o Be sure to review your basic geometry rules before the test; often, questions hinge on knowing that vertical angles are equal or that the sum of the angles in a quadrilateral is 360°.

o On all geometry questions, draw figures on your scratch paper and fill in everything you know.

o When two parallel lines are cut by a third line, the small angles are equal, the big angles are equal, and the sum of a big angle and a small angle is 180°.

o The perimeter of a rectangle is the sum of the lengths of its sides. The area of a rectangle is *length* × *width*.

o The perimeter of a triangle is the sum of the lengths of its sides. The area of a triangle is $\frac{1}{2}$ *base* × *height*.

o Knowing the Pythagorean Theorem, $a^2 + b^2 = c^2$, will help you figure out angles and lengths in a right triangle.

o Similar triangles have the same angles, and their side lengths are proportional.

o The formulas to compute the volumes of many three-dimensional figures are supplied in the reference sheet that can be clicked open at any time during the Math section.

o Look for opportunities to plug in the answer choices or your own numbers on geometry questions.

Part IV
Drill Answers
and Explanations

CHAPTER 6

Reading Drill (page 167)

1. **D** This is a Vocabulary question, as it asks for *the logical and precise word or phrase* to fill in the blank. The blank should describe the Supreme Court case, so look for and highlight clues in the passage about the case. The passage states that *when the Court ruled in favor of Heffernan*, it brought an end to a *truly odd sequence of events*. Therefore, a good word to enter in the annotation box would be "strange" or "odd."

   - (A) and (C) are wrong because *critical* (important) and *trivial* (unimportant) don't match *strange*—it's not known from the passage how important or not the case was.

   - (B) is wrong because *unprejudiced* goes **Beyond the Text**—while the demotion is implied to be unfair, no information is given as to how fairly the case itself proceeded.

   - (D) is correct because *unusual* matches "strange."

2. **A** This is a Purpose question, as it asks for the *overall structure of the text*. Read the passage and highlight the connections between ideas in the passage. The passage is about the work of Alfred Blaschko, who *observed that some patients' skin displays distinctive patterns of patches or streaks*. The passage claims that *one possible cause* of these lines *was later determined to be chimerism*, and that these findings *paved the way for scientists to identify and study chimerism*. Therefore, a good overall structure of the passage to enter in the annotation box would be "describe Blaschko's work and its importance."

   - (A) is correct because it's consistent with the highlighting and annotation.

   - (B) is wrong because it's **Half-Right**—while a hypothesis is offered using the phrase *possible cause*, the passage does not describe Blaschko's *methodology*, or process, for conducting his observations.

   - (C) and (D) are wrong because they're both the **Opposite** of how the passage treats Blaschko's work—his work is the foundation for what later scientists do. No one *rejects* Blaschko's methodology nor is his conclusion *disproved*.

3. **C** This is a Dual Texts question, as it asks what *the author of Text 2* would say about *the underlined portion of Text 1*. Read Text 1 and focus on the underlined portion, which indicates that *these toddlers had adopted what they believed to be the "morality" of the adult experimenters*. Then, read Text 2 and highlight what its author says about the same topic. The author states that children *may seemingly make good moral choices…but only out of fear of punishment, not from any independent moral conclusion*. Therefore, the author of Text 2 would not think the children's choices in Text 1 were based on morality, but rather

the desire to avoid punishment for making the wrong choice. Enter "Text 2 believes the choices were made to avoid punishment" into the annotation box.

- (A) is wrong because it goes **Beyond the Text**—Text 1 only indicates that children may adopt the moral code of adults, not the other way around. Also, neither author criticizes the morality displayed in Text 1 as *questionable*.

- (B) is wrong because it also goes **Beyond the Text**—neither passage suggests that children may have an *innate fear of yellow toys*.

- (C) is correct because it's consistent with the highlighting and annotation—avoiding n*egative consequences* could be the same as avoiding *punishment*.

- (D) is wrong because it also goes **Beyond the Text**—while it's probably true that older children can grasp complex issues better than younger children, no such comparison between older and younger children is made in the passages.

4. **D** This is a Retrieval question, as it asks for a detail about the *development of gwo ka*. Look for and highlight information about gwo ka. The passage states that *Gwo ka emerged* by combining bouladjèl with *two hand drums* and that *Today, a wider variety* of instruments *can be used in gwo ka music, but the same fundamental seven drum beats* are always used. The correct answer should be as consistent as possible with these details.

- (A) is wrong because it goes **Beyond the Text**—it's not possible to know from the passage what would or would not have happened to gwo ka without the French influence.

- (B) is wrong because it's the **Opposite** of the passage—there is a clear difference between gwo ka and bouladjèl, that being that gwo ka uses drums.

- (C) is wrong because it also goes **Beyond the Text**—just because gwo ka has Guadeloupean and French influences does not mean the music style *united multiple cultures through a celebration*.

- (D) is correct because it's consistent with the highlighted descriptions of gwo ka—gwo ka always uses *the same fundamental seven drum beats* even if modern gwo ka uses *a wider variety* of instruments.

5. **B** This is a Main Idea question, as it asks for the *main idea of the text*. Look for and highlight information that can help identify the main idea. The passage states that because of the Johnstown Inclined Plane, *citizens were able to be evacuated safely and efficiently* in a flood and that the *Inclined Plane also helped economically*. Since the other sentences describe the background of the Johnstown Inclined Plane, the last two sentences serve as the main idea. The correct answer should be as consistent as possible with this portion of the passage.

- (A) and (D) are wrong because they each go **Beyond the Text**—it's not known from the passage that anyone created *similar mountain railways* or that *more hillside communities* were founded because of the Plane.

- (B) is correct because it's consistent with the highlighted portion of the passage—the improved safety and boon to the economy would be *multiple benefits*.

- (C) is wrong because it's **Extreme Language**—while the Inclined Plane is a major convenience, it's not known from the passage that it is the *only* practical way to visit the valley.

6. **C** This is a Claims question, as it asks which choice *would most directly support Lowenstam and Skinner's conclusion*. Look for and highlight the conclusion in the passage, which is that *minerals created by living organisms should not be classified as wholly inorganic*. The correct answer should address and be consistent with each aspect of this conclusion.

- (A) is wrong because it does not support the conclusion—if the streaks in calcite *could have been created by organic or inorganic matter*, it is inconclusive to say whether calcite counts as organic or not.

- (B) is wrong because it goes **Beyond the Text**—though minerals can be formed by both *immense pressure* and *water accumulation*, this is outside knowledge and not discussed in the passage.

- (C) is correct because it's consistent with the highlighted conclusion—if calcite were not only created by a living organism but also *contains remnants of organic matter that were integral to its formation*, then it's a mineral that *should not be classified as wholly inorganic*.

- (D) is wrong because it's the **Opposite** of the question task—if calcite's composition was *consistent with formation processes often observed in inorganic matter*, this would weaken, not support, the researchers' conclusion.

7. **A** This is a Charts question, as it asks for *data from the graph* that will *complete the example*. Read the title, key, and variables from the graph. Then, read the passage and highlight the statement containing the same information, which is that *the cost of combined inputs and value of real outputs correlate*, or follow a similar trend. The correct answer should offer accurate information from the graph that provides an example of this statement.

- (A) is correct because it's consistent with the graph and relevant to the statement—from 2008 to 2012, combined inputs and real outputs both increase.

- (B), (C), and (D) are wrong because they're each consistent with the graph but irrelevant to the statement—(B) and (D) only discuss one of the two needed variables, and (C) focuses on a difference between real outputs and combined inputs rather than a correlation.

8. **B** This is a Conclusions question, as it asks what *most logically completes the text*. Look for the main focus of the passage, which is *why humans have phobias*. Then, highlight the main points made regarding this focus: first, the passage states that phobias are *essentially learned behaviors that result from unpleasant experiences with certain objects or situations*. Then, the passage states that *phobic responses can also develop from objects or situations that an individual has never encountered*. Therefore, there are multiple reasons as

to why people have or develop phobias. The correct answer should be as consistent as possible with this conclusion.

- (A) is wrong because it's **Recycled Language**—it combines *unconscious fears* and *strong phobic responses* from different parts of the passage. Furthermore, the passage does not claim that the mind has a *natural tendency* to create these fears.

- (B) is correct because it's consistent with what the two highlighted sentences claim about how phobias form.

- (C) is wrong because it's the **Opposite** of the passage—unconscious fears come despite a lack of exposure, not from having unpleasant experiences. Unpleasant experiences are part of the first reason given for the formation of phobias, not the second.

- (D) is wrong because it goes **Beyond the Text**—the passage makes no predictions about people developing phobias or not *in the future*.

CHAPTER 8

Punctuation Drill (page 201)

1. **B** In this Rules question, periods and question marks are changing in the answer choices, so it's testing questions versus statements. The beginning of the sentence states that *Uno and his team analyzed the fossilized tooth enamel to determine…*, so the second part of the sentence should be a statement. Eliminate answers that aren't correctly written as statements.

    - (A) and (C) are wrong because they are questions.

    - (B) is correct because it's correctly written as a statement.

    - (D) is wrong because it has a period but is written as a question.

2. **B** In this Rules question, verb forms are changing in the answer choices, so it's testing sentence structure. The sentence already contains an independent clause followed by a comma. Thus, the part after the comma must be a phrase that describes *One of her most famous pieces*. Eliminate any answer that does not correctly form this phrase.

    - (A) and (C) are wrong because they are in main verb form, but there is no subject for this verb.

    - (B) is correct because it correctly describes *One of her most famous pieces* as *combining* techniques.

    - (D) is wrong because *to combine traditional oil painting with modern digital image editing* does not provide a clear meaning within this sentence.

3. **B** In this Rules question, punctuation is changing in the answer choices. The sentence explains what *free male residents* would do at an assembly and contains the word *and* toward the end, so look for a list. The list consists of 1) *settle legal disputes,* 2) *approve new laws,* and 3) *listen to a speaker recite a list of all existing laws from memory.* Eliminate any answer that doesn't put commas between the list items.

    - (A), (C), and (D) are wrong because they don't have a comma after *disputes.*

    - (B) is correct because it has a comma after *disputes.*

4. **B** In this Rules question, punctuation is changing in the answer choices. Look for independent clauses. The first part of the sentence says *Soil acidification…can occur due to natural causes…,* which is an independent clause. The second part of the sentence says *though it can also be caused by human activities…,* which is a dependent clause. Eliminate any option that doesn't correctly connect an independent + a dependent clause.

    - (A), (C), and (D) are wrong because independent + dependent cannot be connected with punctuation other than a comma.

    - (B) is correct because independent + dependent can be connected with a comma.

5. **C** In this Rules question, punctuation is changing in the answer choices. Look for independent clauses. The first part of the sentence says *In the late 19th century…plover eggs were a luxurious food item,* which is an independent clause. The second part of the sentence says *and fetched high prices during nesting season,* which is a second piece of information about *plover eggs* that isn't an independent clause. Eliminate any answer that doesn't correctly connect these ideas.

    - (A) is wrong because a colon can't be used with a FANBOYS word after it.

    - (B) is wrong because a comma + a coordinating conjunction (*and*) is used to connect two independent clauses, but the second part isn't an independent clause.

    - (C) is correct because no punctuation should be used here since it's a list of only two things.

    - (D) is wrong because a semicolon is used to connect two independent clauses, but the second part isn't an independent clause. Semicolons can also be used to separate items in a complicated list of three of more things, but this list has only two items.

6. **C** In this Rules question, punctuation is changing in the answer choices. Look for independent clauses. The first part of the sentence says *…Sea Shepherd Conservation Society has been working to protect the vaquita marina…through Operation Milagro…,* which is an independent clause. The second part of the sentence says *despite these efforts, the vaquita population continues to decline…,* which is also an independent clause. Eliminate any answer that can't correctly connect two independent clauses.

    - (A) is wrong because a comma without a coordinating conjunction (FANBOYS) can't connect two independent clauses.

- (B) is wrong because some type of punctuation is needed in order to connect two independent clauses.

- (C) is correct because the period makes each independent clause its own sentence, which is fine.

- (D) is wrong because a coordinating conjunction (*but*) without a comma can't connect two independent clauses.

7.   **C**   In this Rules question, punctuation is changing in the answer choices. The main meaning of the sentence is …*Tagore continued his writing career, bringing Bengali literature to the world through multiple works…that explored love, politics, and philosophy*. The phrase containing a list of the works is a describing phrase that has a long dash before it, so it must have a long dash after it to show that it is Extra Information. Eliminate answers that do not have a long dash after the describing phrase.

- (A), (B), and (D) are wrong because they don't use a long dash.

- (C) is correct because it uses a long dash after the Extra Information.

8.   **D**   In this Rules question, punctuation is changing in the answer choices. Look for independent clauses. The first part of the sentence says *The denomination effect…states that consumers are less likely to spend money in larger cash denominations than in smaller ones…*, which is an independent clause. The second part of the sentence says *this theory was developed over the course of three studies…*, which is also an independent clause. Eliminate any answer that can't correctly connect two independent clauses.

- (A) is wrong because a coordinating conjunction (*and*) without a comma can't connect two independent clauses.

- (B) is wrong because some type of punctuation is needed in order to connect two independent clauses.

- (C) is wrong because a comma without a coordinating conjunction (FANBOYS) can't connect two independent clauses.

- (D) is correct because a semicolon can connect two independent clauses.

9.   **C**   In this Rules question, punctuation is changing in the answer choices. Look for independent clauses. The first part of the sentence says *The Kansas City preventative patrol experiment…yielded some surprising findings*, which is an independent clause. The second part of the sentence says *changing the level of patrol did not significantly affect the frequency of certain crimes…*, which is also an independent clause. Eliminate any option that can't correctly connect two independent clauses.

- (A) is wrong because a comma without a coordinating conjunction (FANBOYS) can't connect two independent clauses.

- (B) is wrong because a coordinating conjunction (*but*) without a comma can't connect two independent clauses.

- (C) is correct because a colon can connect two independent clauses if the second part expands on the first, as it does here.

- (D) is wrong because some type of punctuation is needed in order to connect two independent clauses.

10. **A** In this Rules question, punctuation with a transition is changing in the answer choices. Look for independent clauses. The first part of the sentence says *Zero waste goes beyond reducing, reusing, and recycling.* There is an option to add *however* to this independent clause. This statement does contrast with the previous sentence, which describes zero waste as a movement focused on *repurposing or reusing all products,* so *however* belongs in the first part of the sentence. Eliminate options with *however* in the second part.

- (A) is correct because it puts *however* with the first independent clause and puts a semicolon between the two independent clauses.

- (B) is wrong because it puts *however* with the second independent clause.

- (C) and (D) are wrong because the sentence contains two independent clauses, which cannot be connected with commas alone.

CHAPTER 9

Grammar Drill (page 219)

1. **C** In this Rules question, verbs are changing in the answer choices, so it's testing consistency with verbs. Find and highlight the subject, *pieces*, which is plural, so a plural verb is needed. Write an annotation saying "plural." Eliminate any answer that is not plural.

- (A), (B), and (D) are wrong because they are singular.

- (C) is correct because it's plural.

2. **C** In this Rules question, pronouns are changing in the answer choices, so it's testing consistency with pronouns. Find and highlight the word the pronoun refers back to *architects*, which is plural, so a plural pronoun is needed. Write an annotation saying "plural." Eliminate any answer that isn't plural or doesn't clearly refer back to *architects*.

- (A) and (B) are wrong because they are singular.

- (C) is correct because *they* is plural and is consistent with *architects*.

- (D) is wrong because *any* doesn't refer back to a specific thing.

3.   **B**   In this Rules question, verbs are changing in the answer choices, so it's testing consistency with verbs. Find and highlight the subject, *Atlantic Ocean*, which is singular, so a singular verb is needed. All of the answers work with a singular subject, so look for a clue regarding tense. The sentence says *over the next several hundred million years*, which suggests that the sentence is referring to what is expected to happen in the future. Write an annotation that says "future." Eliminate any answer not in future tense.

   - (A) is wrong because it's in past tense.

   - (B) is correct because it's in future tense.

   - (C) is wrong because it's not in future tense.

   - (D) is wrong because it's in present tense.

4.   **D**   In this Rules question, apostrophes with nouns are changing in the answer choices. Determine whether each word possesses anything. The king possesses the generosity, but the effects don't possess anything. Eliminate any answer that doesn't match this.

   - (A) and (C) are wrong because *effects* shouldn't be possessive.

   - (B) is wrong because *king* should be possessive and not plural.

   - (D) is correct because *king's* is possessive and *effects* is not.

5.   **C**   In this Rules question, pronouns and apostrophes are changing in the answer choices, so it's testing consistency with pronouns. Find and highlight the word that the pronoun refers back to: *recordings*. This word is plural, so in order to be consistent, a plural pronoun is needed. Eliminate any answer that isn't consistent with *recordings* or is incorrectly punctuated.

   - (A) and (B) are wrong because they are singular.

   - (C) is correct because it is plural and possessive.

   - (D) is wrong because it means "they are."

6.   **D**   In this Rules question, apostrophes with nouns are changing in the answer choices. Determine whether each word possesses anything. Neither the *sequences* nor the *scenes* possess anything. Eliminate any answer that doesn't match this.

   - (A) and (C) are wrong because *sequences* shouldn't be possessive.

   - (B) is wrong because *scenes* shouldn't be possessive.

   - (D) is correct because neither *sequences* nor *scenes* is possessive.

7.   **C**   In this Rules question, verbs are changing in the answer choices, so it's testing consistency with verbs. Find and highlight the subject, *bolt of electricity*, which is singular, so a singular verb is needed. All of the answers work with a singular subject, so look for a clue regarding tense. The sentence uses the present tense verb *emit*, and there isn't any shift in tense. Highlight *emit* and write an annotation that says "present." Eliminate any answer not in present tense.

   - (A) and (D) are wrong because they're in past tense.

   - (B) is wrong because it's not in present tense.

   - (C) is correct because it's in present tense.

8.   **D**   In this Rules question, the subjects of the answers are changing, which suggests it may be testing modifiers. Look for and highlight a modifying phrase: *Considered the first organisms to have produced oxygen*. Whatever are *Considered the first organisms* need to come immediately after the comma. Eliminate any answer that doesn't start with an organism.

   - (A) and (C) are wrong because *antennae* are not a type of organism.

   - (B) is wrong because *the oxygenic photosynthesis* is not a type of organism.

   - (D) is correct because *cyanobacteria* are a type of organism.

9.   **A**   In this Rules question, verbs are changing in the answer choices, so it's testing consistency with verbs. Find and highlight the subject, *legitimacy*, which is singular, so a singular verb is needed. Write an annotation saying "singular." Eliminate any answer that is not singular.

   - (A) is correct because it's singular.

   - (B), (C), and (D) are wrong because they are plural.

10.   **D**   In this Rules question, the subjects of the answers are changing, which suggests it may be testing modifiers. Look for and highlight a modifying phrase: *Known for live performances of her poetry*. Whoever is *Known for live performances* needs to come immediately after the comma. Eliminate any answer that doesn't start with a person.

   - (A) is wrong because the magazine is not a person.

   - (B) and (C) are wrong because the magazine cover is not a person.

   - (D) is correct because *Mort* is a person who could be *Known for live performances of her poetry*.

CHAPTER 10

Rhetoric Questions Drill (page 232)

1. **B**   This is a transition question, so follow the basic approach. Highlight ideas that relate to each other. The preceding sentence describes how a whale fall provides *nourishment through multiple stages of decomposition*. This sentence explains one of these stages, and the next two sentences begin with *Second* and *Third*, so the blank should be a time-change transition. Make an annotation that says "time change." Eliminate any answer that doesn't match.

  - (A) and (D) are wrong because this sentence is not a continuation of the preceding sentence.

  - (B) is correct because *First* is appropriate since the next two sentences say *Second* and *Third*.

  - (C) is wrong because this sentence describes an event that happens first in the list of stages.

2. **C**   This is a transition question, so follow the basic approach. Highlight ideas that relate to each other. The preceding sentence states that Seon *broke with tradition by depicting landscapes that were realistic rather than imagined*, and this sentence says that *one of his most famous works…was painted while the artist was facing the mountain*. These ideas agree, so a same-direction transition is needed. Make an annotation that says "agree." Eliminate any answer that doesn't match.

  - (A) and (B) are wrong because they are opposite-direction transitions.

  - (C) is correct because this sentence is an example of a realistic landscape painting.

  - (D) is wrong because this sentence is an example, not an additional point.

3. **D**   This is a transition question, so follow the basic approach. Highlight ideas that relate to each other. The first sentence introduces a *laborious process*, then the second and third sentences begin with *First* and *Next*. This sentence describes another step, so it should be a time-change transition. Make an annotation that says "time change." Eliminate any answer that doesn't match.

  - (A) is wrong because this sentence isn't a logical conclusion based on previously stated evidence.

  - (B) is wrong because this sentence is not a specific detail based on the previous sentence.

  - (C) is wrong because *In conclusion* is used for a logical conclusion, not the final step in a process.

  - (D) is correct because this sentence is the final step in the process described in the first sentence.

4. **C** This is a transition question, so follow the basic approach. Highlight ideas that relate to each other. The preceding sentence states that *Climate change negatively affects birds' breeding season by reducing the availability of food*, and this sentence gives an exception by stating that a certain type of bird is *protected from the negative impacts*. These ideas disagree, so an opposite-direction transition is needed. Make an annotation that says "disagree." Eliminate any answer that doesn't match.

- (A), (B), and (D) are wrong because they are same-direction transitions.

- (C) is correct because *however* is an opposite-direction transition.

5. **A** This is a transition question, so follow the basic approach. Highlight ideas that relate to each other. The first two sentences describe Indonesia's *long history of destructive volcanic eruptions* and state that the volcanic heat can be *harvested to generate geothermal energy*. This sentence states that Indonesia has been using this form of energy. These ideas agree, so a same-direction transition is needed. Make an annotation that says "agree." Eliminate any answer that doesn't match.

- (A) is correct because Indonesia's use of geothermal energy is a result of the fact that volcanoes can produce geothermal energy.

- (B) and (C) are wrong because this sentence is not a restatement of the previous sentence.

- (D) is wrong because this sentence is not a summary.

6. **B** This is a Rhetorical Synthesis question, so follow the basic approach. Highlight the goal(s) stated in the question: *introduce Murasaki Shikibu and her novel*. Eliminate any answer that doesn't fulfill this purpose.

- (A) and (D) are wrong because they don't *introduce Murasaki Shikibu* by providing any biographical details.

- (B) is correct because it introduces *Murasaki Shikibu and her novel* by providing a detail about each.

- (C) is wrong because it doesn't mention the *novel*.

7. **B** This is a Rhetorical Synthesis question, so follow the basic approach. Highlight the goal(s) stated in the question: *specify a reason that some commercial airplanes use turbofan engines*. Eliminate any answer that doesn't fulfill this purpose.

- (A), (C), and (D) are wrong because they don't *specify a reason* that turbofan engines are used by some commercial airplanes.

- (B) is correct because it specifies *a reason that some commercial airplanes use turbofan engines* by stating that they are *the most efficient jet engines* at the speeds commercial airliners travel.

8.   **A**   This is a Rhetorical Synthesis question, so follow the basic approach. Highlight the goal(s) stated in the question: *emphasize the uniqueness of Savage's accomplishment*. Eliminate any answer that doesn't fulfill this purpose.

- (A) is correct because the word *only* emphasizes *the uniqueness of Savage's accomplishment*.

- (B), (C), and (D) are wrong because they don't provide any information on the *uniqueness* of her accomplishment.

9.   **A**   This is a Rhetorical Synthesis question, so follow the basic approach. Highlight the goal(s) stated in the question: *emphasize a difference between the yearly rainfall in two places*. Eliminate any answer that doesn't fulfill this purpose.

- (A) is correct because it has the contrast word *while* and describes a difference in the times of year rain falls in the two places.

- (B) is wrong because it doesn't mention a *difference* between the two places.

- (C) and (D) are wrong because they each mention only one location.

10.   **B**   This is a Rhetorical Synthesis question, so follow the basic approach. Highlight the goal(s) stated in the question: *explain recent research results for an audience familiar with Stradivari's violins*. Eliminate any answer that doesn't *explain recent research results* in a way that assumes the audience is *familiar with Stradivari's violins*.

- (A) and (C) are wrong because they don't *explain recent research results*.

- (B) is correct because it explains the *results* of the *recent research* and doesn't define *Stradivari's violins*, since the audience is already familiar with them.

- (D) is wrong because it doesn't state what the *discovery* from the research was, so it doesn't explain *recent research results*.

CHAPTER 11

Drill 1 (page 243)

1. **c**   Examples: –7, 0, 1, 8

2. **d**   Examples: 0.5, 2, 118

3. **g**   Examples: –0.5, –2, –118

4. **f**   Examples: –4, 0, 10

5. **b**   Examples: –5, 1, 17

6. **a**   Examples: *Factors* of 12 are 1, 2, 3, 4, 6, and 12. Factors of 10 are 1, 2, 5, and 10.

7. **i**   Examples: *Multiples* of 12 include –24, –12, 0, 12, 24, and so on. Multiples of 10 include –20, –10, 0, 10, 20, 30, and so on.

8. **h**   Examples: 2, 3, 5, 7, 11, and so on. There are no negative *prime numbers*, and 1 is not prime.

9. **e**   Examples: 3 and 4 are *distinct* numbers. –2 and 2 are also distinct.

10. **j**   Examples: In the number 274, 2 is the *digit* in the hundreds place, 7 is the digit in the tens place, and 4 is the digit in the ones place.

11. **p**   Examples: –1, 0, 1, and 2 are *consecutive* numbers. Be careful—sometimes you will be asked for *consecutive even* or *consecutive odd* numbers, in which case you would use just the odds or evens in a consecutive list of numbers.

12. **n**   Examples: 6 is *divisible* by 2 and 3, but not by 4 or 5.

13. **l**   Examples: When you divide 26 by 8, you get 3 with a *remainder* of 2 (2 is left over). When you divide 14 by 5, you get 2 with a remainder of 4 (4 is left over).

14. **k**   Examples: When you add 2 and 3, you get a *sum* of 5. When you add –4 and 1, you get a sum of –3.

15. **r**   Examples: When you multiply 2 and 3, you get a *product* of 6. When you multiply –4 and 1, you get a product of –4.

16. **m**   Examples: When you subtract 2 from 3, you get a *difference* of 1. When you subtract –4 from 1, you get a difference of 5.

17. **q**   Examples: When you divide 2 by 3, you get a quotient of $\frac{2}{3}$. When you divide –4 by 1, you get a quotient of –4.

18. **o**   Examples: The absolute value of –3 is 3. The absolute value of 41 is 41.

Drill 2 (page 246)

a. 3^5
b. 3^1
c. 3^6
d. x^8
e. x^4
f. x^{12}

1. **D** The question asks for the value of an expression given an equation. Take the cube root of both sides of the equation $t^3 = -8$ to get $t = -2$. Plug $t = -2$ into the expression t^2 to get $(-2)^2$, which becomes 4. The correct answer is (D).

2. **A** The question asks for the value of an expression. When dealing with exponents, remember the MADSPM rules. The MA part of the acronym indicates that Multiplying matching bases means to Add the exponents. Because both a and b have a base of 3, multiplying 3^a by 3^b becomes 3^{a+b}. The question states that $a + b = 8$, so $3^{a+b} = 3^8$. The correct answer is (A).

3. **D** The question asks for an equivalent form of an expression. Use Bite-Sized Pieces and Process of Elimination to tackle this question. Start with the n terms. When dealing with exponents, remember the MADSPM rules. The MA part of the acronym indicates that Multiplying matching bases means to Add the exponents. A value without an exponent has an implied exponent of 1, so $n = n^1$. Add the exponents to get $(n^1)(n^5) = n^{1+5} = n^6$. Eliminate (A), (B), and (C) because they do not include n^6. The correct answer is (D).

4. **B** The question asks for an equivalent form of an expression. In a fractional exponent, the numerator is the power, and the denominator is the root. Thus, $x^{\frac{2}{3}}$ means taking the third root of x to the power of 2. This can be written as $\sqrt[3]{x^2}$. The correct answer is (B).

Drill 3 (page 255)

1. **B** The question asks for the equation that represents the relationship between two numbers. Translate the English into math one piece at a time, and eliminate answers after each piece. Translate *The number x is* as $x =$. All of the answer choices include this piece, so keep going. Translate *three times the number y* as $3y$. Eliminate (A) because it does not include this piece. Translate *8 less than* as $- 8$. Eliminate (C) and (D) because they do not include this piece. The correct answer is (B).

2. **B** The question asks for an equivalent form of an inequality. Simplify the inequality by finding a common factor. All three numbers—16, 20, and 12—are divisible by 4, so divide both sides of the inequality by 4. Divide $16a$ by 4 to get $4a$, divide $20b$ by 4 to get $5b$, and divide 12 by 4 to get 3. The inequality becomes $4a + 5b > 3$. The correct answer is (B).

3. **A** The question asks for the value of the *x*-coordinate of the solution to a system of equations. One method is to enter both equations into the built-in calculator, then scroll and zoom as needed to find the point of intersection. The graphs intersect at (–2, –1), so the *x*-coordinate is –2, which is (A).

To solve the system for the *x*-coordinate algebraically, multiply the second equation by –1 to get $-2x + 15y = -11$. Now that the two equations have the same *y*-term with opposite signs, stack and add the two equations to make the *y*-terms disappear.

$$\begin{array}{rcr} 4x - 15y = & & 7 \\ + (-2x + 15y = & & -11) \\ \hline 2x \qquad\quad = & & -4 \end{array}$$

Divide both sides of the resulting equation by 2 to get $x = -2$, which is (A).

Using either method, the correct answer is (A).

4. **7** The question asks for the solution to an equation with an absolute value. Start by dividing both sides of the equation by 4 to get $|x - 1| = 6$. With an absolute value, the value inside the absolute value bars can be either positive or negative, so this equation has two possible solutions. To find one solution, either set $x - 1$ equal to 6 or set $x - 1$ equal to –6, and solve for *x*. When $x - 1 = 6$, add 1 to both sides of the equation to get $x = 7$. The question asks for the positive solution, so stop here. The correct answer is 7.

5. **D** The question asks for a system of equations that represents a specific situation. Translate the English into math in Bite-Sized Pieces, and eliminate after each piece. Start with the information about totals. The question states that *the collector purchases 40 cards*. Since the store sells *r rare cards* and *c common cards*, translate this as $r + c = 40$. Eliminate (A) and (C) because they do not include this equation. Compare the remaining answer choices. Both (B) and (D) correctly translate the total cost as = 296, and the difference is the coefficients for *r* and *c*. The question states that the store sells *r rare cards for $20 each and c common cards for $2 each*. Since *r* is the number of rare cards and *c* is the number of common cards, 20 should go with *r* and 2 should go with *c*. Eliminate (B) because it has the coefficients on the wrong variables. The correct answer is (D).

6. **C** The question asks for the solution to an equation. To isolate *x*, distribute the 8 on the left side of the equation and the –5 on the right side of the equation to get $16 - 8x = 10 - 5x - 15$. Combine like terms on the right side of the equation to get $16 - 8x = -5x - 5$. Add $8x$ to both sides of the equation to get $16 = 3x - 5$, and then add 5 to both sides of the equation to get $21 = 3x$. Divide both sides of the equation by 3 to get $7 = x$. The correct answer is (C).

7. **C** The question asks for an inequality that represents a specific situation. Translate the English into math in Bite-Sized Pieces, and eliminate after each piece. Start with the information about the minimum number of calories consumed each day. The question states that *the cat consumed greater than 290 calories...every day for one week*. Since there are 7 days in one week, the minimum number of calories the cat consumed is $(7)(290) = 2,030$ calories. Eliminate (A) and (D) because they do not include this minimum value. Next, calculate the maximum number of calories the cat consumed. If the cat consumed

fewer than 340 calories every day for a week and there are 7 days in one week, the total maximum is (7)(340) = 2,380. Eliminate (B) because it has the wrong maximum value. The correct answer is (C).

8. **14** The question asks for a value given a specific situation. Translate the information in Bite-Sized Pieces. One piece of information states that *the bakery sold 26 funnel cakes and made a total of $1,332*. Another piece states that *one funnel cake costs $27*. Multiply the cost of one funnel cake by the number of funnel cakes sold to get ($27)(26) = $702 made from selling funnel cakes. Subtract this from the total that the bakery made that day to get $1,332 − $702 = $630 made from selling ice cream cakes. Divide $630 by the cost of one ice cream cake, $45, to get $\frac{\$630}{\$45}$ = 14 ice cream cakes sold that day. The correct answer is 14.

Drill 4 (page 263)

a. 6
b. 6
c. −1
d. −1
e. 1

1. **B** The question asks for a value based on a graph. Specifically, the question asks for the value of the y-intercept of a linear graph. This is the point at which $x = 0$ and the graph intersects the y-axis. Look on the graph for the point on the line at which the x-coordinate equals 0 and the graph crosses the y-axis. This point is (0, −4). The correct answer is (B).

2. **D** The question asks for the value of the x-coordinate of the x-intercept on a linear graph. This is the point at which $y = 0$ and the graph intersects the y-axis. Plug $y = 0$ into the equation to get $0 = -\frac{1}{2}x + 4$. Subtract 4 from both sides of the equation to get $-4 = -\frac{1}{2}x$. Multiply both sides of the equation by −2 to get $8 = x$, which is (D).

   Another option is to use the built-in calculator. Enter the equation, and then scroll and zoom as needed to find the x-intercept. The coordinates are (8, 0), so the x-coordinate of the x-intercept is 8, which is (D).

   Using either method, the correct answer is (D).

3. **C** The question asks for the equation of a line based on a point and a graph. Work in Bite-Sized Pieces and eliminate after each piece. The equations in the answer choices are in slope-intercept form, $y = mx + b$, where m is the slope and b is the y-intercept. Use $\frac{rise}{run}$ to find the slope, being sure to

start with the same point for both. The graph contains the points $\left(\dfrac{3}{2}, 0\right)$ and $(0, 1)$. Plug the values

into the equation slope = $\dfrac{y_2 - y_1}{x_2 - x_1}$ to get slope = $\dfrac{0 - 1}{\dfrac{3}{2} - 0}$. Simplify to get slope = $\dfrac{-1}{\dfrac{3}{2}}$, which becomes

slope = $-\dfrac{2}{3}$. In slope-intercept form, m is the slope, so $m = -\dfrac{2}{3}$. Eliminate (A) and (B) because they

have the wrong value of m. The line on the graph crosses the y-axis at $(0, 1)$, so this is the y-intercept,

and in slope-intercept form $b = 1$. Eliminate (D) because it has a different value for b. The correct

answer is (C).

4. **A**   The question asks for the slope of a line that is parallel to another line. When lines are parallel, they

have the same slope. The question provides two points for line m, so start there. Plug the values into the

equation slope = $\dfrac{y_2 - y_1}{x_2 - x_1}$ to get slope = $\dfrac{1 - 7}{3 - 0}$. Simplify to get slope = $\dfrac{-6}{3}$, and then slope = -2. Since

line n is parallel to line m, the slope of line n is also -2. The correct answer is (A).

5. **D**   The question asks for the number of solutions to a system of equations. One method is to enter both
equations into the built-in graphing calculator. Look in the graphing area, and scroll and zoom as
needed to see that the lines never intersect, which makes (D) correct.

To determine the number of solutions algebraically, put both equations into slope-intercept form,

$y = mx + b$, in which m is the slope and b is the y-intercept. For the first equation, subtract $3x$ from both

sides of the equation to get $-6y = -3x + 15$. Divide both sides of the equation by -6 to get $y = \dfrac{-3}{-6}x$

$+ \dfrac{15}{-6}$, which becomes $y = \dfrac{1}{2}x - \dfrac{5}{2}$. For the second equation, subtract x from both sides of the equation

to get $-2y = -x + 10$. Divide both sides of the equation by -2 to get $y = \dfrac{1}{2}x - 5$. The two lines have the

same slope, $\dfrac{1}{2}$, but different y-intercepts, $-\dfrac{5}{2}$ and -5. Thus, the lines are parallel and never intersect,

making (D) correct.

6. **3**   The question asks for the value of the x-coordinate of the solution to a system of equations. One method
is to enter both equations into the built-in graphing calculator, then scroll and zoom as needed to find
the point of intersection. The graphs intersect at $(3, 5)$, so the x-coordinate is 3.

To solve the system for the *x*-coordinate of the solution algebraically, first multiply both sides of the first equation by 5 to get rid of the fraction. The equation becomes $5x - y = 10$. Next, find a way to cancel the *y*-terms and leave the *x*-terms. Multiply the first equation by 2 to get $10x - 2y = 20$. Now that the two equations have the same *y*-term with opposite signs, stack and add the two equations to make the *y*-terms disappear.

$$\begin{array}{r} 10x - 2y = 20 \\ + (24x + 2y = 82) \\ \hline 34x = 102 \end{array}$$

Divide both sides of the resulting equation by 34 to get $x = 3$.

Using either method, the correct answer is 3.

7. **A** The question asks for the slope of a line that is perpendicular to a line shown in a graph. When lines are perpendicular, the slopes are opposite reciprocals. Start by finding the slope of line *a*. There are two points marked on the graph, so plug those values into the equation slope $= \dfrac{y_2 - y_1}{x_2 - x_1}$ to get slope $= \dfrac{4 - 0}{0 - (-7)}$. Simplify to get slope $= \dfrac{4}{7}$. Since line *b* is perpendicular to line *a*, the slope of line *b* is $-\dfrac{7}{4}$. The equations in the answer choices are in slope-intercept form, $y = mx + b$, where *m* is the slope and *b* is the *y*-intercept. For line *b*, $m = -\dfrac{7}{4}$. Eliminate (B), (C), and (D) because they have the wrong slope. The correct answer is (A).

Drill 5 (page 272)

1. **C** The question asks for a percentage based on data. Read carefully to find the correct numbers in the table. The question asks *what percent of the students enrolled in Physics are in 11th grade*. The number of students in 11th grade enrolled in Physics is 36, and the total number of students enrolled in Physics is $36 + 54 = 90$. Divide the number of 11th grade students taking Physics by the total number of students taking Physics to get $\dfrac{36}{90} = 0.4$. To convert the decimal to a percent, multiply by 100 to get $0.4(100) = 40\%$. The correct answer is (C).

2. **B** The question asks for a difference between two values based on a graph. First, check the units on each axis of the line graph. The *x*-axis shows the numbers of years, and the *y*-axis shows the cost per gallon, in dollars. The question asks about two different years, so first find 2007 on the *x*-axis. Move up from there—using the mouse pointer or the edge of the scratch paper—to the point on the line. Move left from there to find the value on the *y*-axis. The value is 3.0, so in 2007 gas cost $3.00 per gallon. Perform the same steps for 2003 to see that the value is halfway between 1.5 and 2.0. Ballpark this as

$1.75 per gallon in 2003. The question asks *how much more*, so subtract the cost per gallon in 2003 from the cost per gallon in 2007 to get $3.00 – $1.75 = $1.25. The correct answer is (B).

3. **D** The question asks for an equation that represents a graph. To find the best equation, compare features of the graph to the answer choices. The equations in the answer choices are in slope-intercept form, $y = mx + b$, where m is the slope and b is the y-intercept. The line is ascending from left to right, so it has a positive slope. Eliminate (A) and (B) because they have negative slopes. The line has a positive y-intercept, at approximately 2.75. Eliminate (C) because it has a negative y-intercept. Choice (D) has a positive slope and a positive y-intercept of 2.75. The correct answer is (D).

4. **B** The question asks for a value on a scatterplot. First, check the units on each axis of the graph. The x-axis shows the price of a cheese pizza, in dollars, and the y-axis shows the price of a veggie pizza, in dollars. The question asks about a *pizzeria that charges $15 for a veggie pizza*, so find 15 on the y-axis. Move right from there—using the mouse pointer or the edge of the scratch paper—to the intersection with the line of best fit. The intersection is just to the right of the vertical gridline for 10 on the x-axis, so the price of a cheese pizza is close to $10. The question asks which is closest, and the closest answer choice is 10. The correct answer is (B).

5. $\dfrac{1}{3}$ The question asks for the slope of a line that is perpendicular to another line. The equation of line p is given, so start by finding the slope of line p. The equation of line p is in slope-intercept form, $y = mx + b$, in which m is the slope and b is the y-intercept. Thus, the slope of line p is –3. The slopes of perpendicular lines are negative reciprocals. Therefore, if the slope of line p is –3, the slope of perpendicular line q is $\dfrac{1}{3}$. The correct answer is $\dfrac{1}{3}$.

6. **3** The question asks for the x-value of the solution to a system of equations. One method is to enter both equations into the built-in calculator, then scroll and zoom as needed to find the point of intersection. The graphs intersect at (3, 0), so the x-coordinate is 3.

To solve algebraically, set the right sides of the two equations equal to each other since they are both equal to y. The new equation is $-8x + 24 = -2x + 6$. Add $8x$ to both sides of the equation to get $24 = 6x + 6$, and then subtract 6 from both sides of the equation to get $18 = 6x$. Finally, divide both sides of the equation by 6 to get $3 = x$.

Using either method, the correct answer is 3.

7. **25 or –25**

The question asks for the value of an expression based on an equation. There is no direct way to solve for $5x$, so start by isolating x. Divide both sides of the equation by 5 to get $x^2 = 25$. This equation has two solutions because both 5 and –5 can be squared to get 25. The question asks for one possible value, so use $x = 5$. The expression becomes 5(5), which equals 25. The other possible value of $5x$ is 5(–5), or –25. Both answers will be accepted as correct. The correct answer is 25 or –25.

8. **2**   The question asks for a value based on an equation and a specific situation. The question states that *there are 5 liters of apple juice in the punch*, and that *a is the volume of apple juice, in liters*. Plug in 5 for *a* in the equation to get $1.9(5) + 2.2c = 13.9$. Simplify the left side of the equation to get $9.5 + 2.2c = 13.9$. Subtract 9.5 from both sides of the equation to get $2.2c = 4.4$. Divide both sides of the equation by 2.2 to get $c = 2$. The correct answer is 2.

CHAPTER 12

Drill 1 (page 283)

1. **A**   The question asks for an equivalent form of an expression. There are variables in the answer choices, so plug in. Make $y = 2$ to keep the math simple. Plug in 2 for *y*, and the expression becomes $(2)^2 - 8(2) + 2$. Simplify the expression to get $4 - 16 + 2$, and then -10. This is the target value; write it down and circle it.

    Now plug $y = 2$ into the answer choices and eliminate any that do not match the target value. Choice (A) becomes $(2 - 4)^2 - 14$. Simplify the expression to get $(-2)^2 - 14$, then $4 - 14$, and finally -10. This matches the target value, so keep (A) but check the remaining answers just in case. Choice (B) becomes $(2 - 4)^2 + 14$. Simplify the expression to get $(2)^2 + 14$, then $4 + 14$, and finally 18. This does not match the target value, so eliminate (B). Choice (C) becomes $(2 + 4)^2 - 14$. Simplify the expression to get $(6)^2 - 14$, then $36 - 14$, and finally 22; eliminate (C). Choice (D) becomes $(2 + 4)^2 + 14$. This will be even larger than (C), so eliminate (D). The correct answer is (A).

2. **B**   The question asks for the relationship between two geometric figures. This is a hidden plug in question. Start by drawing two squares of different sizes. Next, write down the formula for the area of a square, which is $A = s^2$. No numbers are given in the question, only the relationship between side lengths, so plug in. Plug in $s = 2$ for the side length of a child-sized nametag. Plug this into the area formula to get $A = (2)^2$, or $A = 4$ as the area of a child-sized nametag. The question states that *the side length of a child-sized nametag is one-third the side length of an adult-sized nametag*, so the side length of an adult-sized nametag is three times the side length of a child-sized nametag, or $(2)(3) = 6$. Plug this into the area formula to get $A = (6)^2$, or $A = 36$ as the area of an adult-sized nametag. Divide the area of an adult-sized nametag by the area of a child-sized nametag to find that the adult-sized nametag is $\frac{36}{4} = 9$ times the child-sized nametag. The correct answer is (B).

3. **B**   The question asks for an expression that represents a specific situation. The question asks about relative amounts and there are variables in the answer choices, so plug in. Plug in a simple number, such as 10, for d, which represents the cost of John's lunch. The question states that *the total cost of Joan's lunch was $4 less than the total cost of John's lunch*, so Joan's lunch cost $10 – $4 = $6. The total cost of John's and Joan's lunch was $10 + $6 = $16. The question also states that they *split the cost of lunch equally*, so divide $16 by 2 to find that each person paid $\frac{\$16}{2}$ = $8. This is the target value; write it down and circle it.

Now plug $d = 10$ into the answer choices and eliminate any that do not match the target value. Choice (A) becomes $\frac{10}{2} - 4$, then $5 - 4$, and finally 1. This does not match the target value of 8, so eliminate (A). Choice (B) becomes $10 - 2$, or 8. This matches the target value, so keep (B) but check the remaining answers just in case. Choice (C) becomes $2(10) - 2$, then $20 - 2$, and finally 18; eliminate (C). Choice (D) becomes $2(10) - 4$, then $20 - 4$, and finally 16; eliminate (D). The correct answer is (B).

4. **A**   The question asks for an equation that represents a specific situation. There are variables in the answer choices, so plug in. Keep the math simple and plug in 2 for h. The question states that *each hour of play costs $2.50*, so the cost of 2 hours of play is 2($2.50), or $5. Add $5 to the monthly membership fee, $25, to find the total monthly cost: $5 + $25 = $30. Thus, when $h = 2$, $c = 30$.

Now plug $c = 30$ and $h = 2$ into each of the answer choices, and eliminate any that are not true. Choice (A) becomes $30 = 2.50(2) + 25$. Simplify the right side of the equation to get $30 = 5 + 25$, or $30 = 30$. This is true, so keep (A) but check the remaining answers just in case. Choice (B) becomes $30 = 2.50(2) + 27.50$. Simplify the right side of the equation to get $30 = 5 + 27.50$, or $30 = 32.50$. This is not true, so eliminate (B). Choice (C) becomes $30 = 25(2) + 2.50$. Simplify the right side of the equation to get $30 = 50 + 2.50$, or $30 = 52.50$; eliminate (C). Choice (D) becomes $30 = 27.50(2)$. Simplify the right side of the equation to get $30 = 55$; eliminate (D). The correct answer is (A).

5. **B**   The question asks for the interpretation of a number in context. Start by reading the final question, which asks for the meaning of the number 100. To better understand the relationship between the different elements of the equation, plug in. Keep the math simple and plug in 2 for h. The equation becomes $C = 40(2) + 100$. Simplify the right side of the equation to get $C = 80 + 100$, and then $C = 180$. Thus, $180 is the total amount Abigail charges for 2 hours of lessons.

Next, plug in a different number for h to see what happens to C. Make $h = 3$, and the equation becomes $C = 40(3) + 100$, then $C = 120 + 100$, and finally $C = 220$. When h increased by 1 hour, the total charge C increased by $220 - 180 = 40$ dollars. Thus, $40 is the cost of one hour of lessons. Since C is the total cost and $40h$ is the hourly charge times the number of hours, 100 must be the amount of the registration fee. The correct answer is (B).

6. **D**   The question asks for the interpretation of a number in context. Start by reading the final question, which asks for the meaning of the number 1.8. To better understand the relationship between the different elements of the equation, plug in. Keep the math simple and plug in 2 for t. The equation becomes $d = 1.8(2) + 4.5$. Simplify the right side of the equation to get $d = 3.6 + 4.5$, and then $d = 8.1$. Thus, after 2 minutes, the construction worker has reached a depth of 8.1 feet.

Next, plug in a different number for t to see what happens to d. Make $t = 3$, and the equation becomes $d = 1.8(3) + 4.5$. Simplify the right side of the equation to get $d = 5.4 + 4.5$, and then $d = 9.9$. When t increased by 1 minute, the depth d increased by $9.9 - 8.1 = 1.8$ feet. Thus, 1.8 is the number of feet per minute that the construction worker digs. The correct answer is (D).

Drill 2 (page 290)

1. **C**   The question asks for the value of a variable based on its relationship to certain numbers. The question asks for a specific value, and the answers contain numbers in order, so plug in the answers. Rewrite the answer choices on the scratch paper and label them "b." Start with one of the middle answer choices and try (B), 6. If $b = 6$, the product of b and 6 becomes $(6)(6) = 36$, and *4 less than* the product becomes $36 - 4 = 32$. This does not equal 44, so eliminate (B). A larger number is needed, so also eliminate (A) and try (C), 8. If $b = 8$, the product of b and 6 becomes $(8)(6) = 48$, and *4 less than* the product becomes $48 - 4 = 44$. This does equal 44, so stop here. The correct answer is (C).

2. **D**   The question asks for the solution to an equation. The question asks for a specific value and the answers contain numbers in order, so plug in the answers. Rewrite the answer choices on the scratch paper and label them "x." Start with one of the middle answer choices and try (B), 7. The equation becomes $\frac{7-4}{28} = \frac{1}{4}$, or $\frac{3}{28} = \frac{1}{4}$. This is not true, so eliminate (B). The numerator of the fraction on the left was too small, so also eliminate (A) and try (C), 10. The equation becomes $\frac{10-4}{28} = \frac{1}{4}$, then $\frac{6}{28} = \frac{1}{4}$, and finally $\frac{3}{14} = \frac{1}{4}$; eliminate (C). The result was closer, so (D) must be correct. To check, plug in 11 for x, and the equation becomes $\frac{11-4}{28} = \frac{1}{4}$, then $\frac{7}{28} = \frac{1}{4}$, and finally $\frac{1}{4} = \frac{1}{4}$. This is true, so stop here. The correct answer is (D).

3. **A**   The question asks for the solution to an inequality. The question asks for a specific value and the answers contain numbers in order, so plug in the answers. Rewrite the answer choices on the scratch paper and label them "x." Start with one of the middle answer choices and try (B), 24. The inequality becomes $\frac{7}{4}(24 + 8) < 56$. Simplify the left side of the inequality to get $\frac{7}{4}(32) < 56$, and then $56 < 56$. This is not true, so eliminate (B). The result on the left side of the inequality was too large, so try (A) next. Plug in

$x = 20$, and the inequality becomes $\frac{7}{4}(20 + 8) < 56$, then $\frac{7}{4}(28) < 56$, and finally $49 < 56$. This is true, so stop here. The correct answer is (A).

4. **B** The question asks for the solution to an equation. The question asks for a specific value and the answers contain numbers in order, so plug in the answers. Rewrite the answer choices on the scratch paper and label them "x." Start with the easier of the middle answers and try (C), 1. The equation becomes $3 + 2(1) = 1^2 - 5$, then $3 + 2 = 1 - 5$, and finally $5 = -4$. This is not true, so eliminate (C). One side of the equation was positive and the other negative, so see what happens with a negative number for x. Try (B), and plug $x = -2$ into the equation to get $3 + 2(-2) = (-2)^2 - 5$, then $3 + (-4) = 4 - 5$, and finally $-1 = -1$. This is true, so stop here. The correct answer is (B).

5. **A** The question asks for a value based on a specific situation. The question asks for a specific value and the answers contain numbers in order, so plug in the answers. Start with one of the middle answers and try (B), 33. If the gardeners fill 33 jars with 5 tomatoes each, this is a total of $(33)(5) = 165$ tomatoes in the larger jars. The question states that *the gardeners fill 55 jars with 3 tomatoes each*, which is a total of $(55)(3) = 165$ tomatoes in the smaller jars. The total number of tomatoes in jars is $165 + 165 = 330$. The question states that *the community garden produced 295 tomatoes*, but 330 does not equal 295; eliminate (B). A smaller number is needed, so try (A), 26. If the gardeners fill 26 jars with 5 tomatoes each, this is a total of $(26)(5) = 130$ tomatoes in the larger jars. The total number of tomatoes in smaller jars remains 165, so the total number of tomatoes in jars is $130 + 165 = 295$ tomatoes. This matches the information in the question, so stop here. The correct answer is (A).

6. **C** The question asks for the value of a constant based on an expression. The question asks for a specific value and the answers contain numbers in order, so plug in the answers. Rewrite the answer choices on the scratch paper and label them "c." Start with the easier of the middle answers and try (C), 2. Plug $c = 2$ into the first expression to get $x^2 + 2x - 8$. Plug $c = 2$ into the second expression to get $(x - 2)(x + 4)$. Use FOIL to expand the second expression to get $x^2 + 4x - 2x - 8$. Combine like terms to get $x^2 + 2x - 8$. Both expressions are now $x^2 + 2x - 8$, so one is a rewritten form of the other. The correct answer is (C).

Drill 3 (page 303)

a. 90
b. 320
c. 6
d. $x = 8$
e. 5
f. 10
g. 120%
h. 108
i. 1.5

1. **D** The question asks about the mean, or average, of data given in a table. For averages, use the formula $T = AN$, in which T is the *Total*, A is the *Average*, and N is the *Number of things*. The table shows data for five counties, so the *Number of things* is 5. Find the *Total* by adding the values listed for the maximum elevation to get $239 + 289 + 329 + 240 + 195 = 1,292$. The average formula becomes $1,292 = (A)(5)$. Divide both sides of the equation by 5 to get $258.4 = A$. The correct answer is (D).

2. **A** The question asks for an expected value based on data. Since the widgets were randomly selected, the proportion of widgets that are defective will be the same in the total produced by the factory as in the sample. Set up a proportion to determine the number of defective widgets in the total produced by the factory in one day: $\dfrac{41 \text{ defective}}{200 \text{ widgets}} = \dfrac{x \text{ defective}}{5,913 \text{ widgets}}$. Cross-multiply to get $(41)(5,913) = (200)(x)$, which becomes $242,433 = 200x$. Divide both sides of the equation by 200 to get $1,212.165 = x$. The question asks for an approximate number, and the closest number in the answer choices is 1,200. The correct answer is (A).

3. **C** The question asks for a probability based on a situation. Probability is defined as $\dfrac{\text{number of outcomes you want}}{\text{number of possible outcomes}}$. Read carefully to find the numbers that make up the probability. The question states that there are 75 total people in the focus group, so 75 is the *number of possible outcomes*. Use the frequency table to find the number of people that gave a *three-star rating*, which is 31. The question asks for *the probability that the focus group member did not give the game a three-star rating*, so subtract the number that did give a three-star rating from the total number to get $75 - 31 = 44$. It is also possible to add the numbers of focus group members that gave ratings of four stars, two stars, and one star to get $14 + 12 + 18 = 44$. Either way, 44 is the *number of outcomes you want*. Therefore, the probability that a focus group member selected at random did not give the game a three-star rating is $\dfrac{44}{75}$. The correct answer is (C).

4. **C** The question asks for an initial value given a specific situation. Since the question asks for a specific value and the answers contain numbers in increasing order, plug in the answers. Rewrite the answer choices on the scratch paper and label them "original balance." Start with the simpler of the two middle answers and try (C), $4,000. *Percent* means out of 100, so translate 5 percent as $\dfrac{5}{100}$. If the initial balance is $4,000, take 5% of that to get $\dfrac{5}{100}(\$4,000) = \$200$. The interest is added to the initial balance, so the new balance is $4,000 + $20 = $4,200. This matches the current balance given in the question, so stop here. The correct answer is (C).

5. **D** The question asks for a rate in different units. Begin by reading the question to find information about the rate. The question states that the runner runs at a rate of 1 mile per 7 minutes. The question provides the conversion that 1 mile ≈ 1.61 kilometers, so substitute 1.61 kilometers for 1 mile in the rate. Thus, the runner runs at a rate of 1.61 kilometers every 7 minutes. There are 60 minutes in an hour, so set up a proportion to determine how far the runner will go in 60 minutes: $\frac{1.61 \text{ kilometers}}{7 \text{ minutes}} = \frac{x \text{ kilometers}}{60 \text{ minutes}}$. Cross-multiply to get $(1.61)(60) = (7)(x)$, or $96.6 = 7x$. Divide both sides of the equation by 7 to get $13.80 = x$. The runner runs at a rate of 13.80 kilometers per hour. The correct answer is (D).

6. **B** The question asks for the median of a set of data. The median of a list of numbers is the middle number when the numbers are arranged in order. In lists with an even number of numbers, the median is the average of the two middle numbers. The table contains an odd number of numbers, 7, so the median will be the number in the middle. Start by putting the numbers from the table in order: 44, 52, 54, 54, 56, 58, 60. Next, cross out one number at a time from each end until only the middle number is left, like so: ~~44, 52, 54,~~ 54, ~~56, 58, 60~~. The median is 54. The correct answer is (B).

7. **A** The question asks for a ratio based on two other ratios. Ratios are a part-to-part relationship between numbers. Because ratios are about relationships, plug in numbers. The question gives the ratio of x to y as 4 to 3, so plug in 4 for x and 3 for y. The question also gives the ratio of x to z as 1 to 2. A ratio can be written as a fraction, so the ratio of x to z can be written as $\frac{x}{z} = \frac{1}{2}$. Write two equal fractions, plug in $x = 4$, and solve for the second z-value. Make sure to put x in the numerator and z in the denominator of both fractions. The equation becomes $\frac{1}{2} = \frac{4}{z}$. Cross-multiply to get $(1)(z) = (2)(4)$, which becomes $z = 8$. Thus, when $x = 4$, $y = 3$ and $z = 8$. Plug in the values for y and z, and the ratio of y to z is thus $\frac{y}{z} = \frac{3}{8}$. The correct answer is (A).

8. **B** The question asks for a net percentage decrease. No information is given about the initial value, so plug in. Make the initial value $100 because 100 works well with percentages. Next, translate the information in Bite-Sized Pieces. One piece of information says that the value *decreased by 20% from the beginning of 2020 to the beginning of 2021. Percent* means out of 100, so translate 20% as $\frac{20}{100}$. Take 20% of 100 to get $\frac{20}{100}(\$100) = \$20$. Translate *decreased by* as subtraction to get $\$100 - \$20 = \$80$ as the value of the stock at the beginning of 2021. Another piece of information says that the value *increased by 15%*

from the beginning of 2021 to the beginning of 2022. Take 15% of $80 and add it to $80 to get $80 + $\frac{15}{100}$ ($80) = $80 + $12 = $92 as the value of the stock at the beginning of 2022.

The question asks for the net percentage decrease from the beginning of 2020, when the value was $100, to the beginning of 2022, when the value was $92. This is a decrease of $100 – $92 = $8, which is 8% of $100. The correct answer is (B).

CHAPTER 13

Drill 1 (page 315)

1. **D** The question asks for the value of a function with an absolute value. In function notation, the number inside the parentheses is the x-value that goes into the function, or the input, and the value that comes out of the function is the y-value, or the output. The question provides an input value of –3, so plug $x = -3$ into the function to get $f(-3) = |7(-3) - 4|$, which becomes $f(-3) = |-21 - 4|$, and then $f(3) = |-25|$. Absolute value indicates the distance from zero, so the result is always positive. Thus, $|-25| = 25$, and $f(3) = 25$. The correct answer is (D).

2. **C** The question asks for the equation that best models the data shown on a scatterplot. If a line of best fit were drawn, it would ascend from left to right, so the graph has a positive slope. Eliminate (A) and (B) because they have negative slopes. Both (C) and (D) have a negative y-intercept, which matches what the graph looks like, so calculate the slope more precisely. Use two points to calculate the slope of the line using the formula slope = $\frac{y_2 - y_1}{x_2 - x_1}$. There are points at (7, 1) and (9, 2). Plug those values into the slope formula to get slope = $\frac{2 - 1}{9 - 7}$, which becomes slope = $\frac{1}{2}$, or slope = 0.5. Eliminate (D) because it has the wrong slope. Only (C) is left, so it is correct.

    Another approach is to enter the equation from each answer choice into the built-in graphing calculator to see which graph looks most like the graph in the question. The equation in (C) is closest to what the line of best fit would be, so (C) is correct.

    Using either method, the correct answer is (C).

3. **18** The question asks for a value given an equation. In function notation, the number inside the parentheses is the x-value that goes into the function, or the input, and the value that comes out of the function is the y-value, or the output. The question provides an output value of 3, but there are no answer choices to plug in for x. Instead, set $g(x) = 3$ and solve for x. The equation becomes $3 = -\frac{1}{3}x + 9$. Subtract 9 from both sides of the equation to get $-6 = -\frac{1}{3}x$. Multiply both sides of the equation by -3 to get $18 = x$. The correct answer is 18.

4. **10** The question asks for the value of a constant in a function. In function notation, the number inside the parentheses is the x-value that goes into the function, or the input, and the value that comes out of the function is the y-value, or the output. The question states that *the point (–2, 6) lies on the graph of the function*, which means that, when $x = -2$, $f(x) = 6$. Plug both values into the equation of the function to get $6 = 2(-2)^2 + k(-2) + 18$. Simplify the right side of the equation to get $6 = 2(4) - 2k + 18$, then $6 = 8 - 2k + 18$. Combine like terms on the right side of the equation to get $6 = 26 - 2k$. Subtract 26 from both sides of the equation to get $-20 = -2k$, and then divide both sides of the equation by -2 to get $10 = k$. The correct answer is 10.

5. **B** The question asks for the interpretation of a number in context. Start by reading the final question, which asks for the meaning of the number 252. Then label the parts of the equation with the information given. The question states that x represents *the number of days after the book was assigned* and that the function models the number of pages the student has left to read. Rewrite the equation as Number of pages left = 252 – 47(number of days). The number 252 is not multiplied by the number of days, so it must have something to do with the number of pages. Eliminate (A) because it refers to the number of days only. Eliminate (C) and (D) because they relate the number of pages to the number of days. Choice (B) fits the information given in the question: if the student reads 47 pages each day, and that total is subtracted from 252 to give the number of pages left, 252 must be the starting number of pages. The correct answer is (B).

6. **A** The question asks for the table that contains values that are pairs of input and output values in a function. When given an equation and asked for a table of values, plug input values from the tables into the equation to see which tables contain the matching output value. Look at the tables in the answer choices to see that each one has a different value for $f(x)$ when $x = 2$. Plug $x = 2$ into the equation to get $f(2) = 2(2)^2 - 2$, which becomes $f(2) = 2(4) - 2$, then $f(x) = 8 - 2$, and finally $f(2) = 6$. Eliminate (B), (C), and (D) because they have an $f(x)$ value other than 6 when $x = 2$. The correct answer is (A).

7. **C** The question asks for the interpretation of a statement about a function. Start by reading the final question, which asks for the best interpretation of the statement *m(0) is equal to 300*. In function notation, the number inside the parentheses is the x-value that goes into the function, or the input, and the value that comes out of the function is the y-value, or the output. Thus, 0 is an input value and 300 is an output value. The question states that x represents the number of months after the account was opened,

so when $x = 0$, zero months have elapsed since the account was opened. Eliminate (B) and (D) because they refer to 300 months instead of 0 months.

Compare the remaining answer choices. The difference between (A) and (C) is whether the value of the account was $0 or $300. Since 300 is the output, or $m(x)$, and the question states that m is the total amount of money in dollars, the statement means that the amount of money after 0 months was $300. To check, plug $x = 0$ into the function to get $m(0) = 300(1.06)^0$. Any value raised to the power of zero is 1, so the equation becomes $m(0) = 300(1)$, and then $m(0) = 300$. Thus, after 0 months, the amount in the account was $300. The correct answer is (C).

Drill 2 (page 329)

1. **−4** The question asks for the value of the x-coordinate when the graph of a function reaches its minimum. A parabola reaches its minimum or maximum value at its vertex, so find the x-coordinate of the vertex. One method is to enter the equation into the built-in graphing calculator, then scroll and zoom as needed to find the vertex. The vertex is at $(-4, 7)$, so the x-coordinate, represented by a, is -4.

   To find the x-coordinate of the vertex algebraically, recall that, when a quadratic equation is in standard form, $ax^2 + bx + c = 0$, the x-coordinate of the vertex is $-\dfrac{b}{2a}$. In this quadratic, $b = 8$ and $a = 1$, so the x-coordinate of the vertex is $-\dfrac{8}{2(1)}$, or -4.

   Using either method, the correct answer is -4.

2. **C** The question asks for an equivalent form of an expression. Use Bite-Sized Pieces and POE to tackle this question. The answer choices are quadratics in factored form, so use FOIL (First, Outer, Inner, Last) to eliminate answers that are not equivalent to the original expression. Multiply the first terms in (A) to get $(25x)(25x) = 625x^2$. This matches the first term in the original expression, so keep (A). Multiply the first terms in (B) to get $(25x)(125x) = 3{,}125x^2$. This does not match the first term in the original expression, so eliminate (B). Keep (C) because it has the same first terms as (A), and eliminate (D) because it has the same first terms as (B).

   Next, check the last terms in the remaining answer choices. Multiply the last terms in (A) to get $(-12)(-12) = 144$. This does not match the last term in the original expression because the sign is wrong; eliminate (A). Multiply the last terms in (C) to get $(-12)(12) = -144$. This matches the last term in the original expression. The correct answer is (C).

3. **D** The question asks for the sum of the solutions to a quadratic equation. One approach is to enter the equation into the built-in calculator. When graphed, the points where the two vertical lines cross the x-axis, represented by gray dots, are the solutions. Click on each gray dot and write down the x-values: 5 and 15. Add the solutions to get $5 + 15 = 20$, which is (D).

To solve algebraically, the shortcut is to recall that, when a quadratic equation is in standard form, $ax^2 + bx + c = 0$, the sum of the solutions equals $-\dfrac{b}{a}$. In this quadratic, $a = 1$, $b = -20$, and $c = 75$. Plug in the values for a and b to get $-\dfrac{-20}{1} = 20$, which is (D).

Using either method, the correct answer is (D).

4. **1**   The question asks for the solution to a system of equations. The most efficient method is to enter both equations into the built-in graphing calculator, then scroll and zoom as needed to find the point of intersection. Click on the gray dot to see that the coordinates of the point are (1, 2). The x-coordinate is 1, which is correct.

To solve for x algebraically, first add 4 to both sides of the second equation to get $y = 2$. Next, plug in 2 for y in the first equation to get $2 = -x^2 + 2x + 1$. Combine like terms on the left side of the equation and set the equation equal to 0 to get $x^2 - 2x + 1 = 0$. Factor the quadratic to get $(x - 1)(x - 1) = 0$. Set $x - 1 = 0$, and then add 1 to both sides of the equation to get $x = 1$.

Using either method, the correct answer is 1.

5. **17** The question asks for the sum of two constants in a quadratic in standard form. Although the expression is a quadratic, the question is really about combining like terms. The question states that the first expression is subtracted from the second, so write the expressions above each other to keep track of the terms while subtracting.

$$
\begin{array}{r}
3x^2 - 4x + 27 \\
-(\ x^2 + 2x + \ 4) \\
\hline
2x^2 - 6x + 23
\end{array}
$$

The question asks for the value of $b + c$. After subtracting the expressions, $b = -6$ and $c = 23$. Thus, $b + c = -6 + 23$, or $b + c = 17$. The correct answer is 17.

6. **B**   The question asks for the value of a constant in an equation. The left side of the equation is a quadratic in factored form, and the right side of the equation is a quadratic in standard form, so use FOIL (First, Outer, Inner, Last) to expand the left side of the equation and make it look like the right side. Since the question asks for the value of a, start with the first terms. Multiply $(ax)(ax)$ to get a^2x^2. Set this equal to the x^2 term on the right side of the equation to get $a^2x^2 = 25x^2$. Divide both sides of this equation by x^2 to get $a^2 = 25$. Take the square root of both sides of the equation, keeping in mind that a could be positive or negative, to get $a = \pm5$. Only one of these, 5, is in the answer choices, so it is correct. The correct answer is (B).

7. **C**   The question asks for a possible value of the x-coordinate of a solution to a system of equations. The most efficient method is to enter both equations into the built-in graphing calculator, then scroll and zoom as needed to find the point of intersection. The graphs intersect at (2, −6) and (−5, 29), so the value of x is either 2 or −5. Only 2 is in the answer choices, so it is correct. The correct answer is (C).

CHAPTER 14

Drill 1 (page 337)

1. **D** The question asks for the area of a geometric figure. Start by drawing a square on the scratch paper, and then label it with information from the question. Label each side as 26. Next, write down the formula for the area of a square, which is $A = s^2$. Plug in the given side length to get $A = 26^2$, which becomes $A = 676$. The correct answer is (D).

2. **C** The question asks for the perimeter of a geometric figure. Start by drawing a rectangle on the scratch paper, and then label it with information from the question. Label the length as 15 and the width as 30. The opposite sides of a rectangle have the same length, so also label the other length and width as 15 and 30, respectively. The figure should look something like this:

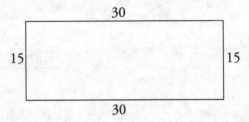

   The perimeter of any geometric figure of the sum of its sides, so the perimeter of this rectangle is $15 + 30 + 15 + 30 = 90$. The correct answer is (C).

3. **A** The question asks for a value based on a figure. Start by redrawing the figure and labels on the scratch paper. When a line intersects two parallel lines, two kinds of angles are created: big and small. All of the small angles are equal to each other, all of the big angles are equal to each other, and any small angle plus any big angle = 180°. The angle labeled $a°$ is a small angle, and the angle labeled 42° is a small angle. Thus, the two angles are equal, and $a = 42$. The correct answer is (A).

4. **6** The question asks for a value in an equation. Although the question refers to the area of a rectangle, very little geometry knowledge is needed to answer the question. To begin to solve for w, multiply the two terms on the right side of the equation to get $72 = 2w^2$. Divide both sides of the equation by 2 to get $36 = w^2$. Because the equation represents the area of a rectangle, the value of w must be positive. Take the positive square root of both sides of the equation to get $6 = w$. The correct answer is 6.

Drill 2 (page 343)

1. **B**   The question asks for an equation that represents the relationship among the side lengths of a triangle. Start by redrawing the figure and the labels. One of the angles is marked with the 90-degree symbol, so this is a right triangle. Write down the Pythagorean Theorem, either from memory or after looking it up on the reference sheet: $a^2 + b^2 = c^2$. Plug in the given values to get $a^2 + 6^2 = c^2$. Square the middle term to get $a^2 + 36 = c^2$. Subtract 36 from both sides of the equation to get $a^2 = c^2 - 36$. Take the square root of both sides of the equation to get $a = \sqrt{c^2 - 36}$. The correct answer is (B).

2. **B**   The question asks for a measure on a geometric figure. Start by redrawing the figure and labels. Next, label the figure with information from the question, and label angle *BCD* as 20°. The figure now looks like this:

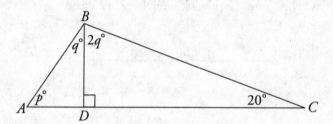

All triangles contain 180°, so subtract the two known angles in triangle *BCD* from 180 to get 180 – 90 – 20 = 70. Thus, $2q = 70$. Divide both sides of this equation by 2 to get $q = 35$. Label angle *ABD* as 35°. Now that two angles in triangle *ABD* are known, solve for the measure of angle *p*: 180 – 90 – 35 = 55. The correct answer is (B).

3. **A**   The question asks for the value of the measure of an angle on a geometric figure. Start by drawing two triangles that are similar to each other, meaning they have the same angle measures but are different sizes. It doesn't matter whether the figures have the exact angle measures given in the question as long as the two triangles look similar. Be certain to match up the corresponding vertices that are given in the question. The drawing could look something like this:

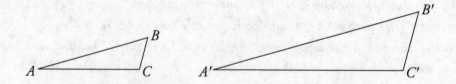

Next, label the figure with the given information. Label angle *B* as 60° and angle *C* as 105°. Because the triangles are similar, corresponding angle measures are the same, so also label angle *B'* as 60° and angle *C'* as 105°. The drawing now looks like this:

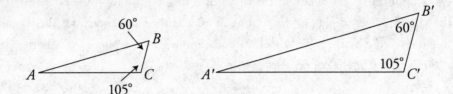

All triangles contain 180°, so find the measure of angle *A'* by subtracting the measures of angles *B'* and *C'* from 180: 180 − 105 − 60 = 15. The correct answer is (A).

4. **C** The question asks for a measure on a geometric figure. Start by redrawing the figure and labels. Next, label the figure with information from the question. Draw arcs at angles *LNP* and *MLP*, then put hashmarks through them to indicate that the angles are similar. Label line segment $\overline{MP}$ as 8. The drawing now looks something like this:

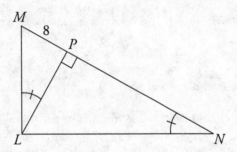

Since angle *LPN* is a 90° angle and $\overline{MN}$ is a straight line, angle *LPM* must also be a 90° angle. Label this on the figure. Since triangles *LPM* and *LPN* have two pairs of equal angles, the third pair of angles, *LMP* and *PLN*, are also equal, and the triangles are similar. It might help to redraw the two triangles next to each other to see how the sides match up. The question states that *the length of* $\overline{LN}$ *is twice the length of* $\overline{LM}$, so the ratio of each side of the larger triangle to the corresponding side of the smaller triangle is 2:1. Set up a proportion, being sure to put the side lengths of the larger triangle in the numerator and the side lengths of the smaller triangle in the denominator, or vice versa. The proportion is $\frac{2}{1} = \frac{\overline{LP}}{8}$. Cross-multiply to get (2)(8) = (1)($\overline{LP}$), or 16 = $\overline{LP}$. The length of $\overline{LP}$ is 16. The correct answer is (C).

Drill 3 (page 348)

1. **A** The question asks for a measure on a geometric figure. Write down the formula for the volume of a rectangular prism, either from memory or after looking it up on the reference sheet. The formula is $V = lwh$. Plug in the given values for the first prism to get $V = (4)(5)(3)$, or $V = 60$. The two prisms have the same volume, so plug in the volume of 60 and the values given for the second prism to get $60 = (6)(10)(h)$. Simplify the right side of the equation to get $60 = 60h$. Divide both sides of the equation by 60 to get $1 = h$. The correct answer is (A).

2. **D** The question asks for a measure on a geometric figure. The question asks for a specific value and the answers contain numbers in order, so plug in the answers. Rewrite the answer choices on the scratch paper and label them "height." Start with one of the middle numbers and try (B), 5. The question states that *the height of the triangle is 1 centimeter longer than the base of the triangle*. If the height of the triangle is 5, the base is $5 - 1 = 4$. Next, write down the formula for the area of a triangle, either from memory or after looking it up on the reference sheet. The formula is $A = \frac{1}{2}bh$. Plug in $b = 4$ and $h = 5$ to get $A = \frac{1}{2}(4)(5)$, which becomes $A = 10$. This does not match the area of 21 given in the question, so eliminate (B).

   The result was too small and not close, so try (D), 7, next. If the height of the triangle is 7, the base is $7 - 1 = 6$. Plug these values into the area formula to get $A = \frac{1}{2}(6)(7)$, which becomes $A = 21$. This matches the area given in the question, so stop here. The correct answer is (D).

3. **B** The question asks for a measure on a geometric figure. It might be difficult to draw a sphere, so start by writing down the formula for the volume of a sphere, either from memory or after looking it up on the reference sheet. The formula is $V = \frac{4}{3}\pi r^3$. No specific values are given for the radius of either sphere, only the relationship between the two volumes, so plug in. Use a multiple of 3 to make it easier to multiply by $\frac{4}{3}$, and plug in 3 for r_1. Plug this value into the volume formula to get $V = \frac{4}{3}\pi(3)^3$, which becomes $V = \frac{4}{3}\pi(27)$, and then $V = 36\pi$. The question states that the volume of the second sphere is 8 times the volume of the first sphere, so the volume of the second sphere is $(36\pi)(8) = 288\pi$. This is the target value; write it down and circle it.

Next, plug $r_1 = 3$ into each answer choice, and then plug the resulting value of r_2 into the volume formula. Eliminate any answers that do not match the target value. In (A), $r_2 = \frac{1}{2}(3)$, or $r_2 = \frac{3}{2}$. The volume becomes $V = \frac{4}{3}\pi\left(\frac{3}{2}\right)^3$, then $V = \frac{4}{3}\pi\left(\frac{27}{8}\right)$, and finally $V = \frac{9}{2}\pi$. This does not match the target value of 288π, so eliminate (A). In (B), $r_2 = 2(3)$, or $r_2 = 6$. The volume becomes $V = \frac{4}{3}\pi(6)^3$, then $V = \frac{4}{3}\pi(216)$, and finally $V = 288\pi$. This matches the target value, so keep (B). Both (C) and (D) multiply r_1 by a number greater than 2, and there are no other differences, so both results will be different than (B) and not match the target. Eliminate (C) and (D). The correct answer is (B).

4. **A** The question asks for a measure on a geometric figure. Start by drawing two squares, and then label them with information from the question. The question asks for a specific value, and the answer choices contain numbers in order, so plug in the answers. Rewrite the answer choices on the scratch paper, and label them "side of plot B." Start with one of the middle numbers and try (B), 8. Label the sides of plot B as 8. The question states that *Each side of plot A is 4 feet longer than each side of plot B*, so if one side of plot B is 8 feet, one side of plot A is 8 + 4 = 12 feet. Label this on the figure, which now looks something like this:

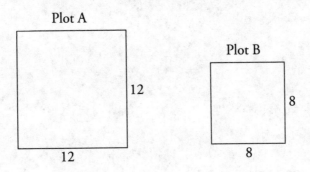

The question compares the areas of the two plots, so write down the formula for the area of a square: $A = s^2$. The area of plot A becomes $A = 12^2$, or $A = 144$. The area of plot B becomes $A = 8^2$, or $A = 64$. The area of plot A is 144 − 64 = 80 square feet greater than the area of plot B, which is more than the 64 square feet greater given in the question, so eliminate (B).

The difference between the areas was too great, so a smaller number is likely correct. Try (A), and relabel the sides of plot B as 6 and the sides of plot A as 6 + 4 = 10. The area of plot A becomes $A = 10^2$, or $A = 100$, and the area of plot B becomes $A = 6^2$, or $A = 36$. The area of plot A is 100 − 36 = 64 square feet greater than the area of plot B. This matches the information given in the question, so stop here. The correct answer is (A).

NOTES

NOTES

NOTES

NOTES

NOTES

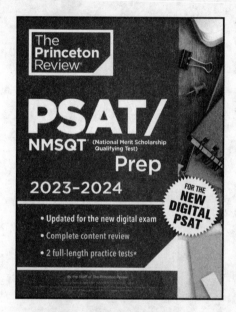